UNLOCKING
THE TORAH TEXT

AN IN-DEPTH JOURNEY
INTO THE WEEKLY PARSHA

DEVARIM

SHMUEL GOLDIN

gefen נפן
publishing house בית הוצאה לאור
JERUSALEM • NEW YORK   Est. 1981

Cover Design Concept: S. Kim Glassman
Cover Layout: Leah Ben Avraham / Noonim Graphics
Typesetting: Raphaël Freeman, Renana Typesetting

ISBN 978-965-229-526-2

1 3 5 7 9 8 6 4 2

Gefen Publishing House Ltd.   Gefen Books
6 Hatzvi Street,   11 Edison Place
Jerusalem 94386, Israel   Springfield, NJ 07081
+972-2-538-0247   516-593-1234
orders@gefenpublishing.com   orders@gefenpublishing.com

www.gefenpublishing.com

Printed in Israel   *Send for our free catalogue*

Library of Congress Control Number: 2014946825

Dedicated with love to our children

Avi and Rena, Yossi and Shifra,
Yehuda and Noa, Donny and Tamara, and Rivka

When we look at you, past and future converge.

You carry the names of those whom we remember;
you shoulder the hopes of those whom we never knew;
you bear our dreams with you.

You have grown into adulthood in an instant.

Suddenly, you are your own independent people, kind and generous,
loyal and steadfast, principled and ethical, accomplished and creative.

Each of you has found your own personal path
of deep commitment to Judaism.

We couldn't be prouder and we couldn't love you more.

And to our grandchildren

Isaac, Benjamin, Temima, Jacob, Chaim, Racheyl,
Mordechai, Julia, Yehudit and Penina

You simply fill us with joy…and we know that
you will continue to fill us with pride…

This set, *Unlocking the Torah Text*,
is lovingly dedicated to the memory of

my parents
Naftali and Lola Goldman
נפתלי בן יוסף הכהן
לאה בת חנניא יום טוב ליפא הלוי

who exemplified love of
תורה, ארץ ישראל ועם ישראל

and my grandparents, aunts and uncles, and great-grandparents
who perished in the Shoah

Josef (Yussel) and Bayla Goldman
Avrum, Ascher and Gittel

Leopold (Lipa) and Rose Weinfeld
Ascher Weinfeld

Yosef and Bina Korn

Shiya and Miriam Weinfeld

and to the memory of
David (Dudek) Fink
אריה דוד בן משה מאיר הכהן
stepfather and *bompa* extraordinaire

JOSEPH (YOSSI) AND GAIL GOLDMAN
NEIL, DANIEL AND MICHAEL

Contents

Acknowledgments

Nine years ago, Ilan Greenfield of Gefen Publishing House took a chance on a project that was only an idea and on a rabbi whom he had never met before. Ilan's unfailing support and encouragement from that moment on, together with the support of Michael Fischberger and the entire Gefen staff, kept me on track throughout the development of these volumes. Gefen boasts a team of consummate professionals. It has been my great fortune to work with them.

I will have to find another writing project to work on soon, if only to maintain my ongoing online partnership with my editor, Kezia Raffel Pride. Her consistent ability to catch each and every inconsistency, to understand and refine a point, and to challenge my thinking on difficult issues has made me a better writer with each successive volume. She is a real talent and a joy to work with.

Lynn Douek, Gefen's project coordinator, doesn't miss a beat as she shepherds all the projects under her care. I can only imagine how hard it must be to keep a bunch of "prima donna authors" focused on the finish line. She performs the difficult job with great finesse.

As this book goes to press, Israel is engaged in its third war in five years against the terrorists of Hamas. Israeli citizens have endured thousands of missiles launched towards their homes, and IDF soldiers are, as I write these words, engaged in fierce fighting on, above and beneath the streets of Gaza in a struggle to protect their families and their homeland. The individuals whom I have thanked in the paragraphs above all live in Israel and have family and friends on the front lines. Their ability to pursue their daily activities under these difficult circumstances is a testament not only to their spirit, but to the spirit of the entire population of the State of Israel. I feel humbled by their courage and strength.

I am deeply gratified by our partnership with OU Press. The OU symbol grants honor to our efforts and greatly expands our reach. I again thank Rabbi Menachem Genack and Rabbi Simon Posner for their confidence in me and in this project.

Once again, a number of dear friends from my Englewood community contributed generously towards the sponsorship of this volume. Thank you to Raphael and Linda Benaroya, Bruce and Hannah-Jean Brafman, Danny and Thalia Federbush, Jeremy and Gail Fingerman, Kenneth and Susan Greif, Jonathan and Mindy Kolatch, Lee and Cheryl Lasher, Solomon and Sharon Merkin, Drew and Careena Parker, and Dina Perry and her family. Your unfailing friendship and support means more to me than you can imagine.

I simply do not know what I would do without the help of my wise and capable administrative assistant, Eileen Gorlyn. For decades she has juggled the various pieces of my professional life with talent and aplomb, enabling me to function effectively on a daily basis and focus on long-term goals. As I have said before, this project, like so many others, is made possible through her diligent, professional, steady management. Thanks are due as well to my entire synagogue office staff – Chavie, Pam and Jill – for their ever-present support.

This has been an unbearably difficult year for my esteemed associate rabbi Chaim Poupko, his wife Shoshana and their entire family. The tragic passing of their cherished younger daughter and sister, Chana Tova, cast a pall upon our entire community and left a void in all of our hearts. At the same time, the faith, courage, strength and sense of perspective that Rabbi Chaim and Shoshana showed during this tragic period taught more to our community than thousands of sermons and classes ever could. I treasure my partnership with Rabbi Chaim, pray that we will share *smachot* with him and his family, and thank him for his unceasing invaluable contributions to our community. I also thank our talented assistant rabbi Mordechai Gershon for his energetic efforts on behalf of our congregation. Knowing that I have a rabbinic team that I can rely on has enabled me to expand my own horizons.

I have, thank God, reached a milestone in my rabbinic career. I have now served as rabbi of Congregation Ahavath Torah in Englewood, New Jersey, for over thirty years. As a young rabbi, nervously entering the service of this major pulpit, I never could have imagined how the experience would shape and enhance my life. This extraordinary community boasts incalculable human treasure and resource. I have been inspired and challenged by the examples of warmth, *chesed*, community activism, personal growth, spiritual striving and more that I have witnessed over the years.

Much of the material in this book emerges from our shared exploration. I sincerely thank the current president of our congregation, Lee Lasher, all the past presidents and officers with whom I have worked, and the entire synagogue membership, for their unstinting support, friendship and partnership in all my endeavors.

Although I have moved from the role of president to the role of honorary president in the Rabbinical Council of America, I continue to gain greatly from my ongoing involvement with my colleagues in that critically important organization. I thank my dear friend Rabbi Lenny Matanky, not only for his exemplary leadership as the RCA's current president, but also for welcoming my continued active participation in the organization. Much of what I have learned from the wise perspective of my colleagues has made its way onto the pages of this volume.

I am endlessly grateful to the Almighty for the continuing *nachat* that my wife Barbara and I experience from our growing family. Our children, Avi and Rena, Yossi and Shifra, Yehuda and Noa, Donny and Tamara, and Rivka fill us with pride. I have often remarked that it is wonderful to see your children become adults and to like the adults that they have become. Each of our children is independent, accomplished, generous and kind and each has found his or her own personal path of deep commitment to the traditions of our people. To see our gifted, exceptional, brilliant (do you think that I am biased?) grandchildren – Isaac, Benjamin, Temima, Jacob, Chaim, Racheyl, Mordechai, Julia, Yehudit and Penina – grow up in the homes that our children are building is an extraordinary experience.

Special thanks are due to my son Yossi for his expert, thoughtful editing of this volume. With insight and honesty he challenged my thinking and made real contributions to many pages of the text.

Finally and most significantly, not one volume of this set would have been written or published had it not been for the manifold contributions of my true partner in all aspects of my life, my wife Barbara. She insisted, over my objections, on taking the year's sabbatical in Israel that launched this project; she encouraged (and when that didn't work, pushed and prodded) me whenever I dragged my feet; she never lost sight of, nor let me forget about, the contribution she felt these volumes could make; and, when it came to this volume, she basically dragged me to the finish line. I don't say it enough, Barbara, but I love you and thank you.

Introduction

In 2003, while on a year sabbatical in Israel, I sat down to write…

I had no idea at the time whether my work would be published. I certainly could not have imagined that nine years later I would be writing an introduction to the final volume in a series of texts that have been received so warmly by the broader community, that have introduced me to a wide range of new friends and fellow travelers in Torah study, and that have brought me tremendous personal and professional satisfaction.

I am humbled by the experience and deeply grateful to all those who have assisted me along the way. Above all, I thank the Creator for allowing me to reach this momentous milestone.

To arrive at this point, however, I had to tackle Devarim. And, as it turns out, Devarim was, for me, the most difficult volume of all…

The first obstacle that I faced was a practical one. As a rabbi and educator, I lecture extensively throughout the year on the first four books of the Torah. Over time, I have therefore accrued a great deal of material, much of which served as the foundation for our studies in the first four volumes of *Unlocking the Torah Text*. During a good part of the summer months, however, when the book of Devarim is read as part of the yearly Torah cycle, I am often away from my congregation and any other teaching position I may have. The sermonic and educational material that I had accumulated over the years on the books of Bereishit, Shmot, Vayikra and Bamidbar was simply not available to me on Devarim. As I began this fifth volume, therefore, I found myself faced with the challenge of "starting from scratch."

Quickly convincing myself that this opportunity for personal growth was an excellent one, I began to look forward to the prospect of exploring and teaching new material…until I started. That's when I realized the full extent of the challenge before us. Devarim, as we will soon discover in our studies, is totally unlike the previous books of the Torah. The entire volume unfolds during the last five weeks of Moshe's life and, written in the first person, consists almost entirely of Moshe's farewell addresses to the nation.

While I had certainly been aware of the book of Devarim's unique character, I had never fully confronted the teaching difficulties that it raises. Substantial questions immediately arise as we approach this volume: How much of the text of Devarim is God's and how much is Moshe's? How does Moshe's role shift in the writing of Devarim? Why does Moshe review some mitzvot in this volume but not others? Why are certain mitzvot apparently commanded in this book for the first time, while others are repeated from previous volumes? Why does Moshe focus on specific topics in his farewell addresses, yet ignore others? Is there a logical structure to Moshe's farewell addresses in the book of Devarim? If so, what is that structure?

And that's even before we open the book…

Once we begin to analyze the text, the problems multiply. The book of Devarim, as we will discover, is a multilayered text. Covering a wide range of significant topics and ideas, this volume contains critical elements of God's unfolding law. At the same time, however, Devarim also subtly chronicles a poignant human drama. Ever present beneath the surface of its words are the roiling emotions of Moshe's last days.

With the text as our eyes, we watch as this commanding leader bids farewell to the people that he has patiently led for over four decades. Destined by divine decree to die at the very edge of the Promised Land, Moshe will not share in the realization of the Israelites' national destiny.

What does Moshe feel as he faces this harsh reality? How does he reconcile his own personal disappointment with the pride, excitement and anxiety that he feels for his people as he watches them ready themselves for the challenges ahead? How do his emotions shape and color his words and messages? What of the conflicting sentiments felt by the people as they prepare to realize their goals, enter an unknown land and simultaneously bid farewell to the only leader that they have known?

Clearly, the challenges that I faced as I started to write this last volume of our series were, therefore, daunting. Could I successfully capture and convey the essence of this unique book? Would I be able to give the halachic elements of the text their due, while not losing sight of the dramatic backdrop against which they appear? Would I successfully provide a glimpse of the harmonious whole into which this last book of the Torah weaves its various strands?

The time has come for you, the readers, to gauge our success. While the challenges have been real, I hope that you will find that we have risen to them. Beyond that, I hope that you will discover what I have discovered: that this last book of the Torah has the power to surprise us with the manifold relevant lessons it conveys. Even more, as we witness the dramatic transmission of our heritage from a teacher to his "students" at the dawn of our nation's history, Devarim has the power to inspire us in the forging our own individual relationships with God.

With excitement and anticipation, therefore, I invite those of you who have been traveling with us to continue – and those who are beginning now to join – our shared journey through the Torah text. Together, we will enter Moshe's world as he spends his last five weeks with his beloved people. We will explore the laws that he presents, the ideas that he conveys, the instructions that he delivers and the hopes that he shares with his people as he bids them farewell. We will strive to understand the relationship between God's will and Moshe's words as the book of Devarim takes its place alongside the other books of the Torah. And, as we go, we will discover some of the timeless lessons that this last book of the Torah so beautifully transmits.

To set the stage for our journey, I repeat a brief review of the parameters of our search. (This review is repeated, with minor changes, from the introductions to volumes 2, 3 and 4. A fuller discussions of these principles can be found in the introduction to volume 1.)

1. While traditional Torah study is based on a fundamental belief in the divine authorship of the text, questioning and challenging the text itself is not only allowed but encouraged. Unless we struggle with the narrative, God's word and God's intent remain distant and unclear and the Torah remains a closed book.

2. The treasures of the Torah can only be uncovered when the narrative itself is seen as the truth, comprised of real events that happened to real people. The heroes of the Bible were human beings, not gods, and the stories of their lives are not fables.

3. No part of the text or its contents will be off-limits to our search. We will probe God's desires for us reflected in His unfolding law and we will attempt to discern what the Torah reveals about His divine will. We will seek to understand why events took place as they did and how the narrative might inform our lives. And we will explore the deep philosophical currents coursing through the laws and events described to us.

4. Two distinct approaches to the Torah text are reflected in rabbinic literature: *pshat* and *drash*.

Pshat refers to the straightforward explanation of the text. When we operate within the realm of *pshat*, we search for the literal, concrete sense of the narrative before us. *Proper understanding of* pshat *reveals deep, unexpected meaning within the text itself.*

Drash refers to rabbinic commentary serving as a vehicle for the transmission of lessons and ideas beyond the literal narrative. Many authorities maintain that Midrashic commentary is not meant to be taken literally, nor is it meant to be seen as an attempt to explain the factual meaning of a specific Torah passage. The key question in the realm of *drash* is: *What are the rabbis trying to teach us?*

When, as unfortunately often happens, we confuse these two approaches to text – when we ignore the *pshat* and instead offer *drash* as the literal interpretation of the text – we end up understanding neither of these interpretive realms. In our studies, therefore, we will make every attempt to distinguish between *pshat* and *drash* and to present each approach appropriately.

5. Each of our studies on the parshiot of Devarim will raise a series of questions designed to strike to the core of a particular passage of the text.

Our search for answers to the questions raised will take us on a journey through traditional commentary and original thought. In each study, a sampling of rabbinic opinion on the issues will be reviewed and original approaches will be offered as we humbly continue our own struggle with the text.

Finally, many studies will include a "Points to Ponder" section in which connections are made between the Torah passage and relevant concerns that touch our lives. This section is specifically designed to encourage ongoing thought and debate.

I close, as I have in the past, with the hope that our continuing journey will be, for each of us, a passionate one, inspiring continuing exploration and thought, sparking conversation, dialogue and debate each week in homes, synagogues, schools and beyond, as together we unlock the treasures of the Torah text.

On this occasion, however, I add one additional wish: that the conclusion of our series should not be an end, but a beginning. I trust that our shared discoveries will be revisited and reexamined, and that our joint exploration will inspire each of us towards further study of the never-ending wonders that lie within the Torah text.

Devarim

CHAPTER 1:1–3:22

דברים

פרק א:א-ג:כב

Parsha Summary

The goodbye begins…

On the first day of the eleventh month of the fortieth year to the Exodus, as the Israelites stand poised to enter the land of Canaan, Moshe opens his farewell addresses. Prohibited by divine decree from entering the land of Canaan, this great leader will spend the last five weeks of his life delivering a series of wide-ranging final messages to his people. These messages comprise the text of the book of Devarim.

Moshe opens his first address by recalling events experienced a generation earlier: the divinely commanded departure from Sinai and the appointment of judges to assist in the governance of the nation. He reminds the people of the sin of the spies and of the painful aftermath of that event, resulting in the nation's long years of wilderness wandering.

Narratively telescoping nearly forty years, Moshe then turns to the recent events experienced by the generation standing before him: the divinely ordained avoidance of conflict with the nations of Edom, Moav and Ammon; and the successful Transjordan battles against Sichon, the king of Cheshbon, and Og, the king of Bashan. The parsha closes as Moshe relates that the land conquered during these battles was divided between the tribes of Reuven, Gad and half the tribe of Menashe, on the condition that after providing habitats for their wives, children and livestock in the Transjordan, the men of these tribes would lead their brothers in the conquest of Canaan before returning to their own land.

1 Author, Author!

Context

The opening words of the book of Devarim immediately set this text apart from the other divinely authored books of the Torah: "And these are the words that Moshe spoke…"[1]

Devarim is Moshe's book. Recorded almost completely in the first person, this volume consists primarily of Moshe's farewell addresses to the Israelites on the eve of his death and their entry into the land of Canaan.

Tellingly absent from Devarim, until the book's closing chapters,[2] are all variations of the familiar phrase "and the Lord spoke to Moshe, saying…"

Much of the text of Devarim, instead, seems to spring spontaneously from Moshe's heart.

Questions

Who is the author of the book of Devarim, God or Moshe?

Normative rabbinic opinion maintains that the first four books of the Torah were dictated by God to Moshe verbatim, each word emanating from a divine source.[3] Are we to understand, however, that the text of Devarim is somehow different, with Moshe taking a more active role in its formulation?

An early Talmudic source seems to weigh in on the issue by drawing a distinction between the two *tochachot*, the Torah's lengthy descriptions of penalties for collective national failure; the first recorded in the book of Vayikra and the second in the book of Devarim. The first of these sets of warnings, the Talmud maintains, was transmitted by Moshe upon divine

---

1. Devarim 1:1.
2. Ibid., 31:14, 31:16, 32:48.
3. See among other sources Ramban, introduction to the book of Devarim.

command. In contrast, the second set, found in the book of Devarim, was "conveyed by Moshe, of his own accord."[4]

Is this observation reflective of the rabbinic approach to the book of Devarim as a whole? Do the rabbis view the primary content of this book as text "conveyed by Moshe, of his own accord"? Furthermore, if Moshe actually authored sefer Devarim, what place does this volume have as part of the divinely authored Torah text?

Approaches

— A —

A number of classical scholars briefly address the issue of the authorship of Devarim. An initial review of their comments, however, seems to yield confusing, even contradictory results.

The Ramban, for example, argues with Rashi concerning the interpretation of the introductory biblical phrase *ho'il Moshe be'er et haTorah hazot*.[5] While Rashi renders this phrase as "Moshe *began* to explain this Torah,"[6] the Ramban, supporting his position from texts in the prophets, insists that these words mean "Moshe *desired* to explain this Torah." Moshe, explains the Ramban, wants the nation to know that "he, himself, decided to [explain the law]. He was not commanded to do so by God."[7]

Similarly, Rabbi Saadia Gaon understands this phrase to mean that Moshe "waxed lengthy in his explanation of the Torah" (apparently of his own volition),[8] while the Sforno sees this passage as indicating that Moshe "explained those areas of law concerning which he was worried there would be uncertainty after his death."[9]

While the above disputants with Rashi seem to accept a degree of independence on Moshe's part in the authorship of Devarim, the Ramban himself, in his introduction to the book of Bereishit, clearly disabuses the reader of this notion. After discussing Moshe's exceptional use of the first person in the book of Devarim, the Ramban emphatically declares:

---

4. Talmud Bavli Megilla 31b.
5. Devarim 1:5.
6. Rashi, ibid.
7. Ramban, Devarim 1:1.
8. Saadia Gaon, Devarim 1:5.
9. Sforno, Devarim 1:5.

> Moshe served as a scribe copying from an ancient book...for it is true and clear that the entire Torah, from the beginning of the book of Bereishit until the words "to the eyes of all Israel" [the final words of the book of Devarim], were spoken from the mouth of the Holy One Blessed Be He directly to the ears of Moshe.[10]

The Ramban's position on the authorship of Devarim seems unclear. If, as he and the other commentaries quoted above accept, much of this volume consists of text that "[Moshe] himself decided" to include, how can the Ramban also claim that the entire Torah, including the book of Devarim, was "spoken from the mouth of the Holy One Blessed Be He directly to the ears of Moshe"?

A possible explanation of the Ramban's position may well emerge from an unlikely source. In his introduction to the book of Devarim, the Abravanel strenuously disagrees with much of the Ramban's view concerning the general character of the book (see Devarim 2, *Approaches* C). His explanation of Moshe's authorship role in the volume, however, may help clarify the Ramban's position on this subject. Devarim, the Abravanel maintains, consists primarily of Moshe's explanations of laws and concepts about which uncertainty had developed during the years in the wilderness. After Moshe offers his independent analysis concerning these laws, however, God then commands him to include that analysis in the final redaction of the text. By doing so, God weaves Moshe's contributions into the divinely authored text of the Torah.[11]

Perhaps the Ramban also maintains that Moshe's independent contributions to the text are granted the quality of divine authorship when God decides to include them in the text. They are ultimately woven into the fabric of a text which, in its entirety, is "spoken from the mouth of the Holy One Blessed Be He directly to the ears of Moshe."

— **B** —

If the Ramban's position concerning the authorship of Devarim needs elucidation, the position of the Ohr Hachaim, at first glance, does not. This scholar accepts the revolutionary idea of Moshe's authorship of Devarim as

---

10. Ramban, introduction to the book of Bereishit.
11. Abravanel, introduction to the book of Devarim.

emerging from the first words of the book: *V'eileh hadevarim asher diber Moshe*, "And *these are* the words that Moshe spoke."

Applying the well-known exegetical principle that the introduction of a biblical passage with the word *eileh* (these are) indicates a distinction from previous text,[12] this scholar interprets this opening phrase of Devarim as follows:

> Because the Torah is about to introduce words that Moshe spoke of his accord…the text deliberately clarifies that only *eileh hadevarim*, these words, were spoken independently by Moshe.
>
> Concerning the preceding four volumes of the Torah, however, [Moshe] did not speak one letter on his own; rather, [those texts contain] words emerging from the [heavenly] obligator, unchanged in any way, without even one letter added or omitted.[13]

—— C ——————————————————————————————

Not all scholars, however, are willing to take the Ohr Hachaim's seemingly clear position at face value. Rabbi Chaim Elazar Shapira, the Munkatcher Rebbe in the late nineteenth–early twentieth centuries, for example, declares, "Let the heart of each reader tremble at the possibility of arriving at the mistaken conclusion that these words could have emerged as they seem from the Holy Ohr Hachaim."[14]

The Ohr Hachaim could not possibly believe that Moshe authored the book of Devarim independently, Rabbi Shapira maintains, when the Talmud clearly condemns an individual who denies the divine authorship of even one sentence of the Torah.[15] After mentioning and rejecting another possibility, suggested by an unnamed kabbalist, that the Ohr Hachaim was actually punished for creating this mistaken impression, the Munkatcher insists on reinterpreting the Ohr Hachaim's position in line with that of the Maharal and the Vilna Gaon, cited below.[16]

---

12. Midrash Rabba Bereishit 12:3.
13. Ohr Hachaim, Devarim 1:1.
14. Quoted in Yehuda Nachshoni, *Hagot B'parshiot HaTorah* (Tel Aviv: Zohar Publishing, 1979), vol. 2, pp. 719–720.
15. Talmud Bavli Sanhedrin 99a.
16. Quoted in Nachshoni, *Hagot B'parshiot HaTorah*, vol. 2, pp. 719–720.

—— **D** ——————————————————————————————

Perhaps the most detailed approach to the uniqueness of the book of Devarim is proffered by the famed sixteenth-century scholar the Maharal of Prague, later quoted in the name of the Gaon of Vilna. The text of the first four books of the Torah, these scholars maintain, is "placed by God into Moshe's mouth." Throughout Bereishit, Shmot, Vayikra and Bamidbar, *God literally speaks through Moshe.* With the advent of the book of Devarim, however, Moshe's role changes to that of a prophetic *shaliach*, messenger. God transmits the substance of this volume to Moshe and then takes a step back, allowing Moshe to convey each divine message to the Israelites in his own words.

In order to appreciate the singular character of the book of Devarim, the Maharal explains, a fundamental reality must be understood. Every communication in human experience is shaped by the unique perspectives of both the *notein* (communicator [literally, giver]) and the *mekabel* (recipient). When two parties involved in a communication are of equal stature, their perceptions tend to converge. As the gap in standing between them widens, however, so do their individual assessments of the interchange.

The transmission of the Torah represents a phenomenon unique to world history: an ongoing, extensive, detailed communication between God and man. Because of the monumental gap between the *notein* and the *mekabel* in this interchange, the perspectives of the participants, God and man, are obviously "worlds apart."

The first four books of the Torah, the Maharal continues, reflect God's perspective in the communication that shapes the Torah text. With regard to these volumes, man is relegated to a passive role. He is the recipient of a finished product. With the book of Devarim, however, everything changes. This last, closing book of the Torah is designed to include the perspective of the recipient. Known in rabbinic literature as *Mishneh Torah*, the repetition of the Torah, Devarim contains the elaborations and explanations that are necessary for man's understanding of God's law. Here, Moshe is not simply a scribe but an active participant in the formulation of the text. He does not simply transmit God's words unchanged. He is a *shaliach*, shaping the text from his own viewpoint, the viewpoint of man.[17]

———————

17. *Tiferet Yisrael* 43.

—— E ——

The nineteenth- and twentieth-century scholar Rabbi Meir Dan Plotski, in *Kli Chemda*, his commentary on the Torah, offers a nuanced yet significant variation on the position of the Maharal and the Vilna Gaon.

Rabbi Plotski points out that although Moshe's primary role vis-à-vis the first four volumes of the Torah is that of faithful scribe of God's Word, even those volumes, at times, reflect Moshe's own contributions. Moshe's dramatic directive to the Levi'im to summarily execute the perpetrators in the sin of the golden calf, his mistaken interpretation of a ritual law following the death of Nadav and Avihu, his addition of an extra day to the period of preparation preceding Revelation, his numerous discussions with God are but a few examples of the many passages in Shmot, Vayikra and Bamidbar that mirror autonomous dialogue and action on the prophet's part.

The distinction drawn by the Ohr Hachaim and other commentaries between the book of Devarim and the earlier texts, Rabbi Plotski therefore maintains, is actually more subtle than might first appear. Moshe's independent words and deeds certainly contribute to the narrative of three of the four initial volumes of the Torah. *His final recording of the law in those texts, however, mirrors God's instructions, word for word, without change.* Similarly, towards the end of his life, Moshe independently embarks upon a series of lengthy explanations and elaborations of Torah law, in order to cement the people's understanding and appreciation of specific mitzvot before his death. After Moshe offers these analyses, *God eventually directs him to record them in the book of Devarim, as part of the Torah text.*

God's commandment to transform the words of the Torah into a complete written record thus ultimately includes not only God's contributions to the text, but Moshe's, as well. These separate threads are woven into one cohesive whole, as God dictates to Moshe each volume of the Torah, word by word and letter by letter. While Moshe's contribution to the book of Devarim, therefore, is more extensive; the actual authorship of this fifth volume of the Torah does not differ from the first four. By accepting and incorporating Moshe's contributions into a *divinely authored Torah text*, God makes those contributions an integral part of His divine law.[18]

As we will see in the following study (Devarim 2, *Approaches* c), the Kli Chemda's position builds upon the earlier observations of the Abra-

---

18. *Kli Chemda*, Parshat Devarim 4.

vanel, who views the book of Devarim primarily as a volume featuring Moshe's clarification of earlier transmitted concepts and laws. Like the Kli Chemda, the Abravanel maintains that God ultimately commands Moshe to include the prophet's own analysis and explanation in the final redaction of the text.[19]

—— F ——

Finally, mention must be made of one powerful scholar who adopts an approach to the authorship of Devarim diametrically opposed to those cited above.

Referencing a suggestion in the text of Rashi,[20] Rabbi Menachem Mendel Schneerson, the most recent Lubavitcher Rebbe, maintains that Moshe actually serves not simply as a scribe, but as a prophetic messenger vis-à-vis the first four books of the Torah. In the formation of these texts, Moshe receives God's messages and then proceeds to transmit those messages to the people in his own words. With the advent of the book of Devarim, however, Moshe experiences a "joining" with the Divine that he has not experienced before. "In the latter instance, the Divine Presence enclothed itself in his [Moshe's] conceptual processes until the two were united in a bond so powerful that 'the Divine Presence spoke from his [Moshe's] throat.'"[21]

From the Lubavitcher Rebbe's perspective, *God's direct involvement in the authorship of the Torah text increases, rather than decreases, with the advent of the book of Devarim.* In this volume, and in this volume alone, God's words emerge directly and unchanged through Moshe.

Points to Ponder

As we have seen in our study, while debate rages as to the exact nature of the phenomenon, rabbinic opinion overwhelmingly maintains that there is "more of Moshe" in the book of Devarim than in any other volume of the

---

19. Abravanel, introduction to Devarim.
20. Rashi, Megilla 31b.
21. Rabbi Eliyahu Touger, trans., *Likkutei Sichot: An Anthology of Talks Relating to the Weekly Sections of the Torah and Special Occasions in the Jewish Calendar by the Lubavitcher Rebbe Rabbi Menachem M. Schneerson*, vol. 10, Devarim (New York: Sichos in English).

Torah text. Apparently, God could not allow the Torah to close without a more complete glimpse into the heart and mind of this great leader.

The inclusion of the book of Devarim thus embeds in the Torah's structure a fundamental truth that will shape the development of our nation's tradition across time. *The fabric of Jewish experience is as much a product of people and personalities as it is a product of technical statute and law.*

We have noted before (see *Bereishit*: Toldot 5, *Approaches* E) that the concept of *mesora*, the passing of tradition, is often inaccurately seen as a two-step process – as the receiving of a heritage from the past generation and the handing of that heritage to the next. There is, however, a pivotal third step. We receive tradition from the past generation, *that tradition courses through us*, and we then pass that tradition to the future. Inexorably, as the corpus of Jewish life courses through each individual, family and community in each generation, it is altered by a myriad of variables. The personal experiences, challenges, perceptions aspirations and dreams of parents, teachers, grandparents, rabbis, communal leaders and whole communities all shape the continually developing character of our people's legacy.

Even in the seemingly technical arena of Jewish law, the human component is starkly evident. As we have explained in greater detail (see *Shmot*: Yitro 5), Judaism is unique in its insistence upon a foundational partnership between man and God in the determination of religious law. Once God establishes the basic legal and methodological foundations of halacha, He hands the law over to the rabbis for continuing interpretation and application. Human beings all, the rabbis naturally bring to bear their own perceptions and personalities as they apply their expertise to the delineation of our nation's legal path.

The Torah would not have been complete without a glimpse of Moshe. That glimpse is provided by the book of Devarim. With this book, God teaches us to be mindful of the partnership between God and man in the defining of Jewish experience until the end of time.

2 Deciphering Devarim

Context

Moshe's farewell addresses, recorded in the book of Devarim, feature a diverse and seemingly disconnected amalgam of components, among which are the following:

1. Words of rebuke concerning the nation's past sins and shortcomings.
2. Messages of encouragement as the nation prepares to enter the land of Canaan.
3. General recollections of shared experiences with the people.
4. Exhortation towards continued Torah observance.
5. A review of and elaboration upon specific mitzvot already recorded in previous volumes of the text.
6. Introduction of a number of mitzvot that appear in this volume for the first time.

Questions

A number of overarching questions emerge as we consider both the structure and content of the book of Devarim.

Is there any pattern to the arrangement of Moshe's final addresses to the nation and is there any logical structure to the book itself?

By what criteria are certain previously commanded mitzvot chosen for review in the book of Devarim while others are not?

Why are some mitzvot introduced in this volume for the first time? Why would God wait until the weeks before Moshe's death for the presentation of these particular commandments?

Approaches

—A—

Our effort to answer these questions is hindered by the very character that sets the fifth book of the Torah apart from the previous volumes. This is a sweeping, dramatic and emotionally charged text, filled with the lofty prose of a towering leader bidding farewell, during a five-week period, to the people whom he has faithfully lead for decades.

The conflicting emotions that course beneath the surface of the book of Devarim cannot be ignored: the excitement of a nation on the verge of a journey's end; their anticipation and trepidation as yet another unknown path opens before them; their sorrow at bidding farewell to the only leader they have ever known; the pride of that leader as he views his people about to claim their national destiny; his own personal, devastating disappointment that he will not accompany them on the final leg of the journey…

Such a text defies quantification and technical analysis, bidding us instead to step back in appreciation of its eloquence and majesty. The separate components of Devarim cannot easily be classified into a neat, clear structure. The flow of ideas and emotions continuously overlap in the text as Moshe attempts, for this last time, to move his people forward.

And yet, Devarim is the fifth book of the Torah – a text, like its sister volumes, meant to be examined, analyzed and studied for the eternal lessons that lie within.

A balance must therefore be struck as we approached this unique, final book of God's law. Armed with the observations of the sages across the ages, we will dissect and analyze the text of Devarim for lessons that God would have us learn. Such analysis, however, must never blind us to the majestic personal drama unfolding before our eyes.

—B—

Among those who attempt to organize the text of Devarim, the Vilna Gaon suggests a tripartite structure to the book, based upon three distinct areas of focus in Moshe's addresses to the nation. While later commentaries strive to further refine the Gaon's suggestions, few stray far from his basic overview of the text:

1. Moshe's first discourse (1:6–4:40), the Gaon maintains, focuses on words of *mussar* (moral teachings). In this address, Moshe reviews shared

past experiences with the nation and contrasts the abortive attempt of the previous generation to enter the land with the recent military victories experienced by this generation. Rebuking the people for past failings, he exhorts them to recognize and remain loyal to the true source of their strength: God and His law.[1]

2. During the course of his second discourse (5:1–27:8), Moshe focuses on the mitzvot he intends to convey to the nation. Recalling the Revelation at Sinai, he underscores the foundations of the law through a repetition (with various emendations; see Va'etchanan 1) of the Aseret Hadibrot (the Ten Declarations), and declares God's oneness in the first paragraph of the Shma. He then segues into a lengthy discussion of the practical consequences attached to obedience and/or neglect of the law. He transmits the obligations that will be incumbent upon the people upon entry into the land and outlines a wide array of mitzvot on a variety of themes. As noted above, some of these obligations have been communicated before in the previous volumes of the Torah, while others are apparently introduced here for the first time.

3. Finally, Moshe closes his addresses to the nation with *bracha* and *tochacha*, a reiteration of the potential blessings and misfortunes that will hinge upon observance of the mitzvot; *kritat brit*, a renewal of the covenant between God and the nation; and *shira* and *bracha*, lofty words of song and blessing, as he bids farewell to his people (27:9–33:29).

With typical incisiveness, the Gaon uses this three-part division of the text to solve a puzzling repetitiveness in the first five sentences of the book of Devarim. The volume opens with the statement "These are the words that Moshe spoke to all Israel…,"[2] then reiterates, "And it was in the fortieth year, in the eleventh month, on the first of the month that Moshe spoke to the Children of Israel…,"[3] then reiterates again, "On the other side of the Jordan, in the land of Moav, Moshe began explaining this Torah, saying…."[4]

In the Gaon's eyes the textual flow is clear. The first five sentences of Devarim serve as a preface to the entire volume. By referencing Moshe's

---

1. Centuries earlier, the Ramban also sees 4:40 as the demarcation between Moshe's introductory address to the nation and his exposition of the mitzvot (Ramban, Devarim 1:2).
2. Devarim 1:1.
3. Ibid., 1:3.
4. Ibid., 1:5.

verbal communication with the nation three separate times in this introductory paragraph, the Torah alludes to the three major sections of the book as a whole. Each introductory allusion, the Gaon continues, contains language appropriate to the later corresponding section of text.

Finally, the Gaon cites one last phenomenon concerning the tripartite division of the book of Devarim. Each of the three sections of Devarim opens, in order, with a term that corresponds to the opening word of one of the three previous volumes of the Torah in which Moshe has played an active role. The first section opens with the word *eileh* (these are), the first word of the book of Shmot; the second section opens with the word *va'yikra* (and he called), the first word of the book of Vayikra; and the third section opens with the word *va'yedaber* (and he spoke), the first word of the book of Bamidbar. As Moshe bids farewell to the nation, the Gaon maintains, he poignantly references their shared history, recorded in three earlier volumes of the Torah.[5]

——— C ———

While the Vilna Gaon's tripartite division of the book of Devarim certainly aids in our understanding of this last book in the Torah, it fails to address our significant questions concerning the two separate categories of mitzvot contained in this volume: "repeated" commandments that had been previously recorded in earlier volumes of the Torah and "new" mitzvot that are transmitted in this volume for the first time. By what criteria are these mitzvot chosen for review or for first mention in this final book of the Torah?

The Ramban addresses this issue directly in the first passages of his commentary to the book of Devarim.

The text of Devarim, the Ramban explains, is shaped in large measure by Moshe's perception of the needs of the Israelites on the eve of their entry into the land of Canaan. Recognizing the challenges facing his people at this critical moment, Moshe decides to repeat specific mitzvot to the nation and to explicate others.

He selects, for example, commandments that are regularly incumbent upon the nation as a whole and concerning which he feels there is a need for continued encouragement. He weaves prohibitions, such as the ban on

---

5. The Vilna Gaon as quoted in *Haktav V'hakabala*, Devarim 1.

idolatry, into general warnings concerning the dangers awaiting the people upon entry into the land. He entirely omits, however, all laws for which the Kohanim bear direct responsibility, such as the laws of *korbanot*. The priests, he reasons, will be punctilious in their observance, and therefore need no further admonition at this time.

The Ramban argues that the commandments recorded in Devarim for the first time could not possibly be "new." These mitzvot must have been transmitted to Moshe during the first two years following the Exodus, together with all the other commandments of the Torah. The delay in their transmission to the nation, the Ramban reasons, can perhaps be attributed to one of two alternative explanations: either the fulfillment of these mitzvot becomes incumbent upon the Israelites only after they enter the land, or the observance of these commandments is not commonplace.[6]

— **D** ———————————————————————

The Ramban's contentions, however, come under serious attack from numerous other authorities, including the Abravanel and the Radbaz. Moshe, these scholars argue, would not have waited until the weeks before his death to transmit commandments that he had received at Sinai close to forty years earlier. Additionally, the Ramban's suggestion that the only laws introduced in Devarim are those incumbent after entry into the land or those not practiced regularly also belies the evidence. Numerous edicts apparently recorded for the first time in this volume were commonly practiced by the people throughout their wilderness sojourns. Other commandments, such as the laws of Shmita (the sabbatical year) and Yovel (the Jubilee year), obviously obligatory only in the land of Canaan, appear in the Torah in the volumes preceding the book of Devarim.[7]

The Abravanel, therefore, offers an entirely different perspective upon the character of this last volume of the Torah. Devarim is neither a book of rebuke nor a text that introduces new legal doctrine. It is, instead, an exercise in clarification. In the weeks before his death, Moshe sets out to elucidate any law or concept concerning which an uncertainty or misunderstanding may have developed during the Israelites' years in the wilderness. No law, the Abravanel insists, is actually introduced in Devarim for the first

---

6. Ramban, introduction to the book of Devarim.
7. Abravanel, introduction to the book of Devarim.

time. All laws recorded in this volume are actually "repeated laws." Every edict mentioned has already been recorded outright or subtly alluded to in one of the previous volumes of the Torah.[8]

—— E ——

Finally, Rabbi Shimshon Raphael Hirsch, based on the unusual phrase "Moshe spoke to the Children of Israel according to everything that Hashem had commanded him to them,"[9] maintains that Moshe, before his death, reviewed with the nation *all 613 mitzvot of the Torah with full explanation.* Of these mitzvot, however, only those new or repeated laws most relevant to the Israelites' new life in the Land of Israel are actually recorded in the text of Devarim. As a case in point, Hirsch notes that when the laws of the festivals are repeated in Devarim,[10] the holidays of Pesach, Shavuot and Succot are mentioned while Shabbat, Rosh Hashana, Yom Kippur and Shmini Atzeret are omitted. The festivals absent from the text, Hirsch explains, "originate from the relationship of the individual to God" and are therefore not affected at all by the nation's entry into the land. Pesach, Shavuot and Succot, however, are deeply connected to the Land of Israel, both as pilgrimage festivals requiring ascent to the Temple in Jerusalem and as agricultural festivals marking milestones of the harvest season. While Moshe reviewed all the laws of all the festivals before his death, Hirsch explains, only the laws of Pesach, Shavuot and Succot, the holidays affected by the Israelites' entry into the land, are actually recorded in the text of Devarim.[11]

—— F ——

The above observations are representative of the numerous global approaches suggested by the commentaries towards deciphering what may be the most multilayered book of the Torah. As our journey through this text continues, we will walk along the path of Moshe's parting from the Israelites, a path replete with human drama and eternal messages that reverberate across the ages.

---

8. Ibid.
9. Devarim 1:3.
10. Devarim 16:1–17.
11. Rabbi Shimshon Raphael Hirsch, Devarim 1:3.

3 Commencing a Farewell

Context

Moshe opens his first farewell address to the nation with a review of events experienced by the previous generation, close to forty years earlier:

1. God's commandment to depart from Mount Sinai following Revelation.
2. The appointment of judges to share in the burden of governing the nation.
3. The sin of the spies, God's resultant decree of wilderness wandering and death upon the generation of the Exodus, and the nation's abortive attempt to defy that decree by immediately entering the land.[1]

Moshe then turns his attention towards experiences that he has shared with the new generation standing before him:

1. God's commandment to turn northward from Mount Seir towards the eastern bank of the Jordan, the nation's point of entry into the land of Canaan.
2. The avoidance of conflict with the inhabitants of Seir and the nations of Moav and Ammon, as per God's instructions.
3. The military victories over Sichon, the king of Cheshbon, and Og, the king of Bashan, at God's command.
4. The granting of land on the Jordan's east bank to the tribes of Reuven, Gad and one half the tribe of Menashe, following their agreement to participate in the conquest of the land of Canaan.[2]

---

1. Devarim 1:6–2:1.
2. Ibid., 2:2–3:22.

Questions

Moshe's choice of events for review, as he opens his first farewell address to the nation, seems arbitrary and difficult to understand.

If, as many commentaries suggest,[3] Moshe's primary goal in his first discourse is to chastise the nation for past sins, why does he limit his opening narrative to the sin of the spies? Why doesn't he cite the people's prior tragic failing, the sin of the golden calf? Why does he omit other national rebellions, such as the revolt of "the graves of desire" (see *Bamidbar*: Beha'alotcha 6) or the insurrection of Korach (see *Bamidbar*: Korach 1–6)?

If, on the other hand, Moshe's primary intent at this point is not to chastise but simply to recall shared experiences with the Israelites, *why does he leave so much out*? Why doesn't he reference the "rest of the journey"; the all-important formative events of the Exodus, the Revelation at Sinai, the building of the Mishkan and more? While some of these events are discussed in later sections of the book of Devarim, why aren't they mentioned here, in their order of occurrence? Why does Moshe begin his narrative *in the middle of the story*, with the departure from Sinai?

Furthermore, why is the selection of judges important enough to "make the cut" for this initial discourse? This incident seems to pale in comparison to the above-mentioned omitted events.

Finally, why does Moshe suddenly jump from events that occurred thirty-eight years earlier to current experiences, without so much as a preamble? What is the connection between the two sets of events, the past and the current, and why do the decades between them disappear in Moshe's narrative with hardly a mention?

Approaches

—A—

A penetrating approach to Moshe's opening words is laid out by a number of commentaries, including Rabbi David Tzvi Hoffman.[4] The approach of these scholars, combined with some additional observations, reveals a clear, logical structure to Moshe's initial message to the nation.

As Moshe views the scene before him, he is overcome by an unrelent-

---

3. Rashi, Devarim 1:1; Chizkuni, Devarim 1:1 and others.
4. Rabbi David Tzvi Hoffman, *Sefer Devarim* 1:22–28.

ing fear. He sees a people surrounded by circumstances uncannily similar to circumstances experienced by their parents close to forty years earlier. Then, as now, the Israelites stood poised to enter the land of Canaan.

Perhaps, Moshe reasons apprehensively, *this generation will fail, as did their parents, on the very brink of success. Perhaps they too will lose heart in the face of the challenges before them, causing God to deny them their national destiny again.*

Recognizing the challenge that he confronts, Moshe sets out to capture and compare two corresponding moments in time, separated by decades. Employing parallel language, he introduces his two sets of recollections, reflecting the past and the present:

> The Lord, our God, spoke to us in Horev, saying: "You have dwelt by this mountain [Mount Sinai] long enough! Turn yourselves and journey…"[5] *Close to forty years ago, with these words, God launched your parents' journey towards Canaan.*
>
> And the Lord said to me: "You have circled this mountain [Mount Seir] long enough! Turn yourselves northward…"[6] *With these words, God has now launched our journey towards Canaan.*

In a powerful effort to underscore the promise and peril that lies before the people, Moshe relates the failures of the past to the present. He speaks to this generation as if they are complicit in decades-old events, as if they are responsible for the sins of their parents. He then connects those events to the current challenge facing the nation.

In this way, he emphatically conveys his message:

This is not history of which I speak, a series of events that happened to a different people at a different time. It could happen again. You are vulnerable to the same weaknesses that ensnared your parents.

We have been here before, you and I… Do not fall into the same trap. Recognize the opportunity that God is giving to you; seize that opportunity with strength and courage; succeed where your parents failed…

---

5. Devarim 1:5.
6. Ibid., 2:2.

—— **B** ————————————————————————————

The logical structure of Moshe's opening remarks to the nation, as he begins the heartbreaking process of bidding his people farewell, now becomes readily apparent.

Moshe's goal is neither remonstration nor recollection, but moral instruction. He is desperate that the people learn, not only of the missteps of the past, *but of the real possibility of their own failure.* He therefore focuses on the one event that prevented their parents' entry into the land, the turning point of the past generation, the sin of the spies (see *Bamidbar*: Shelach 1–3). This moment is not the time for a review of other sins. Such episodes, important though they may be, are irrelevant to Moshe's message. Nor does Moshe now speak of the glorious events of the Exodus or Revelation; there will be time enough for such recollections. Moshe has one focus, and one focus alone. He is determined that the people understand that they have lost this opportunity before and that only their own efforts will ensure that they do not lose it again.

—— **C** ————————————————————————————

We can now understand how other aspects of Moshe's discourse convey ideas that are ancillary – yet essential – to this basic message. Carefully, Moshe includes details designed to both instruct and encourage the nation at this pivotal juncture.

1. Military triumph is clearly possible, Moshe insists, as evidenced by the dramatic victories over Sichon and Og. *Such successes, however, will consistently be dependent upon obedience to God's will.*

Had the people entered Canaan from the outset, as God desired, a generation ago, Moshe explains, they would have triumphed. Upon the sin of the spies, however, such entry became divinely prohibited. The nation's failure to recognize the reality of that divine decree led to their abortive attempt to enter the land against God's will and resulted in devastating defeat.

The current generation, Moshe continues, has witnessed success on the battlefield only because it has embarked upon those wars permitted by God. At God's word, the nation avoided conflict with the inhabitants of Seir and the nations of Moav and Ammon. At His word, they defeated Sichon and Og. And, at His word, Moshe promises, they will defeat the nations of Canaan.

2. No one, Moshe continues, can be allowed to shirk personal respon-

sibility in the face of the challenges that lie ahead. The nation's success will depend upon total participation. As a case in point, he cites the agreement contracted with the tribes of Reuven, Gad and half the tribe of Menashe to fight alongside their brothers in the conquest of the land.

3. Finally, even Moshe's seemingly strange inclusion of the appointment of judges in his initial discourse now seems on point, as well. As Moshe recalls the departure from Sinai that was to lead directly to Canaan, he underscores that the Israelites' failure to enter the land cannot be blamed on external circumstances. *All was in place to allow for their success.* Critical to the endeavor was the structuring of a legal system enabling the people to live in the land under God's law. Even that system was established from the outset through the selection of judges to assist in the nation's governance.

The failures of the past, Moshe argues, can be blamed only on the nation's shortcomings. And now, once again, all is in place for success. *If, God forbid, you fail, you will have only yourselves to blame.*

Additionally, as Moshe begins his emotional farewell to his people, his reference to the appointment of judges may well resonate poignantly on another level. *I will have to leave you but you will not be alone. God will guide you from the heavens and you will be blessed with wise, capable leadership here on earth.*

— **D** —————————————————————————————

Far from a series of arbitrary recollections, Moshe's initial words of farewell to the Israelites are pointedly direct. With sweeping prose and powerful rhetoric he drives home one significant message: *We have been here before and we failed then. Do not repeat past mistakes. Seize this moment with courage and strength and, with God's help, you will succeed!*

Points to Ponder

Parshat Devarim is read each year in the synagogue on Shabbat Chazon, the Shabbat immediately preceding the mournful day of Tisha B'Av, the ninth day of the month of Av, the saddest day on the Jewish calendar. This day marks numerous calamities, the most significant of which are the tragic destructions of the two Temples, the first at the hands of the Babylonians in 586 BC and the second at the hands of the Romans in 70 CE. The second of these tragedies launched thousands of years of exile and torment for the Jewish nation.

As we have noted previously (see *Bamidbar*: Shelach 3), however, the Talmud maintains that the roots of Tisha B'Av stretch to an even earlier point in Jewish history, to the moment when the generation of the Exodus lost its opportunity to enter the land of Canaan through the *chet hameraglim*, the sin of the spies.

"That very night [when the Israelites wept in response to the report of the spies] was the eve of Tisha B'Av. Said the Holy One Blessed Be He to them [the Israelites]: 'You have cried for naught and I shall establish for you crying across the generations.'"[7] Rooted in the nation's first failure to claim its national destiny is the tragedy and sorrow that will visit their descendents, over and over again, throughout the ages, on the mournful day of Tisha B'Av.

No Torah reading could, therefore, be more appropriate for Shabbat Chazon than Parshat Devarim. Consisting wholly of Moshe's first parting message to the Israelites, with its focus on the earlier failure of the sin of the spies, this parsha serves as a perfect prelude to the sad day born through that event, the mournful day of Tisha B'Av.

Our analysis of Moshe's words, however, demonstrates that the connection between Parshat Devarim and the fast that follows runs even deeper, particularly in our day. For Tisha B'Av reminds us that in order to meet present and future challenges, we must first recognize the painful failures of the past.

As Moshe challenged the Israelites in his first words of farewell, Tisha B'Av challenges us.

We have been here before, you and I. Jewish history is, after all, replete with opportunities presented, lost, and presented again. At other points in your journey God afforded you with the opportunity to succeed. Yet, you failed – through lack of belief, an absence of vision, disloyalty to God and His commandments, and sinat chinam, *reasonless hatred among yourselves.*

And, now, here we are again, at a time when you have returned to the land and your destiny is achievable.

Will you learn from the past? Will you correct your flaws? Will you succeed where your ancestors failed?

Your fate rests in your hands...

---

7. Talmud Bavli Ta'anit 29a.

4 Editing History

Context

A number of variations emerge between Moshe's recollections of *chet hameraglim* (the sin of the spies) and the details of the events themselves, as recorded in the book of Bamidbar. While some of these differences can be easily explained, two glaring discrepancies must give the reader pause.

The narratives diverge completely both concerning the origin of the spies' mission and concerning the quality of their report upon returning from the land.

BAMIDBAR	DEVARIM
1. The Sending of the Spies	*1. The Sending of the Spies*
"And the Lord spoke to Moshe, saying, 'Send for yourself men, and let them spy out the land of Canaan...'"[1]	"And all of you [the Israelites] approached me [Moshe] and said, 'Let us send men before us and let them spy out the land for us and bring us back word.... And the idea was good in my eyes...'"[2]
2. The Spies' Report	*2. The Spies' Report*
"We came to the land to which you sent us and indeed it flows with milk and honey, and this is its fruit. But the nation that resides in the land is powerful, and the cities are fortified and very great; and also the descendents	"They brought back word to us and said, 'Good is the land that the Lord our God gives us.'"[3]

1. Bamidbar 13:1–2.
2. Devarim 1:22–23.
3. Ibid., 1:25.

BAMIDBAR	DEVARIM
of the giant we saw there. Amalek resides in the Southland; the Hittites, the Yevusites and the Emorites reside in the mountains; and the Canaanites reside by the sea and on the bank of the Jordan."[4] "We cannot ascend against that people for they are stronger *mimenu* (than we)."[5] "The land through which we passed to spy out is a land that devours its inhabitants, and all the people that we saw in it were of great stature; and there we saw… the sons of giants…and we were in our own eyes as grasshoppers and so were we in theirs."[6]	

Questions

In our time, many within the Jewish community and beyond rail against perceived inaccuracies in the media's reporting of world events, particularly concerning the State of Israel. We are quick to point out that the boundary between objective reporting of facts and editorializing on those facts has become increasingly blurred.

These current concerns only serve to highlight the questions before us.

How can we explain the discrepancies in Moshe's recollections of the sin of the spies? We hesitate to make the charge, but could Moshe be guilty of historical revisionism or, at the very least, selective memory, in his representation of the events?

What are the facts? Whose idea was it to send the spies – God's or the Israelites'?

---

4. Ibid., 13:27–28.
5. Ibid., 13:31.
6. Ibid., 13:32–33.

And why does Moshe glaringly omit the majority of the report brought back by the spies upon the conclusion of their mission to Canaan? This omission cannot be construed as a minor oversight on the prophet's part. By leaving out the overwhelmingly negative aspects of the spies' testimony, Moshe effectively changes the quality of the entire story. According to the reality that he presents, the spies seem to bear no blame at all, while the nation is fully at fault, having had no reason to lose heart and rebel.

Approaches

—A—

Faced with these glaring issues, the scholars rise to address the differences between the two versions of the sin of the spies. To a one, the classical commentaries are emphatic in their acceptance of Moshe's version of the initial sending of the spies: *contrary to appearances in the original account of the episode, the Israelites, not God, initiated the spies' mission.*

Rashi, quoting the Midrash, finds allusion to this fact at the opening of the Bamidbar narrative, in the very wording of God's commandment to send the spies: *Shelach lecha anashim*, "send for yourself men."[7] Focusing on the seemingly superfluous word *lecha* (for yourself), the Midrash explains that the term in this context means *l'da'atcha* (according to your wishes).

I am not commanding you to do so, God says to Moshe, *but since the people have asked, if you so desire, send…*

The Midrash quoted by Rashi goes on to explain that the people's request, itself, constituted a sin. The Israelites should have implicitly trusted God's word without further inquiry, both concerning the quality of the land and concerning their ability to defeat its inhabitants.[8]

---

7. Bamidbar 13:2.
8. Midrash Tanchuma Shelach 5. Going one step further, a number of commentaries perceive in the word *lecha* additional divine messages to Moshe concerning the selection of the spies. The Sforno and the Kli Yakar, for example, maintain that God instructs Moshe to choose the spies *lecha* (for himself), rather than grant the right of selection to the people. The Kli Yakar offers another approach, as well, perceiving a prophetic dimension within the wording of God's command. *The sending of the spies, Moshe, will be "lecha" – for your benefit – not for the benefit of the Israelites. They will perish in the wilderness as a result of this event. Your life, however, will be extended another forty years to enable you to lead the nation through that wilderness.*

The Ramban, however, disagrees emphatically with Rashi's categorization of the people's request for spies as a sin. The Israelites, this scholar claims, acted in a natural fashion, as would any nation attempting to determine the best approach to an impending battle. God, in fact, fully requires that we not rely on miracles in such endeavors, but that we do our part. Moshe, therefore, agreeing with the people's appeal, consults with God and receives the response "*Shelach lecha anashim.*"[9]

Nehama Leibowitz explains that, according to the Ramban, the nature of the people's request for spies is so obvious that there is no need for a mention of that request in the original Bamidbar narrative of the episode. In Moshe's recollections, recorded in the book of Devarim, this great leader does refer to the people's request, in order to emphasize their ancestors' direct responsibility for the unfolding events.[10]

—— **B** ——

The rabbis struggle, as well, to explain the glaring discrepancies in Moshe's account of the spies' report upon their return from the land. Why, they ask, does Moshe omit the overwhelmingly negative aspects of that report?

In order to maintain historical accuracy, Rashi tersely limits Moshe's recollections to the testimony of the two spies who supported entry into Canaan: Calev and Yehoshua. Moshe, Rashi maintains, refers solely to the account delivered by these two heroes when he states, "They brought back word to us and said. 'Good is the land that the Lord our God gives us.'"[11]

Objecting to Rashi's approach, the Ramban argues that, appearances aside, Moshe actually does allude to the entire report of the spies, including its negative aspects, in his recollections to the nation. The Ramban bases this contention on the thesis that the spies, as a group, originally delivered their account to the nation in two distinct stages and in two very different settings.

At first, speaking in a public forum before Moshe and the nation, the twelve spies together conveyed their initial positive assessment of the quality of the land. Still in this public setting, ten of their number (excluding Calev and Yehoshua) then injected a powerfully pessimistic note

---

9. Ramban, Bamidbar 13:2.
10. Nehama Leibowitz, *Studies in Devarim* (Jerusalem: World Zionist Organization, 1980), pp. 19–20.
11. Rashi, Devarim 1:25.

concerning the strength of the land's inhabitants. In reaction, Calev rose to urge the people forward.

The ten spies then changed their tactics. Sensing that the nation, bolstered by Calev's encouraging words, was still considering the possibility of entering the land, the spies began to speak to the people in private, entering their tents and "bringing forth an evil report" concerning the land.[12] These efforts succeeded in moving the nation to absolute, total despair.

Thirty-eight years later, the Ramban explains, Moshe recalls the events in two stages, as well. He alludes to this first, public report when he recalls, "They brought back word to us and said, 'Good is the land that the Lord our God gives us.'"[13] He does not, however, omit the devastating second stage of the spies' report from his account, as might first seem. His accusation, "And you murmured in your tents, saying, 'Because the Lord hates us he has taken us out of Egypt...,'"[14] refers not only to the people's reaction to the spies' report. This "murmuring" is also a direct, full reference to the portion of the report that was "delivered in the tents of the nation."[15]

— C —

In stark contrast to the scholars quoted above, who struggle to correlate Moshe's version of the sin of the spies in Devarim with the events as recorded in Bamidbar, a number of other commentaries, including Rabbi David Tzvi Hoffman, maintain that *the two versions of the episode do not and need not match at all.* The nature and purpose of each of the two narratives, these scholars claim, are totally different. While the text in Bamidbar presents *a historical accounting of the events* surrounding the sin of the spies, the narrative in Devarim presents *Moshe's interpretation of these events.*

As noted in our previous study, Moshe refers to the sin of the spies in his opening farewell address to the nation for only one purpose. He is intent on ensuring that this episode does not recur, and that the nation standing before him does not fail on the brink of success, as did their parents. To accomplish his goal, Moshe must convince each Israelite that he or she alone is responsible for the moral decisions to be made; "the

---

12. Bamidbar 13:32.
13. Devarim 1:25.
14. Ibid., 1:27.
15. Ramban, Devarim 1:25.

existence of a provocateur does not absolve the subject of the provocation from responsibility."[16]

Moshe, therefore, deliberately shades his retelling of the story to minimize the role played by the spies and to emphasize the personal decisions made by each individual Israelite at the time. He does not claim to deliver a full historical account, but rather a moral discourse with a clear message at its core:

Do not make the mistake of blaming what occurred on the spies themselves. Each of your parents, after all, had a choice between believing the evil report of a malicious few or trusting in the word of God. Their failure was their own and can be blamed on no one else.

You, as well, will be continually tested to make the right choices in the face of temptation and seduction as your journey continues. Trust in God and in your own moral compass, and you will succeed.[17]

Points to Ponder

A number of years ago, facing the ruins of a Roman aqueduct near a beach in Israel, an Israeli tour guide taught me a dramatic lesson that I remember clearly to this day.

The guide pointed to a panel on the aqueduct upon which an inscription had once been etched and, subsequently, deliberately obliterated.

This panel, the guide explained, had originally identified the Roman legion responsible for the aqueduct's construction. When this legion later suffered humiliating defeats in battle, however, the Roman authorities erased all vestiges of their identity from structures throughout the empire. Such failure could only be dealt with by Roman society in one way: by totally eradicating the memory of those responsible, as if those individuals had never existed. Roman history was to be continually revised, to reflect only Roman success.

"This distinction between the Jews and the Romans in our attitudes towards history," the guide suggested, "may well have contributed towards our respective fates. The Romans, who were unable to admit fault or failure, eventually atrophied as a people and disintegrated as a nation. We Jews – who embraced failure as well as success in our collective memory, and

---

16. Leibowitz, *Studies in Devarim*, p. 22.
17. Hoffman, *Sefer Devarim* 1:22–28.

who conveyed history honestly across the generations, warts and all – are still here to tell the tale. You can only learn from history if the record you transmit is honest and complete."

Historical transmission can be complex even within the Jewish world, however, with considerable controversy frequently surrounding the process. Facts are subject to interpretation and multiple "possible truths" commonly emerge from different observers. Complicating matters further, issues of boundaries arise, as authorities debate the appropriateness of including specific "truths" in the historical record.

Our own studies have often reflected the tension, for example, between those commentaries who accept the human foibles attributed in the Torah to biblical heroes and those scholars intent on explaining those apparent weaknesses away.

Far from being relegated to a distant past, however, this tension carries to our own time. The controversy surrounding a two-volume set authored by Rabbi Nathan Kamenetsky, son of the renowned sage Rabbi Yaakov Kamenetsky, serves as a perfect example.

In 2002, the younger Rabbi Kamenetsky published a two-volume work, *The Making of a Gadol*. The product of over fifteen years of extensive research culled from over eight hundred sources, this work featured detailed biographical information on the lives of the author's father and numerous other prominent Jewish sages of the nineteenth and twentieth centuries.

Shortly after the work's publication, however, controversy erupted. Ten leading Haredi (fervently Orthodox) rabbis in Israel signed a letter banning the book for containing disrespectful material concerning its rabbinic subjects. The ban initially remained unofficial, pending discussion between the leading opponent of the book, Rabbi Yosef Shalom Elyashiv, and the work's author. The letter, however, was soon leaked to the public and, in spite of Rabbi Kamenetsky's objection that none of the rabbinic signatories to the letter had actually read the volumes, the ban took hold.

The issuing of a second, revised edition of *The Making of a Gadol*, an attempt by the author to address the objections to the work, only resulted in a reissuing of the ban. As a result of these events only one thousand volumes of the work are extant today.

At the core of this conflict lies not only the obvious question "how much news is fit to print," but a deeper concern. How do we best pay tribute to the great personalities of our tradition? Are these great individuals best served through the recording of "sanitized" versions of their lives? Or as Rabbi Kamenetsky himself argued in his defense of his work, does fuller disclosure about these personalities help achieve more complete appreciation of their greatness? Will we be inspired more by the tales of unblemished heroes or by the accomplishments of real human beings who rise to monumental accomplishment?

The rabbinic struggle to correlate Moshe's recollections with the earlier historical record foreshadows the complex challenge of historical transmission across the ages. At the dawn of Jewish national history, our greatest leader faced the challenge of conveying history in a way that would most benefit future generations. How well we meet this challenge, and the decisions we make when we do so, will help determine the character of our people for years to come.

Va'etchanan   ואתחנן

CHAPTER 3:23–7:11   פרק ג:כג-ז:יא

Parsha Summary

Poignant pleas, powerful exhortations, pivotal memories, timeless text…

Moshe highlights his pleas to God for a reversal of the divine decree prohibiting him from entering the land together with the people. Although his request is refused, God will allow him to view the length and breadth of the land from atop a mountain.

Moshe issues a general exhortation towards observance of the divinely given law. Warning the nation to neither add to nor subtract from God's decrees, he recalls the character of the Revelation at Sinai, where God directly spoke to the people, but revealed no divine image. He cautions the nation, therefore, to create no images in their worship of God but to focus on obedience to His law.

Urging the people to recognize their unique relationship with the Divine, Moshe asks: Has there ever been any other nation that has experienced what you have experienced; any other people that have witnessed what you have witnessed? *"You have been shown in order to know that the Lord, He is the God! There is none beside Him!"*[1]

After designating three cities in the Transjordan to serve as cities of refuge for individuals convicted of negligent homicide (see Shoftim 5), Moshe opens his second major farewell discourse to the nation, focusing on the mitzvot to be conveyed before his death. He begins by underscoring the foundations of the law as he repeats the Ten Declarations with minor variations (see Va'etchanan 2).

Towards the end of Parshat Va'etchanan Moshe transmits a passage destined to become one of the best-known paragraphs of the entire Torah text. Known popularly as the first paragraph of the Shma, this paragraph is the first of the biblical texts recited daily by the Jew in fulfillment of the mitzva of Kriat Shma, the recitation of the Shma. The passage opens with the powerful

---

1. Devarim 4:35.

proclamation "Shma Yisrael, *Hear O Israel: the Lord is our God, the Lord is One*" *and goes on to underscore a series of ideas fundamental to Jewish thought (see Va'etchanan 3–5).*

1 Why Not?

Context

As the curtain rises on Parshat Va'etchanan, Moshe recounts his unsuccessful pleas to God to reverse the divine decree prohibiting him
from entering the land of Canaan:

> And I beseeched God at this time, saying: "My Lord, God, You have
> begun to show Your servant Your greatness and Your strong hand....
> Let me now cross and see the good land that is on the other side of
> the Jordan, this good mountain and the Lebanon."
>
> But God turned angrily against me for your sakes and He did
> not listen to me; and God said to me: "It is too much for you! Do
> not continue to speak to Me concerning this matter. Ascend to the
> top of the cliff and raise your eyes westward, northward, southward,
> and eastward, and see with your eyes, for you will not cross this
> Jordan."[2]

Questions

The tragedy of Moshe's fate, the fulcrum upon which the entire book of
Devarim turns, continues to haunt us across the centuries. This humble,
reluctant leader, who has patiently and painstakingly brought his people
to the very edge of their dreams, will, as a result of divine mandate, not
realize those dreams with them.

Why does God reject Moshe's supplications? Is Moshe's sin so great
that he must be denied forgiveness? Are the gates of prayer and repentance
truly closed to our most sainted leader? If so, what hope have we that God
will hear our prayers?

We have previously noted the struggle of the commentaries to identify
the exact sin of Moshe and Aharon at the scene of Mei Meriva, the waters

---

2. Devarim 3:23–27.

of strife, where God issues His decree concerning the fate of these great leaders.[3] The suggested possibilities for Moshe and Aharon's failure include deviation from God's instructions, unwarranted anger against the nation, assumption of credit for a divine miracle, and more (see *Bamidbar*: Chukat 3, for a full discussion).

Whatever the catalyst for God's verdict against Moshe at Mei Meriva, however, why can't that verdict be set aside now?

Approaches

— A —

Deeply troubled by God's continuing rejection of Moshe's pleas for forgiveness, numerous rabbinic sources suggest that God is actually *unable*, as opposed to *unwilling*, to forgive Moshe. These authorities note the use of the term *lachen* (therefore) in God's original verdict at Mei Meriva.[4] According to Midrashic tradition, the presence of this term invariably indicates that an oath has been enacted.[5] At the scene of Mei Meriva, God actually swears that Moshe and Aharon will not enter the land. This divine oath, once taken, cannot be abrogated.[6]

Building on this approach, the Sifrei suggests that Moshe's entreaty to God at this time is based upon a misapprehension of the extent of God's original vow. Once Moshe sees that he has been allowed to participate in the battles for the conquest of the Transjordan, he assumes that the divine oath decreeing his fate has been abrogated and that he will now be allowed to participate in the subjugation of Canaan, as well. God, however, informs him that the vow remains in place and that Moshe's entry into the land remains prohibited.

The Da'at Zekeinim Miba'alei Hatosafot offers a poignant Midrashic play on God's rejoinder to Moshe, "*Rav lecha*, it is too much for you." Departing dramatically from the *pshat* of the text, the Tosafists note that the words *rav lecha* can be interpreted to mean "[Moshe,] you have a master."

The Tosafists postulate that, in the face of God's rejection of his pleas,

3. Bamidbar 20:1–13.
4. Ibid., 20:12.
5. Midrash Tanchuma Shmot, Va'era 2.
6. Rashi, Bamidbar 20:12, Devarim 3:23; Chizkuni, Bamidbar 20:12; Abravanel, Devarim 3:23–26.

Moshe argues: *Master of the universe, please release Yourself from Your vow – as You have released me from my vows, in the past. God responds: Moshe, rav lecha, you have a master, Someone above you Who can release you from your vows. I, in contrast, have no master. No one, therefore, can annul the vows that I take upon Myself. They must remain in place.*[7]

——— **B** ————————————————————————————————————

Other authorities focus on Moshe's puzzling claim, "God turned angrily against me *for your sakes.*" This statement mirrors an equally troubling comment made by Moshe in Parshat Devarim where, in recounting the sin of the spies, he states, "With me, as well, did God become angry *because of you*, saying, 'You, too, shall not come there [into the land of Canaan].'"[8]

Can it be that Moshe, at these critical moments, tries to evade responsibility for his own past failures? Why would God reject Moshe's pleas "for the sake of the Israelites" or "because of the Israelites"?

This puzzle is solved, the Abravanel argues, if we accept his claim that the events at Mei Meriva do not truly determine the fate of Aharon and Moshe. As previously noted, the Abravanel maintains, contrary to the apparent evidence of the text, that these great leaders are actually punished for earlier offenses: Aharon for his involvement in the sin of the golden calf and Moshe for his participation in the sin of the spies (see *Bamidbar*: Chukat 3, *Approaches* A). In each of these cases, the actions of these great leaders are well intentioned; and yet in each case they inadvertently contribute to the national disasters that ensue.

God, therefore, calibrates His responses carefully. In order to protect the reputation of both Moshe and Aharon, He does not punish them immediately, together with those guilty of intentional rebellion. He instead waits for them to commit an intentional sin, however minor, in order to punish them for their original transgressions. When Moshe deviates from God's commandment at Mei Meriva, by striking the rock instead of speaking to it, God seizes the opportunity to exact retribution upon these leaders for their previous, more substantial failings.[9]

Now, as he recounts his unsuccessful attempts to overturn God's decree,

---

7. Da'at Zekeinim Miba'alei Hatosafot, Devarim 3:26.
8. Devarim 1:37.
9. Abravanel, Bamidbar 20:1–14.

Moshe turns to the nation and declares: *I am being punished "for your sake."* *Because of your flawed reaction to the report of the spies, I must now pay the price for my initial involvement in that tragic episode.*[10]

— C ———

Moving in a different direction, other commentaries suggest that Moshe is forbidden from entering the land at least in part because of the powerful effect that his presence would have upon the people's ultimate fate. According to these authorities, this great leader literally suffers "for the people's sake."

The Sforno and the Kli Yakar, for example, maintain that Moshe wants to prevent, through his towering presence and personal involvement in the conquest of Canaan, any possibility of the nation's eventual exile from the land. Moshe's plan, however, runs counter to God's intentions. God knows that, in the future, the people are destined to sin and that their ultimate exile will be both unavoidable and necessary. He therefore ensures that the conquest of Canaan takes place only after Moshe's death, under the weaker leadership of Yehoshua. Consequently, the Israelites' continued possession of the Land of Israel will not be assured but will forever remain dependent upon their own merits.[11]

— D ———

Combining aspects of the approaches of the Abravanel, on the one hand, and of the Sforno and Kli Yakar, on the other, the Malbim makes a revolutionary claim. *God's decree concerning Moshe is not the result of any sin on this great leader's part at all.* Moshe's fate is instead sealed by the failings of the nation. Under God's original plan, the Israelites were to conquer the land of Canaan under Moshe's continuing leadership. Moshe's very involvement would have resulted in a miraculous chain of events. No physical battles would have been fought, as God would have miraculously destroyed the nation's enemies before them. Moshe would have supervised the building of a Temple destined to stand in perpetuity. And, finally, the messianic era would have been reached.

The realization of these miracles, however, remained dependent on the nation's continuing faith in God…

_____

10. Abravanel, Devarim 3:26.
11. Sforno, Devarim 3:26; Kli Yakar, Devarim 3:26.

When the nation, through the sin of the spies, tragically demonstrates itself to be unworthy of God's supernatural intervention, God has no choice but to ensure that Moshe will not enter the land. He decrees that the generation of the Exodus will perish in the desert, clearly excluding only Yehoshua and Calev (the two spies who withstood the evil counsel of their colleagues) from the decree.[12] For their part, Moshe and Aharon are to share the fate of the rest of their generation.

One last chance for redemption, however, remains. If the next generation, the generation that matures in the wilderness, can prove the strength of its commitment to God, the decree sealing Moshe and Aharon's fate can yet be reversed. These great leaders will be able to lead the nation into the land and all of the promised miracles will still unfold.

These final hopes, however, are dashed at the scene of Mei Meriva. There, once again, as they "gather against Moshe and Aharon," the people prove unworthy of God's trust. Moshe, in addition, affected by the turmoil, misses the opportunity to fully sanctify God's name by speaking to the rock. Consequently, the original decree against Moshe and Aharon is reaffirmed and raised to the status of a divine oath that cannot be subsequently reversed. Moshe and Aharon will perish "for the sake of" and "because of" the people.[13]

— **E** —————————————————————————

One final approach to Moshe's contention that his prayers are rejected "for the people's sake" can be offered by reinterpreting, yet again, the events at Mei Meriva. Adapting the insights of Rabbi Harold Kanatopsky, a brilliant teacher and my community rabbi during my teenage years, we have previously suggested that Moshe's failure at Mei Meriva consists of an inability to transition from the leadership of one generation to the leadership of the next (see *Bamidbar*: Chukat 3, *Approaches* H).

The first generation of Israelites with whom Moshe deals, the generation of the Exodus, relates to God only through the primitive emotion of fear. When, therefore, shortly after the Exodus, this generation finds itself without water at a location known as Refidim, God commands Moshe to speak to the people in the only language that they will understand. *Strike*

———————————

12. Bamidbar 14:30.
13. Malbim, Bamidbar 20:7–13, Devarim 3:26.

the rock, He commands, *and let the Israelites recognize the power of their heavenly master.*

Forty years later, however, at Mei Meriva, Moshe stands before a generation that has come to relate to God through the more mature dimension of love. God therefore commands Moshe: *Take the staff. Show the people that you can use it, but that you deliberately will not. Instead, speak to the rock and, in doing so, "speak" to the people. Demonstrate to them, at this critical moment, that the power of love is infinitely stronger than the power of brute force.*

Moshe, however, slips…

Confronted again by the bitter complaints of the Israelites, he flashes back to Refidim. He sees before him not the Israelites of the day, but their parents and grandparents of yesteryear. And in that one fateful instant, as Moshe lifts his staff to strike the rock, he fails to transition with his people from one generation to the next, from one relational level to another. This failure seals his fate. He and Aharon (who makes no move to stop his brother) will remain forever part of their generation, consigned to perish in the desert without entry into the land.

"For the sake of the people," Moshe cannot enter the land. A new generation needs a new leader – one who will be able to transition with his people in their march towards a glorious future.

— **F** —

The above interpretations, however, create an opening for a powerful question. If Moshe's fate is sealed "for the sake of the nation," because his leadership would somehow compromise the people's destiny, why can't he enter the land as a common man? This humble leader has already requested that God appoint a successor in his stead and, at God's command, has publicly appointed Yehoshua as that successor.[14] Surely Moshe would now agree to join in the conquest of Canaan under the stewardship of his trusted student. Why doesn't God simply pass the mantle of leadership to Yehoshua without insisting on Moshe's death in the Transjordan?

The Mechilta imagines a powerful conversation in which this argument,

14. Bamidbar 27:15. The Ramban maintains that the appointment of Yehoshua, although instructed in Parshat Pinchas, actually takes place immediately before Moshe's death. Nonetheless, the instructions for this transfer of leadership have already been clearly conveyed.

among others, is actually raised by Moshe to God: *Master of the universe, when You initially decreed my fate You stated: "Therefore you shall not bring this congregation to the land…"*[15] *Since I cannot bring the people into the land as a king, please allow me to enter with them as a commoner.*

God's response, the Midrash continues, is short and to the point: *A king may not enter [the land] as a commoner.*[16]

Elaborating on this Midrashic approach, the Abravanel suggests that God's declaration to Moshe in Parshat Va'etchanan, "*Rav lecha*, it is too much for you…," can be reinterpreted as a rhetorical question. *Rav lecha? Would it really be appropriate*, God asks Moshe, *for Yehoshua to teach while you sit and watch? Would it really be appropriate for Yehoshua to be your teacher* (rav) *and master?*[17] Having risen to the grandeur of leadership, Moshe cannot now descend from its heights.

The poignant picture painted by the Midrash and the Abravanel highlights the powerful challenges that often emerge at times of personal transition and change. When an individual must step aside from a specific life arena and allow someone else to "take his place," the questions often abound.

What can I hold onto; what must I let go? How will I feel when he does things differently? Can I stay, or must I leave? How much space does my successor need in order to be his own man?

Through the rabbis' eyes, we watch Moshe struggle with these questions after over forty years of extraordinary personal investment and sacrifice. As he does so, our own potential struggles come to light, as well.

— G —

Finally, in a telling observation elaborated upon by many later authorities,[18] the Talmud overturns our original assumptions concerning the opening narrative of Parshat Va'etchanan. From the point of view of the Talmudists, the text does not emphasize God's rejection of Moshe's prayers, but, rather, His acceptance of those prayers – at least, in part:

---

15. Ibid., 20:12.
16. *Mechilta D'bei Rebbi Yishmael*, Beshalach 2.
17. Abravanel, Devarim 3.
18. Kli Yakar, Devarim 3:25, and others.

The power of prayer is greater than the power of good deeds – for no one was greater than Moshe in good deeds, yet he was only answered through prayer. As the text relates: "Do not continue to speak to Me concerning this matter. Ascend to the top of the cliff [and raise your eyes]…"[19]

Here, then, is a very different take on the results of the dialogue between God and Moshe. *Moshe's prayers are answered, after all.* His words do have an effect, as God relents. Although this great leader will still be prohibited from entering Canaan, he will now be allowed to view the land from afar.[20]

Sometimes the answers God provides to our prayers are painted in shades of gray, rather than in black or white.

Point to Ponder

Three powerful ancillary lessons emerge from the rabbinic conversation surrounding Moshe's interchange with God at the beginning of Parshat Va'etchanan.

1. *Our word is our bond.* The suggestion that God may be bound by the strictures of His own vows underscores the seriousness with which we should view our own spoken commitments. If an almighty deity will not stray from the path determined by His word, how careful must we be to fulfill the verbal obligations that we take upon ourselves?

2. *It's not all about us.* The contention that Moshe's fate is decreed, at least in part, for the sake of others sensitizes us to the fact that an individual's destiny is determined not only by his own needs but by the valid needs of others, as well.

As we have previously noted (see *Bereishit*: Noach 4, *Approaches* A), this idea is dramatically underscored during the Covenant between the Pieces enacted by God with Avraham at the dawn of Jewish history. In predicting the eventual return of Avraham's descendents to the land of Canaan, God states: "And the fourth generation will return here, for the iniquity of the

---

19. Talmud Bavli Brachot 33b.
20. God's allowance to Moshe regarding the viewing of the land is actually recorded in a prior passage in Bamidbar (27:12). Apparently the Midrash believes that passage, as well, reflects God's response to Moshe's prayers. Moshe now recapitulates his request and God's response in his farewell speeches in Devarim.

Emorites will not be complete until then."[21] *You will not be able to acquire the land of Canaan until the indigenous inhabitants deserve to lose it.*

There are times when what is "best" for us is not "best" for those around us. God will factor our competing needs and rights into the equation as He determines our respective destinies.

3. *It's never too late to pray.* The proposition that Moshe changes God's mind through prayer marks this incident as one of a number of occasions in the text where Moshe's prayers seem to sway God's judgments. This phenomenon, however, highlights a fundamental philosophical problem. How can an all-perfect God be moved to "change His mind" by the words of man? God is, by definition, not capable of error. Whatever He decides is correct, or He would not decide it. What is the mechanism by which such prayer works?

We have noted before (see *Bereishit*: Toldot 3, *Approaches* A) that, according to some authorities, the roots of this phenomenon can be traced to the words that launch Jewish history. God's initial promises to the patriarch Avraham include the phrase "And you will be a blessing."[22] The Midrash interprets this phrase to mean, "Blessings are given to your hand. Until now they were in My hand. I blessed Adam and Noach. From this time on, you will bless whom you wish."[23]

By granting man the power to bless, God withdraws and deliberately limits His own power. As part of a divine partnership agreement with humanity, God will respect the words spoken by man and reckon with them when He makes his decisions. Man thus acquires the power of blessing and prayer. God Himself grants effectiveness to our prayers, both on behalf of ourselves and for the welfare of others.

Other authorities suggest that the effectiveness of prayer and repentance in swaying God's judgments can be viewed from an entirely different perspective. Prayer, these scholars argue, transforms the supplicant. An individual who engages in heartfelt prayer and in true repentance emerges from the experience a different person than he was before. *In effect, therefore, the subject of God's original decree no longer exists.* God has not changed His mind; man has changed himself.

---

21. Bereishit 15:16.
22. Ibid., 12:2.
23. Midrash Rabba Bereishit 39:11.

Whether as a mechanism for changing God's mind or as an experience through which a supplicant changes himself, prayer remains, for the Jew, a tool that never loses its potential effectiveness. "Even if a sharp sword lies upon his neck," the Talmud maintains, "an individual should never refrain from [asking for God's] mercy."[24]

While we recognize that God's answer to our requests may well, at times, be no, *Moshe's poignant supplications at the beginning of Parshat Va'etchanan remind us that it's never too late to pray.*

---

24. Talmud Bavli Brachot 10a.

2 Second Edition?

Context

Moshe's recollections bring him back to the pivotal moment at Sinai, when, amidst thunder, lightning and the sounding of the shofar, God conveyed the Ten Declarations to the Israelites (see *Shmot*: Yitro 4).

As Moshe repeats these declarations in retrospect, a series of variations upon the original text recorded in the book of Shmot emerge. These textual discrepancies are inconsistent in nature. While the first and third declarations are repeated without any change at all, the other eight contain variations ranging from the nuanced to the substantial.[1]

Questions

We have repeatedly noted (see *Bereishit*: Bereishit 3; Chayei Sara 3; Miketz 1) that whenever the Torah replicates a conversation or event, we are challenged to carefully compare the two versions presented. Invariably, the differences that emerge are important and instructive.

The passages before us, however, are uniquely problematic. With Moshe's retrospective recording of the Ten Declarations, we are effectively confronted with a "second edition" of the divine communication that launched Revelation and changed the world.

How can we explain the textual discrepancies between the two versions of the Aseret Hadibrot? These declarations are, after all, God's own words. A perfect God must have fashioned a perfect text through which to introduce His law to His people. Communication shared by such a Deity should need neither further editing nor improvement.

Our questions are further complicated by the singular nature of the book of Devarim as a whole. We have previously noted (see Devarim 1) that a spectrum of rabbinic opinion exists concerning the authorship of this volume. While all traditional scholars accept the divine nature of Devarim,

---

1. Devarim 5:1–18.

they argue over Moshe's role in the narrative. Does Devarim, they ask, uniquely consist of Moshe's words, agreed to by God in retrospect; or does Moshe continue in the role that he has played until now, faithfully recording a text dictated by his Divine Master? Our position on these issues will clearly affect our posture concerning the "dueling editions" of the Aseret Hadibrot. Numerous possibilities emerge. Did the textual emendations found in Devarim originate from God, from Moshe or from a partnership between the two? Is the source of all these variations consistent; or were some changes determined by God and others suggested by Moshe?

Approaches

— A —

Faced with these glaring issues, the rabbis accept as a given that the second version of the Aseret Hadibrot is neither an improvement upon nor a replacement for the first. *Both versions are authentic.* The changes that appear are, instead, designed to convey critical lessons and ideas that could not be derived from one consistent text.

Armed with this understanding, the scholars painstakingly study the differences between the two versions of the Aseret Hadibrot and offer explanations for each.

Our discussion must, of course, begin with a review of the textual discrepancies themselves.

THE TEN DECLARATIONS: VERSION I (SHMOT)	THE TEN DECLARATIONS: VERSION 2 (DEVARIM)
1. I am the Lord your God, Who has taken you out of the land of Egypt, from the house of slavery.	1. I am the Lord your God, Who has taken you out of the land of Egypt, from the house of slavery.
2. You shall have no other gods in My presence. You shall not make for yourself *a graven image nor any likeness* of that which is in the heavens above or on the	2. You shall have no other gods in My presence. You shall not make for yourself *a graven image of any likeness* [the letter *vav* is omitted] of that which is in the heavens

THE TEN DECLARATIONS: VERSION 1 (SHMOT)	THE TEN DECLARATIONS: VERSION 2 (DEVARIM)
Earth below or in the water beneath the Earth. You shall not bow down to them nor shall you serve them, for I am the Lord your God, a jealous God, Who visits the sin of fathers upon children to the third and to the fourth generations of those who hate Me; and Who shows kindness to thousands of those who love Me and to those who keep My commandments.	above or on the Earth below or in the water beneath the Earth. You shall not bow down to them nor shall you serve them, for I am the Lord your God, a jealous God, Who visits the sin of fathers upon children *and* to the third and to the fourth generations of those who hate Me; and Who shows kindness to thousands of those who love Me and to those who keep My commandments.
3. You shall not take the name of the Lord, God, in vain, for the Lord will not absolve anyone who takes His name in vain.	3. You shall not take the name of the Lord, God, in vain, for the Lord will not absolve anyone who takes His name in vain.
4. *Remember* the Sabbath day to sanctify it. Six days shall you labor and perform all your work; but the seventh day is Sabbath to the Lord your God; you shall not do any work – you, and your son, and your daughter, your slave, and your maidservant, *and your animal*, and your convert who is within your gates – *for in six days the Lord made the heavens and the earth, the sea and all that is within them, and He rested on the seventh day. Therefore the Lord blessed the Sabbath day and sanctified it.*	4. *Safeguard* the Sabbath day to sanctify it, *as the Lord your God has commanded you.* Six days shall you labor and perform all your work; but the seventh day is Sabbath to the Lord your God; you shall not do any work – you, and your son, and your daughter, *and* your slave, and your maidservant, *and your ox, and your donkey, and your every animal,* and your convert who is within your gates; *in order that your slave and your maidservant shall rest like you. And you shall remember that you were a slave in the land of Egypt, and the*

THE TEN DECLARATIONS: VERSION 1 (SHMOT)	THE TEN DECLARATIONS: VERSION 2 (DEVARIM)
	Lord your God took you out from there with a strong hand and an outstretched arm. Therefore, the Lord your God has commanded you to make the Sabbath day.
5. Honor your father and your mother so that your days may be lengthened upon the land that the Lord your God gives to you.	5. Honor your father and your mother, *as the Lord your God has commanded you*, so that your days may be lengthened *and so that it will be good for you*, upon the land that the Lord your God gives to you.
6. You shall not murder.	6. You shall not murder.
7. You shall not commit adultery.	7. *And* you shall not commit adultery.
8. You shall not steal.	8. *And* you shall not steal.
9. You shall not bear *false* witness against your fellow.	9. *And* you shall not bear *vain* witness against your fellow.
10. You shall not covet your fellow's wife, *nor his manservant, nor his maidservant, nor his ox, nor his donkey, nor anything that belongs to your fellow.*	10. *And* you shall not covet your fellow's wife, *and you shall not desire your fellow's house, his field, nor his manservant, nor his maidservant, his ox, nor his donkey, nor anything that belongs to your fellow.*

The textual variations between the two versions of the Aseret Hadibrot can be summarized as follows:

1. On six occasions the conjunctive letter *vav* is added to the text (second, fourth, seventh, eighth, ninth, and tenth declarations), while on two occasions that letter is omitted (second and fifth declarations).

2. On two occasions the Torah substitutes one word for another (fourth and ninth declarations).
3. On three occasions the Torah adds a totally new phrase to the text (fourth and fifth declarations).
4. On two occasions the Torah substantially changes a passage of existing text (fourth and tenth declarations).
5. On two occasions slight written variations appear in the text, but are not vocalized (second and fifth declarations). [Note: As these variations do not result in a change in meaning, they are not reflected in the above translation. One of the variations results in the omission of another letter *vav* from the Devarim text, in a variant spelling of the word *ya'arichun* (shall be long; see below).]

— B —————————————————————————

In predictable fashion, the rabbis approach these textual variations from all ends of the interpretive spectrum, offering explanations that range from the mystical and Midrashic to the pragmatic and halachic. Differing perspectives concerning the divine or human origin of the emendations found in the Devarim text can also be discerned.

At one end of the spectrum, a fascinating Midrashic source takes note of an easily missed transformation in the Aseret Hadibrot as a whole. The first "edition" of the declarations, the rabbis point out, contains the entire Hebrew alphabet with the exception of one letter, the letter *tet*. This omission is subsequently rectified in the second "edition" through the insertion of two phrases: *u'vizro'a netuya*, "and with an outstretched arm" (third declaration) and *u'lma'an yitav lach*, "and so that it will be good for you" (fifth declaration). The words *netuya* and *yitav*, each containing the letter *tet*, provide one such letter to compensate for the original omission and one to complete the alphabet in the second edition of the *dibrot*.

These nuanced distinctions, the rabbis explain, hardly occur by chance. God intentionally omits a letter of the alphabet when the Aseret Hadibrot are first given at Sinai in order to protect the Israelites from the full consequences of their impending sin – the sin of the golden calf. *By rendering His contract with the people incomplete and thereby technically "invalid," God deliberately minimizes the impact of their subsequent betrayal of that contract.*

A corrected version of the Sinaitic covenant, complete with all letters of the alphabet, is granted to the next generation of Israelites, as they stand poised to enter the land of Canaan and to succeed where their fathers failed.[2]

A second Midrashic tradition attributes yet another omission in the initial version of the Aseret Hadibrot to potential consequences of the sin of the golden calf. The word *tov* (good), the rabbis note, is absent from the declarations inscribed on the tablets at Sinai. Had those tablets – ultimately smashed by Moshe in response to the sin of the golden calf – contained the word *tov* in any form, God would have been compelled to strip away all future "goodness" from the fledgling Jewish nation.

Any direct allusion to the concept of "goodness" must wait until a new, more deserving generation receives its version of the declarations. This condition is fulfilled when the phrase *l'ma'an yitav lach*, "so that it shall be good for you," is incorporated into the fifth declaration recorded in the book of Devarim.[3]

Finally, a third Midrash focuses on the addition of a total of four conjunctive letters, *vavs*, in the Devarim text.[4] The numerical value of the letter *vav* is six.[5] The inclusion of these four *vavs*, therefore, carries the cumulative effect of symbolically adding the number twenty-four to the *dibrot*. Twenty-four is also the number of volumes contained in Tanach, the Jewish scriptural canon. The entire corpus of Torah She'bi'chtav, the Written Law, is thus alluded to within the text of the Ten Declarations.[6]

It should be noted that, as is often the case with Midrashim, all these sources ignore the literal significance of the additions in question, choosing instead to see the inclusions as "carriers" of divine lessons that are external to the straightforward meaning of the text.

— C —

While the Midrash offers countless other observations concerning these textual variations, we now turn our attention to the opposite end of the

---

2. Pesikta Zutarta (Lekach Tov) Shmot 20, Devarim 10:1.
3. Yalkut Shimoni, Va'etchanan 830:5.
4. Six such letters are actually added but two *vav*'s that were in the first *dibrot* are deleted; resulting in the final addition of four *vav*'s in the Devarim declarations.
5. Each letter of the Hebrew alphabet carries a numerical value as well, from *alef* (one) to *taf* (400).
6. Pesikta Zutarta (Lekach Tov), Devarim 10:1.

interpretive spectrum. Here, numerous scholars struggle to discern logical explanations for the emendations to the *dibrot*. Particularly noteworthy in this regard is the general approach of Rabbi Yehuda Loew, the Maharal of Prague.

As previously noted (Devarim 1, *Approaches* A), the Maharal maintains that Moshe's role is transformed with the advent of the book of Devarim. The first four books of the Torah, the Maharal explains, are designed to reflect God's perspective, as the transmitter of the law. The text of those volumes is therefore transmitted by God directly, literally speaking through Moshe. The book of Devarim, however, is different. This text is devised to more closely parallel the perception of man, the recipient of the law. Now Moshe serves as a prophetic messenger, receiving God's messages and recording them in his own words. Devarim presents God's truths – seen through Moshe's eyes.

The emendations found in the Devarim version of the Aseret Hadibrot thus reflect Moshe's desire to add "commentary" to the text. Upon receiving God's word and perceiving its thrust, Moshe sets out to shape the text as necessary, so that all of God's messages will be clear to the nation.[7]

While the Maharal's overall approach to the variations in the *dibrot* is rooted in logic, however, this scholar's explanation of the individual emendations remains somewhat esoteric.

As a case in point, the Maharal notes that the phrase *l'ma'an yitav lach*, "so that it shall be good for you," is added to the fifth declaration in the Devarim edition of the *dibrot*. This phrase is omitted from the first edition, the Maharal explains, because of the unique nature of Revelation at Sinai. In that setting, God speaks to the nation "face to face," addressing the divine dimension of the Israelites' souls. The heavenly dimension in mortal man, however, is by nature incomplete and cannot be referred to by the term *tov* (good), a term that uniformly connotes wholeness and completeness. The phrase *l'ma'an yitav lach*, therefore, with its reference to "goodness," can only be included in the second edition of the *dibrot*, when Moshe addresses the Israelites as earthly equals, one mortal speaking to another.[8]

The Maharal also observes that in contrast, the next phrase, *u'l'ma'an ya'arichun yamecha*, "so that your days will be long," is included in the fifth

---

7. *Tiferet Yisrael* 43.
8. Ibid.

declaration of both editions of the *dibrot*. Strangely, however, the word, *ya'arichun* (shall be long) is written incompletely in the Devarim edition, with a *vav* omitted and a smaller letter, *yud*, added. This emendation, the Maharal explains, is created by Moshe to reassure the nation. Generally, when the Torah speaks of a lengthy period of time, the connotation is one of sorrow. The time period involved may actually be short, but it "feels endless," due to the difficult nature of its passage. Conversely, when the text speaks of a short duration of time, the days spoken of are pleasurable.[9] The Torah thus informs us that Yaakov toiled seven years in expectation of marrying Rachel, yet the time period "seemed to him a *few days* because of his love for her."[10]

Moshe, recognizing the negative connotation associated in the text with a lengthy period of time, deliberately shortens the word *ya'arichun*. The reward for performing the commandment of *kibbud av va'em*, he conveys, will be "long days" that don't possess the usual character of "long days" in the Torah. An individual who honors his parents will be rewarded by God with a long yet gratifying life. He will be blessed with an abundance of pleasurable days that will not seem endless.[11]

— **D** —

Numerous other commentaries follow the Maharal's general approach to the text in Devarim, yet offer specific explanations that cleave closer to the *pshat*.

Rabbi Shimshon Raphael Hirsch, for example, maintains that Moshe tailors the *dibrot* in Devarim in order to address the unique challenges faced by a generation about to enter its Promised Land.

By adding the phrase *l'ma'an yitav lach...al ha'aretz*, "so that it shall be good for you...on the land," to the declaration concerning obedience to parents, Moshe conveys that "every contemporary generation in Israel

---

9. An objection to the Maharal's contention could be raised from Yaakov's famous complaint upon meeting Pharaoh: "Few and difficult were the years of my life..." (Bereishit 47:9). That statement, however, is a subjective observation on Yaakov's part as opposed to an objective observation made by the text. In addition, Yaakov's conversation with Pharaoh is replete with hidden agendas that shape his comments (see *Bereishit*: Vayigash 4).
10. Bereishit 29:20.
11. *Tiferet Yisrael* 43.

[will only achieve] happiness and prosperity if it takes over, with honoring obedience, the tradition of its history and laws from the hands of its parents, as a heritage to be carried on forever..."[12]

Hirsch also offers a logical explanation for Moshe's joining together of the last five *dibrot* – the prohibitions against murder, adultery, theft, false testimony and coveting another's property – into *one long collective statement* in the Devarim text. He does so, Hirsch argues, in order to include and prohibit all crimes against the property of others "in one and the same utterance of God." In addition, by connecting these transgressions, Moshe consciously roots all such crimes in the last declaration, the ban on "coveting" the property of another. Envy towards others, Moshe emphasizes to the people, inexorably leads to greater sin. Such emphasis, Hirsch explains, is particularly necessary at this juncture, as the people prepare to leave behind the controlled, centralized authority of the desert encampment in favor of a scattered existence over the whole of a country.[13]

—— E ————————————————————

Once we accept Hirsch's suggestion that Moshe tailors the *dibrot* in Devarim to suit the needs and perceptions of a new generation, we can offer other explanations for some of the variations found in the declarations.

Moshe adds, for example, the phrase "as God commanded you" specifically to the fourth and fifth declarations dealing with the observance of Shabbat and *kibbud av va'em*, obedience to parents, respectively. Based on a Talmudic tradition,[14] Rashi and others explain that this phrase references the fact that the mitzvot of Shabbat and *kibbud av va'em* were actually introduced to the nation shortly after the parting of the Reed Sea, *before the Revelation at Sinai*.[15]

If these commandments preceded the Sinaitic Revelation, however, why is the phrase "as God commanded you" not included in the first edition of the *dibrot* communicated at Sinai, as well? By the time Revelation occurred, these imperatives had already been shared.

We might argue, perhaps, that, for the generation of the Exodus, Revelation at Sinai was a stand-alone event, designed to impress the people with

---

12. Rabbi Shimshon Raphael Hirsch, Devarim 5:6–18.
13. Ibid., Devarim 5:6–18; Shmot 20:14.
14. Talmud Bavli Sanhedrin 56b.
15. Rashi, Devarim 5:12, 16.

its power and strength. As we have noted before, this generation, shaped in the cauldron of Egyptian slavery, relates to God through the primitive dimension of *yira*, fear (see *Bamidbar*: Korach 6, *Approaches* B, *Points to Ponder*; Chukat 2, *Approaches* D; Chukat 3, *Approaches* H). Immediacy and power, rather than slow, painstaking processes, speak to the erstwhile slaves. The Ten Declarations are therefore presented in isolation to the generation of the Exodus, as a powerful independent statement of binding law.

Their children, however, come to see God through the continuing prism of *ahava*, love. Raised for almost four decades under God's watchful eye, surrounded by the Clouds of Glory, nurtured on the heaven-sent manna, patiently traveling towards a destiny and a destination, this generation now understands that a true relationship develops over time, in incremental fashion. Against this backdrop they are able to view the unfolding of the law itself as a process, with Sinai as a dramatic but by no means isolated event. This generation has witnessed laws enacted following the Revelation at Sinai during their own wilderness travels. They can readily understand that the development of law could have preceded Sinai, as well.

The shift of generations potentially explains the greater emphasis on material possessions in the second edition of the *dibrot*, as well. In the fifth declaration, as recorded in Devarim, the commandment of Shabbat applies not only to "your animal," but to "your ox, and your donkey, and your every animal." In the tenth declaration the list of possessions that we are forbidden to covet expands to include "your fellow's house" and "his field." Additionally, while the Israelites are prohibited from "coveting" another's possessions in the first *dibrot*, in the second version they are also warned not to "desire" those possessions. The generation of the wilderness has begun to comprehend the reality of personal ownership in a way that their parents, raised in slavery, could scarcely imagine. Moshe therefore specifies material possessions in greater detail, including "real estate" where applicable. He also warns this new generation not only against "coveting" that which is clearly beyond their reach, but against "desiring" prohibited possessions that they believe they could potentially attain.

Finally, the shifting emphasis in the fourth declaration from creation to the Exodus as the philosophical foundation for Shabbat observance may also reflect generational change. Momentous events can only be fully appreciated and understood in retrospect. To the generation of the Exodus, therefore, Shabbat is presented as a remembrance of the creation of the world. To the wilderness generation, however, Shabbat also becomes a remembrance of the Exodus itself.

———**F**———

No discussion concerning the variations between the two editions of the Aseret Hadibrot would be complete without mention of the most famous distinction: the transition from "*Zachor* (remember) the Sabbath day to keep it holy…" in the first edition to "*Shamor* (safeguard) the Sabbath day to keep it holy…" in the second. Rabbinic commentary on this glaring shift is extensive. One basic approach, however, stands out, weaving Midrashic and halachic analysis into a fascinating interpretive tapestry.

The rabbis begin with a foundational Midrashic suggestion: "'Remember' and 'safeguard' were delivered in one utterance."[16]

These two imperatives, the rabbis suggest, were miraculously communicated at Sinai simultaneously. Rashi and others explain this claim to mean that the two words were somehow pronounced by God as one, yet each word was separately and distinctly discerned by the assembled Israelites.[17]

What, however, is the import of these two separate imperatives? What specific obligations do the commandments of "remembering" and "safeguarding" the Sabbath entail?

While various suggestions are offered within rabbinic literature, one basic approach is of particular significance. The commandment to "remember" the Shabbat obligates us to perform the positive acts that underscore the significance of the Sabbath day, such as the recitation of Kiddush (the blessing proclaiming the sanctity of Shabbat recited over a cup of wine).[18] The commandment to "safeguard" the Shabbat, on the other hand, obligates us to observe the restrictions that define the day. By refraining from thirty-nine basic prohibited activities and their derivatives on Shabbat, we effectively "safeguard" the sanctity of the day.[19]

Combining the legal distinction between these two imperatives with the Midrashic tradition that they were transmitted in "one utterance," the

---

16. Mechilta, Shmot 20:8. A less well-known Midrashic tradition has God transmitting the entire Ten Declarations "in one utterance" and then transmitting each one separately. Yalkut Shimoni, Yitro 285.
17. Rashi, Devarim 5:11.
18. Talmud Bavli Pesachim 106a.
19. Ramban, Shmot 20:9.

rabbis arrive at a practical halachic conclusion. Although women are normally exempt from time-bound positive biblical commandments, they are nonetheless obligated in the biblical mitzva of Kiddush. This exception to the rule, the rabbis explain, emerges from the divinely ordained connection between *zachor* and *shamor*: "All those who are included in the commandment to 'safeguard [the Shabbat]' are also included in the commandment to 'remember [the Shabbat].'"[20]

Since women are obviously as responsible as men in maintaining the sanctity of the Sabbath through refraining from prohibited activity, they are also obligated in the positive acts, such as Kiddush, that underscore the holiness of the day.

Taken together, the rabbis maintain, the imperatives of *zachor* and *shamor* summarize each Jew's relationship with Shabbat. *Shamor* directs our attention to the restrictions through which we create the behavioral boundaries that define the circumference of the Sabbath day. *Zachor* commands us towards the positive actions through which we fill the newly created circle with meaning.

—— G ——

Our search for answers concerning the two editions of the Aseret Hadibrot has been extensive but hardly exhaustive. Numerous other sources comment on these textual emendations, and further insights remain to be revealed through continuing study and analysis.

Points to Ponder

How does a divinely ordained legal system transcend the ages? We examined this question in depth in our review of the structure and process of the Oral Law (see *Shmot*: Yitro 5). In short, however, the secret lies in the delicate balance between continuity and change – in immutable foundational laws that remain open to constant interpretation and application across the generations.

Can it be that the Torah hints at this essential balance through the differing editions of the Aseret Hadibrot? No section of text would seem riper for rigidity than these declarations, pronounced at Sinai by a powerfully present God. Nonetheless, the Torah allows for controlled transformation

---

20. Talmud Bavli Brachot 20b; Shevuot 20b.

even in this divinely transmitted code. While the laws remain unchanged in the second version, new ideas are added and the text is consciously shaped to better address a new generation.

Apparently, the balance that preserves the law is embedded in the law from the outset.

3 Kriat Shma: A Mitzva for the Ages

Context

Following the review of the Ten Declarations, the Torah records a textual passage that is destined to attain unmatched significance within Jewish thought.

Among the first words learned at a parent's knee and among the last recited when life's journey ends, the verses of this paragraph are more familiar to the Jew than any others in the entire biblical text:

> *Shma Yisrael, Hashem Elokeinu, Hashem Echad,* Hear O Israel: the Lord is our God, the Lord is One!
>
> And you shall love the Lord your God with all your heart and with all your soul and with all your might. And these words which I command you this day shall be upon your heart, and you shall teach them diligently to your children; and you shall talk of them when you sit in your house and when you walk by the way and when you lie down and when you rise up. And you shall bind them for a sign upon your hand, and they shall be as frontlets between your eyes. And you shall write them upon the doorposts of your house and upon your gates.[1]

Most significantly from a halachic perspective, this paragraph, along with two other biblical passages,[2] is eventually incorporated into the morning and evening prayer services of the Jewish nation.[3] While clearly central to each of these prayer services, these paragraphs remain distinct from their surroundings. Their full or partial recitation (see below) constitutes the fulfillment of a foundational mitzva,

---

1. Devarim 6:4–9.
2. Devarim 11: 13–21; Bamidbar 15:37–41.
3. Mishna Brachot 1:1–5.

separate from prayer, known as the mitzva of Kriat Shma, the "recitation of the Shma."[4]

Questions

What is the source of the mitzva of Kriat Shma?

Why have these paragraphs become so central to Jewish thought? Why are they singled out from among all other passages of the Torah for obligatory daily recitation?

What are the parameters of this mitzva? Are all three paragraphs of the Shma included in the basic obligation?

Approaches

—A—

So integral is the mitzva of Kriat Shma to Jewish thought that the entire Talmud opens with a discussion concerning its observance: "From when," the Mishnaic sages ask with their opening words, "may we recite the Shma in the evenings?" *At what moment of the daily cycle does the mitzva of reciting the evening Kriat Shma begin?*[5]

Centuries later, the Gemara[6] objects to the fact that, with this question, the Mishna jumps to the second stage of a halachic discussion without addressing the first: "Where is the Tanna [Mishnaic sage] 'standing' when he asks 'When may we recite…'?" In other words, how can the Tanna question the time for the recitation of Kriat Shma without first establishing the source of the mitzva itself?

Answering its own question, the Gemara explains that the Mishna accepts the existence of a biblical mitzva of Kriat Shma as a given, based on an obvious source: "The Tanna derives his position from the text: '[and you shall speak of them…] when you lie down and when you rise up.'" The mitzva of Kriat Shma emerges directly from a phrase found in the first passage of the Shma itself. This phrase evidently establishes a biblical

---

4. Rambam, *Sefer Hamitzvot*, positive commandment 10.
5. Talmud Bavli Brachot 2a.
6. The Talmud consists of two distinct sections: the Mishna, compiled in 200 CE, and commentary thereon called the Gemara, compiled in 500 CE.

obligation to recite the Shma each day, "when you lie down and when you rise up," in the morning and in the evening.[7]

—— **B** ——

In this opening discussion, the Talmud accepts the biblical origin of the mitzva of Kriat Shma without question. Not all Talmudic authorities, however, are sanguine with this conclusion, as evidenced by a debate recorded later in the tractate of Brachot. There, Rabbi Elazar does agree that the mitzva of Kriat Shma emerges directly from the biblical source cited above. Rabbi Yehuda, however, demurs and, quoting the towering sage Shmuel, argues that the obligation to recite the Shma is of rabbinic, rather than biblical, derivation.[8]

A series of later scholars, ranging from the thirteenth-century Spanish authority Rabbeinu Yona to the eighteenth-century Lithuanian halachist Rabbi Aryeh Leib ben Asher Gunzberg, add another layer of complexity to the discussion. These authorities insist that even Rabbi Yehuda and Shmuel, who define the mitzva of Kriat Shma as rabbinic, accept the existence of a biblical mitzva mandating the recitation of Torah passages in the morning and evening. The only area of dispute between Rabbi Yehuda and Shmuel, on the one hand, and Rabbi Elazar, on the other, is whether or not the Torah requires the recitation of *these particular passages* of text.

Rabbi Elazar interprets the phrase "and you shall speak of them…when you lie down and when you rise up" in narrow terms. From his point of view, the Torah mandates a specific obligation to "speak of" the Shma each morning and evening.

Rabbi Yehuda and Shmuel, on the other hand, interpret this same phrase in general terms. On a biblical level, these scholars maintain, one fulfills the mitzva of Kriat Shma through the recitation *of any passage of Torah text* at the appointed times. The requirement to read the specific paragraphs of the Shma (and as we are about to see, there is some discussion about exactly which passage or passages these are), they insist, is of later rabbinic origin.[9]

---

7. Talmud Bavli Brachot 2a.
8. Ibid., 21a.
9. Rabbeinu Yona commenting on the Rif, Brachot 12b; *Responsa Sha'agat Aryeh* 1.

—— C ————————————————————————————————

Across the centuries, as countless authorities add their voices to the debate surrounding this mitzva, a strong pattern emerges. The preponderance of rabbinic opinion weighs in on the side of Rabbi Elazar, citing *a clear biblical requirement to recite the specific passage or passages of the Shma each morning and evening.*[10]

In spite of this majority conclusion, however, the exact parameters of this biblical mitzva still remain open to debate. Exactly which passages of text, ask the scholars, are included in the Torah obligation?

The Shma that we recite daily, after all, does not emerge from one unified source, but is culled, instead, from three disparate sections of text:

1. *Shma* and *V'ahavta* (Parshat Va'etchanan) contain the declaration of God's oneness and the commandments to love and worship God, study and teach Torah, bind words of Torah on one's arm and between one's eyes (the mitzva of tefillin) and place words of Torah upon the doorposts of our homes and gates (the mitzva of mezuza).[11]

2. *V'haya im shamo'a* (Parshat Ekev) contains an exposition concerning divine reward and punishment and a reiteration of the commandments of Torah study, Torah teaching, tefillin and mezuza.[12]

3. *Va'yomer* (Parshat Shelach) contains the mitzva of tzitzit (the obligation to place fringes on a four-cornered garment (see *Bamidbar:* Shelach 4, for commentary) and the commandment to remember the Exodus.[13]

Which of these three paragraphs, the rabbis ask, is essential to the fulfillment of the Torah mandate to recite the Shma? Does the biblical mitzva require the recitation of all three passages; or is the obligation to recite some of these passages rabbinic in origin?

—— D ————————————————————————————————

Before we can begin to answer this question, we must first remove one paragraph from the discussion. Textually, the third paragraph of the Shma emerges as the "outlier," the only one of the three paragraphs in question

———————————————

10. Rambam, *Sefer Hamitzvot*, positive commandment 10; *Sefer Hachinuch*, mitzva 119; and numerous other sources.
11. Devarim 6:4–9.
12. Ibid., 11:13–21.
13. Bamidbar 15:37–41.

that does not contain any version of the critical phrase *v'dibarta bam…*, "and you shall speak of them…when you lie down and when you rise up."

As we have noted, this phrase is identified by many scholars as the source of the biblical obligation to recite the Shma in the morning and in the evening. It stands to reason, therefore, that only passages containing this phrase would be considered for inclusion in any formulation of the biblical mitzva of Kriat Shma.

Why, then, is the third paragraph, *Va'yomer*, a passage that *does not contain* the critical language "*v'dibarta bam…*," incorporated into the daily recitation of the Shma?

A glance at the halachic sources reveals a startling answer. The "third paragraph of the Shma" is technically *not part of the Shma* at all. This passage is not recited in fulfillment of the mandate to "speak of" biblical passages in the morning and evening. Instead, the paragraph of *Va'yomer* is recited in fulfillment of a separate biblical obligation: the mitzva to re-member the Exodus on a daily basis.[14] In order to ensure the regular execu-tion of this second daily responsibility, the rabbis append the paragraph of *Va'yomer* to the first two paragraphs of the Shma for recitation in the morning and the evening.[15] In spite of its separate derivation, this passage becomes known as "the third paragraph of the Shma."[16]

— E —

Even when the paragraph of *Va'yomer* is removed from the discussion, however, debate continues over the parameters of the biblical mitzva of Kriat Shma.

At one end of the halachic spectrum lie the "minimalists" who main-tain that the biblical obligation of Kriat Shma is limited to the recitation of the one sentence *Shma Yisrael, Hashem Elokeinu, Hashem Echad*, "Hear O Israel: the Lord is our God, the Lord is One!" An individual fulfills the mitzva of Kriat Shma on a Torah level, these authorities claim, upon pro-nouncing this single familiar phrase.[17]

A second series of other scholars adopt an intermediate position; ar-

---

14. Rambam, *Mishneh Torah*, Hilchot Kriat Shma 1:3.
15. Talmud Bavli Brachot 12b; Rambam, *Mishneh Torah*, Hilchot Kriat Shma 1:2–3.
16. Rambam, *Mishneh Torah*, Hilchot Kriat Shma 1:1–3.
17. Rashba, Brachot 21a.

guing that the entire first paragraph must be recited to satisfy the biblical requirement.[18]

Finally, yet other authorities seem to indicate that the recitation of the entire first two paragraphs of the Shma is essential to the fulfillment of the biblical mitzva of Kriat Shma.[19]

Even those authorities who hold the minimalist and intermediate positions agree that, on a practical level, *all three paragraphs* of the Shma must be recited to satisfy the combination of biblical and rabbinic requirements associated with this mitzva.

——— **F** ———————————————————————————————

Whatever the parameters of the mitzva, the existence of a biblical or rabbinic mandate requiring the reading of specific passages of Torah text on a daily basis raises an obvious question: *Why are these passages singled out from all others in the Torah for obligatory daily recitation?*

——— **G** ———————————————————————————————

A fascinating debate recorded in the Jerusalem Talmud concerning this very question highlights two global approaches to this and other biblical or biblically inspired mandates: "Why do we read these two paragraphs [the first two paragraphs of the Shma] each day? Rabbi Levi and Rabbi Seemon each offered an answer. Rabbi Seemon maintained: 'Because they each speak of lying down [in the evening] and arising [in the morning].' Rabbi Levi argued: 'Because the Ten Declarations are incorporated in them.'"[20]

According to Rabbi Seemon, the selection of the passages of the Shma is best understood in technical terms. These paragraphs are chosen for recitation because they are the only passages in the Torah that include any variation of the phrase "and you shall speak of them…when you lie down and when you rise up." *That phenomenon alone ensures their selection as passages for daily recitation.*

Rabbi Levi disagrees. If the passages of the Shma are selected above all others for obligatory twice-daily recitation by the Jewish people across time, this scholar argues, *a reason beyond the technical must motivate their*

———————————

18. Rashi, Brachot 21a.
19. Rambam, *Mishneh Torah*, Hilchot Kriat Shma 1:2. Some authorities dispute this reading of the Rambam's position, as his language leaves itself open to interpretation.
20. Jerusalem Talmud Brachot 1:5.

choice. Upon examination, Rabbi Levi determines that the Ten Declarations, God's introduction to the entirety of Torah law (see *Shmot*: Yitro 4), are all subtly referenced within the first two passages of the Shma. This foundational content marks these paragraphs as a most appropriate choice for daily recitation.[21]

Rabbi Levi's philosophical approach to the selection of the paragraphs of the Shma may be foreshadowed by an earlier discussion, recorded in the Babylonian Talmud.

In the tractate of Brachot, the Mishnaic sages Rabbi Yehoshua ben Korcha and Rabbi Shimon bar Yochai are quoted as offering explanations for the sequencing of the paragraphs of the Shma during their recitation. The opinions they offer, the Talmud maintains, are not mutually exclusive.

Rabbi Yehoshua ben Korcha explains that the first paragraph of the Shma, reflecting an individual's *acceptance of the yoke of the kingdom of heaven*, logically precedes the second paragraph, reflecting an individual's *acceptance of the yoke of the mitzvot*. Rabbi Shimon bar Yochai cites a different phenomenon: a descending pattern of obligations as the Shma unfolds. The Shma opens with a paragraph containing three basic obligations: *to learn, teach and practice the mitzvot*. The second paragraph follows because it contains only two obligations: *to teach and to practice*; the third paragraph contains the sole obligation of *practice*.[22]

In this discussion, Rabbi Yehoshua ben Korcha and Rabbi Shimon bar Yochai focus on the content of the Shma solely as an explanation for the order in which the paragraphs of the Shma are to be recited. Nonetheless, the significant subject matter these scholars cite may help explain why the passages of the Shma are selected for daily recitation in the first place.

---

21. According to Rabbi Levi's position that the paragraphs of the Shma are read each day because of their reference to the Ten Declarations, why not read the declarations themselves? The Talmud explains that the Ten Declarations were, indeed, originally recited each morning as part of the daily liturgy. This practice, however, was eventually suspended by the rabbis when subversive elements within the nation cited this daily recitation as proof of their erroneous claim that only the Ten Declarations were divinely transmitted to the Israelites at Sinai, and not the entire Torah.
22. Talmud Bavli Brachot, 13a, 14b.

— H

Yet another critical dimension to the recitation of the Shma is introduced through Rabbi Yehoshua ben Korcha's observation that the first paragraph of the Shma reflects an individual's acceptance of the yoke of the kingdom of heaven.

Numerous authorities, including the Rambam, count this conscious acceptance of God's authority – synonymous with the affirmation of God's unity – as a *separate, distinct, daily mitzva* within the list of the 613 biblical commandments.[23]

This separate mitzva of affirmation can certainly be fulfilled in ways other than the recitation of Kriat Shma. Nonetheless, these scholars note that by reading the first sentence of the Shma, "Hear O Israel: the Lord is our God, the Lord is One," with proper intent, an individual automatically affirms God's unity and accepts His majestic will. The recitation of Kriat Shma thus allows for the simultaneous fulfillment of yet another fundamental daily mitzva.

— I

Finally, as countless later authorities indicate, the manifold overarching ideas embedded in the paragraphs of the Shma clearly recommend these paragraphs for daily recitation. The Oneness of God, the obligation to love God, the mitzva of Torah study, the obligation to teach Torah to one's children, the obligation to accept all the mitzvot of the Torah as a whole, the concept of divine reward and punishment, the presence of God's hand in nature and in history, and the practical mitzvot of tefillin and mezuza are among the many essential themes to be found in these rich passages.

While formally no section of biblical text is meant to be seen as more important than another, one can clearly understand why the passages of the Shma were chosen for daily recitation and why they have become so central to Jewish practice, thought and experience across the ages.

---

23. Rambam, *Sefer Hamitzvot*, positive commandment 2.

4 The Dialogue of Prayer

Context

Although a distinct, separate obligation, the mitzva of Kriat Shma (see previous study) is not performed in isolation. Instead, the three paragraphs of the Shma are woven into, and recited as part of, central sections of the morning and evening prayer services.

Questions

Why is the mitzva of Kriat Shma incorporated into the daily liturgy?

At first glance, the paragraphs that constitute the Shma can hardly be classified as prayer. Within these passages, *man does not speak to God at all. God, instead, speaks to man.* The Shma consists of instructional verses, chosen from countless others in the Torah text, informing the nation of its responsibilities. Whatever benefits might accrue from the daily recitation of the Shma, they would seem to be separate and distinct from the experience of prayer.

Even if a practical argument can be made for attaching this mitzva to the prayer service as an expedient way to ensure its performance, the weaving of the Shma into the most central sections of the *tefilla* remains difficult to understand. Why didn't the rabbis append the recitation of the Shma to the conclusion of the service? Why insert these biblical passages at a point in the prayers where they would seem to be an intrusion, breaking the flow of each prayer service as it moves towards a crescendo. What connection is there between the mitzva of Kriat Shma and the experience of prayer?

Approaches

—A—

Our search for answers begins with the prayers that surround and weave the Shma into both the morning and evening services. Known as the Birchot Kriat Shma (Blessings of the Kriat Shma), these prayers are thematically connected to the passages of the Shma and are clearly referenced in the Mishna: "In the morning, one recites two blessings before [the Shma] and one after it. In the evening, one recites two blessings before [the Shma] and two after it."[24]

The Gemara and later halachic works identify these seven blessings as follows:

1. *Yotzer ohr*, "He Who forms light" (said in the morning, before the Shma), describes and praises God's creation of the physical world, beginning with His creation of light and darkness.
2. *Ahava raba*, "abundant love" (said in the morning, before the Shma), praises God's bestowal of the Torah upon the Jewish people and requests the wisdom to appreciate and understand that gift.[25]
3. *Emet v'yatziv*, "true and certain" (said in the morning, after the Shma), praises God's faithfulness across the generations, with particular focus on the miracles of the Exodus.
4. *Hama'ariv aravim*, "He Who brings on evenings" (said in the evening, before the Shma), praises God's control of the passage of time, with emphasis on the transition from day to night.
5. *Ahavat olam*, "eternal love" (a shortened version of the morning prayer, said in the evening, before the Shma), praises God's bestowal of the Torah and its commandments upon the Jewish people.
6. *Emet v'emuna*, "true and faithful" (said in the evening, after the Shma), praises God's protection of the Jewish nation from its enemies, with particular focus on the Exodus.
7. *Hashkiveinu*, "lay us down to sleep" (said in the evening, after the Shma), requests God's protection from danger.

—— **B** ——

A puzzling statement in the Mishna forces the later Talmudic authorities to scrutinize the technical relationship between these blessings and the Shma itself.

After establishing that the appropriate time for the recitation of the morning Shma ends when three daylight "halachic hours" have passed[26] (or

---

24. Mishna Brachot 1:4.
25. In communities that follow the liturgy known as Nusach Sfard and in the Sephardic community, this blessing begins with the words *Ahavat olam*.
26. For the purpose of determining the time periods for daily obligations, the halachic

in other words a quarter of the day),[27] the Mishna asserts: "If one recites [the Shma] from that point on, *he has not lost*; he is like an individual who reads from the Torah."[28]

The Mishna's halachic position is clear. Upon missing the appropriate time for the recitation of Kriat Shma in the morning, an individual *loses the opportunity to fulfill the mitzva properly.* Nonetheless, the Shma may yet be recited at any point throughout the day. One may, after all, always read passages from the Torah.

Less clear, however, is the meaning of the puzzling Mishnaic statement "he has not lost." If this individual has *lost the opportunity* to perform the mitzva properly, what then, has he *not lost*?

In a striking move, the scholars of the Gemara quote sources from the Mishnaic period that connect this phrase to the blessings surrounding the Kriat Shma. If, on any particular day, an individual fails to recite the morning Shma in its appropriate timeframe, *he has not lost* the opportunity to recite the Shma's blessings. These blessings may still be recited, together with the biblical passages of the Shma, even after the time for the mitzva has passed.[29]

— C —

Following the close of the Talmud, however, rabbinic disagreement develops as to the extent of this allowance concerning the Shma's blessings. Until what point of the day, the authorities query, may these blessings yet be recited?

Taking the Mishna at face value, the Rambam is among those authorities who maintain that the Birchot Kriat Shma can and should be recited whenever the Shma itself can yet be said, throughout the entire day.[30]

Numerous other scholars, however, including the towering fourteenth-century halachist Rabbeinu Asher (the Rosh), adamantly disagree. The

---

authorities divide the daylight hours of each day into twelve equal units or *shaot zemaniyot* (halachic hours). The length of each halachic hour varies according to the time of the year, with the smallest units during the winter months when the "days are shorter" and the longest during the summer months when the "days are longer."

27. Mishna Brachot 1:2.
28. Ibid.
29. Talmud Bavli Brachot 10b.
30. Rambam, *Mishneh Torah*, Hilchot Kriat Shma, 1:13.

blessings of the Shma, these authorities argue, are not governed by the time frame that governs the Shma. Instead, these blessings may be recited *only within the appropriate time frame for the morning prayers.* This time frame, also established in the Mishna, extends one daylight hour after the temporal endpoint for the mitzva of Kriat Shma, namely until one third of the day has passed.[31]

If an individual misses the appropriate time for the morning Shma, these authorities thus conclude, he can yet recite the Shma itself at any point during the day. The Shma consists of biblical verses, and the recitation of biblical verses is always allowed. *The Shma's blessings, however, may only be recited for one more daylight hour, until the time for the morning prayers has passed.* Past that point, the recitation of these blessings is prohibited and an individual who recites them transgresses the sin of "saying God's name in vain." This latter position is codified as law by Rabbi Yosef Caro in the *Shulchan Aruch* and is accepted as normative practice today.[32]

—— **D** ——

The normative position outlined above concerning the Birchot Kriat Shma seems confusing. *What exactly is the nature of these blessings?*

If these blessings are, as their title indicates, "Blessings of the Kriat Shma," why then are they governed by the time frame for the morning prayers and not by the time frame for the Shma itself? Logically, one of two other options should be chosen. Either the recitation of these blessings should be prohibited once the optimal time for Kriat Shma has passed, or the recitation should be allowed as long as the Shma can still be recited, throughout the day.

And if, conversely, these blessings are considered part of the morning prayers and are, in fact, governed by the rules of those prayers, why are they referred to as the "Blessings of the Kriat Shma"?

—— **E** ——

The tension mirrored in the above ruling may well be a product of a fundamental internal tension in the nature of the blessings themselves.

On the one hand, a review of the content of these blessings quickly

---

31. Rabbeinu Asher, Brachot 10.
32. *Shulchan Aruch*, Orach Chaim 58:6.

reveals that, unlike the Shma itself, the blessings are prayers in the full, formal sense. Upon reciting these blessings we find ourselves in the familiar territory of classical *tefilla*, where man reaches out to his Creator with majestic words of tribute and heartfelt appeal.

At the same time, however, the blessings are clearly connected to the Shma. Carefully and consciously, the rabbinic authors of these *brachot* rework and expand upon the themes of the Shma, fashioning them into prayer. To cite a few examples:

1. While the Shma proclaims God's oneness, the blessings of the Shma lead the supplicant to praise the unity of God's physical and philosophical creations.

2. The commandment of Torah study repeatedly embedded in the Shma is transformed in the blessings into a request for the wisdom to engage in such study.

3. The Shma's focus on God's hand in history leads to appeals in the *brachot* for "a new light shining upon Zion" and an ingathering of the exiles from the "four corners of the earth."

The blessings of the Shma move from one realm to the next. Thematically rooted in the paragraphs of the Shma, they transform the themes of those biblical passages into classical prayer. Although they retain their identity as Birchot Kriat Shma, therefore, these blessings are ultimately governed by the laws that regulate the morning prayers, as a whole.

— F —

The unique rabbinically designed bridging role of Birchot Kriat Shma may help us understand how the scholars view the inclusion of Kriat Shma itself in the prayers. Far from an alien intrusion, Kriat Shma and its surrounding blessings enable a *two-way, man-God conversation* to unfold at the core of the morning and evening prayer services. At the center of this exchange lies the Shma itself – Torah passages through which God daily conveys His aspirations for and challenges to His people. At the conversation's peripheries lie the blessings of the Shma, the people's contribution to the discussion: each supplicant wrestles with the themes embedded in God's words, transforming them into personal prayers of praise and request.

The Shma thus helps shape the very paradigm of Jewish prayer: a dialogue, not a discourse. *Just as certainly as man speaks to God during prayer, God speaks to man.*

Three times daily, as the Jew approaches his Creator in prayer, God draws near, as well. An intimate conversation unfolds. Hopes, expectations, requests and challenges are freely exchanged, and an agreement to sanctify the world in partnership is renewed. The parties then part ways, with an implicit promise to return shortly, armed with additional life experience, for further conversation and dialogue.[33]

Points to Ponder

The story is told of a security guard serving at the Kotel (the Western Wall) in Jerusalem. Over time, he takes note of one elderly man who arrives at the wall each day at the same time, prays with obvious devotion for an hour and leaves.

Finally, after decades of witnessing this scene, the guard stops the man and asks him, "Excuse me, sir, but I have taken note of the constancy of your commitment. Can you please tell me what you have been praying for each day over these many years?" "Well," answers the man, "for years I have approached the Kotel to pray to God that He grant our people peace, security and the wisdom to deal with each other with sensitivity and respect." "And now," continues the guard, "as you look back on all these years of fervent prayer at the Western Wall, how do you feel about the experience?" "I feel," answers the man, "like I've been talking to a wall."

Tefilla is tough. We find ourselves locked in a continuing struggle. Can we breathe new life into the same words recited day after day? Can we continue to regularly approach a mysterious God, only to be answered with silence, never quite knowing if, when or how our prayers will be answered? Can we, who live in a world governed by intellectual search, learn to open our hearts to an unfathomable God?

Like most of my colleagues, I have shared, over the years, a multitude of ideas with my congregants and students as to how we might more meaningfully experience *tefilla* (all the while speaking to myself as much as to them). I have counseled concentration, the study of the prayers, introspection, arriving to synagogue on time, a cessation of conversation with our neighbors during the services and much more.

---

33. For a beautiful essay on Rabbi Soloveitchik's view of prayer as a dialogue, see Abraham Besdin, *Reflections of the Rav*, vol. 1, *Lessons in Jewish Thought – Adapted from the Lectures of Rabbi Joseph B. Soloveitchik* (Jerusalem: Jewish Agency, Alpha Press, 1979).

As important as all those steps may be, however, I would argue that another potential action can have even more far-reaching consequences upon our search for more meaningful *tefilla*.

We can decide to listen, as well as to speak, during prayer.

So many voices, after all, clamor for our attention as we engage in *tefilla*: the voices of our earliest progenitors – Avraham, Yitzchak and Yaakov – whose own search for God at the dawn of our history leads them, according to Talmudic tradition, to establish the three basic daily prayer services, Shacharit, Mincha and Ma'ariv; the voice of King David, whose impassioned Psalms take us on a journey through the turbulent events that marked his life and thus through the myriad human emotions that color our own; the voices of scholars and sages across the ages, whose contributions to the prayer services preserve in perpetuity their struggles, priorities and dreams; and above it all, the voice of God, speaking to us of His hopes for His people, individually and collectively, and of the tasks that we must fulfill if we are to bring about their realization.

And if we listen hard enough, we might even hear the voice of our own hearts, urging us to reflect upon our own place in this rising crescendo. Who are we to approach God in prayer? What aspirations do we have for ourselves and how do they relate to the dreams of those who came before? How can we shape our priorities so that they reflect an understanding of the truly important things in life? As we wrestle with these and other critical issues, we naturally turn to God in heartfelt prayer, asking that He aid us in our search for direction.

Rabbi Shimshon Raphael Hirsch notes that the root of the Hebrew verb *l'hitpallel*, to pray, is *pallel*, literally, to judge. The verb is conjugated reflexively. *L'hitpallel*, to pray, thus means to judge oneself. "Jewish praying, says Hirsch, "is not from within outwards, but from without inwards.... *Hitpallel* means to penetrate oneself, ever afresh again, with eternal, essential lasting truths and facts."[34]

If the *tefilla* experience becomes a process through which we gauge our lives and our actions against the backdrop of our nation's ongoing search for God and God's reciprocal search for us, then our thrice-daily approach to the Almighty will acquire new and powerful meaning.

---

34. Rabbi Shimshon Raphael Hirsch, Bereishit 48:11.

5 Commanded Love

Context

Immediately after recording the overarching declaration "Hear O Israel: the Lord is our God, the Lord is One," the Torah continues with the commandment "And you shall love the Lord your God with all your heart and with all your soul and with all your might…"[1]

Questions

Two powerful objections, raised by the classical commentaries, strike to the very foundations of the mitzva of *ahavat Hashem*, the mitzva to "love the Lord."

How can a mitzva concerning emotions and "feelings" possibly have been issued? After all, as the Akeidat Yitzchak notes, "Man cannot be commanded concerning matters [such as love] that are not dependent upon his conscious will."[2]

Once commanded, can the directive of *ahavat Hashem* possibly be fulfilled? "How can the commandment to love apply," Rabbi Eliyahu Mizrachi wonders, "to something that man has neither seen nor ever recognized?"[3]

Approaches

— A —

Judaism's extraordinary range – its ability to encompass widely varied approaches to thought and life – is showcased in the disparate reactions of the scholars to the issues raised above. Both the starkly intellectual Litvak (Jew of Lithuanian heritage) and the deeply emotional Chassid can carve out a halachically acceptable path towards the love of God.

---

1. Devarim 6:5.
2. Akeidat Yitzchak, Devarim, sha'ar 90.
3. Mizrachi, Devarim 6:6.

At opposite ends of the philosophical spectrum lie two groups of schol-ars who, instead of grappling with the questions concerning the mitzva of *ahavat Hashem*, choose instead to dismiss them. Strikingly, the justifica-tion offered by each group for this "dismissal" is the polar opposite of the rationale suggested by the other.

—— **B** ————————————————————————

At one extreme stands the nineteenth-century Chassidic master the Sfat Emet (Rabbi Yehuda Aryeh Leib Alter), who argues that the question concerning the Torah's commanding of emotions "is itself the answer."[4]

The very existence in the Torah of a commandment to love God, the Sfat Emet maintains, is proof positive of each Jew's innate ability and natu-ral inclination to do so. *Love of the Divine is deeply rooted in man's basic nature, waiting to be activated through heartfelt search and diligent effort.* By "placing God's words upon his heart" continuously, an individual will uncover the love of God already embedded in his heart.[5]

Yehuda Nachshoni notes that the Sfat Emet's approach to the mitzva of *ahavat Hashem* reflects a fundamental principle of Chassidic philosophy, recorded in the works of the students of the Ba'al Shem Tov (the founder of the Chassidic movement).[6] Basing their approach on the kabbalistic concept of *tzimtzum*,[7] the Chassidic masters maintain that all human ten-dencies, beliefs and aptitudes are actually fragments of the Divine Presence buried deeply in our souls. Man is challenged to kindle these internal divine sparks into flames that ultimately unite with the heavenly blaze above.

Yet another Chassidic scholar, Rabbi Chaim of Chernovitz, draws a parallel to an individual who determines to pipe pure stream water into his home. To succeed in this endeavor he must ensure both the purity of the water's source and the integrity of the transmitting pipeline. Similarly, an individual who wishes to benefit from the love resting in his soul must

---

4. Sfat Emet, Va'etchanan, *shnat* 5634.
5. Ibid.
6. Nachshoni, *Hagot B'parshiot HaTorah*, vol. 2, p. 733.
7. The concept of *tzimtzum* posits that as God withdraws during the process of Creation, to allow space for that which He creates, pieces of the Divine remain woven into the fabric of Creation.

cultivate his personal integrity and spiritual purity. Only then will he be able to taste the sweetness of his own instinctive *ahavat Hashem*.[8]

The Chassidic approach to the mitzva of *ahavat Hashem* may well be foreshadowed in the writings of a brilliant luminary, penned centuries before the birth of the Ba'al Shem Tov. Rabbi Yehuda Loew (the Maharal), a sixteenth-century scholar and one of the most influential thinkers of the post-medieval period, comments on the Torah's recording of the mitzva of *ahavat Hashem* directly after the proclamation of Shma Yisrael, emphasizing the oneness of God. God's "oneness," the Maharal explains, means that He is "one" with His creations.

"Because He is One, there is nothing in existence that is separate from Him, for all depends on and is attached to Him, for He is the foundation of all. And that is why love is relevant to God."[9]

Like the Chassidic masters centuries later, the Maharal maintains that man's love of God rises out of man's fundamental inseparability from the Divine.

— C —

A fascinating contemporary corollary to the Chassidic view of *ahavat Hashem* can be found, perhaps, in the scientific debate concerning the "God gene." Postulated by geneticist Dean Hamer, the "God gene" hypothesis maintains that spirituality in man is quantifiable, partially heritable, and can be largely traced to the presence of a specific gene, VMAT2. The development of this gene through natural selection, Hamer argues, may well be encouraged by the innate sense of optimism of spiritual individuals, which increases general health and the likelihood of reproduction.[10]

The publication of this hypothesis in 2004 generated the expected criticism and debate within the scientific community. More to the point of our study, however, numerous religious authorities also objected to the reductionist thinking they saw mirrored in the concept of a God gene. Some saw Hamer's contentions as inherently sacrilegious, a scientific attempt to redefine spiritual enlightenment as the product of the brain's electrical impulses. Others maintained that an individual's spirituality is determined

---

8. Quoted in Nachshoni, *Hagot B'parshiot HaTorah*, vol. 2, p. 733.
9. *Netivot Olam*, Netiv Ahavat Hashem, chapter 1.
10. Dean Hamer, *The God Gene: How Faith Is Hardwired into Our Genes* (New York: Anchor Books, 2005).

by a constellation of forces – personal, societal, educational – and cannot be relegated to genetic factors.[11]

One could argue, however, that Hamer's hypothesis might be seen as a modern iteration of the Chassidic approach to the man-God relationship. Perhaps God embeds in man an innate capacity for *ahavat Hashem* and other spiritual strivings through the creation of a "God gene." Hamer himself insists that "religious believers can point to the existence of God genes as one more sign of the creator's ingenuity – a clever way to help humans acknowledge and embrace a divine presence."[12]

Does a "God gene" exist? Is this gene God's way of implanting His divine sparks within man's soul? The verdict is still out, but the idea is tantalizing…

—— **D** ——————————————————————————

At the opposite end of the interpretive spectrum lie other scholars who, like the Chassidic masters, totally dismiss the questions concerning the mitzva of *ahavat Hashem*. In stark contrast to the Chassidic approach, however, these scholars do not accept man's capacity and inclination to perform this mitzva as a given. They instead maintain that *the mitzva does not exist as a separate imperative in the first place.*

The observations of Shmuel David Luzzatto (the Shadal) reflect, perhaps, the clearest iteration of this view:

> Once the Divine Torah has seen fit to speak in the language of man and to paint for us [the picture] of a God Who acts concretely and possesses the traits of love, hate, anger and conscious will, it is understandable that [the text] should also portray man as "loving" or "hating" his God.…
>
> An individual who places God's presence before him and desires to please Him and to observe His statutes, laws and commandments, will [by definition] be referred to as a "lover of God".…
>
> The love of the Lord is not an independent mitzva, but, instead,

---

11. "Geneticist Claims to Have Found 'God Gene' in Humans," *Washington Times*, November 14, 2004.
12. Ibid.

generally informs all the mitzvot, for a commandment could not [literally] apply to [the emotion of] love.[13]

Acknowledging the impossibility of "commanded love," Luzzatto maintains that there is no separate, distinct mitzva of *ahavat Hashem*. The Torah's mandate to love God is, instead, an overarching reference to the general attitude an individual should adopt in his relationship with his Creator. Citing the well-known Talmudic maxim that the Torah speaks in "the language of man,"[14] Luzzatto argues that just as the biblical references to God's love, anger or hate cannot be interpreted literally, the text cannot mean that man should literally "love God." Instead, the Torah informs the reader that *an individual who lives a God-present life is, by definition, a "lover" of God.*[15]

— E —————————————————————————

While the scholars cited above dismiss, albeit for broadly different reasons, the questions concerning *ahavat Hashem*, other authorities are not sanguine with this approach. Wrestling with the deep philosophical issues surrounding this mitzva, these sages identify a wide variety of potential pathways leading towards love of the Divine.

— F —————————————————————————

Noteworthy among those who struggle to define a concrete path towards the love of God is the Rambam, who discusses this commandment in a number of his major works.

In the first section of his halachic magnum opus, the *Mishneh Torah*, the Rambam enumerates the basic concepts and laws that, to his mind, comprise the "foundations of the Torah." Tellingly, the Rambam not only includes the mitzva of *ahavat Hashem* in this chapter of fundamentals, but also identifies the primary source from which, he believes, both the fear and love of God can naturally emanate:

And what is the path towards the love and fear [of God]? When a man contemplates His [God's] wondrous and great deeds and creations

---

13. Shmuel David Luzzatto, Devarim 6:5.
14. Talmud Bavli Brachot 31b and numerous other locations.
15. Shmuel David Luzzatto, Devarim 6:5.

and sees in them His unequaled and infinite wisdom, immediately he loves and praises and exalts Him and is overcome by an overwhelming desire to know the Great Name.... And according to these ideas do I explain great principles concerning the actions of the Master of the world – that they provide an opening for a wise person to love God....[16]

Ever the rationalist, the Rambam argues that *intellectual search* – openness to the wonders of creation – will automatically give rise to a love of God and a desire to "know" Him more intimately.[17]

Lest we think, however, that the nature of intellectually based "love" of the Divine must be limited by the cold logic from which it emanates, the Rambam, in a later section of the *Mishneh Torah*, describes the passion that should characterize an individual's love of the Almighty:

> And what is the love [of God] that is appropriate? [An individual] should love the Lord with an exceedingly great and mighty love so that his very soul shall be bound by the love of God, being constantly consumed [by this love], as someone who is lovesick does not cease to pine after his beloved....[18]

Three paragraphs later, however, the Rambam quickly returns to his central theme, arguing that, no matter how passionate, an individual's love of God can only emerge from intellectual contemplation:

> [An individual] can only love the Lord in the measure of the knowledge that he has gained of Him. According to the knowledge so shall be the love, whether little or much. Therefore, a man must set aside [time] to understand and comprehend the [various areas of] wisdom and study that will impart to him the knowledge of his Creator....[19]

The Rambam's approach to the mitzva of *ahavat Hashem* remains consis-

---

16. Rambam, *Mishneh Torah*, Hilchot Yesodei HaTorah 2:2.
17. The Rambam recognizes that such intellectual contemplation also causes man to fear God. This unavoidable and necessary fear reaction, however, will always remain subordinate to the more essential response of love.
18. Rambam, *Mishneh Torah*, Hilchot Teshuva 10:3.
19. Ibid., Hilchot Teshuva 10:6.

tent when we turn to his major philosophical work, the *Moreh Nevuchim* (*Guide to the Perplexed*). There, the Rambam argues that many of Judaism's foundational philosophical principles are revealed in the Torah solely in general terms and can be fully understood only "after the acquisition of many kinds of knowledge." He reiterates that love of the Divine is only possible when "we comprehend the real nature of things, and understand the divine wisdom displayed therein."[20]

A subtle yet significant shift in the Rambam's approach emerges, however, when we move from the *Mishneh Torah* and the *Moreh Nevuchim* to the Rambam's *Sefer Hamitzvot*: "And the third mitzva is that He has commanded us to love Him, and that [means] that we should contemplate and strive to comprehend *His commandments, statements and works….*" [italics mine][21]

While the Rambam continues to maintain that love of the Divine can only be achieved through intellectual exploration, the scope of that exploration is expanded in *Sefer Hamitzvot*. The path towards God still includes study of "His works," but here the Rambam places greater emphasis upon *analysis of the mitzvot, God's behavioral blueprint for the Jew*. To bolster this inclusion, the Rambam cites a Midrash that derives support from the text of the Shma itself:

> Although the text states, "And you shall love the Lord your God with all your heart and with all your soul and with all your might," I might wonder, how does one come to love the Creator? Therefore the text immediately continues: "And these things that I command you today shall be upon your heart." Through this [the contemplation of the mitzvot] you shall come to recognize the "One Who spoke and the world came into being."[22]

Rabbi Dr. Norman Lamm, in his volume on the Shma, suggests that the variations in the Rambam's texts may well reflect his targeted audiences. When speaking to "ordinary Jews, who wish to observe what is required of them and what is within their ability to understand," the Rambam focuses

---

20. Rambam, *Moreh Nevuchim* 3:28.
21. Rambam, *Sefer Hamitzvot*, positive commandment 3.
22. Sifri, Devarim 6:6.

on the mitzvot as the source of *ahavat Hashem*. When addressing the intellectual elite, however, the Rambam delineates a higher standard. These
individuals must turn to other disciplines, as well, if they are to forge the
unique relationship with their Creator that is open only to them.[23]

─── **G** ───────────────────────────────────

In stark contrast to the Rambam, Rabbeinu Bachya Ibn Pakuda, in his classic work, *Duties of the Heart*, insists that love of God can only be achieved
through withdrawal from all earthly contemplation. *Complete surrender to
God's will*, as opposed to *intellectual struggle and search*, illuminates Bachya's
path towards *ahavat Hashem*:

> What does the love of God consists of? The complete surrender of the
> soul to the Creator in order to cleave to His transcendent light…and
> thus the soul, spiritual in its essence, shall turn towards similar [heav-
> enly] spiritual fires and shall distance itself, by its very nature, from the
> crude physicality that confronts it.… Its eyes will be opened and freed
> from the cloud that hides the understanding of God and His Torah, it
> will distinguish truth from falsehood, and the true nature of its Creator
> will be revealed…and then, the cup of love of God will be filled.…[24]

─── **H** ───────────────────────────────────

A unified approach to *ahavat Hashem*, weaving together the seemingly
antithetical mystical and rational threads mentioned above, is offered by
Rabbi Shneur Zalman of Liadi, the Ba'al Hatanya and founder of Chabad-
Lubavitch Chassidism.

Mirroring the Chassidic masters before and after him (see *Approaches
B* above), Rabbi Shneur Zalman postulates the existence of *ahava tiv'it
u'mesuteret*, a natural, hidden love of the Divine that resides innately in
the soul of each human being. This latent love, indigenous to all, emerges
automatically upon the removal of obstacles and impediments to its expression. The Torah's commandment to love the Lord becomes understandable
in light of this preexisting natural love.

──────────

23. Norman Lamm, *The Shema: Spirituality and Law in Judaism* (Philadelphia: Jewish
    Publication Society, 1998).
24. Rabbeinu Bachya Ibn Pakuda, *Chovot Halevavot*, The Gate of Love of the Lord 1.

There is, however, to Rabbi Shneur Zalman's mind, a second category
of *ahavat Hashem*: *ahava sichlit*, rational love. This love emerges when an
individual, as a result of intellectual contemplation and rational insight,
comes to recognize God as the Creator of all and as the ultimate source of
goodness. Upon reaching this recognition, the individual understandably
develops a love of, and a desire to draw closer to, the Divine.

Perhaps the most intriguing aspect of Rabbi Shneur Zalman's approach,
however, is not his delineation of these two paths towards *ahavat Hashem*,
but the contrast and interplay that he finds between them.

On the one hand, the superiority of natural over rational love of the
Divine can be seen in natural love's selflessness and constancy. Natural love
exists without any agenda. Rational love, in contrast, is inherently self-
serving. Along the rational path, an individual draws closer to God only
after recognizing the benefits of that closeness. In addition, while rational
love requires continued attention and concentration, natural love is ever
present, whether we pay attention to it or not.

On the other hand, Rabbi Shneur Zalman argues, the superior elements
of rational love are evident, as well. This contemplative path towards love
of the Divine is uniformly open to all, while the extent of an individual's
natural love of God is predetermined by inborn qualities that remain outside his control. Rational love, in addition, has the capacity to grow, while
natural love is circumscribed at birth.

The two paths towards *ahavat Hashem*, Rabbi Shneur Zalman maintains, are therefore complementary. The natural love of God embedded in
our souls must be augmented by a rational love that can only be attained
through intellectual search. Such search, however, should never blind us
to the instinctive emotional connection to the Divine that is latent within
our hearts.[25]

— I —

Finally, a transformative layer to the mitzva of *ahavat Hashem* is delineated
by the rabbis in a powerful Talmudic passage:

---

25. Shneur Zalman of Liadi, *Tanya*, Shaar Hayichud Veha'emuna, introduction (Brook-
    lyn: Kehot Publication Society).

"And you shall love the Lord your God," *that the name of heaven shall become beloved through you*. That a Jew should study Written and Oral Law, minister to Torah scholars, deal faithfully in business and interact pleasantly with his fellow man: what do others say of him? "Fortunate is this individual who has studied Torah! Fortunate is his father who taught him Torah! Fortunate is his teacher who taught him Torah! This individual who studied Torah, see how pleasant are his ways and how appropriate his actions."

However, he who studies Written and Oral Law, ministers to Torah scholars, but does not deal faithfully in business, nor interact pleasantly with his fellow man, what do others say of him? "Woe to this individual who studied Torah! Woe to his father who taught him Torah! Woe to his teacher who taught him Torah! This individual who studied Torah, see how corrupt are his ways and how repugnant his behavior."[26]

To the rabbinic mind, our understanding of the mitzva to love the Lord remains incomplete if we see this commandment only in a self-centered fashion. A Jew's personal relationship with God must ultimately connect with the fundamental responsibility of the Jewish nation as a whole: to increase God's sanctified presence in the world.

How does one "love God"? By recognizing one's capacity to increase or (God forbid) decrease the love of God among those around him.

How does one "love God"? *By being a mensch!* (See Ekev 2, *Points to Ponder*, for an elaboration on this theme.)

Points to Ponder

I have an admission to make. A popular six-word Hebrew song often featured at Jewish weddings and other celebrations makes me uncomfortable.

Hakadosh Baruch Hu, anachnu ohavim Otcha, "Holy One Blessed Be He, we love You!"

In the middle of a crowd dancing to these words, I often find myself questioning: "Love God? What does that mean? How does one love God? Do I love Him more if I sing this song?"

Part of the problem certainly lies with my biological heritage. I am a Litvak, of Lithuanian descent, from both sides of my family. Known for our

---

26. Talmud Bavli Yoma 96a.

cerebral approach to the world, we Litvaks often have difficulty connecting to our emotional core. It stands to reason, therefore, that, unlike those around me, I might fail to be moved by the fervor of this song. It stands to reason, even more, that I would react negatively to what I perceive as the reduction of a deeply challenging philosophical issue, such as the love of God, to a musical sound bite.

I have, however, over the years become comfortable with my discomfort. As many of our studies indicate, the greatness of our religion lies, in large measure, in its embrace of varying approaches to the same ideas and concepts. For some of us, the mitzva of *ahavat Hashem* speaks to a deep emotional connection felt within our hearts that transcends logic. Others, like me, feel more at home wrestling with the issues surrounding this mitzva, as we try to apply its parameters to our lives.

While all Jews share the same halachic obligations, we do not all travel along the same spiritual road. Judaism recognizes this fundamental truth and allows us each to find our own way to God.

Ekev

CHAPTER 7:12–11:25

עקב

פרק ז:יב-יא:כה

Parsha Summary

Careful cautions, promising reassurances, difficult memories, reward and punishment…

Moshe continues his second farewell address by warning the nation that their ultimate success upon entering the land will be dependent upon their continuing obedience to God's law. He reminds the people of God's constant care during their wilderness travels and describes the beautiful nature of the land that they are about to acquire. "Be careful," he desperately warns, "lest you forget the Lord your God…lest you eat and be satisfied, and build good homes and settle down. And your cattle and your sheep will increase, and silver and gold will increase for you, and all that you have will increase. And your hearts will become haughty and you will forget the Lord your God, Who took you out of the land of Egypt, from the house of slavery.… And you will say in your heart: 'My strength and the might of my hand has made me all this wealth!'"[1] To avoid this eventuality, Moshe instructs the nation to be ever mindful of their reliance on God. Their powerful enemies, he promises, will fall before them at God's hands, if the nation remains loyal.

Moshe explains to the Israelites that they are acquiring the land, not because of their own worthiness, but because the inhabitants on the land merit destruction due to their own evil actions. "And you should know, he declares, that not because of your righteousness does God give you this good land to acquire, for you are a stiff-necked people."[2]

Moshe reminds the nation of their numerous provocations against God from the time of the Exodus, and returns in detail to the seminal sin of the golden calf. He describes his own poignant prayers on behalf of the nation on that occasion and chronicles God's instructions concerning the second Tablets of Testimony.

---

1. Devarim 8:12–17.
2. Ibid., 9:6.

After briefly noting the death of Aharon, the elevation of the Levites to leadership and a small portion of the nation's travels, Moshe again exhorts the people by declaring, "And now, O Israel, what does the Lord your God ask of you? Only to fear the Lord your God, to walk in His paths and to love Him and to serve the Lord your God, with all your heart and with all your soul."[3] Moshe continues in this vein and, towards the end of the parsha, conveys the "second paragraph of the Shma." Beginning with the phrase V'haya im shamo'a tishme'u el mitzvotai, "And it will be if you hearken to My commandments...," this paragraph focuses on the critical theme of divine reward and punishment (see Ekev 2, 3).

---

3. Ibid., 10:12.

1 Anatomy of a Blessing

Context

Towards the beginning of Parshat Ekev Moshe describes the land of Canaan's physical bounty and warns the nation against taking God's role in that bounty for granted:

> For the Lord your God is bringing you to a good land: a land of streams of water, of springs and underground pools emerging forth in the valley and in the mountain; a land of wheat and barley and grapes and figs and pomegranates; a land of olive oil and honey; a land where you will eat bread without scarceness; you will lack nothing within it; a land whose stones are iron and from whose mountains you will mine copper.
>
> And you will eat, and you will be satisfied, and you will bless the Lord your God upon the good land that He has given you.
>
> Take care lest you forget the Lord your God by not observing His commandments, His laws and His statutes, which I command you today...and your hearts will become haughty, and you will forget the Lord your God, Who took you out of the land of Egypt, from the house of slavery... And you will say in your heart: "My strength and the might of my hand has made me all this wealth!"[4]

The Talmudic authorities identify one sentence from this passage as the source of a fundamental biblical commandment: "From where do we learn a Torah obligation to bless God? As it is said: 'And you will eat, and you will be satisfied, and you will bless the Lord your God, concerning the good land that He has given you.'"[5]

Aside from the Priestly Blessing, this blessing, known as Birkat Hamazon (Grace after Meals), is the only blessing of *uncontested biblical origin* in Jewish tradition. Some authorities maintain that

---

4. Devarim 8:7–17.
5. Talmud Bavli Brachot 21a.

the recitation of Birkat HaTorah, the blessing recited before Torah study, is also commanded in the Torah text;[6] while others consider the Bracha me'ein Shalosh, the blessing recited after foods containing at least one of the seven species associated with the Land of Israel, to be of Torah origin, as well.[7]

A myriad of other *brachot* are mandated by the rabbis, regularly punctuating the daily life of the Jew.

Questions

At first glance, the phrase "and you will bless" seems descriptive in nature, part and parcel of Moshe's prediction concerning the nation's eventual reaction to the bounty of the land. What, then, compels the Talmudic authorities to interpret the phrase "and you will bless" as an imperative, mandating a biblical obligation of Birkat Hamazon?

What is the nature of this commandment? Why would man be commanded to bless God? Clearly, man requires God's blessing; God does not require man's. As Rabbeinu Bachya ben Asher emphatically declares, "Given that God is the source of all blessing…were [man] to bless Him all day and all night, how would God benefit at all?"[8]

How did the multi-paragraph Grace after Meals regularly recited by Jews today emerge from the vague commandment "and you will bless…"?

Approaches

—A—

Immediately sensing the objections that might be raised to the derivation of a mitzva from this text, the Ramban refers the reader to other commandments derived from parallel phrases in the book of Devarim: "*and you will make* a fence for your roof,"[9] "*and you will perform* the Pesach offering for your God,"[10] "*and you will take* of the first of every fruit of the ground."[11]

6. *Sefer Hachinuch*, mitzva 430.
7. Rashba, Brachot 35a; Rosh, Brachot 6:16; Tur, Orach Chaim 209.
8. Rabbeinu Bachya ben Asher, Devarim 8:10.
9. Devarim 22:8.
10. Ibid., 16:1.
11. Ibid., 26:2.

At the same time, this scholar notes that the Torah is not consistent in its application of the formula "and you will…" While the phrase "and you will bless the Lord your God" constitutes a mitzva, the preceding phrases, "and you will eat, and you will become satisfied," are clearly not meant to be seen as distinct imperatives themselves, but as helping to define the obligation to bless.[12]

—— **B** ——

In spite of the Ramban's observations, the question of context in our case still remains. Given the descriptive nature of the preceding text, why are the rabbis insistent upon interpreting the phrase "and you will bless…" not simply as part of Moshe's narrative, but as a separate, distinct biblical imperative?

A rereading of the passage before us may provide an answer. This is a carefully structured presentation in which Moshe describes both the benefits and dangers presented by the natural resources of the land of Canaan. *The very bounty meant to sustain you*, Moshe warns the Israelites, *could well prove to be your undoing.*

The paragraph pivots on an apparent "cause-and-effect" structure established by the transition between three sentences:

A land where you will eat bread without scarceness; you will lack nothing within it; a land whose stones are iron and from whose mountains you will mine copper.

And you will eat, and you will be satisfied, and you will bless the Lord your God upon the good land that He has given you.

Take care lest you forget the Lord your God by not observing His commandments, His laws and His statutes, which I command you today.

Sated and satisfied by the wondrous natural wealth of the land, and filled with pride over your own accomplishments, Moshe warns, *you could easily forget your dependence upon God for the countless gifts that you have received.*

A problem, however, emerges from the text. One phrase does not fit the otherwise seamless "cause-and-effect" structure presented by Moshe.

---

12. Ramban, Devarim 8:10.

The insertion of the words "and you will bless the Lord your God" in the second sentence strikes an incongruous note. Blessing God can hardly be seen as a step along the path towards abandonment of our dependence upon Him. In fact, the opposite would seem to be true. If upon reaching a point of comfort and satiation, we bless God for the bounty that we have received, we will be *less likely* to forget His role in our good fortune.

Perhaps that is exactly the point recognized by the rabbis. In their eyes, "and you shall bless the Lord your God" cannot be understood as part of Moshe's description of the potential problem facing the nation, but instead must be seen *as a corrective for that problem*. In the words of the Meshech Chochma, "When one eats and is satisfied, one is likely to rebel. God, therefore, commands the nation to recall His name and to bless Him, specifically at the point of satiation, and to remember that He is the One Who gives man power to succeed."[13] Precisely because of the context in which it is found, the rabbis interpret the phrase "and you shall bless the Lord your God" as a commandment.

— C —

The above interpretation suggests an answer to another of our questions. Why does the Torah command man to "bless" God? What possible purpose could there be in such an act?

According to the approach of the Meshech Chochma and others, *man blesses God for man's sake*, in order to enable man to achieve and maintain proper life perspective. The recitation of Birkat Hamazon, specifically at a point of contentment and satiation, serves as a critical reminder of man's dependence upon God for sustenance and success. Similarly, all *brachot*, recited at various points during the daily life of the Jew, are designed to help an individual maintain proper spiritual balance.

Other authorities take this approach one step further. *Brachot*, these authorities maintain, do not only serve man's spiritual needs, but his physical requirements, as well. When an individual, through the act of blessing God, testifies to God's personal care for all life forms, God responds by increasing the bounty provided.[14] This phenomenon, Rabbeinu Bachya ben Asher maintains, explains the Talmudic assertion that if an individual eats without

---

13. Meshech Chochma, Devarim 8:10.
14. *Sefer Hachinuch*, mitzva 428; Rabbeinu Bachya ben Asher, Devarim 8:10.

a prior blessing, "it is as if he steals from God and from the assembly of Israel."[15] He steals from God by denying the Almighty's Providence over all living things, and he steals from the Assembly of Israel by denying them the physical benefit that would have accrued as a result of his blessing.[16]

—— D ——

Swimming against the tide, Rabbi Shimshon Raphael Hirsch argues that *man actually possesses the power to bless God.* As the only creature granted free will by his Creator, man is capable of furthering God's purposes and wishes in this world or of retarding and thwarting them. *Man blesses God when, through his actions, he increases God's sanctified presence in the world around him.* The *bracha* recited after eating, Hirsch continues, is to be understood as a verbal commitment, or even a vow, to bless God through action. "As often as you strengthen yourself with that which God has granted you...," this scholar asserts, "you are to dedicate the whole of your being to His service, to [the fulfillment of] His purposes and to the realization of His Will on earth. And this promise of dedication you are to pronounce in the words of *bracha*, of blessing Him."[17]

—— E ——

Having established that the phrase "and you will bless the Lord your God" serves as the source of the mitzva of Birkat Hamazon, the rabbis proceed to derive basic details of this mitzva from the surrounding text.

1. Two positions emerge in the Mishna, for example, as to *how much food must be consumed to obligate* the recitation of Birkat Hamazon. These opinions, the Talmud explains, reflect a fundamental disagreement as to where the emphasis should be placed in the sentence "And you will eat, and you will be satisfied, and you will bless the Lord your God."

The opinion of Rabbi Meir, recorded anonymously in the Mishna,[18] emphasizes the word *v'achalta* (and you will eat). As the Torah clearly bases the mitzva of Birkat Hamazon on food consumption, Rabbi Meir maintains, the obligation should be gauged by the normative minimum

15. Talmud Bavli Brachot 35b.
16. Rabbeinu Bachya ben Asher, Devarim 8:10.
17. Rabbi Shimshon Raphael Hirsch, Devarim 8:10.
18. Note: Anonymous sources in the Mishna are generally attributed to Rabbi Meir.

food measurement throughout Jewish law: the amount equivalent to the bulk of an olive.

Rabbi Yehuda, however, disagrees. Focusing on the word *v'savata* (and you will be satisfied), this scholar maintains that the key condition governing the mitzva of Birkat Hamazon is not food consumption, but, instead, satiation. The minimum standard for this mitzva must therefore be higher than the normative halachic minimum. An individual must eat food equivalent to the bulk of an egg, Rabbi Yehuda insists, in order to incur the obligation to recite Birkat Hamazon.[19]

Later halachic authorities disagree as to the parameters of the dispute between Rabbi Meir and Rabbi Yehuda.

According to some, these Mishnaic scholars are not debating the Torah law at all. Both Rabbi Meir and Rabbi Yehuda agree that, on a biblical level, *no objective minimum standard for the mitzva of Birkat Hamazon exists.* The Torah obligation of Birkat Hamazon is literally delineated by the term *v'savata* (and you will be satisfied). Biblically, an individual is only obligated to recite the blessing after a meal *that leads to his own personal satiation.* The amount that must be consumed to trigger this obligation varies, dependent upon the person and the situation. Uncomfortable with this lack of practical definition, the rabbis later issue an edict designed to create a uniform minimum standard. Rabbi Meir and Rabbi Yehuda argue about the scope of this edict. Rabbi Meir maintains that the rabbinic obligation to recite Birkat Hamazon takes effect once an individual consumes food equivalent to the bulk of an olive. Rabbi Yehuda, in contrast, argues that the rabbinic obligation only "kicks in" upon the consumption of an egg-sized portion. The textual proofs from the Torah derived by these scholars in support of their respective positions fall into the category of *asmachtot*, biblical hints used by the rabbis to support later mandated rabbinic laws.[20]

Other scholars adamantly disagree and insist that Rabbi Meir and Rabbi Yehuda disagree about biblical, not rabbinic, law. Their debate is

---

19. Talmud Bavli Brachot 45a; Rashi, ibid. Note: The Talmudic authorities debate whether the positions attributed to Rabbi Meir and Rabbi Yehuda in the Mishna are accurate as recorded, or whether they should be reversed.

20. Rashi, Brachot 20b, 48a; Tosafot, Brachot 49b, Pesachim 49b; Rambam, *Mishneh Torah,* Hilchot Brachot 1:1.

straightforward, focusing on the minimum standard required for the biblical obligation of Birkat Hamazon.[21]

2. The question of *which foods give rise to the biblical obligation* of Birkat Hamazon generates three opinions recorded in the Mishna and Gemara.

Basing his position on the word *v'achalta* (and you will eat), Rabbi Akiva maintains that the Torah requires the recitation of Birkat Hamazon after the consumption of *any food* that an individual considers a meal.

Rabbi Gamliel chooses a different path by noting that the biblical passage containing this mitzva specifically mentions the *seven species* associated with the Land of Israel, "a land of wheat and barley and grapes and figs and pomegranates, a land of olive oil and honey." The blessing is obligatory, Rabbi Gamliel therefore argues, *only after the consumption of a meal containing at least one of these seven species.*

Finally, the majority rabbinic opinion insists that the obligation to recite the full Grace after Meals is limited to *a meal containing bread.* This opinion is based on the fact that bread is the foodstuff listed in closest proximity to the commandment itself: "a land where you will eat bread without scarceness..."[22]

3. On a practical level, the law concerning these issues is codified according to the majority rabbinic opinion, that Birkat Hamazon must be recited after consumption of *an olive-sized portion of bread* or after *a meal containing that amount of bread.*[23]

——— F ———

Moving into the area of the mitzva's structure, the Talmudic scholars also discern references in the text to the number and content of the individual blessings meant to be incorporated into Birkat Hamazon.

The word *u'veirachta* (and you will bless), the Talmudists maintain, indicates that Birkat Hamazon must include a blessing referring to the physical sustenance provided by God to all living creatures; the phrase *al ha'aretz* (upon the land) mandates the inclusion of a blessing concerning the Land of Israel; and the reference to *ha'aretz hatova* (the good land) indicates that a blessing should be recited concerning Jerusalem.

---

21. Ra'avad on Rambam, *Mishneh Torah*, Hilchot Brachot 5:15; Rashba, Brachot 49b.
22. Talmud Bavli Brachot 44a.
23. Rambam, *Mishneh Torah*, Hilchot Brachot 1:1, 3:2; *Shulchan Aruch*, Orach Chaim 183:6, 208:1.

According to some scholars, these biblical references indicate that the thematic structure and content of Birkat Hamazon are actually of biblical origin.[24] Other scholars, however, maintain that the quoted textual allusions fall into the category of *asmachtot* (see above) and that the thematic structure of Birkat Hamazon is rabbinically rather than biblically mandated.[25]

G

Even those scholars who view the structure and general content of Birkat Hamazon to be of biblical origin acknowledge that the actual texts of the blessings recited today are of later prophetic derivation.

Originally, each individual fulfilled the mitzva of Birkat Hamazon through his own blessings, in his own words. As time went on, however, the paragraphs of Birkat Hamazon were standardized by pivotal Jewish leaders at critical moments in Jewish history:

> Moshe established the blessing concerning sustenance when the manna began to descend [for the Israelites in the wilderness]; Yehoshua established the blessing concerning the land upon the [Israelites'] entry into the land; David and Shlomo established the blessing concerning the building of Jerusalem, with David authoring the words "upon Israel Your nation and Jerusalem, Your city" [reflecting the conquest of Jerusalem during David's reign] and Shlomo authoring the words "upon the great and sanctified House" [reflecting the construction of the Holy Temple during Shlomo's rule].[26]

The Talmud explains that a fourth blessing, over and above those alluded to in the Torah, was added to Birkat Hamazon in response to a series of dramatic events roughly fifty years after the destruction of the Second Temple. At that time, Shimon Bar Kosiba, renamed Shimon Bar Kochba by Rabbi Akiva, led an ultimately unsuccessful and costly revolt against continuing Roman rule. So devastating were the results of this failed rebellion that many authorities mark Bar Kochba's final defeat, the fall of the city of

---

24. Tosafot, Brachot 16a; Lechem Mishneh, Hilchot Brachot 2:2.
25. *Shulchan Aruch*, Orach Chaim 194:6.
26. Talmud Bavli Brachot 48b.

Beitar, as the true onset of the Jewish nation's exile from their land. For a period of time following the fall of Beitar, the Roman authorities prohibited the Judeans from burying those killed in the city's siege. When this ban was finally lifted, the sages of Yavneh (see *Vayikra*: Emor 5, *Approaches* E–H) established the fourth blessing of Birkat Hamazon, *Hatov v'Hameitiv*, "He Who is good and bestows goodness." This blessing was instituted in gratitude to God for the lifting of the Roman ban and for the miraculous preservation of the bodies of the victims, allowing for their proper burial.[27]

Rabbi Meir Simcha of Dvinsk explains that the events surrounding the fall of Beitar delivered a profound message to a shattered people: God's providence will extend to the nation even during tragedy and exile. This message, Rabbi Meir Simcha explains, warranted the addition of a fourth blessing to Birkat Hamazon, a prayer built entirely upon the concept of God's providence towards man.[28]

—— **H** ————————————————————————

The mitzva of Birkat Hamazon emerges from Moshe's farewell messages to his people, only to accrue a myriad of halachic, philosophical and historical subtexts as it travels across the generations. The richness of Jewish experience is thus mirrored in the blessing that a Jew offers to his God.

---

27. Ibid. It should be noted that while the vast majority of scholars consider the fourth blessing of Birkat Hamazon to be totally of rabbinic origin, one tradition in the Talmud does suggest a biblical reference.
28. Meshech Chochma, Devarim 8:10.

2 One Small Detail

Context

As Moshe recounts the events following the sin of the golden calf, he adds a detail not mentioned in the original version of these events, recorded in the book of Shmot.[1]

Moshe relates that when God commanded him to carve a second set of Tablets of Testimony to replace the first, God also instructed him to fashion an *aron etz*, a wooden ark, in which to house the new tablets. Strikingly, Moshe mentions this wooden ark no less than four times within the span of five sentences:

> At that time the Lord said to me, "Carve for yourself two stone tablets like the first and ascend to Me to the mountain *and make for yourself a wooden ark*. And I shall inscribe on the tablets the declarations that were on the first tablets that you shattered, *and you shall place them in the ark*."
>
> *And I made an ark of cedarwood* and I carved two stone tablets like the first, and I ascended the mountain with the two tablets in my hand. And He inscribed on the tablets, according to the first writing, the Ten Declarations that the Lord spoke to you on the mountain from the midst of the fire, on the day of the congregation, and the Lord gave them to me. And I turned and I descended from the mountain *and I placed the tablets in the ark that I made*, and they remained there as Hashem had commanded me.[2]

Questions

Why is the creation of the *aron etz* mentioned by Moshe here, yet omitted in the original narrative concerning these events?

---

1. Shmot 34:1–4.
2. Devarim 10:1–5.

Why does Moshe place repeated emphasis on the fashioning and use of the ark? What aspect of the *aron etz* captures the attention and fires the imagination of this great leader? And again, if the ark is so important, why isn't it mentioned until now?

Why did Moshe apparently alter the sequence of God's instructions surrounding the *aron etz*? God commanded Moshe to first carve Tablets of Testimony and then to fashion the ark. Moshe, however, responded by first fashioning the ark and only subsequently carving the tablets.

Why did God command Moshe to fashion an ark only in connection with the second set of Tablets of Testimony and not in connection with the first?

Finally, what ultimately happens to the *aron etz*? Does it continue to be used? What is the relationship between this wooden ark and the gold-covered Ark first detailed in Parshat Teruma as part of the overall construction of the Sanctuary and its utensils?[3]

Approaches

— A —

Addressing our last question first, a dispute emerges among the classical commentaries concerning the ultimate role and fate of the *aron etz* fashioned by Moshe at Sinai.

Mirroring a position quoted in Talmud Yerushalmi[4] and elsewhere, Rashi and the Da'at Zekeinim Miba'alei Hatosafot identify Moshe's wooden ark as one of two arks that were destined to stand in the Sanctuary. These scholars explain that for a short period of time – after Moshe's descent from Sinai until the creation of the Mishkan – the simple wooden ark held both the shards of the first tablets as well as the complete second set. With the building of the Mishkan, a primary, gold-covered Ark was created at God's command to serve as the permanent home for the second complete set of tablets. Fashioned by Betzalel and his artisans, this second ark was designed to remain in the Sanctuary as the centerpiece of the Holy of Holies. The creation of Betzalel's Ark, however, did not render Moshe's first ark obsolete. The wooden ark remained in use as the lasting home for the

---

3. Shmot 25:10–16.
4. Talmud Yerushalmi Shekalim 6:49.

shards of the shattered first tablets. Housed in the Sanctuary as well, this humble ark was periodically removed to accompany the nation in battle.[5]

─── **B** ───────────────────────────────────────

Noting that the Talmudic view postulating two arks in continual use is a minority opinion, the Ramban insists that only one ark, Betzalel's Ark, stood in the sanctuary. This gold-covered Ark housed both the shards of the shattered first tablets as well as the complete second set. Moshe's wooden ark was meant to be temporary from the outset. Once the Sanctuary's Ark was created, the *aron etz* was stored away in preparation for respectful burial, as are all sanctified items that have fallen into disuse. The absence of a similar temporary *aron* in connection with the first tablets, the Ramban adds, reflects God's awareness that those tablets were destined for immediate destruction by Moshe at the base of the mountain.

The Ramban also offers a second, alternative reading for this entire passage – a reading that completely changes our understanding of God's message to Moshe at this critical moment.

In his second approach the Ramban contends that *God did not command Moshe to create a separate wooden ark at all*. Only one ark was built at Sinai: the Ark fashioned by Betzalel as part of the Sanctuary's construction. This Ark, although covered and lined with gold, was primarily built out of cedarwood and could be rightfully referred to as a "wooden ark." The divine instruction to Moshe, "Make for yourself a wooden ark," therefore, does not refer to a new ark at all, but to Betzalel's Sanctuary Ark. God deliberately repeats the instruction to create this ark in conjunction with the second tablets, in order to put Moshe's mind at ease.

Moshe, explains the Ramban, was uncertain as to the extent of God's forgiveness in the aftermath of the sin of the golden calf. Did that forgiveness, he wondered, extend to the building of the Sanctuary, as well, or would that sanctified edifice be denied to the nation as a result of their failing? God, therefore, simultaneous with His instructions concerning the second set of tablets, commands Moshe, "make for yourself a wooden ark. *I reiterate, Moshe, the first mitzva associated with the Sanctuary's creation – the fashioning of the Ark – as an indication of the extent of My forgiveness. Rest*

───────────────

5. Rashi, Devarim 10:1; Da'at Zekeinim Miba'alei Hatosafot, ibid.

assured that the nation will not be denied the Mishkan as a result of the sin of the golden calf.[6]

— **C** —

If we accept the Ramban's second reading of the text, the question as to why the *aron etz* only seems to appear in conjunction with the second set of tablets becomes moot. God is not commanding the construction of a new ark, but instead reaffirming His commitment to the ark that has already been mentioned.

Also understandable is Moshe's preoccupation with the construction and use of this ark in his recollections of these events in the book of Devarim. Traumatized by the nation's sin, Moshe was deeply afraid that the Mishkan would be denied to the Israelites. His profound joy and relief upon realizing that his fears were unfounded are now expressed by his repeated emphasis on the ark.

— **D** —

The Ramban refers to his second approach – that only one ark was created at Sinai – as the *pshat* of the text. The vast majority of scholars, however, accept the more obvious reading: that God commands Moshe to fashion a separate wooden ark at Sinai, distinct from the primary Ark of the Sanctuary.

If we reconsider the creation of this wooden ark against the backdrop of surrounding events, another explanation for its significance can be suggested.

Travel back for a moment to the scene at Sinai, to the swiftly moving events following the sin of the golden calf. The nation has failed grievously at the very foot of Sinai, moving Moshe to smash the first tablets at the mountain's base; the primary perpetrators of the sin have been punished; God has threatened further penalties against the nation as a whole; Moshe has prayed; God has fundamentally forgiven. And now, God commands Moshe to begin again, to carve a second set of tablets. Only one question

---

6. The Ramban's second approach adheres to this scholar's stated position that God's commandments concerning the construction of the Mishkan precede the sin of the golden calf, as indicated by the flow of the text. An alternate, midrashically based position maintains that the entire concept of the Sanctuary emerges as a divinely ordained response to that sin (see *Shmot*: Teruma 1).

remains: *What will be different this time? What must the nation learn from their previous failure, so that they will not fail again?*

To convey the essential changes that must occur if the second attempt at Sinai is to succeed, God subtly varies His instructions concerning the tablets. These variations allow for the transmission of two critical lessons with the giving of the second tablets: *the lessons of partnership and context.*

The first of these lessons emerges from an obvious distinction between the tablets themselves. While the first Tablets of Testimony were both carved and inscribed by God, the second set is to be fashioned by Moshe himself, and only inscribed by divine hand.[7] To a people whose sin may well have been an unwillingness to relate directly and closely to God,[8] God's primary message is clear:

This is a partnership that we are forging, you and I. You cannot be passive, distant participants in the process. I am giving you a living law that you will be required not only to obey, but to study, analyze and apply to ever-changing circumstances.

You are full partners in the task of bringing My sanctity into the world. To symbolize that partnership, we will create these second tablets together. Moshe will carve the tablets and I will inscribe My word upon them.

If the nation is to succeed in this second attempt, however, another lesson must be taught as well. It is the lesson of context: the Torah is value-less in a vacuum. *The words of God's law are only significant when they find a ready home in the heart of man, shaping the actions of those who receive them.* As we have previously suggested (see *Shmot*: Ki Tissa 4, *Approaches* E), this second critical lesson is conveyed not only through the second tablets themselves, but also through the newly commanded *aron etz.*

Moshe recognized a hard truth upon descending from Sinai with the first set of tablets in his hands. Confronted by the horrific scene of his nation celebrating before a golden calf, he realized that they were unready to accept God's word. The Torah had no place to "land," no ready context within which to exist. Had the law been given to the people in their present state, the Torah itself would have become an aberration, misunderstood and even misused. Moshe had no choice but to publicly destroy the Tablets

---

7.   Shmot 34:1.
8.   For a full discussion of this approach to the sin of the golden calf, see *Shmot*: Ki Tissa, *Approaches* C and *Points to Ponder.*

of Testimony before the eyes of the people. Only then, at God's command, could he begin the process of their reeducation.

This teaching process begins as God alters the details concerning the Tablets of Testimony. God will inscribe His decrees upon this second set, but this time, only on stone carved by Moshe. The tablets thus represent the word of God finding a home in the actions of a man. To further convey this point concretely, God also commands that these new tablets be immediately placed into a physical home, Moshe's *aron etz* – a simple ark of wood. The symbolism is clear. *Only if the contents of these tablets also find their home (in the humble hearts of man) – only if the Torah finds context – will this Torah be worthy of existence.*

——— E ———

If these lessons of partnership and context are so critical, however, why does God wait until the transmission of the second set of tablets to convey them? Couldn't the horrific failure of the *egel hazahav* and the devastating ensuing pain and punishment have been avoided had these points been shared from the outset, with the transmission of the first tablets?

With these questions we once again enter difficult territory that we have already explored (see *Bereishit*: Noach 1, *Approaches* A; Shmot: Teruma 1, *Approaches* B; Bamidbar: Shelach 1, *Points to Ponder*). Why does God allow man to fail, at times educating him to his errors only after the failures have occurred? Why not avoid, through divine intervention, the devastation of the flood in Noach's time, the sin of the spies after the Exodus or the sin of the golden calf at Sinai?

As we have previously suggested, it would seem that God's education of man does not follow a linear course. By creating a world predicated upon the existence of free will, God accepts the inevitability of human failure. In such a world certain values cannot be taught frontally but must emerge through a process of human trial and error. Like the wise parent who hurts for his child's pain, yet recognizes that his child must experience failure, God stands back and allows his creations to stumble, knowing that upon rising they will be better for the process. The values embedded in the second set of tablets and the accompanying *aron* could not have been fully appreciated by the Israelites until after their failure at Sinai. God therefore waits until the transmission of the second Tablets of Testimony to convey the lessons critical to the nation's success.

—— **F** ——————————————————————————

God also appreciates the powerful impact that Moshe's own dawning realizations can have upon the people. He therefore holds back any mention of the wooden ark in the initial narrative of the events, instead allowing this powerful symbol to emerge only in Moshe's recollections. The repeated stress that Moshe places upon the *aron* as he speaks to the nation in retrospect drives home this great leader's own critical recognition of the ark's importance. Telling, as well, is Moshe's self-admitted deviation from God's instructions. While God commands Moshe to create the second tablets and then to fashion the ark, Moshe insists on creating the *aron* first. This great leader recognizes that the Tablets of Testimony cannot exist even for a moment outside of their proper spiritual context. For the nation to learn that lesson, these tablets must be placed immediately in their physical home, as well.

Points to Ponder

Every once in a while, we rabbis hit what we consider to be a sermonic "home run," a critical speech that truly finds its mark.

From the reactions received, it seems that my Kol Nidrei drasha this past year was one such "home run." This drasha, in fact, hit such a sensitive nerve with so many of my congregants that, with a bit of editing, I submitted it as an op-ed to my local area Jewish newspaper, again to strong reaction.

This piece deals in its own way with the lesson of context that we have discussed in our study, the recognition that Torah is only valuable when it shapes the character and actions of man. I therefore offer it for your attention, as well.

*   *   *

So there we were, Barbara and I, on a two-week vacation to the Canadian Rockies.

The trip was exceeding even our high expectations: majestic mountains, roaring crystal rivers, emerald lakes in hanging valleys, and wildlife – bear, elk, deer, bighorn sheep, an elk that we thought was a moose (we never did see a moose) – a nature lover's dream. *Ma nora ma'asecha, Hashem*, How awe inspiring are Your works, God!

But as the days wore on, I unexpectedly found myself captivated by a different "life form." I began to take note of the people we met along the way – non-Jews, mostly – along the trails, in the parks, at the picnic tables…

And you know what I found? *They were nice! I mean, really nice!* They were open, friendly, pleasant and engaging. Their children were polite, well mannered and cooperative. And strangely enough, the more people I met, the more uncomfortable I became. *Because I began to feel that in some ways, they are nicer than us.*

Now I know what some of you are saying to yourselves. *Wow, the rabbi is skating on thin ice. He goes on a two-week vacation, meets a couple of people in passing, and returns to insult us.* So let me make some things abundantly clear from the outset: Our congregations are exemplary in so many ways. The extraordinary human resource and wealth of spirit that exist within them are incomparable. The personal support that we extend to each other at critical life moments, whether joyous or challenging, sets a standard towards which other faith communities can aspire. When the chips are down, there is no one I would rather be with than the members of our Jewish community.

I also recognize that my chance meetings with a series of people on vacation in the Canadian Rockies hardly qualify as a scientific survey of the non-Jewish world.

Nonetheless, the High Holy Day season is a time for honest self-appraisal. Let me, therefore, ask you a question. Don't you sometimes feel that we Jews could use an attitude adjustment? Don't you sometimes think, and I don't know how else to put it, that we need to get over ourselves a bit?

The signs are readily apparent: How many of you in the service fields have come to me over the years and told me that you would rather deal with your non-Jewish customers than with Jews? How many of us, in the public arena, from the shul to ShopRite, have acted, or seen our coreligionists act, in ways that are a bit condescending, entitled, even pushy? And what about our children? Are we pleased with the way they talk to each other, to us, or to other adults?

If you are not convinced yet, try this little litmus test. Some of you may know the story of the El Al plane landing at Tel Aviv during Chanukah, in a year when Chanukah falls when it most often does. As the plane taxis towards the gate, the copilot announces over the loudspeaker, "Ladies and gentlemen, please stay in your seats. The plane is still moving; we have not yet reached the gates." A few moments later, he says, "Ladies and gentlemen, once again, the plane is still moving. It is not safe. Please be considerate of yourselves and others – please remain in your seats." And a few moments later: "Ladies and gentlemen, stay in your seats!" Finally, he announces, "Ladies and gentlemen, I am pleased to tell you that we have arrived at the gate. To all of you who are standing, happy Chanukah! To all of you who are still seated, merry Christmas!"

The litmus test: Could this story be true?

I almost feel as if there is an attitudinal veneer that blocks the basic goodness in our hearts from rising to the surface. It seems to automatically kick in, like a switch that's pulled, whenever we feel a bit stressed, tense, harried or pushed.

The reasons for this phenomenon are potentially manifold: Perhaps we have been pushed so often and so long throughout our history that given the opportunity, we naturally tend to push back. Perhaps we still feel a bit uncertain and vulnerable. Clearly many of us misinterpret our role as God's chosen people to mean that we are inherently superior, rather than that we have greater responsibility. And to be honest, for some of us, it's simply our affluence and our success that makes us feel that we can do anything or say anything with impunity. *After all, there is no mitzva to be nice.* Six hundred thirteen commandments, and not one of them says outright that we have to be nice, right?

Wrong! Dead wrong!

During this holiday period, as we return to basics, let me tell you what one of our greatest scholars has to say about the mitzvot. Rav Abba bar Aivu, who is known within Talmudic literature simply as Rav ("teacher"), emphatically declares: "The sole purpose of the mitzvot is to refine mankind." He goes on to explain that our detailed performance of the mitzvot does not make a difference to God. It makes a difference to us. The mitzvot simply are created to refine us. To make us nice.[9]

Let's understand what this means. If we are punctilious in the performance of the mitzvot, yet that performance does not change us, refine us, make us better human beings, then the system simply isn't working. If the performance of mitzvot doesn't knock the chip off our shoulder, if it doesn't bring us down a peg by making us realize that we stand on equal footing

---

9. Midrash Rabba Bereishit 44:1.

with all human beings before an all-powerful God, if it doesn't bring us up a notch by making us recognize the majestic potential that lies within our souls, then we are not performing mitzvot properly. If the system of Jewish law does not produce nicer people, then something is desperately wrong.

The reason there is no specific mitzva to be nice is that *the purpose of all the mitzvot is to make us better human beings.*

Now, you may say, *You know, the rabbi is right. This is all fine and good. How, however, can we act upon this knowledge? How can we break through our own familiar attitudinal veneer?* I would like, therefore, to prescribe a simple exercise.

This exercise is not mine. It was prescribed by the rabbis of the Talmud, centuries ago. Thankfully, they even hinged this drill upon an abundantly familiar biblical passage, so that it is very easy for us to remember: *V'ahavta et Hashem Elokecha b'chol levavcha u'v'chol nafshecha u'v'chol me'odecha*, "And you shall love the Lord your God with all your heart and with all your soul and with all your might…"[10]

How, ask the rabbis, is it possible to "love God"? How can love apply to an entity that lies so far beyond our understanding? Among the answers they propose is the following powerful suggestion: "And you shall love… that the name of heaven should become beloved through you." In other words, you should act in such a way that your very actions increase the awareness of and the love of God in this world. Others should see your behavior as a Jew and say, "How wonderful! What a mensch! If this is what Judaism produces, what a beautiful system it must be."[11]

So here's the exercise: This year, every time you are about to lash out at the person next to you, every time you feel entitled to be rude, every time you become frustrated because the cashier at ShopRite (who is so obviously inferior to you in your mind, because she needs to work behind the counter to put herself/her children through college and you don't) is too slow, every time you feel righteously entitled to criticize someone in your synagogue and you don't feel the need to do so in a non-hurtful way (because you so obviously know better than the person you are about to criticize), every time you are about to be rough on your housekeeper (who is also so obviously lesser than you, although she is only doing the work

---

10. Devarim 6:5.
11. Talmud Bavli Yoma 96a.

that your grandmother once had to do for someone else; and there, but for the grace of God, go you)…

Every time, stop and ask yourself: "Is this really what God wants? Is what I'm about to do or say going to increase God's presence in this world? Are my actions or words going to enhance the appreciation of God's will and the love for His word?"

If the answer is no, then don't do it. Don't say it. Period!

And, who knows, maybe if we stop and regularly ask ourselves these questions, we will succeed in being nicer to each other, to those with whom we regularly deal, to those whom we glancingly meet on the journey.

We will succeed in bringing out the innate goodness that lies in each of our hearts. We will fill the world with a bit more love and respect for the Divine.

We will truly do "what God wants" and we will show our love for Him by bringing Him *nachat*.

3 An Unusual Sales Pitch

Context

On two separate occasions in Parshat Ekev, Moshe describes the nature of the land promised to the Israelites.

Towards the beginning of the parsha, Moshe declares:

> For the Lord your God is bringing you to a good land: a land of streams of water, of springs and underground pools emerging forth in the valley and in the mountain; a land of wheat and barley and grapes and figs and pomegranates; a land of olive oil and honey; a land where you will eat bread without scarceness; you will lack nothing within it; a land whose stones are iron and from whose mountains you will mine copper.[12]

Further in the parsha, Moshe states:

> For the land to which you come, to possess it, is not like the land of Egypt from which you left, where you would plant your seed and water it on foot, like a garden of vegetables. And the land to which you cross over to possess it is a land of mountains and valleys; from the rain of the heavens you shall drink water. A land that the Lord your God seeks out; constantly the eyes of the Lord your God are upon it, from the beginning of the year to year's end.[13]

Questions

Moshe's first description of the land in Parshat Ekev is uniformly positive. Canaan, he explains, is a well-irrigated land of plenty that will produce a multitude of important crops and is rich in natural resources. Clearly, this

---

12. Devarim 8:7–9.
13. Ibid., 11:10–12.

description is designed to encourage the nation as it prepares, with both excitement and trepidation, for its entry into an unknown land.

Moshe's second description of Canaan, however, might well give the Israelites pause. The land from which you have come, says Moshe, is sustained through a regular source of irrigation, the overflow of the Nile. The land towards which you travel, however, is not automatically irrigated with such regularity. This land depends instead upon rain from the heavens. *God's constant care is needed for those who live upon this land to thrive.*

Why would Moshe deliberately share this unsettling information with the nation? In what way does it help the Israelites to know in advance that life in Canaan will be uncertain? We have seen that Moshe is desperately afraid that this generation might, like their parents before them, fail on the very brink of success; that they might lose heart in the face of the challenges before them (see Devarim 3, *Approaches* A). Why, then, would this great leader transmit discouraging information to the people at a time when encouragement is so desperately needed?

Approaches

—— A ——

After clearly rejecting the possibility that Moshe would deliberately compare Canaan unfavorably to Egypt, Rashi searches for and discerns in this great leader's words an allusion to the agricultural superiority of Canaan. Irrigation in Egypt through the Nile's overflow, Rashi explains, does not create consistent results. While low-lying areas in Egypt are automatically well watered, elevated terrain remains dry. Water, therefore, must be manually carried by farmers and workers to the higher terrain, as they are required to "water [the land] on foot, like a garden of vegetables."[14] In contrast, the land of Canaan is irrigated "from the rain of the heavens."[15] God will water the fields of the Israelites while they "lie comfortably in their beds."[16]

Across the ages, other scholars follow Rashi's lead by suggesting additional benefits to the agricultural model of Canaan as compared to the Egyptian model. The nineteenth–twentieth-century scholar Rabbi Zalman

14. Devarim 11:10.
15. Ibid., 11:11.
16. Rashi, Devarim 11:10.

Sorotzkin, for example, maintains that the man-made canals dug in Egypt to spread the waters of the Nile over distant areas create an unhealthy, damp environment that breeds disease. In contrast, the natural topography of Israel allows for water to flow from mountains to valleys, yet remain long enough to benefit each area before escaping to the sea.[17]

—— B ——

Other scholars, including the Ramban and the Rashbam, adopt a totally different approach to Moshe's second depiction of Canaan in Parshat Ekev. Moshe's words in this case, these authorities argue, are not designed to reassure and encourage the Israelites but *to warn them*.[18]

Couched directly after an admonition to observe the mitzvot and directly before the second paragraph of the Shma, with its clear description of divine reward and punishment, Moshe's message to the people concerning Canaan is succinctly summed up in the words of the Rashbam: "This land is the best of all lands for those who observe the mitzvot, and the worst of all lands for those who do not."[19]

You are entering a land, Moshe tells the nation, *that will be completely responsive to your actions. Vastly unlike Egypt, which is irrigated regularly by the Nile, Canaan is a land that requires God's constant attention. If you obey His law, He will cause the rain to fall and you will thrive. Conversely, if you rebel against His will, disaster will result.*

This warning, the Ramban maintains, serves as a perfect introduction to the passage that immediately follows, the second paragraph of the Shma, which outlines a clear vision of divine reward and punishment in response to man's actions (see next study).[20]

—— C ——

Yet other scholars go a striking step further in their interpretation of Moshe's words. Representative of this group, the Malbim asks: Why didn't God simply bequeath the land of Egypt to the Israelites instead of orchestrating their journey into the land of Canaan? Egypt is a fertile land in its own right. Given the collective guilt of the Egyptians, it certainly would

---

17. *Oznaim LaTorah*, Devarim 11:11.
18. Ramban, Rashbam, Devarim 11:10.
19. Rashbam, ibid.
20. Ramban, ibid.

have been appropriate (and simpler) for the Israelites to dispossess their erstwhile masters and acquire their land.

The answer, suggests the Malbim, is embedded in Moshe's description of the land of Canaan. Unlike Egypt, where irrigation occurs with regularity, Canaan is a land clearly dependent upon daily Divine Providence. Rain, in appropriate measure and in appropriate season, is essential for the sustenance of those living within its borders. After their entry into Canaan, therefore, the Israelites will be forced to continually turn their hearts heavenward in search of God's blessing.[21]

God, Moshe emphasizes, wants the Israelites to live in a land where their dependence upon Him will be clearly before them, front and center, each day of their lives.

— **D** —

If we accept the approach represented by the Malbim, we can combine the positions of the earlier quoted scholars by suggesting that Moshe's description of Canaan is consciously multi-textured, *designed to both encourage and warn the nation at once.* Canaan, Moshe emphasizes, is the Israelites' geographical destination, not only because of its physical attributes, but also because of its spiritual character:

The land to which God takes you does not lie. The fundamental truth that has been taught to you through the daily delivery of the manna in the wilderness (see Shmot: Beshalach 4, Approaches c) will now confront you daily upon your entry into Canaan, as well.

You are dependent upon God's Providence each and every day of your lives.

This fact would be true, of course, no matter where you might live. But in a land like Egypt, where sustenance seems guaranteed, it is a truth easily forgotten. God, therefore, in His kindness, takes you into a land that does not lie, a land where the truth of your dependence upon heaven is inescapable, where that truth will confront you each and every day of your lives.

There is, of course, a price to be paid for living in a land that does not lie. You will be held directly accountable for your actions in ways that will concretely affect your physical destiny. This is, however, a small price to pay

---

21. Malbim, Devarim 11:10–12.

*for the gift of living in a land where God's presence is so clearly felt each and
every day.*

Points to Ponder

Many of us spend our days in worlds where it is easy to forget our dependence upon God. Concrete cities and suburban enclaves shield us from
the rhythms of the natural world; abundant produce fills the shelves of
our stores, regardless of the season; we surround ourselves with creature
comforts designed to distance us from any uncertainty that might touch
our lives. Striking scientific advances, particularly in the health-related
fields, make it easy to lose our way – to stumble, as Moshe warns us we
might, into believing that "our strength and the might of our hands has
brought us all this wealth."[22]

In such worlds, the ongoing rituals of Jewish tradition become critical aids in the maintenance of a Jew's spiritual balance. Daily contact with
God through study, prayer and concrete observance prompts each Jew to
regularly consider his own vulnerability and the truth of his reliance upon
God for the most basic essentials of life.

In this struggle for perspective, the Land of Israel plays a central role,
as well. Not only has this land retained the unique spiritual character referred to by Moshe so many centuries ago, but the concrete manifestations
of that character have dramatically increased. Israel remains to this day a
land that does not lie, a land that conveys dependence upon God on so
many levels and in so many ways.

Agriculturally, in spite of the State of Israel's world-leading techno-
logical advances, the Israeli farmer must still rely upon rain in its season;
the water level of the Sea of Kineret is closely monitored each year and
water rights remain a consistent point of contention between Israel and
its neighbors.

Historically, not only did the dream of return to the Land help sustain
the nation through its turbulent exile journey, but God's promise of that
return helped refine each Jew's awareness of his continued reliance upon
his Creator.

Politically, with the restoration of the Jewish homeland, the pattern
continues. Ensconced in a region of perpetual instability, surrounded by

---

22. Devarim 8:17.

intractable foes, often isolated within the world community, the State of Israel continues to defy the odds through the grace of God and the strength and ingenuity of its citizens. Why does this small country, described by one observer as a tiny beauty mark on the face of an expansive globe, command so much of the world's attention? Why has this land, across the flow of history, consistently been at the center of so much religious, political and emotional conflict? Why does the Jew constantly find himself praying for true peace within its borders and for the safety and security of its citizens?

Perhaps because, from the beginning of time, the Land of Israel was always meant to be a land that does not lie, *a land in which our dependence upon God confronts us front and center, each and every day of our lives.*

4 Dealing with Doubt

Context

Embedded in Parshat Ekev is a passage familiar to many Jews as the second paragraph of the Shma (see Va'etchanan 2). Like many passages in Parshat Ekev and beyond, this section outlines a clear biblical vision of divine reward and punishment in response to man's actions:

V'haya im shamo'a… And thus it shall be if you hearken to My mitzvot that I command to you today, to love the Lord your God and to serve Him with all your heart and with all your soul. And I shall provide the rain of your land in its proper time, the early and late rains, and you shall gather your grain and your wine and your oil. And I shall provide grass in your field for your cattle and you will eat and you will be satisfied.

Beware for yourselves, lest your hearts be seduced and you will stray and serve other gods and bow down to them. And the anger of the Lord shall be kindled against you, and He will hold back the heavens and there will be no rain, and the ground will not yield its produce, and you will be swiftly banished from the goodly land that the Lord gives you.

And you shall place these words of Mine upon your hearts and upon your souls, and you shall bind them for a sign upon your hands and they shall be as frontlets between your eyes. And you shall teach them to your children that they shall speak of them, when you sit in your house and as you walk by the way and when you lie down and when you rise up. And you shall write them upon the doorposts of your house and upon your gates. In order that your days and the days of your children shall be long upon the land that the Lord has promised to your forefathers to give to them, like the days of the heaven over the earth.[1]

---

1. Devarim 11:13–21.

Questions

Passages such as the second paragraph of the Shma present us with a wrenching dilemma. Can we maintain belief in the axiom of divine reward and punishment in light of the physical evidence before our own eyes?

How do we deal with the doubts that are raised in our hearts when we confront a world filled with illness, natural disasters and man-made horrors, a world in which the righteous often seem to suffer while the evil seem to flourish?

Approaches

—A—

I clearly remember a point made by Dr. Norman Lamm many years ago in a presentation to a group of fledgling rabbis (of which I was one). While the quote is not verbatim, it went something like this: *Any meaningful philosophical discussion you eventually have with any member of your congregation will ultimately boil down to the issues raised by our belief in divine justice.*

After thirty years in the rabbinate, I find Dr. Lamm's point to be unerringly on target. No religious concern touches our lives more personally. Our own experiences and the experiences of those around us, past and present, regularly move us to question God's justice. Furthermore, unlike other philosophical queries, the questions raised in this arena are often not distant or esoteric, but emotionally charged, poignantly personal and powerfully real.

These pressing questions, however, are hardly new. The issue of theodicy (the problem of reconciling God and religion in the face of evil) has been examined, discussed and debated by Jewish and non-Jewish scholars since time immemorial. Innumerable classical and contemporary Jewish sages have weighed in on the topic, introducing variables to the discussion that include the role of the world to come in the application of divine justice, causes other than direct punishment that might account for human suffering, the necessary existence of evil in a world based upon man's free choice, the contention that the very performance of a mitzva is its own reward, the boundaries of personal Divine Providence (see *Bamidbar*: Chukat 4) and more. Clearly these and other points will continue to be discussed and debated until the end of days, when God sees fit to reveal the secrets of His relationship with man.

Rather than retread this familiar territory, we will approach the issues from a different perspective, by narrowing the discussion to a more personal set of questions: How did our earliest sages deal with doubt? Did the rabbis of the Talmud experience the wrenching questions that plague us? Did they personally struggle with the chasm between the biblical vision of divine justice and the reality of the world that surrounded them? If so, can their personal spiritual journeys inform our own?

B

At first blush, the task that we have set for ourselves is a daunting one. As we have noted before (see *Bamidbar*: Chukat 4, *Approaches* F and G), the structure of the Talmud does not easily lend itself to categorization of its contents. In order to preserve its character as Oral Law, this monumental work is written in the form of a sort of conversation in suspended animation. Free association characterizes the flow of the text as it moves from one topic to another without pause. Those who wish to determine the Talmudic approach to any philosophical topic are forced to cull together disparate rabbinic statements on the subject from across the Talmud's many tractates.

Similarly, the Talmud does not present coherent, structured biographies of the many authorities who populate its pages. Such information is deemed peripheral to the text's central task of conveying Jewish law. Nonetheless, from its pages biographical hints do emerge of the colorful, pivotal giants who set the course of Jewish law. The glimpses that the Talmud provides of these great men, albeit incomplete, can help guide us in our own personal religious searches, centuries later.

The stories of three Talmudic scholars will prove instructive as we navigate the unstable byways of faith and doubt.

C

The first of our scholars to emerge from the mists of history may, at first, seem peripheral to our discussion. His story nevertheless serves as a cautionary tale of the dangers that can arise when the place of divine justice in Jewish tradition is misunderstood.

Antignos Ish Socho (Antigonus from Socho [an ancient town near Hebron]) lived in the early second century BCE. Little is known about his personal life, yet we do know that he served as an important teacher during the critical transitional period between the Anshei Knesset Hagedola, the Men of the Great Assembly, and the Zugot, five pairs of halachic authorities who, in succession, steered the course of Jewish law until the years directly before the destruction of the Second Temple. Among Antignos's students were Rabbis Yossi ben Yo'ezer and Yossi ben Yochanan, the first set of these Zugot.[2]

Antignos is directly quoted only once in the Talmud, in Pirkei Avot. His singular statement, however, remains one of the best-known maxims to emerge from the Talmudic era: "Do not be like servants who serve their master in order to receive reward; rather be like servants who serve their master not in order to receive reward, and let the fear of heaven be upon you."[3]

Antignos cautions his students that they should not let the promise of divine reward motivate their actions. God's will, this scholar maintains, should be fulfilled *simply because it is His will.*

Had Antignos's story ended there, we would have been left with the legacy of a shadowy, powerful teacher whose one primary teaching is preserved for posterity. Unfortunately for the Jewish people as a whole, however, his story does not end there. A source in *Avot D'Rabi Natan* relates that two other students of this great teacher, Tzadok and Boetus, publicly promulgate a misinterpretation of Antignos's central teaching.

Why did Antignos instruct us to follow God's will "as a servant who works in order not to receive reward?" Would a servant work all day, yet refuse reward in the evening? Clearly not! Rather, it must be that there is no expectation of reward – that there is no reward to be received for divine obedience at all. If the rabbis truly believed in a world to come, Antignos would never have preached as he did.

Why should we follow rabbinic dictate and deny ourselves in this world, if there will be no ultimate payback in any world beyond our own?

So powerful and persuasive are the arguments of these two rebellious students that they and their followers establish two breakaway sects from

2. Pirkei Avot 1:4.
3. Ibid., 1:3.

traditional rabbinic Judaism: the Tzedukim (the Sadducees), followers of Tzadok, and the Boetussim, followers of Boetus. These two groups continue to challenge and plague the adherents of rabbinic Judaism for centuries to come.[4]

The Talmud strikes a delicate balance in dealing with Antignos's legacy. This sage's central teaching is preserved for posterity in Pirkei Avot, because it is absolutely correct. Obedience to God should be maintained, as Antignos argues, for its own sake and not for the purpose of ultimate reward. The Talmud also preserves, however, the tragic story of Antignos's students to remind us that his maxim should not be misunderstood or misinterpreted. Fundamentally, *there can be no lasting faith in the existence of a just God without a concomitant belief in the eventual dispensation of His justice.* Absent such belief, Jewish thought and tradition cannot survive.

—— **D** ———————————————————————————

The recognition that Judaism cannot be sustained without a belief in the ultimate execution of divine justice, however, does not begin to answer our basic question. Are there models within the Talmud as to how our sages personally dealt with doubt? For direction we turn to a seemingly strange source: the story of our second personality, Elisha ben Avuya, who emerges from the Talmud as one of the most controversial figures in the history of Jewish law.

A respected contemporary and colleague of such outstanding scholars as Rabbi Akiva, Elisha eventually experiences an existential crisis of faith so profound that he renounces Jewish belief and becomes known within Talmudic literature by the appellation Acher, "the other."

Numerous traditions are offered in the Talmud as to the catalysts for Elisha's descent into heresy.

Some authorities posit a gradual trajectory to Elisha's spiritual rebellion. In a lengthy narrative concerning Elisha in the tractate of Chagiga, the Talmud Bavli reports that "a Greek song never ceased from his mouth" and that when he stood up from his seat in the house of study, "many heretical texts would fall from his lap."[5] Even before his full severance from Jewish tradition, Elisha was toying with ideas antithetical to his faith.

---

4. Avot D'Rabi Natan 5:2.
5. Ibid., Chagiga 15b.

Others maintain that Elisha's path was at least partially shaped earlier in his childhood, perhaps even before he was born, as a result of missteps and failures on the part of his parents.[6]

The Talmudic narrative in Chagiga offers a more detailed, mystical approach to Elisha's rejection of Judaism. The Talmud relates that four sages, including Elisha, embark upon a journey of exploration into esoteric Jewish thought, reaching into the vault of the heavens. Elisha's encounter with the unknown leaves him deeply shaken and, according to one tradition, ultimately leads him to doubt the central tenet of Jewish belief, the oneness of God, thus causing a complete break with Jewish tradition.[7]

Other authorities, however, posit a more abrupt breakdown on Elisha's part. Elisha abandons Judaism, these scholars claim, when he comes face-to-face with the overwhelming question of theodicy.

Some trace Elisha's trauma to the harsh persecution of the rabbis at the hands of the Romans after the Bar Kochba revolt. The Jerusalem Talmud relates that, upon seeing the tongue of the recently executed Rabbi Yehuda Hanachtom in a dog's mouth, Elisha bitterly concludes, "Is this Torah and is this its reward? This tongue that brought forth flawless words of Torah, this tongue which occupied itself with Torah all its days... There is no [heavenly] reward!"[8] The Babylonian Talmud similarly records that Elisha witnesses a pig dragging the tongue of Chutzpit the Meturgeman (the translator)[9] and exclaims, "The mouth that brought forth pearls now licks the dust!"[10]

Another well-known tradition, of which there are a few variations, traces Elisha's disillusionment to a less historically dramatic yet similarly heartbreaking incident. According to a narrative in the Babylonian Talmud, two sages, Elisha ben Avuya and Rabbi Yaakov ben Bartai, each independently witness a father instructing his child to climb a tree and retrieve chicks from a nest after performing the mitzva of *shiluach hakan*, sending away the mother bird. The child complies, but upon his descent, falls to his death. Compounding the mystery of this tragedy for these sages is their

---

6. Talmud Yerushalmi Chagiga 2:1.
7. Talmud Bavli Chagiga 14b–15a.
8. Talmud Yerushalmi 2:1.
9. So named because of his ability to repeat the lecture for all to hear. Talmud Bavli Brachot 27b.
10. Talmud Bavli Kiddushin 39b.

awareness that only two mitzvot in the Torah specifically bear the promise of long life: the mitzva of *kibbud av va'eim* (honoring one's parents) and the mitzva of *shiluach hakan. How it is possible in a just world*, each scholar agonizes, *for a child to die so suddenly and tragically while engaged in the very two biblical mitzvot that carry the Torah's promise of longevity?*

Rabbi Yaakov, the Talmud continues, is moved by this incident to conclude that heavenly reward is not granted in this world. Such reward, he insists, is reserved for the righteous in the world to come. Elisha, in contrast, unwilling to accept his colleague's solution to the riddle of divine justice, descends into heresy.[11]

——— **E** ———————————————————————————————

Other aspects of Elisha's life are vigorously debated by the authorities.

The character and extent of his apostasy, for example, is apparently viewed differently within the Babylonian Talmud and the Jerusalem Talmud, respectively. The Talmud Bavli portrays Elisha as spending his days primarily in the pursuit of physical pleasure.[12] The Talmud Yerushalmi contends, however, that he deliberately attempts to lead other Jews astray, forces them to desecrate the Shabbat during the period of religious persecution at the hands of the Romans, and is directly responsible for the death of a number of sages.[13]

Even the origin of the term Acher, "the other," the appellation by which Elisha becomes known in the Talmud, becomes the subject of dispute. The Talmud Bavli traces the term to the consternation of a harlot, who, when solicited by Elisha asks, "Are you not Elisha ben Avuya [the renowned sage]?" When Elisha wordlessly responds by committing an act of Shabbat desecration, she exclaims, "He must have become *acher*, another!" Later authorities, however, interpret the name as a form of ostracism by the rabbis in response to Elisha's apostasy.[14]

——— **F** ———————————————————————————————

Certainly, one of the most fascinating aspects of Elisha's story is the continuing relationship forged with him by his most loyal student, the towering

---

11. Ibid.
12. Talmud Bavli, Chagiga 15b.
13. Talmud Yerushalmi Chagiga 2:1.
14. Geonim, recorded in *Encyclopedia Judaica.*

sage Rabbi Meir. When all other scholars sever connection with Elisha in response to his apostasy, Rabbi Meir alone refuses to abandon his teacher.

As time goes on, a complex relationship develops between the disenfranchised teacher and his brilliant student. Earning criticism from some and accolades from others,[15] Rabbi Meir stubbornly continues to learn, discuss and debate with Elisha, repeatedly begging his mentor to repent. Elisha, for his part, refuses to return, claiming that he is no longer redeemable.

Boundaries, drawn in the breach between the protagonists, are respected against all odds. The Talmud, for example, describes a remarkable incident in which Elisha, riding a horse on Shabbat, is followed on foot by Rabbi Meir, who is seizing the opportunity to learn Torah from his master.

By and by, Elisha turns to his student and says: "Meir, go back, for I have calculated the footsteps of my horse and determined that we have now reached the Shabbat boundary [the point beyond which one is not allowed to walk on Shabbat]." *I no longer respect the law, but I want to spare you the pain of inadvertently breaking it.*

Rabbi Meir responds: "You, too, go back, to your earlier Torah observance."

Elisha insists: "I have already heard from behind the [heavenly] partition: 'Return, O my sons'[16] – except for Acher." *It is too late for me, Meir. I have gone too far.*

When Rabbi Meir continues to press, Elisha manages to prove, through a variety of means, the truth of his own spiritual irretrievability.[17]

Yet another Talmudic source places Rabbi Meir at Elisha's deathbed, once again urging his master to repent. When Elisha cries at the moment of his soul's departure, Rabbi Meir quietly rejoices: "It appears to me that in the midst of repentance he died."[18]

—— **G** ——

The rabbinic comments concerning Elisha's final journey reflect the deep ambivalence with which the sages viewed their wayward colleague.

The Talmud relates that when Acher died, the heavenly court found itself in a quandary, unable to consign Elisha to the fires of hell because

15. Talmud Bavli Chagiga 15b.
16. Yirmiyahu 3:14.
17. Talmud Bavli Chagiga 15a–b.
18. Talmud Yerushalmi Chagiga 2:1.

of the merit of his Torah study yet unable to admit him to the world to come because he had sinned. In order to break the impasse, Rabbi Meir declared: "Better that he be judged [through hellfire] so that he will then be able to enter the world to come. When I die I will cause smoke to rise from his grave [to indicate that I have been successful in causing his judgment to begin]."[19] And indeed, upon Rabbi Meir's death, smoke began to rise from Elisha's grave.

Subsequently Rabbi Yochanan asked, "Does it show strength to burn one's teacher? There was one among us [who stumbled and strayed], can we not save him? If I take him by the hand [to lead him to the world to come], will anyone stand in my way? When I die, I will extinguish the smoke from his grave." And indeed, when Rabbi Yochanan died the pillar of smoke rising from Elisha's grave disappeared, indicating that Rabbi Yochanan had been successful in escorting Elisha into the world to come.[20]

—— H ——

While the tale of Elisha ben Avuya is certainly compelling, even more compelling is the mystery of its very existence. Why do the rabbis record the detailed story of a "failed scholar"? Given the Talmud's primary focus on the preservation and perpetuation of Jewish thought and law, isn't the story of Acher exactly the kind of narrative that Talmudists would choose to avoid?

On one level, the answer is simple. As we have noted before (see Devarim 4, *Points to Ponder*), a good deal of the strength of Jewish thought lies in its honesty. We do not rewrite history to suit our needs. If Elisha ben Avuya existed, then his story must be told. Only in this way can we learn from our successes and failures alike.

On a deeper level, however, I believe there might well be another reason for the inclusion of Elisha's story in the Talmud. *Perhaps the rabbis found this tale to be a safe vehicle for reflection upon their own religious questions and struggles.* Through a mixture of fact and supposition, the rabbis enter territory they could not otherwise easily enter and entertain possibilities they could not normally entertain.

Consider some of the powerful issues that swirl through the Talmudic

---

19. Talmud Bavli Chagiga 15b.
20. Ibid.

recording of Elisha's journey: What could cause a loyal sage to break with tradition? Are there circumstances under which such a break can be excused? Can belief withstand a battle with doubt? What would life be like on the outside (outside the circle of scholarly friendship, outside the limitations of Jewish law, outside the system of faith that sustains us)? Would such a life be empty or pleasurable? At what point, if any, does someone become irredeemable? Should an apostate be shunned? What are the limitations of God's forgiveness?

By projecting these and other issues onto the life of their own wayward colleague, the rabbis of the Talmud reflect a keen awareness of their shared vulnerability. Elisha ben Avuya is not a distant figure, but one of "their own." The myriad potential forces that lead him astray are not alien to the rabbis' experience, but exceedingly familiar, ever present in their lives. A thin line separates Elisha's choices from their own, his fate from theirs. Far from living in ivory towers, the Talmudic scholars are thinking men who wrestle with questions and challenges each day. They are men who *choose to believe*, in spite of their own uncertainties and in the face of clear alternatives that surround them.

Can we, however, discern their approach in the face of doubt? How do the rabbis manage to withstand the very uncertainties and temptations to which their own colleague, Elisha, falls prey?

For direction, we turn to our third and final scholar, an individual whom we have already met, Elisha ben Avuya's loyal student, Rabbi Meir.

— I —

We enter Rabbi Meir's life and thought through the portal provided by a dramatic debate in Brachot, the first tractate of the Babylonian Talmud (see *Shmot*: Ki Tissa 5, *Approaches* E).[21]

At issue is the substance of Moshe's conversation with God at Sinai, in the aftermath of the sin of the golden calf. Rabbi Yochanan, quoting Rabbi Yossi, builds upon evidence in the biblical text to identify three requests submitted by Moshe to God at this fluid, critical moment of Jewish history:

1. "[I]s it not that You will go with us…"[22] Moshe requests that God continue to rest His presence upon the Israelites.

---

21. Talmud Bavli Brachot 7a.
22. Shmot 33:16.

2. "And I and Your people will be made distinct from every people that are on the face of the earth."[23] Moshe requests that God not rest His presence (in the same way) upon other nations.

3. "[S]how me Your ways…"[24] Moshe requests that God reveal why there are righteous individuals for whom things are good, righteous individuals for whom things are bad, wicked people for whom things are good, evil people for whom things are bad. (In short, Moshe's third request is for an understanding of the issue of theodicy.)

Contending that God responds affirmatively to each of Moshe's requests, Rabbi Yochanan proceeds to offer a possible solution to the mysteries of divine justice.

His colleague, Rabbi Meir, however, dissents. The first two of Moshe's requests, Rabbi Meir argues, are indeed granted. *The third request, however, Moshe's plea for an understanding of theodicy, remains unanswered.*

— J —————————————————————————————

Before touching on the dispute between Rabbi Yochanan and Rabbi Meir, we must first address a more basic question. From what source does either of these sages determine the substance of Moshe's third request? Moshe's first two appeals emerge clearly from the text. The biblical phrase upon which Rabbi Yochanan bases the third request, however, is general and vague. What evidence exists that with the words "show me Your ways," Moshe is asking for a solution to the puzzle of theodicy?

The answer, I would suggest, is obvious. *The rabbis cannot imagine that Moshe, given the opportunity to ask any question of God, would have asked anything else.* To their minds, the issue of theodicy remains the single most perplexing issue to confront any thinking person of belief. The question that haunted the rabbis themselves is the question that, to their minds, must have haunted Moshe, as well.

— K —————————————————————————————

What, however, motivates Rabbi Meir to disagree with Rabbi Yochanan concerning God's response to Moshe's third plea? Why does this sage insist that even Moshe, whose access to the Divine exceeded that of all others

_____
23. Ibid.
24. Ibid., 33:13.

across the face of history, was denied an answer to the riddles surrounding divine justice? No unambiguous evidence emerges from the text that Moshe's plea for understanding is refused…

Rabbi Meir's contribution to this discussion may well be forged by the nature of his own life journey. No personal story emerging from the Talmudic period is more tragic than Rabbi Meir's. During his lifetime, this great sage experiences the loss of his beloved teacher, Elisha ben Avuya, to apostasy (see above); the sudden death of two sons over the course of one Shabbat; the equally sudden death of his brilliant wife, Beruriah, under particularly devastating, guilt-provoking circumstances;[25] and a resultant self-imposed exile to Asia, where he dies.[26]

The Talmudic passage before us thus acquires new, powerful urgency as we reimagine Rabbi Meir's response to Rabbi Yochanan.

You, my colleague, may feel that Moshe received answers to the riddles raised concerning the application of divine justice in this world. I, however, must insist that he did not. My own bitter experience has shown me that no human being has been granted, or will be granted, answers to these questions until the end of days.

Does Rabbi Meir experience the questions and doubts to which his beloved mentor, Elisha ben Avuya, falls prey? I would argue that, obliquely yet firmly, the Talmud tells us that he does. Perhaps that is why Rabbi Meir alone most closely identifies with and remains loyal to "Acher."

Rabbi Meir consciously chooses a middle road in his approach to the issues of theodicy. On the one hand, he rejects what he sees as the facile solutions offered by his colleagues in their struggle to reconcile belief in divine justice with the evidence from a surrounding world. On the other hand, in spite of his own tragic life experience, he equally rejects the surrender of his mentor, Elisha, to the overwhelming power of doubt. Rabbi Meir instead chooses *to live with the questions of faith, fully aware of the pain that those questions will bring.*

—— **L** ——————————————————————————

We should not be surprised that we end our journey of exploration haunted by the same questions with which we began. The issues of theodicy will plague the thinking believer until the end of days.

———————————

25. Rashi, Talmud Bavli Avoda Zara 18b.
26. Talmud Yerushalmi Kilayim 9:4.

We have, however, picked up some interesting and important company along the way. Antignos, Rabbi Meir, Elisha ben Avuya's contemporaries, and others walk with us. Their presence provides the reassurance that we do not question alone. Their struggles inform ours across the ages…

Points to Ponder

Issues of belief are intensely personal. We each walk along a unique path of faith – a path that is shaped by personality, background and experience; a path that can twist and turn as life's journey progresses. While some among us may achieve a level of *emuna temima*, pure unwavering faith in an omniscient Creator, others will struggle with belief daily, as they attempt to reconcile the existence of that Creator with difficult personal experience or troubling observed events. Some will ultimately accept one of the many approaches raised within Jewish tradition to the issue of theodicy. Others will prefer, as did Rabbi Meir, to live with the "questions of belief."

Recognizing the disparity in personal faith paths can be critically important, particularly when dealing with those in the throes of painful personal challenge. I have often been approached by individuals after occasions of loss or illness, deeply disturbed by well-intentioned comments that have come their way. Even remarks as seemingly innocuous as "It's all for the best" or "I know how you feel" can be painful for a struggling individual to hear.

Not by chance, the rabbis mandate initial silence upon entering the home of a mourner. A visitor, they maintain, is enjoined from speaking until the mourner speaks first[27] (see *Vayikra*: Shmini 2, *Points to Ponder*). This "etiquette of sorrow" forces the visitor to focus on the needs of the mourner, rather than on his own. *Consolation emerges not when we impose our beliefs or opinions upon those in pain, but when we reflect and validate their own feelings and struggles.*

---

27. *Shulchan Aruch*, Yoreh Deah 376:1.

5 A Strange Segue

Context

A puzzling textual connection is apparently drawn between two separate themes in the second paragraph of the Shma.

> Beware for yourselves, lest your hearts be seduced and you will stray and serve other gods and bow down to them. And the anger of the Lord shall be kindled against you, and He will hold back the heavens and there will be no rain, and the ground will not yield its produce, *and you will be swiftly banished from the goodly land that the Lord gives you.*
>
> And you shall place these words of Mine upon your hearts and upon your souls, and you shall bind them for a sign upon your hands and they shall be as frontlets between your eyes. And you shall teach them to your children that they shall speak of them, when you sit in your house and as you walk by the way and when you lie down and when you rise up. And you shall write them upon the doorposts of your house and upon your gates. In order that your days and the days of your children shall be long upon the land that the Lord has promised to your forefathers to give to them, like the days of the heaven over the earth.[28]

Questions

What connection is there between the threat "you will be swiftly banished" from the land and the instructions that immediately follow: "You shall place these words of Mine upon your hearts and upon your souls, and you shall bind them for a sign upon your hands and they shall be as frontlets between your eyes…"?

Why does the text apparently link Torah study and the performance

---

28. Devarim 11:16–21.

of mitzvot to the eventuality of exile? Aren't the commandments eternally incumbent upon the Jewish people, whether they find themselves in the Land of Israel or in the diaspora?

Approaches

—A—

So troubling is this textual flow that a number of commentaries, including the Malbim and the Netziv, refuse to accept it at face value. The directives concerning mitzva observance contained in this passage, these scholars claim, reflect "backward," textually, rather than "forward." The obligation to mitzvot is not to be seen as a product of exile but as a preventative to exile.

How can you avoid seduction, sin, punishment and exile? God rhetorically asks the nation. "And you shall place these words…" *By observing My commandments, you will lengthen your days upon the land.*

As proof of his position, the Malbim notes the final, seemingly disconnected sentence of the passage: "In order that your days and the days of your children shall be long upon the land that the Lord has promised to your forefathers to give to them, like the days of the heaven over the earth." This sentence, the Malbim maintains, reflects "backwards," as well, and is actually the culmination of all that comes before. *Through the observance of mitzvot*, God promises, *you will avoid the tragedy of exile; and together with your children you will enjoy length of days on the land.*

—B—

In stark contrast to the above scholars, the Midrash embraces the straightforward textual connection between exile and the mitzvot by interpreting God's message as follows: "Even though I exile you from the Land, continue to distinguish yourself in the performance of mitzvot *so that when you return they will not seem new to you….* As [the prophet] Yirmiyahu instructs: Set for yourselves signposts…"[29]

This Midrashic interpretation, however, raises more problems than it solves.

Are the rabbis really suggesting that the performance of mitzvot in exile

---

29. Sifrei, Devarim 11:17–18.

is simply "a practice run" for when the nation returns to the land? This contention flies in the face of our fundamental understanding of Jewish law.

There are, after all, two categories of halachic obligations:

1. *Mitzvot hateluyot ba'aretz* (mitzvot that are connected to the land): commandments, such as the agricultural laws of Shmita (the seventh sabbatical year) and Yovel (the Jubilee year), that can only be properly fulfilled within the Land of Israel.

2. *Mitzvot she'einam teluyot ba'aretz* (mitzvot that are not connected to the land): commandments, such as mezuza, tefillin, kashrut and Shabbat observance, that are incumbent upon the Jewish people, wherever they may be.

How can the Midrash suggest that this second group of mitzvot (including tefillin and mezuza, which are clearly mentioned in the text of the Shma) are only observed by Jews in exile so that these commandments "will not seem new" to the nation upon their return to the land?

This contention seems to openly contradict the halachic reality that these mitzvot are binding upon all Jews, wherever they may be.

Rashi compounds the mystery by accepting this Midrashic thesis without question. Commenting on the Torah passage before us, this great sage simply declares: "[God commands:] 'Even after you are exiled continue to distinguish yourself through the performance of mitzvot. Put on tefillin, affix mezuzot in order that they should not be new to you when you return.' As [the prophet Yirmiyahu] states: 'Set for yourself signposts…'"[30]

Is it possible that Rashi, a citizen of France, considered his own observance of mitzvot such as tefillin and mezuza to be only a "practice run," preparatory to his people's eventual return to the Land of Israel?

— C —

The towering sixteenth-century scholar Rabbi Yehuda Loew (the Maharal of Prague) quotes an opinion in his supercommentary on Rashi that addresses the questions concerning this Midrash directly. The Midrash can be understood, according to this view, by narrowing the focus of our discussion to the two physical mitzvot mentioned in the second paragraph of the Shma, the mitzvot of tefillin and mezuza.

The Torah specifically connects tefillin and mezuza to the threat of

---

30. Rashi, Devarim 11:18.

exile because these commandments possess characteristics that *might have logically exempted the diaspora Jewish community from their observance.* Although tefillin and mezuza are independent of the land of Israel and are thus certainly incumbent upon Jews everywhere; the realities of exile could easily prevent their proper observance. The mitzva of mezuza entails the rights of homeownership, often denied to diaspora Jews. Tefillin, for their part, must be worn without mental distraction. "And how," asks the Maharal, "is it possible [when living in exile among foreign nations] not to be distracted when wearing tefillin?"

Had the critical mitzvot of tefillin and mezuza fallen into disuse because of these diaspora realities, however, the people would have lost their ability to properly perform these commandments even upon their return to the land. The Torah therefore urges the nation to exert all efforts to overcome the obstacles and perform these commandments even in the diaspora: to purchase and settle in homes that will require mezuzot, to rise above the daily travail of diaspora existence and focus without distraction on the messages inherent in the tefillin. *Even though you might rightfully have been exempt from these mitzvot due to the exigencies of exile,* God commands, *find your way to their observance. If you do so, upon your return to the land these commandments will not seem new and strange.*

——— **D** ———————————————————————————————

A much more direct approach to the Midrash, however, is offered by the Ramban, who sees this rabbinic teaching as an earlier iteration of his own revolutionary position connecting Jewish observance to the Land of Israel. As we have previously noted (see *Bereishit:* Vayeitzei 2, *Approaches* c), the Ramban maintains that *all mitzvot fulfilled outside the Land of Israel are fundamentally incomplete.* While commandments such as mezuza and tefillin are certainly obligatory upon the Jewish people wherever they may be, this scholar argues, even these mitzvot can only be observed in their fullness in the land.[31]

This singular connection between Jewish observance and the Land of Israel, the Ramban maintains, is acknowledged at the dawn of Jewish history by the patriarch Yaakov. On the morning following his dramatic dream of a ladder stretching from the earth heavenward, as he prepares to leave

---

31. Rambam, Bereishit 24:3, 26:5; Vayikra 18:25.

the land of Canaan for the first time, Yaakov enacts a vow: "If God will be with me and will guard me on this path upon which I go, and [if He] will give me bread to eat and clothing to wear, and [if] I will return in peace to the home of my father and the Lord will be my God, then this stone that I have set up as a pillar will be as a house of God; and all that You give to me I will repeatedly tithe to You."[32]

A multitude of scholars struggle with this vow, asking how the patriarch could possibly make his worship of God conditional upon material gain (see *Bereishit*: Vayeitzei 2). The Ramban, however, solves the problem in a manner consistent with his overall position on the singularity of the Land of Israel. The phrase "and the Lord will be my God," this scholar argues, is not a condition that Yaakov places upon his own volitional behavior. This phrase, instead, reflects a newfound awareness on the part of the patriarch as a result of God's promise to bring him back to the land. *Now, I recognize*, Yaakov declares, *that the Lord will fully be my God only upon my return to the Land of Israel. I and my progeny can only be complete with our God when we are within the land.*[33]

The Ramban thus accepts the Midrash connecting exile and the mitzvot at face value. God commands the Jewish nation to observe mitzvot such as tefillin and mezuza in exile, not only in fulfillment of their fundamental obligation to do so wherever they may be, but also in preparation for another time. Their daily observance of these mitzvot will be "practice" for the time when they will be able to observe these commandments in their fullness, upon a return to the land of Israel.[34]

— E —

Moving past the Midrashic approach, another explanation can be offered, from the vantage point of historical hindsight, for the connection drawn in the text between the themes of exile and mitzva observance.

---

32. Bereishit 28:20–22.
33. Ramban, Bereishit 28:21.
34. Ramban, Devarim 11:18. Note: As we have noted before (see *Bereishit*: Vayeitzei 2, *Approaches* C), in a perfect example of practicing what you preach, the Ramban's philosophical commitment to the Land of Israel was concretely mirrored in his own life decisions. At the age of seventy-three, the Ramban embarked on the difficult and dangerous journey to the Land of Israel, thereby fulfilling his lifelong dream of settling in the Holy Land. Once in Israel, the Ramban worked diligently to restore the Jewish community in Jerusalem. He is considered by many to be the father of modern Jewish settlement in that holy city.

After centuries of exile and unimaginable persecution, an identifying Jew today can walk into a Jewish community anywhere in the world and feel at home. The traditions he observes will vary from place to place, the atmosphere will be different, but the essential experience will be familiar and the welcome he receives will be real. From Hong Kong to Berlin to Bombay to Kiev to Melbourne to New York, a Jew can find his people.

This phenomenon is nothing short of miraculous. A nation long ago dismissed by its enemies as destroyed continues to thrive after those enemies are long gone.

While rooted in God's plan, this miracle of survival is very much a product of man's effort. A Jew can recognize another Jew today for one reason, and one reason alone. He is – or somewhere along the line his recent ancestors were – loyal to Jewish tradition and practice. During the centuries of separation, when Jewish communities across the globe had little or no physical contact with each other, the mitzvot united them. That is why in our day, when so many of the walls have come down, Jews from vastly different cultural worlds are recognizable to each other.

The brilliance of the Torah is clear to see. God warns the nation of exile, then prescribes the one process that will allow them to survive that exile as a people: "And you shall place…" *Be loyal to your tradition, perform the mitzvot, and even in the diaspora, you will endure.*

Point to Ponder

As I write these words, the American Jewish community is carefully analyzing the results of yet another survey concerning the state of Jewish life in America. This report, conducted by the Pew Research Center, delineates significant changes in the nature of Jewish identity in the United States, where, as of 2013, one in five Jews now describe themselves as having no religion.

This trend towards secularism becomes even more pronounced when the survey's results are analyzed by generation. Among older Jews, 93 percent identify as Jewish on the basis of religion, while only 7 percent describe themselves as having no religion. In contrast, a full 32 percent of identifying Jews in the youngest generation of adults describe themselves as having no religion, choosing instead to define their Jewishness on the basis of ancestry, ethnicity or culture.

The ramifications of this shift are perhaps most clearly reflected in one staggering statistic contained in the report: if the Orthodox community is removed from the equation, *the current intermarriage rate for the remaining Jewish population in America is 71 percent.*[35]

In the face of these statistics, numerous observers have suggested a clear strategic response. *Meet the Jews where they are,* the argument goes. *Since a growing number of Jews affiliate culturally, eschew the religious approach and focus, instead, on cultural identification.*

While this argument might sound logical at face value, upon consideration, its flaws become readily apparent. The American Jewish community finds itself in its current difficult state specifically because of the gradual, steady deterioration in Jewish observance and practice. As study of the Torah texts and concrete observance of the mitzvot has waned, the glue that held the Jewish people together across the millennia has disappeared. If we further divorce *Judaism* from our definition of *Jewishness,* we can fully expect the statistics to be even more tragic when the next report on the state of the American Jewish community is issued.

Ancestry, ethnicity and culture are critical components of Jewish identity. They are also excellent portals of entry through which unaffiliated and disenfranchised Jews might be motivated to pass. Once through those portals, however, these individuals must be provided with reasons to stay. These reasons can only emerge with discovery of the powerfully relevant ideas embedded in the traditional texts and practices of our people.

Centuries ago, with frightening prescience, the Torah predicted the challenges of exile that would face us for centuries: "…and you will be swiftly banished from the goodly land that the Lord gives you."

With equal prescience, the Torah also prescribes the key to our continued survival in the face of those challenges: "And you shall place these words of Mine upon your hearts and upon your souls, and you shall bind them for a sign upon your hands and they shall be as frontlets between your eyes…"

35. Pew Research Center, "A Portrait of Jewish Americans: Findings from a Pew Research Center Survey of U.S. Jews," October 1, 2013.

Re'eh

CHAPTER 11:26–16:17

ראה
פרק יא:כו–טז:יז

Parsha Summary

Centralizing ritual, external and internal challenges, foods and festivals, communal concerns, festive occasions…

As the curtain rises on Parshat Re'eh, Moshe continues his second discourse with a mention of the dramatic ceremony designated for performance on the mountains of Gerizim and Eival, after the nation's entry into the land. The details of this ritual, consisting of the public recitation of blessings and curses, will be further explained in Parshat Ki Tavo.

Moshe commands the nation to destroy all vestiges of idol worship in Canaan and outlines the requirement for the centralization of Jewish worship: "And it shall be the place that the Lord your God will choose to rest His name there, there you shall bring all that I command you…"

Moshe issues a dispensation allowing for the consumption of unconsecrated meat (meat slaughtered outside the context of the Sanctuary/Temple service) upon entry into and settlement of the land, but cautions the nation to refrain from eating the blood of any animal, "for the blood, it is the life; and you shall not eat the life with the meat."

After warning the Israelites not to be attracted by the evil ways of the peoples that they will conquer, Moshe outlines the halachic response to a series of potential internal threats: a navi sheker *(false prophet)*, a meisit u'meidiach *(a member of the community who entices others towards idolatry)*, and an ir hanidachat *(a city that succumbs in its entirety to idolatrous practice)*.

Moshe then reviews the laws governing kosher and non-kosher animals, fish and fowl, the various tithes to be separated from a farmer's produce, the suspension of debts during the Shmita (the Sabbatical year), the freeing of Jewish indentured servants at the end of their seven-year period of servitude, and the offering of firstborn animals to God.

Parshat Re'eh closes as Moshe outlines a series of laws pertaining to the Shalosh Regalim (the three pilgrimage festivals): Pesach, Shavuot and Succot.

1 The Times, They Are A-changing

Context

After commanding the nation to destroy all vestiges of idolatry upon entering the land, Moshe informs them that the rules of their own worship will ultimately change. The nation's ritual worship will eventually be centralized in a place of God's choosing.

You shall not do this to the Lord your God. For only at the place that the Lord your God will choose from among all your tribes to place His name there shall you seek His presence and come there. And there you shall bring your elevation offerings and feast offerings…

You shall not do as we do here today, every man what is proper in his own eyes. For you have not yet come to the *menucha* (resting place) and to the *nachala* (heritage) that the Lord your God gives to you…

And it shall be the place that the Lord your God will choose to rest His name there, there shall you bring all that I command you…

And you shall rejoice before the Lord your God – you and your sons and your daughters and your servants and your maidservants and the Levite who is in your gates, for he has no share and inheritance with you.

Beware for yourself lest you bring up your offerings in any place that you will see.…

You may not eat, in your cities, the tithes of your grain, and your wine and your oil; the firstborn of your cattle and your flocks… Rather you shall eat them before the Lord your God in the place the Lord your God will choose; you, your son your daughter, your slave, your maidservant, and the Levite who is your cities; and you shall rejoice before the Lord your God in your every undertaking."[1]

---

1. Devarim 12:4–19.

Questions

Why is centrality of worship so critical to Jewish thought? The harsh warning issued in the text, "Beware for yourself…," seems to foreshadow severe repercussions if this requirement for centrality is disobeyed.

What was the status of Jewish worship from the time of entry into the land until the erection of the first Beit Hamikdash in the days of King Shlomo, three centuries later?

What is the meaning of Moshe's statement "You shall not do as we do here today, every man what is proper in his own eyes"? Are we to assume that at the time of Moshe's address to the nation the Israelites were worshiping "as they saw fit"? Wasn't worship at that time centralized in the portable Mishkan constructed in the wilderness?

What specific location or locations are referenced by Moshe when he states, "For you have not yet come to the *menucha* (resting place) and to the *nachala* (heritage) that the Lord your God gives to you…"?

The text seems to indicate that in the absence of a central location, localized worship becomes permitted. Why is such ritual worship (e.g., grain and animal offerings) forbidden today?

Approaches

─── **A** ───

Any discussion concerning the development of centralized ritual worship in Jewish practice must begin with a short timeline, summarized in a series of Mishnayot in the tractate of Zevachim. The Mishna delineates a series of historical periods during which the character of Jewish ritual worship repeatedly changes. While specific aspects of the Mishnaic rulings are disputed by other sources quoted both in in the Talmud Bavli and the Talmud Yerushalmi,[2] most authorities view the decisions quoted in the Mishna as authoritative:

1. *First period*: "Once the Mishkan was constructed, *bamot* (localized altars) were prohibited."[3] From the beginning of time, man worshiped God through sacrifices offered on localized altars (see *Vayikra*: Vayikra 1, *Approaches* A–C). The patriarchal progenitors of the Jewish nation and the

─────────────────

2. Talmud Bavli Zevachim 119 a–b; Talmud Yerushalmi Zevachim 1:12.
3. Mishna Zevachim 14:4.

earliest Jews (from the time of the Exodus until the construction of the Mishkan) permissibly engaged in such practices, as well. These practices ended, however, with the building of the portable Sanctuary in the wilderness. At that point ritual worship became centered in the Mishkan.

2. *Second period*: "When the nation arrived at Gilgal, *bamot* were [again] permitted."[4] Gilgal marked the Israelites' point of entry into the land of Canaan. From the moment of the nation's arrival in Canaan through the fourteen-year period of conquest and division of the land,[5] localized ritual worship was again permitted. This allowance was granted, in spite of the fact that the Mishkan was erected in Gilgal, both because Gilgal was not a divinely selected formal site for the Sanctuary and in order to accommodate the Israelites who were engaged in battle throughout the land.[6]

3. *Third period*: "When the nation arrived at Shilo, localized altars were [again] prohibited."[7] At the end of fourteen years of conquest and land division under Yehoshua's leadership, the nation congregated at Shilo, where the Mishkan was erected and where it remained for 369 years.[8] At that point, worship once again became centralized within the Mishkan and personal altars were again prohibited. The Mishna explains this prohibition by identifying Shilo as the *menucha* (resting place) referred to in Moshe's message to the nation. Unlike Gilgal, Shiloh is identified as an official site of the Mishkan and, once the Sanctuary is erected there, centralized worship again becomes the order of the day.

4. *Fourth period*: "When the nation arrived at Nov and Givon, *bamot* were [again] permitted."[9] In the days of the prophet Shmuel, the Philistines defeated the Israelites in battle, temporarily captured the Holy Ark[10] and destroyed the city of Shilo. The Sanctuary structure, however, was saved and erected at Nov, a city of Kohanim, where it remained for thirteen years. When Nov was destroyed by King Shaul, in retribution for the Kohen

---

4. Ibid., 14:5.
5. Talmud Bavli Zevachim 118b.
6. Rashi, Zevachim 112b.
7. Mishna Zevachim 14:6.
8. Talmud Bavli Zevachim 118b.
9. Mishna Zevachim 14:7.
10. After a seven-month period, the ark was returned to the Israelites by the Philistines, who had endured a number of tribulations as a result of their illicit possession of this holy object. Shmuel I chapters 5–6.

Achimelech's support of David,[11] the Sanctuary was relocated to Givon, where it remained for another forty-four years. During this combined period of fifty-seven years, when the sanctuary stood at Nov and Givon,[12] localized ritual worship was again permitted.

5. *Fifth period*: "When the nation arrived at Jerusalem, the localized altars were [again] prohibited and were never allowed again."[13] Once the First Temple was built in Jerusalem under the leadership of King Shlomo, localized worship became permanently prohibited. The Mishna identifies Jerusalem as the *nachala* (heritage) referred to by Moshe in his message to the nation. Jerusalem becomes the eternal central location for Jewish ritual worship. Once established, this permanence mandates against localized ritual worship, even after the Temple is destroyed.

— B —

The sequence of edicts quoted in the Mishna creates a clear, decisive pattern. Optimally, Jewish ritual worship is meant to be centralized in the Mishkan and later in the Beit Hamikdash. Allowances, however, are initially made for practical constraints. When the Sanctuary cannot be erected in one of its divinely designated locations, localized worship becomes allowed. This situation continues until the sanctification of Jerusalem, when a permanent reality is established. Once the first Beit Hamikdash is erected and consecrated on the Temple Mount, localized ritual worship is prohibited forever, even when the Temple is no longer standing.

A critical caveat is added to the Mishnaic timeline, however, limiting the function of the *bamot* even during the periods when their use is allowed. This limitation, the rabbis explain, emerges from Moshe's puzzling remark, "You shall not do as we do here today, *every man what is proper in his own eyes.*"

Clearly, the Talmudic scholars argue, this statement cannot be taken at face value as referring to unstructured ritual practices during Moshe's time. At the point when Moshe addresses the nation, the Mishkan is standing as the physical and ritual center of the nation's encampment and all ritual worship is centered within. Instead, the rabbis maintain, Moshe refers to

11. Shmuel I 22:16–19.
12. Talmud Bavli Zevachim 14:7.
13. Mishna Zevachim 14:8.

the time period directly ahead of the nation when, during the conquest and division of the land, localized worship will be allowed. This allowance, Moshe explains, will be limited:

Although private altars will be permitted, you will not be allowed to offer upon them "as we do here today." The only offerings that will be permissible upon the bamot *will be voluntary offerings, concerning which "every man [brings] what is proper in his own eyes." Furthermore, even during the period when* bamot *are allowed, obligatory offerings such as guilt and sin offerings must be offered only at a central location.*[14]

Two major questions, however, remain. Why is the concept of centralized worship so "central" to Jewish thought? And why does localized worship remain forbidden even after the Temple is tragically destroyed?

—— C ——

The issue of centralized worship clearly intertwines with the visual and experiential lessons potentially derived from the Sanctuary, the Temples, their respective appurtenances, and the rituals performed within their confines (for a more detailed discussion of these lessons, see *Shmot: Teruma* 1–4). The powerful teaching impact of a visit to the Sanctuary or Temple may well, in and of itself, have been one of the primary motivations for the insistence on centralized worship in Jewish thought.

—— D ——

Other, independent reasons for the emphasis on centralized worship, however, are also suggested by the scholars.

The Kli Yakar, for example, notes that Moshe's discussion of the issue of centralization immediately follows his description of the idolatrous practices of the nations of Canaan, who worshiped their gods "on the high mountains and on the hills, and beneath every leafy tree."[15] In response to these practices, Moshe warns, "You shall not do this to the Lord your God.… For only at the place that the Lord your God will choose to rest His name there, there shall you bring all that I command you…" *The nations of Canaan seek specific places of significance for worship because they believe that these locations "lend honor" to their gods. Our belief is vastly different.*

---

14. Talmud Bavli 117b.
15. Devarim 12:2.

Our God is above time and place. He does not draw honor from a specific location. The opposite is, in fact, true. He honors any place that He chooses. Your goal, therefore, will be to work towards the time when you will merit worshipping God in a central location of His choosing.

The Kli Yakar's interpretation of the passage before us echoes a well-known ethical teaching rooted at Sinai. The Torah states that although the nation may not approach Mount Sinai during Revelation, "Once an extended shofar blast is sounded [signaling the end of Revelation and the departure of God's presence], they may ascend the mountain."[16]

Commenting on this phenomenon, the rabbis declare: "The place does not does not honor the individual; the individual honors the place."[17]

What is true for God, the rabbis suggest, must be true for man, created in God's image. God's presence lends significance to a location. Similarly, man should recognize that he does not derive true significance or honor from the external trappings of his environment. Instead, man, through sanctified thought and action, has the capacity to honor his surroundings.

—— E ——

Perhaps, however, the most straightforward rationale for the centralization of ritual worship in Jewish thought is one suggested by a number of other authorities, including Rabbi Shimshon Raphael Hirsch. According to these scholars, the Torah strives to achieve two interconnected goals through the selection of a single site for worship: uniformity of religious practice and unity of the nation.

By obligating the nation to converge on one central location for the performance of ritual worship, the Torah "underscore[s] the conviction that God can only be sought by devotion to all the traditional laws handed down by God to the nation."[18]

A people spread throughout its land can easily splinter into cultish sects, with each family or group performing rites and rituals created "exclusively through the medium of one's own mind and opinion."[19] Left unfettered, these groups will develop increasingly different practices and beliefs, to the point where the worship of one sect will become unrecognizable to the

---

16. Shmot 19:13.
17. Talmud Bavli Ta'anit 21b.
18. Rabbi Shimshon Raphael Hirsch, Devarim 12:9.
19. Ibid.

next. The Torah's demand for centralization of worship is meant to ensure that the "Judaism" observed by the people will remain recognizable as Judaism – true to its roots, reflective of the demands and values of God's law, and consistent in practice. We have noted previously that diversity of thought and idea enriches the character of Jewish experience. That diversity must be balanced, however, with the ritual unity essential to the nation's survival (see Bamidbar 2, *Approaches* H, I, *Points to Ponder*).

The "pernicious subjectivity"[20] that shapes the performance of localized ritual, however, can also cause deeper problems to emerge. Not only do individuals engaged in localized worship separate from each other in the area of religion, but their overall sense of connectedness steadily dissipates, as well. Each group begins to believe that it holds a lock on the truth, and the disparagement of others becomes increasingly acceptable. Step by step, the nation's social fabric begins to fray. The text of Tanach testifies to the societal damage caused when the demand for centralization is ignored, by repeatedly characterizing the period of national division following the death of King Shlomo as a time when "the *bamot* were not taken away; the people still sacrificed and burned incense on the *bamot*."[21]

Entirely different is the vision of centralized worship described by Rabbi Shimshon Raphael Hirsch, within which the Torah "becomes the center point elevated above the nation and its individuals, drawing everything and everybody up to it, uniting everything and everybody in equal obligation to dutifulness, and affecting everything and everybody with equal responsibility…"[22]

Not by coincidence, the Torah clearly and repeatedly connects the theme of centralized worship to the themes of national unity and social justice.[23]

By coming together as one people to worship one God, Moshe tells the nation, *you will strengthen not only your bond with God but your bonds with each other, as well*. This sentiment is mirrored centuries later when the Talmudic sage Rabbi Yehoshua ben Levi interprets the verse in Psalms,

---

20. Ibid.
21. Melachim I 22:44; Melachim II 12:4, 14:4, 15:4, 35.
22. Rabbi Shimshon Raphael Hirsch, Devarim 12:9.
23. Devarim 12:12, 12:17–18, 16:11, 16:14, 26:11.

"Jerusalem, the built, is like a city that is united together,"[24] to mean: *Jerusalem the built, is a city that unites Israel, one with the other.*[25]

———— **F** ————————————————————————————

Interpersonal relationships will be enhanced on other levels, as well, as the nation joins together geographically. A particularly poignant teaching recorded in the Mishna brings this human dimension of centralized worship to life. The Mishna explains that two staircases connected the Temple with the surrounding area, one staircase upon which all ascended to the Temple Mount and a second staircase upon which all descended – *with two glaring exceptions.* In a practice that seems, at first, abundantly strange, individuals in mourning and in *nidui* (official ostracism from the community due to a specific transgression) were halachically mandated to walk *against the flow of traffic*, to "go up the down staircase" and "down the up staircase."[26]

The touching reason for this seemingly strange mandate becomes, upon consideration, abundantly clear. A mourner or a *menudeh* walked against the flow of traffic *to alert others to his status.*

Picture, for a moment, the scene at the Temple on a pilgrimage festival, one of three such annual occasions upon which the people are commanded to ascend en masse to the Temple in Jerusalem. Thousands throng to the Holy City. Friends encounter and greet each other for the first time in months. Warm embraces, hearty handshakes and the excited sharing of personal news are the order of the day. Suddenly, one among the group sees "Yankel" in the distance, ascending or descending the Temple Mount the "wrong way." In an instant, the mood shifts. Yankel is approached quietly and sensitively. Questions are asked and condolences are shared. The mourner is spared the initial discomfort of having to explain himself to those who are in a totally different emotional world. Similarly, the ostracized individual is greeted appropriately with a prayer that, through his repentance, he be returned to the bosom of the community.

And the Temple visit works its magic…uniting the people in worship of the Divine and in personal support for each other.

———————————————

24. Tehillim 122:3.
25. Talmud Yerushalmi Bava Kama 7:7.
26. Mishna Middot 2:2.

—— **G** ——

Jewish liturgy is replete with prayers reflecting sorrow and frustration over the absence of classical worship due to the Temple's destruction. Although the Temple service seems distant from our lives, we nonetheless regularly pray for its return (see *Vayikra*: Vayikra 1, *Approaches* E).

But does it have to be that way? Why can we not return to a system of localized ritual worship until the Temple is rebuilt, as we did following the destruction of Shilo? Why did the *bamot* become permanently prohibited upon the sanctification of the Temple in Jerusalem, never to be allowed again?[27]

—— **H** ——

On a technical level, the answer to our question is clear. Majority halachic opinion mandates that, once established, the sanctity of Jerusalem never wanes.[28] Unlike Shilo, the Temple Mount retains its position as the central location for Jewish ritual worship even when it lies in ruins. Jerusalem's continued sanctity and centrality preclude the allowance of localized ritual.

Deeper currents, however, may well course beneath the surface of Judaism's ultimate decision to limit Jewish ritual worship to the Temple in Jerusalem. Like so much else in Jewish life, this area of observance is informed by the historical journey of the nation.

Early in Jewish history, the push and pull between centrality and localization of worship embeds a balance between *what is* and *what should be* in the psyche of the people. While accepting central worship as a goal, Judaism makes allowances for reality. Over and over again, *bamot* become permissible, but only as a stopgap measure. The goal of centrality remains clear, even when it is unattainable.

With the destruction of the Temples, however, everything changes. Judaism enters a new phase, shaped by the tragic reality of diaspora existence. Exiled from its land, first in Babylon and then across the globe, the Jewish nation must now be nurtured by its dreams. The aspiration for *what should be* becomes a powerful force, uniting a scattered people in disparate lands. Even during comfortable times, the clarion calls of "Next year

———————————

27. Note: According to a minority position quoted in the Talmud (Talmud Bavli Megilla 10a), *bamot* are actually permitted after the destruction of the Temple.
28. Rambam, *Mishneh Torah*, Hilchot Beit Habechira 6:15.

in Jerusalem" remind each Jew that everything in diaspora is not "right," and that the present reality cannot be accepted, even temporarily. Jewish ritual worship cannot be allowed to take root in this exile world, even as a stopgap measure.

The very dream of a Temple rebuilt – of a people united on its land, worshipping its God as one nation with one voice – will power the Jewish nation to achieve its goals. The time for temporary solutions has passed. Only a return to Jerusalem will suffice.

Points to Ponder

Close to twenty years ago, as my family and I stood on line at the airport, waiting to board a Tower Air[29] flight to Israel, I was approached by a fellow Orthodox passenger who was waiting to board the same flight.

"Excuse me," he asked, "but would you like to sit in the *mehadrin* section?"[30]

"The *mehadrin* section?" I responded, "What's the *mehadrin* section?"

"No movies and no *pritzus* [immodest attire]," he replied, apparently referring to the dress of many of the female passengers.

My twins, the youngest of our children, who were at that time about six years old, immediately exclaimed: "No movies and no pizzas? We want the pizzas!"

While our family still laughs at this story decades later, we also often comment on the sad reality lying at its core. I turned down the offer to sit in the *mehadrin* section that day, saddened by the realization that we Jews were fast becoming *a people who could no longer even sit together on an airplane.* The attitudes and behaviors of individuals at both ends of the religious spectrum had pushed us so far apart that we were no longer comfortable associating with each other, even in passing.

To be sure, stark internal divisions have continually marred our long march through history. The Kingdom of Judah versus the Kingdom of Israel, Sadducees versus Pharisees, Loyalists versus Hellenizers, Chassidim versus Mitnagdim, Haskalists versus Traditionalists – the list goes on and on.

One might have hoped, however, that after centuries of forced exile,

---

29. For those too young to remember, Tower Air was a charter and schedule US airline that offered discounted flights to Israel and other destinations from 1983 until 2000.

30. The term *mehadrin* derives from the verb *l'hadeir* (to beautify) and conveys the obligation to beautify the mitzvot through meaningful practice and observance.

after the unspeakable trauma of the Shoah, after the miraculous return to our land, a unity of purpose would emerge, overshadowing the fractures dividing us. One might have hoped that the age-old vision of Jerusalem in its prime, nearer to reality now than it has been for centuries, would have brought us together.

"All dreams," the rabbis maintain, "follow their interpretation."[31] Images and dreams have no power of their own. They achieve significance only through the impact that they have upon our "waking" lives. The divisions within the Jewish world are wide and reconciliation will require real effort. If the vision of a rebuilt Jerusalem, however, does not inspire us to work diligently towards the social unity that the rebuilding itself is meant to produce, our nation's journey towards Jerusalem will, tragically, be much longer than it needs to be…

---

31. Talmud Bavli Brachot 55b.

2 Meat Eaters?

Context

Immediately after instructing the nation concerning the eventual centralization of worship in a place of God's choosing (see previous study), Moshe makes the following puzzling proclamation:

> When the Lord your God will broaden your border…and you shall say, "I will eat meat" – for you will have a desire to eat meat – you may eat meat to your entire soul's desire.
>
> If the place that the Lord your God will choose to place His name will be far from you, you may slaughter from your herd and from your flock that the Lord has given you, as I have commanded you, and you shall eat in your gates whatever your soul desires.[1]

Questions

Why must Moshe, as the nation prepares to enter Canaan, issue a special dispensation allowing the consumption of unconsecrated meat, meat slaughtered outside the context of the Sanctuary/Temple service? Meat has, after all, been permitted for centuries, by dint of a divine decree in the aftermath of the flood of Noach's time.

Does Moshe's proclamation provide any indication concerning the Torah's general attitude towards the consumption of meat? Is such consumption ideal, or is the dispensation for *basar ta'ava* (meat of desire) a grudging concession to man's primitive desires?

---

1. Devarim 12:20–21.

Approaches

---A---

Two giants of the Mishnaic era arrive at polar opposite conclusions concerning Moshe's comments in this passage.

Rabbi Akiva maintains that what appears to be a dispensation is no dispensation at all. In fact, this scholar argues, Moshe's words actually represent a *tightening of the rules*. Throughout the Israelites' desert travels, the consumption of meat was allowed in completely unfettered fashion, without any regulations governing the slaughter of animals for food. Now Moshe explains, however, that the rules are about to change. Upon the nation's entry into the land, all animals designated as food will require preparation through *shechita*, halachically acceptable slaughter, "as I have commanded you."[2]

Rabbi Yishmael adamantly disagrees. Moshe's proclamation at this critical moment, this scholar maintains, actually conveys the allowance that it appears to convey. *For the first time since Sinai, the Israelites will be permitted to consume unconsecrated meat.* Throughout the nation's sojourn in the wilderness, the Israelites were permitted to eat meat only in conjunction with the Sanctuary services. Any individual desiring to eat meat was obligated to dedicate an animal as a "peace offering." The animal, after its slaughter, was then divided three ways. A portion of the animal was burnt on the altar, a portion was set aside for consumption by the Kohanim, and a portion was eaten by the owner and his family. Thus, no consumption of meat was allowed to the Israelites without an element of "sanctification." No Israelite could derive personal benefit from meat unless the altar and the priests "benefited," as well.

Upon entry into the land, Moshe now informs the nation, everything will change. The private consumption of *basar ta'ava* will now be permitted without connection to the Sanctuary/Temple service.

---

2. No explicit instructions are found in the Torah concerning *shechita*, halachically acceptable slaughter of animals. The rabbis, therefore, posit that the laws of *shechita* were orally transmitted by God to Moshe and then orally transmitted by Moshe to the people. These laws therefore serve as one of the proofs that Torah She'b'al Peh, Oral Law, existed from the time of Moshe onward, alongside the Written Law (see *Shmot*: Yitro 5 for a fuller discussion of the origins and development of the Oral Law).

——— **B** ———

A fascinating divide develops in the flow of later Jewish scholarship as the rabbis continue to discuss the dispute between Rabbi Akiva and Rabbi Yishmael.

On the one hand, the normative halachic position is recorded by the Rambam, who outlines the law's development according to the opinion of Rabbi Akiva: "When the Israelites were in the wilderness, they were not commanded concerning the ritual slaughter of unconsecrated animals, but were instead allowed to stab, slaughter and eat [these animals in any way], as were the nations of the world."[3] Moshe's declaration on the eve of the nation's entry into the land, the Rambam continues, changes the rules by mandating for the first time an obligation for *shechita*, halachically acceptable slaughter, in the preparation of unconsecrated meat.

The vast majority of textual commentaries, on the other hand, disagree with the halachic position staked out by the Rambam. Recognizing that the straightforward reading of the text favors the opinion of Rabbi Yishmael in this dispute, these scholars choose his position over that of Rabbi Akiva. According to these authorities, Moshe is now permitting the consumption of unconsecrated meat to a nation that had previously been forbidden such meat entirely.[4]

While these later authorities agree on their understanding of Moshe's dispensation to the nation, however, they offer a wide variety of opinions as to the philosophical significance of this new allowance to eat meat.

——— **C** ———

Alone among the halachic authorities, Rabbi Saadia Gaon offers the startling opinion that Moshe's words to the nation convey *not only allowance, but obligation*. The consumption of meat, Saadia maintains, is actually one of the 613 biblical mitzvot.

Struggling to determine a basis for this strange position, Rabbi Yerucham Perlow cites a declaration in the Talmud Yerushalmi indicating that all individuals are destined to undergo "a divine judgment and reckoning" for deliberately failing to experience and enjoy any permissible aspect of

---

3. Rambam, *Mishneh Torah*, Hilchot Shechita 4:17; S. Y. Zevin, ed., *Encyclopedia Talmudit* (Jerusalem: Talmudic Encyclopedia Publishing Ltd., 1980), vol. 4, s.v. *basar ta'ava*.
4. Rashi, Ramban, Rabbeinu Bachya ben Asher, Rabbi Shimshon Raphael Hirsch and others, Devarim 12:20–21.

God's great creations.[5] Saadia, Perlow argues, understands this rabbinic statement literally, as reflecting a real halachic responsibility. There exists, according to this sage, a positive mitzva to eat meat in fulfillment of the obligation to enjoy God's gifts to man.[6]

—— **D** ——

At the opposite end of the spectrum lie the many authorities who view the allowance for the eating of meat as *a concession* rather than *an obligation*. For many of these authorities, the key to the Torah's view concerning the consumption of meat lies in a much earlier transition, rooted at the dawn of human history. The character of Moshe's dispensation to the Israelites prior to their entry into Canaan may well find its roots in this earlier transition.

The first indication of a divine attitude towards the consumption of meat is found on the sixth day of the world's formation when, immediately after creating man, God instructs him concerning his sustenance: "And God said, 'Behold, I have given to you all grass-yielding seed that is on the face of the entire land, and every tree that bears seed-yielding fruit, for you shall they be for food.'"[7] *Man is to sustain himself, God decrees, solely through the consumption of plant life.*

Ten generations later, however, when Noach exits the ark to reenter a world devastated by the flood, God outlines a dramatic change in the rules:

> And the fear of you and the dread of you shall be upon all of the animals of the land and upon all the birds of the heavens, in everything that treads upon the earth and in all the fish of the sea; in your hand they are given. *Every moving thing that lives shall be to you for food; as the green grass I have given to you everything.*[8]

What sparks the change in God's instructions to man? Why are Noah and his descendents granted the permission to consume meat whereas Adam and his descendents were not?

Multiple opinions are offered by the commentaries.

---

5. Talmud Yerushalmi Kiddushin 4:12.
6. Rabbi Yerucham Perlow, commentary on Rav Saadia Gaon's *Sefer Hamitzvot*, quoted in Nachshoni, *Hagot B'parshiot HaTorah*, vol. 2, p. 761.
7. Bereishit 1:29.
8. Ibid., 9:2–3.

——— **E** ————————————————————————————

The Ramban, for example, explains that the initial prohibition concerning the consumption of animal products stemmed from the unique, superior character of animals themselves. "All creatures that possess a moving soul have a small measure of superiority within their souls, resembling in a way those who possess a rational soul [i.e., mankind]. [Animals] have the power of choice concerning their welfare and they flee from pain and death."[9]

When, however, the members of the animal kingdom sin, along with man, through the "corruption of their ways upon the earth,"[10] God decrees their total destruction in the flood, sparing – for Noach's sake – only those beasts required for the perpetuation of the species. Since these creatures survive solely for the sake of Noach and his descendents, having lost their own independent right to exist as a result of their sins, God now grants man complete supremacy over the animal kingdom.

Nonetheless, the Ramban continues to explain, indications of God's sensitivity to the animal world remain embedded in the unfolding law. All people are immediately prohibited, as part of the Noachide Code, from eating the limb of a living animal. Centuries later, the Israelites are eventually prohibited from consuming blood, the "soul of an animal." *Shechita*, halachically acceptable slaughter, becomes a required step in the preparation of all kosher meat. And a general, positive obligation to relieve the suffering of animals is mandated upon the Israelites, as well.[11]

——— **F** ————————————————————————————

Rabbi Yosef Albo, in his monumental work *Sefer Ha'ikkarim*, offers a fascinating alternative explanation. God originally prohibits the eating of meat, Albo explains, because of the deleterious effects that the slaughter and consumption of animals can have upon man's spiritual health. Within one generation, however, this divinely ordained prohibition is sorely misinterpreted. Kayin, the eldest of Adam and Chava, arrives at the erroneous conclusion that God prohibited meat because of man's fundamental lack of superiority over the beast. *Man has no right to take the life of an animal for any reason*, Kayin concludes, *because man is only an animal himself.*

---

9. Ramban, Bereishit 1:29.
10. Bereishit 6:12.
11. Talmud Bavli Shabbat 128b; Rambam, *Mishneh Torah*, Hilchot Rotzei'ach U'shmirat Hanefesh 13:13.

Kayin's erroneous belief explains the contrast between his eventual offering to God and the offering brought by his brother, Hevel. While neither
brother, according to Albo, fully apprehends the delicate balance meant to
govern man's complex relationship with the animal kingdom, Hevel does
recognize a degree of man's preeminence. He realizes that, despite God's
decree prohibiting this consumption of meat, man has the right to take
the life of an animal for specific purposes other than food. This realization
is reflected in his decision to bring God an offering "from the firstlings of
his flock and from their choicest."[12] Kayin, in contrast, viewing man and
beast as synonymous, only offers "of the fruit of the ground."[13] The horrific
ramifications of Kayin's mistaken perceptions soon become evident…

When Kayin witnesses God's acceptance of his brother's animal offering,
he is forced to reassess his position. He concludes that his brother is right;
God indeed allows the slaughter of animals for purposes other than food.
Steadfastly refusing to differentiate between man and the beast, however,
Kayin now becomes convinced that, if killing is acceptable, killing his
brother is not distinguishable from killing any other living creature. This
conviction leads to tragic action as Kayin murders his brother. Kayin's
divinely ordained punishment, in the aftermath of this horrific act, causes
him to undergo one last philosophical conversion. Stubbornly refusing to
acknowledge any superiority on the part of man over the beast, he reverts
back to his original posture. He returns to the belief that the punishment
meted out for the murder of his brother would have been mandated for
the killing of any animal. At no point, throughout these multiple changes
of heart, is Kayin ever willing to entertain the possibility of a distinction
between man and animals. *No matter the evidence*, in the eyes of this tragic
figure, *man is simply no better than the beast.*

The catastrophic consequences of Kayin's perceptions extend well beyond his own tragic story. The generations of men that follow adopt and
build upon Kayin's erroneous beliefs. Failing to discern the majestic spark
that separates man from the beast, they eventually descend into the bestial
behaviors that directly lead to the flood.

In the aftermath of the flood, God wants to ensure that Kayin's erroneous perceptions will never again take root in the heart of man, that man

---

12. Bereishit 4:4.
13. Ibid., 4:3.

will never again lose sight of the majestic spark and heavenly potential that distinguishes him from all else in creation. Immediately upon Noach's reemergence into the world, God announces a change in the rules. The slaughter of animals and the consumption of their meat, which had been prohibited from the time of Adam, will now be allowed. Man's dominion over the animal kingdom will remain forever clear.

God's allowance to Noach and his descendents, Albo concludes, is grudging. Born out of man's failure, the allowance to eat meat is a necessary concession to his own urges and desires.[14]

G

Numerous other commentaries across the ages add their views to those of the Ramban and Rabbi Yosef Albo concerning God's shifting approach to the consumption of meat. While the particulars of their explanations differ widely, all share one basic thrust. God's allowance to Noach and his descendents develops in response to unfortunate changes in circumstance. During the period between Adam and Noach, man and/or beast fall from the high plane upon which they were created. The divine allowance to eat meat is a reflection of that descent.

The approaches of these scholars lend credence to the idea that Moshe's allowance to the Israelites centuries later, permitting the consumption of *basar ta'ava*, further reflects a grudging concession on God's part to the desires of man.

H

It remains, however, for Rabbi Avraham Yitzchak Hacohen Kook, the first Ashkenazic chief rabbi of the yet-to-be-born State of Israel, to draw a straight line between the deterioration of man's moral fiber and the shift in God's initial instructions concerning the consumption of meat.

With man's descent from the spiritual perfection that marked his creation, Rav Kook maintains, man can no longer be required to expend the moral energy necessary to refrain from the slaughter of animals for food. In a world filled with violence and corruption, all of man's moral strength must be directed towards the maintenance of an ethical standard in his dealings with his fellow man. *As long as man must exert his energies towards*

---

14. Rabbi Yosef Albo, *Sefer Ha'ikkarim* 3:15.

the avoidance of violence against his fellow, he cannot be required to refrain from the slaughter of animals.

The Torah's underlying antipathy towards the consumption of meat, Rav Kook continues, can be discerned, centuries later, in the dispensation verbalized by Moshe to the Israelites, on the eve of their entry into Canaan. Moshe predicates the people's consumption of meat upon their own stated needs and desires: "When the Lord your God will broaden your border... *and you shall say, 'I will eat meat' – for you will have a desire to eat meat –* you may eat meat to your entire soul's desire."

God's implicit message to the nation, Rav Kook maintains, is clear: *Were you able to inhibit your appetite for meat, such consumption would be forbidden to you. This act of moral control on your part, however, cannot be demanded of you at this time.*

God's message to the Israelites is also embedded in the intricate network of halachic edicts governing the Jew's consumption of meat. Halachically acceptable slaughter, the abstention from blood, the covering of blood after the slaughter of specific animals and other laws are all designed, in the eyes of Rav Kook, to sensitize the consumer to the fundamental injustice being perpetrated upon the animal kingdom. Properly understood, these laws drive home the recognition "that you are not dealing with a worthless object, with an inanimate automat, but rather with a living being."[15]

Finally, God's allowance, Rav Kook maintains, is temporary in character. The time will come when the words of the prophet Yirmiyahu predicting a fuller God-awareness on man's part[16] will come to fruition. At that point, Rav Kook insists, "man's latent desire for justice towards the animal kingdom will emerge [and the consumption of meat will end]."[17]

Unlike the vegetarians of our day, Rav Kook is not promoting the immediate abstention from meat. Consistent with his stated view concerning the reinstatement of animal sacrifice (see *Vayikra*: Vayikra 1, *Approaches* E), this scholar argues that such abstention must wait until man reaches the level of moral refinement appropriate for such a step. Only then, will the "mute protest" built into the philosophical and halachic legacy of the Jewish nation, "be transformed into a mighty shout and succeed in its

15. Rabbi Avraham Yitzchak Hacohen Kook, *Tallelei Orot*, chapter 8.
16. Yirmiyahu 32:34.
17. Rabbi Avraham Yitzchak HaKohen Kook, *Tallelei Orot*, chapter 8.

aim."[18] Only when man has fully realized his moral responsibility to other human beings, will he be able to treat all living creatures with the justice they truly deserve.

Points to Ponder

On October 26, 1984, a fourteen-day-old infant, known as Baby Fae, became the first recipient of a baboon-to-human heart transplant. Three other humans had previously received animal heart transplants, but none survived more than three and one half days. Baby Fae survived the operation, but succumbed to kidney failure twenty days later.

The operation and Baby Fae's subsequent struggle for life garnered international attention and raised serious ethical questions, particularly among "animal rights" groups. Was it moral, questioners asked, to sacrifice an "intelligent animal," such as a baboon, in an attempt to save the life of a human infant?

Among the ethical arguments raised in support of the operation was the concept of "intellectual relativity" (my term). Proponents of this approach argued that it is ethically acceptable to sacrifice creatures of lower intelligence to save the lives of creatures of higher intelligence. Since the intellectual capacity of a baboon, although high for an animal, is certainly lower than that of a human being, these thinkers maintained, one could ethically sacrifice a baboon to save the life of a human child.

Numerous other ethicists, rabbis among them, strenuously objected to this approach. Such logic would dictate, they argued, that a human child born with a serious brain defect, producing an intellectual capacity lower than that of a baboon, could ethically be sacrificed to save the baboon. Such a conclusion, these thinkers insisted, is unconscionable. A continuum does not exist between animals and human beings when considering the value of life. No matter what his or her intellectual capacity, a human being occupies a higher plane than a member of the animal kingdom. As long as the need for the animal's sacrifice is real and defensible, an animal may be sacrificed to ensure the survival of a human being.

A delicate balance is meant to be maintained in the relationship established between man and the animal kingdom. Without question, man is obligated to respect and cherish all forms of life created by God. Jewish

---

18. Ibid.

law not only prohibits acts of wanton cruelty towards animals, but also mandates that every possible effort be made to alleviate the suffering of all living things.[19] At the same time, however, a clear distinction must be made between man and beast. When that distinction is forgotten, when the divine spark that sets mankind apart from all other creatures is ignored, man runs the risk of descending to the level of the beast he purports to cherish. One need look no further than the example of the Nazis and other murderers across the ages, who often treated their pets with gentle kindness, yet proved themselves capable of committing all forms of atrocities against their fellow man.

As understood by the rabbis, the Torah's blueprint for the man-animal relationship is carefully calibrated. On the one hand, man must be sensitive to the value of the wide myriad of life forms with which he shares the world. On the other hand, man must never forget the divine spark that sets him and all mankind apart.

---

19. Talmud Bavli Shabbat 128b; Rambam, *Mishneh Torah*, Hilchot Rotzei'ach U'shmirat Hanefesh 13:13.

3 Truth or Consequences

Context

As Moshe turns his attention to a series of internal forces that might endanger the nation after his death, he begins by outlining the potential challenge presented by a *navi sheker*, a false prophet.

He warns of the possibility that "a prophet or a dreamer of a dream" might successfully produce "a sign or a wonder" in an attempt to convince the people to follow the gods of others.

"Do not listen to the words of that prophet," he cautions, "for the Lord your God is testing you to know whether you love the Lord your God with all your heart and with all your soul."[1]

Questions

If the individual in question is a charlatan, why does the Torah refer to him as a "prophet or a dreamer of dreams"? Shouldn't the appellation "prophet" be reserved for someone who is telling the truth?

Even more importantly, why would God grant this individual the power to produce "a sign or a wonder"? Shouldn't such power be divinely granted only to a true prophet? Would God truly grant supernatural powers to an imposter, simply to "test" the people's belief? Given that God knows from the outset what lies in man's heart, what would be the purpose of such a test?

Finally, Moshe indicates in this passage that the production of "a sign or a wonder" by a possible prophet does not, in and of itself, confirm the veracity of the messenger. In Parshat Shoftim, however, when the Torah discusses the general method for determining the truthfulness of a potential prophet, the text states that veracity is determined by whether or not an event predicted by the prophet "comes about."[2]

---

1. Devarim 13:2–5.
2. Ibid., 18:21–22.

Under what circumstances is the production of "a sign or a wonder" proof of a prophet's truthfulness and under what conditions is it not?

Approaches

——A———————————————————————————————

A number of commentaries, Rabbi Saadia Gaon and Rabbeinu Bachya ben Asher among them, maintain that the Torah labels the false prophet as a "prophet" as a reflection of his own claims. From the perspective of these authorities, the term *prophet* in this case refers to someone who "claims prophecy."[3]

After first considering the above interpretation, the Ramban offers an alternative approach. Perhaps the text refers to an individual who possesses a natural talent for divination. Such an individual, who in our day might be referred to as a psychic or a medium, could justifiably be called a "prophet" by the Torah because of his innate ability to predict the future. Unlike a true prophet, however, this individual remains unaware of the source of his talent and enjoys no special relationship with God.[4]

——B———————————————————————————————

Whatever explanation we accept for the Torah's reference to the false prophet as a "prophet," the deeper question remains. What is the source of this individual's power? Why would God grant an imposter the power to produce "a sign or a wonder"?

This question serves as the focus of a debate recorded in the Babylonian Talmud between two towering figures of the Mishnaic period:

> Rabbi Yossi the Galilean stated: "The Torah understood the intentions of idolaters and therefore granted them dominion. Even if he [the false prophet] causes the sun to stand still in the middle of the heavens, do not listen to him."
>
> Rabbi Akiva said: "God forbid that the Holy One Blessed Be He would cause the sun to stand still in the heavens on behalf of those who transgress His will. Instead, [the Torah passage that references

---

3. Rabbi Saadia Gaon, Rabbeinu Bachya ben Asher, Devarim 13:2.
4. Ramban, Devarim 13:2.

miracles generated by a false prophet] speaks of an individual such as Chanania ben Azur,[5] who began his career as a true prophet and subsequently became a false prophet."[6]

Rashi explains Rabbi Akiva's position to mean that the "sign or wonder" attributed in the text to the *navi sheker* was actually performed before this individual rebelled against God, while he was still a true prophet.[7]

The debate between these two great Talmudic luminaries is clear. Rabbi Yossi the Galilean maintains that, at times, God will grant transgressors the ability to perform miraculous acts, in order, as the Torah testifies, to test the nation's loyalty. Rabbi Akiva demurs and insists that under no conditions would God grant supernatural power to those who disobey His will. Any apparent evidence to the contrary is simply incorrect.

─── C ───────────────

With the above Talmudic debate serving as a backdrop, scholars across the ages continue their struggle to understand what, if any, powers God might grant a false prophet, and why.

As noted above, for example, the Ramban suggests that the power of a *navi sheker* rises out of a natural talent for divination. God allows such abilities to develop even among those who would use them for ill, the Ramban insists, in order to "test" and ultimately benefit those targeted by the false prophet. Consistent with his general approach to God-administered tests, the Ramban explains that *God tests man to increase man's awareness of his own capabilities and to actualize man's own potential* (see *Bereishit*: Vayeira 4, *Context*). Through their resistance to the words of the *navi sheker*, in the face of the "wonders" that he performs, the people will become more aware of their own attachment to God. More than that, the very experience of crisis will transform them. The potential love of God that exists in their hearts will be converted into concrete behavior that will subsequently shape their future actions and character.[8]

In contrast to Rashi, who appears to accept the possibility that God would grant supernatural strength to a *navi sheker* in order to test the

---

5. Yirmiyahu 28:1–17.
6. Babylonian Talmud Sanhedrin 90a.
7. Rashi, ibid.
8. Ramban, Devarim 13:4, Bereishit 22:1.

Israelites,[9] the Rambam views any seemingly miraculous sign generated by a false prophet to be the product of magic or sorcery.[10] As to the purpose of the encounter with the *navi sheker*, the Rambam, like the Ramban, remains true to his own general approach to divinely administered tests, explaining as follows:

"If a man should rise, pretend to be a prophet, and show you his signs…"
Know that God intends thereby to prove to the nations how firmly you believe in the truth of God's word, and how well you have comprehended the true essence of God, that you cannot be misled by any tempter to corrupt your faith in God.
Your religion will then afford a guidance to all who seek the truth, and of all the religions man will choose that which is so firmly established that it is not shaken by the performance of a miracle. For a miracle cannot prove that which is impossible; it is useful only as a confirmation of that which is possible…"[11]

God tests an individual, or a group, the Rambam believes, *in order to proclaim that individual or group's greatness to others* (see *Bereishit*: Vayeira 4, *Context*). This interpretation is reflected in the fact that the biblical term for test, *nissayon*, comes from the root *nes* (banner). God will test the nation as a whole through their encounter with false prophecy, in order to "raise the banner" of the nation's greatness to the world. When surrounding nations discern the Jewish people's ability to retain their belief in God's word, they will be moved to explore a religion that is "so firmly entrenched" in the hearts of its adherents "that it is not shaken by the performance of a miracle." In the Rambam's eyes, successful resistance to the words of the *navi sheker* furthers the Jewish nation's mission to the world.[12]

Unwilling to accept the prospect that God would grant any unusual power to a *navi sheker*, the Ibn Ezra offers two possible explanations for the *navi*'s apparent ability to produce "a sign or a wonder." Perhaps the false prophet, this scholar suggests, overhears the predictions of a true prophet and "steals them," presenting them as his own to bolster his reputation

9. Rashi, Devarim 13:2.
10. Rambam, *Mishneh Torah*, Yesodei HaTorah 7:7, 8:1.
11. Rambam, *Moreh Nevuchim* 3:24.
12. Ibid.

and position. Alternatively, the Torah's terms *ot* (sign) and *mofet* (wonder) may not refer to miraculous signs at all, but to volitional acts performed by the *navi*. The *navi* Yeshayahu, for example, proclaims: "Behold, I and the children whom the Lord has given me are signs and wonders for Israel…"[13] *The unique acts that I perform and the unusual names that I have bestowed upon my children are all "signs and wonders," God-commanded deeds designed to represent events that will befall the nation of Israel.*[14]

Similarly, says the Ibn Ezra, the "signs and wonders" associated with the false prophet in the text may well refer to conscious acts that he performs in order to convey his message. God's "test" of the nation, the Ibn Ezra concludes, does not consist of granting powers to the *navi sheker*, but simply allowing him to survive in spite of his designs against the nation. The purpose of the test is to "demonstrate the righteousness of those tested."[15]

Likewise maintaining that "the Holy One Blessed Be He would not strengthen the hand of evildoers by granting them the power to change the course of nature or to perform wonders for the purpose of perpetuating lies,"[16] the Abravanel notes a nuance in the text concerning the false prophet's approach to the nation. The Torah states: *V'natan lecha ot o mofet,* "and *he will present to you* a sign or a wonder," and not *V'asa lecha ot o mofet,* "and *he will create for you* a sign or a wonder." The power of a *navi sheker*, the Abravanel explains, is limited to the presentation through magic or sorcery of that which already exists, while the power of a true prophet extends to the creation of wonders that transcend the natural world. The test of the nation consists of God's refusal to sabotage the *navi sheker*'s presentation by changing the course of natural events.[17]

——— D ———

Ultimately, however, the role of seemingly miraculous signs in the realm of prophecy remains confusing.

On the one hand, as we have seen, the Torah clearly informs us that such signs are not to be believed when determining the character of a *navi sheker*. *The litmus test of a prophet's veracity is the content of his prophecy,*

13. Yeshayahu 8:18.
14. Rashi, ibid.; Metzudat David, ibid.; Ibn Ezra, Devarim 13:2–3.
15. Ibn Ezra, Devarim 13:2–3.
16. Abravanel, Devarim 13:2.
17. Ibid.

rather than the wonders that he performs. Thus, the Talmud clearly proclaims, "He who prophesies to uproot anything that is in the Torah is culpable and we pay no heed to his 'signs and wonders.'"[18]

On the other hand, as noted before, the text in Parshat Shoftim indicates that the presentation of signs is a critical component in the process of a true prophet's self-identification. This point is legally codified by the Rambam in his *Mishneh Torah*, where he states that when a *navi* is divinely sent to speak to a people, "*he is given a sign or a wonder [to present] so that the nation will know that God has sent him.*"[19]

Are signs and wonders acceptable proof of a prophet's veracity, or not? The evidence seems contradictory. If the validation of a potential prophet is based on the content of his prophecy, why must the candidate present a sign? And if signs are significant, how are we to discern which signs are truthful and which are not?

Our guide in this area will be the Rambam, who, in his *Mishneh Torah*, outlines a halachic approach to a nation's encounter with prophecy. In his unique, brilliant style, this great sage marries the esoteric realm of prophetic vision to the rational world of Jewish law.

Public awareness of a potential prophet's personal characteristics and spiritual dedication, the Rambam maintains, is an essential prerequisite towards this individual's acceptance as a true *navi*. Not everyone is worthy of becoming a prophet. Prophecy will only visit an individual who is innately wise, strong of character and in full control of his passions; who possesses an extremely wide breadth of true knowledge; and who consciously cultivates communication with the Divine through separation from the outside world and full immersion in the contemplation of heavenly mysteries.[20] Only such an individual, known to be "worthy of prophecy in his wisdom and actions," can be considered a candidate for prophecy from the outset. If an individual who is not known to possess these qualities claims prophecy, he is not to be heeded by the people, no matter what signs or wonders he may produce. If, on the other hand, an apparently worthy individual does present himself to the nation as a prophet, *they cannot ignore his approach*.

---

18. Talmud Bavli Sanhedrin 90a.
19. Rambam, *Mishneh Torah*, Hilchot Yesodei HaTorah 7:7.
20. Ibid., 7:1.

Upon his successful production of a sign or a wonder the nation is *bound by law to accept his prophecy.*[21]

At this point in his analysis, the Rambam makes a striking assertion. Even an apparently worthy individual who claims to be a prophet may be a charlatan, and the sign that he produces may be sleight of hand. "We are nonetheless commanded to heed him," the Rambam asserts. "Since he is great, wise and [apparently] deserving of prophecy, we accept him upon his assumed merit."[22]

This situation is actually comparable, the Rambam explains, to a much more familiar set of circumstances. Throughout Jewish jurisprudence, a fact is established through the testimony of two halachically acceptable witnesses. Although it remains completely possible that these witnesses are testifying falsely, we rely upon their established legal acceptability. In these matters, the Rambam concludes, the operant Torah passage is: "The hidden things belong to the Lord our God, but the things that are revealed belong to us and to our children forever, to carry out all the words of this Torah."[23] *The "truth" is immaterial to our actions, the Rambam argues, because we can never be certain of the truth.* Certainty remains in God's realm and not in ours. Our behavior is determined by the law. When that law is satisfied in cases of uncertainty, whether through the testimony of two "kosher" witnesses or through a sign produced by a seemingly worthy *navi*, we have no choice but to follow the mandated path. We accept a potential *navi's* sign, not because we are convinced by the sign itself, but because the Torah commands that a "worthy" candidate for prophecy must be accepted upon his presentation of a sign.

There is one circumstance, however, under which even a seemingly worthy *navi's* sign will not be accepted: if the candidate preaches the overturning of any aspect of the Torah.[24]

Once again, the Rambam maintains, this ruling is eminently logical. We accept the prophecy of Moshe, not because of the miraculous signs that he produced, but ultimately because of the monumental corroborating evidence that we ourselves saw and heard, together with Moshe, at Sinai. The situation of a *navi sheker*, therefore, is comparable to two halachically

---

21. Ibid., 7:7.
22. Ibid.
23. Devarim 29:28.
24. Talmud Bavli Sanhedrin 90a.

acceptable witnesses who offer testimony that *directly contradicts what we ourselves have observed*. Such testimony is clearly not acceptable, no matter how reliable the witnesses themselves may seem to be. Similarly, the signs presented by a potential *navi* who directly contradicts the prophecy of Moshe will not sway us, no matter how worthy that candidate for prophecy seems to be. "Given that we only accept a potential *navi*'s signs because we are commanded to do so [by God through Moshe], how can we accept such a sign from one who endeavors to refute the very prophecy of Moshe, prophecy that we ourselves have seen and heard?"[25] Here again, the law leads us. *Just as we are mandated by law to accept the sign of a worthy candidate for prophecy who does not contradict Torah law, we are equally mandated by law not to accept the sign of an apparently worthy candidate who does contradict Torah law.*

When all is said and done, the ultimate veracity of a prophet will be determined by what he says and not by how he says it. Substance, and not form, the halacha mandates, should convince us of the truth.

---

25. Rambam, *Mishneh Torah*, Hilchot Yesodei HaTorah 8:1–3.

4 Absent Presence:
A Personal Retrospective

Context

By rabbinic mandate, the section of Parshat Re'eh detailing the agricultural and festival cycle of the Jewish year[1] is among the Torah passages read in synagogue on the festivals of Pesach, Shavuot and Shmini Atzeret (the independent holy day attached as an eighth day to the Succot festival).[2]

Questions

While the rabbinic decision to read this section of text on the festivals of Pesach and Shavuot is readily understandable, one fact makes the mandate to read this passage on Shmini Atzeret abundantly strange: *the Torah reading chosen by the rabbis for public reading on Shmini Atzeret makes no direct mention of Shmini Atzeret at all.*

Why would the rabbis deliberately choose to read on a specific holiday a section of biblical text that excludes any direct reference to that holiday?

To make matters even more troubling, the omission seems to be deliberate. Although this section of Parshat Re'eh clearly references the Shalosh Regalim (the three pilgrimage festivals), including the holiday of Succot, it is described as a seven-day festival, with no clear allusion to an eighth day. This, in spite of the fact that Shmini Atzeret, the eighth day, is directly referenced in other biblical passages discussing the Succot festival.[3]

The question is, of course, even more basic. In its review of the holiday cycle in Parshat Re'eh, why does the Torah fail to mention the festival of

---

1. Devarim 14:22–16:17 (on Shmini Atzeret and on the seventh day of Pesach and second day of Shavuot when they coincide with Shabbat); Devarim 15:19–16:17 (on the seventh day of Pesach and the second day of Shavuot that fall on weekdays).
2. Talmud Bavli Megilla 31a.
3. Vayikra 23:36; Bamidbar 29:35.

Shmini Atzeret? Why omit this significant festival from the list of pilgrim-age festivals?[4]

Approaches

——A——

For me, this issue is informed by a powerfully painful personal experience that recently touched my life. As mentioned in the introduction to our volume on Bamidbar, my mother passed away a little over two years ago. Our family lost a warm, loving, wise and courageous matriarch and life teacher whom we all miss deeply.

At the age of seventy-nine, a few years after my beloved father's pass-ing, my mother made aliya to Jerusalem, Israel, where she lived for ten wonderful years. Her funeral, therefore, was conducted in that holy city. Having experienced funerals in Israel before, albeit not so personally, I was prepared to encounter ceremonies vastly different in feel from those to which I had become accustomed in America. In Israel, the entire expe-rience surrounding death is simpler, more austere and, I believe, healthier, than it is elsewhere. In Israel, there is no cushion created by pomp and circumstance. The emotional distance between the living and the stark reality of their loss is almost nonexistent.

One ritual during the proceedings, however, took me completely by surprise. As we left the modest chapel on the cemetery grounds where the eulogies were delivered, our journey to the grave was abruptly inter-rupted by a member of the *chevra kadisha* (literally "holy society"), the group of volunteers tasked with the burial arrangements. Without a word of explanation this stranger blocked my path, hurling a piece of pottery to the ground, shattering it into shards. I was stunned and bewildered by this dramatic yet puzzling act, and a sobering phrase from the High Holy Day liturgy came unbidden to my mind: *mashul k'cheres hanishbar*, "[man is] likened to shattered pottery…" Clearly, I reflexively reasoned, this graphic, destructive ritual was designed to underscore the finality of my mother's passing from this world; the totality of her absence from our lives.

---

4. The Midrash does interpret the phrase "and you will be completely joyous" (Devarim 17:15) as a reference to Shmini Atzeret. The question remains, however, as to why the text does not openly mention the festival.

In the weeks that followed, I found myself returning over and over again to that moment in my mind, reassessing my initial reactions.

Is this what we really believe? Is an individual's physical departure from this world truly "total" and "final," or is the transition at the moment of death actually more nuanced? Death is a shift, after all, not from presence to absence, but, rather to a unique state that can only be called "absent presence." As anyone who has experienced the death of a loved one can testify, a person may be physically absent, yet remain present in the most powerful ways.

One could actually argue that the most important chapter of my mother's life in this world began when she "passed away." At that moment the true test began. What of my mother's life remains behind? How has the world changed because she was here? What lasting legacy did she leave in the hearts and minds of the many whose lives she touched?

As Jews, we believe in "life after death," a spiritual afterlife in a world that we can scarcely begin to comprehend.[5] We also recognize as equally important, however, the continued *absent presence* of an individual in this world – a world forever changed because of the life that person lived. The pottery may be shattered, but its imprint remains.

— **B** —————————————————————————————

None of this, of course, was totally new to me. As a rabbi, I had shared similar ideas with countless families, counseling them at times of loss. Never, however, had the formulation been sharper in my mind. My thoughts inexorably led me towards another conclusion that, at least for me, broke new ground: *while the transition to absent presence is clearest at the time of death, we actually deal with the phenomenon of absent presence throughout our lives.*

In the arena of childrearing, for example, *we train our children primarily towards the moments when we are absent.* We hope that the morals, ethics, principles and values that we instill in and model for our children will be present in their lives even when we are not. Thus the parents of young children ask, "How did our children behave at someone else's house?" The parents of older children worry, "Will our children maintain their commitment to Jewish observance on the college campus and beyond?" And the parents of young adults wonder, "Who will our children choose as

---

5. Numerous rabbinic sources, including the Rambam's Thirteen Principles of Faith.

life partners? What will their homes be like? Will those homes mirror the ideals that we hold dear?"

School, as well, is designed to teach our children to deal with the world outside the classroom, when teachers are not present to guide them. Friendships and marriages are tested by the loyalty and fidelity we show when our partners are not present. Even our relationship with God is often defined by our struggle to discern His presence in a world where His absence often feels pronounced.

Every sphere of our lives is marked by the challenge of making our presence felt in the lives of others even when we are physically absent. Death thus becomes another step in a natural process, the ultimate iteration of a test that we have faced over and over again, throughout our lives.

—— C ——

We can now return to our original questions concerning the omission of Shmini Atzeret from the passage outlining the holidays in Parshat Re'eh.

Shmini Atzeret is the most "absent" festival of the year, a holiday that in many ways is simply "not here." The very character of the day remains unclear, the nature of the celebration elusive. Attached as an eighth day to the Succot festival, it is, nonetheless, a "festival unto itself," independent of Succot.[6] Alone in the Shalosh Regalim cycle, this festival commemorates no historical or agricultural event. Rabbinic sources define the festival only in general terms, as marking the relationship between God and His people.[7] *Shmini Atzeret is absent not only from the Torah reading of the day. Instead, the day seems to be strangely "absent" in character and focus as well.*

Yet perhaps that is the point. Shmini Atzeret marks not only the culmination of the Shalosh Regalim cycle, but the culmination of the High Holy Day period at the beginning of the Jewish year, as well. In that position, as the year begins, *Shmini Atzeret serves as a day of transition to a state of absent presence in our relationship with God.*

Each year, with the passage of Shmini Atzeret, the majestic observances associated with the holiday season come to a close and the true test begins. Will the year to come be shaped by the introductory experience of the High

---

6. Talmud Bavli Succa 47a, 48a.
7. Rashi, Vayikra 23:36, Bamidbar 29:36; Ramban, Vayikra 23:36; and numerous other commentaries based upon an observation in the Talmud Bavli Succa 55b.

Holy Days and Succot? Will the lessons learned during our encounter with the Divine remain with us even when God's presence is not so keenly felt? Will the resolutions and commitments that we have made while in the rarefied atmosphere of the festivals take hold once we enter the everyday world? Will God be present in our lives even when we must work to seek Him out?

Shmini Atzeret moves us along, preparing us for the challenges ahead – a final holiday, perpetuating our relationship with God. *Remain with Me one more day*, the rabbis picture God telling His children, *your parting from Me is too difficult to bear.*[8] As God and His people start to pull away from each other, only this day remains – one last day in each other's presence, a celebration of the relationship itself.

Yet even now, on this final holy day, subtle changes begin to emerge, as God moves a small step away and becomes a bit more "inaccessible" to us. With no special rituals to guide us, no unique holiday traditions to illuminate our path, Shmini Atzeret – the very celebration of our bond with the Divine – forces us to find our own way, to define our own relationship with God. And if we make use of this last day of *yom tov* in this way, we will be better able to extend that relationship to the times of God's absent presence throughout the year, when God's apparent distance will challenge us to find His continuing presence in our lives.

---

8. Ibid.

Shoftim

שופטים
פרק טז:יח-כא:ט

CHAPTER 16:18–21:9

Parsha Summary

Societal righteousness, courtroom justice, rabbinic authority, kings and priests, the rule of law…

In Parshat Shoftim, Moshe turns his attention to the critical laws designed to shape a society built upon the dictates of Torah law. He opens with the instruction to appoint judges and officers in cities throughout the land and exhorts those appointed officials to apply the law righteously and without favor. Tzedek, tzedek tirdof, *he declares,* "Justice, justice shall you pursue!"[1]

After a short segue dealing with the prohibition of idolatry and the consequent punishment, Moshe returns to the legal system as a whole. In a seminal passage outlining the concept of rabbinic authority, he commands the nation to consult with the leaders of their day across the generations when facing situations of uncertainty. "You shall not deviate," *he insists,* "from the word that they will tell you, right or left."[2]

Turning to other areas of communal leadership, Moshe outlines the laws concerning the appointment, role and limitations of a Jewish king, and delineates the obligatory gifts to be provided to the Kohanim, who will not be granted their own land during the subdivision of Canaan. He exhorts the people to eschew all forms of sorcery and divination and explains that God will make His will known to the people through the aegis of true prophets.

Returning again to the general theme of jurisprudence, Moshe instructs the nation to set aside three arei miklat (cities of refuge) upon entry into the land; in addition to those cities already designated in the Transjordan (see Vaetchanan, Parsha Summary). Exile to the arei miklat *will serve as punishment, atonement and protection for individuals guilty of a specific level of unintentional manslaughter, the parameters of which Moshe proceeds to*

---

1. Devarim 16:20.
2. Ibid., 17:11.

outline (see Shoftim 5). Moshe then contrasts these laws with the laws governing an intentional murderer who, upon conviction, is to be put to death.

After dealing briefly with additional laws of jurisprudence, including the rules of testimony, Moshe turns to the laws governing warfare, including the encouragement to be given to soldiers before battle by a Kohen specifically anointed for that task; the various exemptions from active army service; the overtures for peace to be made before battle; and the obligation to protect the environment, particularly fruit trees, when besieging the enemy.

The parsha ends as Moshe outlines the ritual laws of egla arufa, the "axed heifer," to be conducted by the elders of a town closest to the site of discovery of an unidentified corpse. These rituals underscore the obligation of each Jewish community to care for the welfare of strangers in their midst.

1 Poetry or Practicality?

Context

We have previously noted and discussed the tension created by the multilayered character of the book of Devarim (see Devarim 1).

On the one hand, as we have noted, Devarim chronicles the poignant human drama of Moshe's farewell to his people. Within his public addresses, this great leader waxes eloquent as he searches for words that will remain with his "flock" long after he is gone.

On the other hand, Devarim is an integral part of God's eternal law. As such, this text is bound by the rules that govern the interpretation of the entire Torah. Every word is essential; each phrase is divinely chosen to convey a particular eternal message to the reader.

While this dual unfolding is felt throughout the book of Devarim, there are times when it rises more clearly to the surface, complicating the nature of specific imperatives appearing in the text. Two powerful examples of such commandments are found in Parshat Shoftim:

> *Tzedek tzedek tirdof*, "Justice, justice shall you pursue, so that you will live and possess the land that the Lord your God gives to you."[3]

> *Tamim tihiyeh im Hashem Elokecha*, "Wholehearted shall you be with the Lord your God."[4]

Questions

How are we meant to view commandments such as those quoted above?

Are they general, spontaneous products of Moshe's passion as he strives to penetrate the hearts of a listening people? Or are they mitzvot, or elements of mitzvot, divinely fashioned, like all other Torah imperatives, to

---

3. Devarim 16:20.
4. Ibid., 18:13.

convey specific behavioral requirements across the ages? If the latter is true, what are those concrete requirements?

Approaches

The first and most important answer to our questions is clearly "*all of the above.*" As we often have noted before, the Torah text unfolds on multiple levels simultaneously.

The narrative in the book of Bereishit, for example, chronicles the birth of a nation through the stories of individual families. The national saga coursing beneath the surface of these personal tales does not in any way diminish the poignant private journeys described therein.

Similarly, any halachic requirements conveyed by Moshe's imperatives to the nation in the book of Devarim should not blind us to the dramatic passion reflected in his words. To fully appreciate this book of the Torah, we must always keep the scene of its unfolding before our eyes. An aged, powerful leader bids farewell to the people that he has shepherded from slavery to freedom. Powerful sentiments course through each sentence as Moshe shares his personal regrets with the nation over his inability to join in entering the land; desperately tries to teach final, critical lessons before his death; and delivers, one last time, words of encouragement, warning, support, remonstration and so much more. Clearly Moshe's eloquent choice of words mirrors a myriad of personal emotions.

At the same time, however, these are words of Torah text and, as such, transcend the moments of their delivery. Concrete, eternal instructions are contained within the commandments shared by Moshe throughout the book of Devarim. Every phrase uttered by this great leader, no matter how dramatic, is therefore fair game for halachic analysis by scholars across the ages.

The two phrases before us provide telling examples of the varied rabbinic approaches to Moshe's dramatic words in Sefer Devarim.

I. *Tzedek tzedek tirdof*

——— **A** ———

The phrase *Tzedek tzedek tirdof…*, "Justice, justice shall you pursue, so that you will live and possess the land that the Lord your God gives to you," appears at the end of the short opening passage of Parshat Shoftim. Serving as an introduction to the entire parsha, this three-sentence passage conveys the general admonition to establish a righteous system of governance upon entering the land.

——— B ———————————————————————————————————————

While the scholars of the Talmud do not derive an independent mitzva from the words *tzedek, tzedek tirdof*, they do view this phrase as potentially broadening the Torah's demand for justice in multiple ways. A number of interpretations in this vein are suggested in the tractate of Sanhedrin.[5]

The rabbis open the Talmudic discussion by questioning the demands presented by two separate biblical verses. In the book of Vayikra, the Torah commands, "with justice shall you judge your fellow,"[6] while the text in Devarim demands, "Justice, justice shall you pursue…" Perceiving seemingly contrasting requirements emerging from these verses, the rabbis ask: In which cases does "judging with justice" suffice? And in which cases must we "pursue justice, justice" with extra vigor?

Answering their own question, the scholars explain that through the use of these variations, the text challenges judges to follow their own instincts. In straightforward situations, where the facts match the judges' internal perceptions; "judging with justice" will suffice. When the judges suspect deceit, however, they must dig deeper, moving past the apparent facts before them, as they "pursue justice" with further force. A judge cannot fulfill his task in pro forma fashion. He must always invest his full capacities as God's agent in the administration of the law.

——— C ———————————————————————————————————————

Rabbi Ashi demurs, negating the textual question raised by his colleagues. The two Torah passages are not in conflict, this sage argues, as the repetitive language in the phrase "Justice, justice shall you pursue" does not reflect a call for extraordinary effort in specific cases. At all times, a judge must apply himself fully towards the rendering of a just verdict. Instead, the reiteration "Justice, justice…" references the *legitimacy of two distinct judicial paths: justice and compromise*. Based upon the circumstances and the judgment of the bench, either of these paths can be followed.

———————————————

5.   Talmud Bavli Sanhedrin 32:2.
6.   Vayikra 19:15.

Rabbi Ashi's acceptance of compromise as a legitimate judicial path is carried one step further by another Talmudic scholar, Rabbi Yehoshua ben Korcha, earlier in this same tractate, Sanhedrin. Rabbi Yehoshua maintains that, when possible, *a judge is obligated to negotiate or arbitrate a compromise between two disputants.* To buttress his position, this scholar quotes the pronouncement of the prophet Zecharia, "Truth and a judgment of peace shall you execute in your gates."[7]

How, Rabbi Yehoshua asks, *is a "justice of peace" attainable? One could argue that these two terms are mutually exclusive. Is it not true that when a decision is determined through strict justice, peace has not been achieved? One of the disputants will inevitably be dissatisfied the verdict.*

What, then, is the "judgment of peace" to which the prophet refers? Obviously, answers Rabbi Yehoshua, *the prophet is referencing the path of compromise.*[8]

Rabbi Yehoshua's embrace of compromise as the preferred legal path, however, is not without controversy. In the same passage of Talmud, Rabbi Eliezer the son of Rabbi Yossi the Galilean maintains that a judge is *absolutely forbidden to arbitrate a compromise.* While disputants can certainly find a middle ground between themselves, Rabbi Eliezer maintains, once they approach a court for a ruling, strict justice must rule the day.[9]

Strangely enough, Rabbi Eliezer's position prohibiting courtroom compromise would seem to find support from the very sentence that Rabbi Yehoshua quotes to buttress his own position in support of such compromise: "Truth and a judgment of peace shall you execute in your gates." For while conciliation satisfies the need for both "peace" and "judgment," *it does not satisfy the third component cited by the prophet, "truth."* If a judge arbitrates a compromise between two litigants, he does not arrive at the truth. He creates, in effect, a legal fiction through which neither of the parties completely loses. Such a fiction is an acceptable settlement, Rabbi Eliezer argues, only before the court becomes involved. Once the legal process is engaged, a judge can only choose one path. He is obligated to strive for the truth through the *strict application of Torah law.*

In spite of Rabbi Eliezer's compelling argument against judicial negotia-

---

7. Zechariah 8:16.
8. Talmud Bavli Sanhedrin 6b.
9. Ibid.

tion, however, the halacha, as codified both in the Rambam's *Mishneh Torah*[10] and in Rabbi Yosef Caro's *Shulchan Aruch*,[11] adopts Rabbi Yehoshua's embrace of compromise as the *preferred courtroom path*.

In the words of the Rambam,

> It is a mitzva [for a judge] to ask the litigants, at the onset of the legal process, "Do you wish a legal ruling or a compromise?" If they desire to compromise, [the court] should effect a compromise between them.
>
> And any court that consistently effects compromise is a laudatory court about which [the prophet] states: "Truth and a judgment of peace shall you execute in your gates." What justice is accompanied by peace? Let us say that it is [the justice of] compromise.[12]

The halachic support of judicial compromise, even at the expense of the truth, mirrors the powerful priority placed upon *shalom*, interpersonal peace, in countless other scholarly texts. Most telling, perhaps, is the rabbinic decision to close the entire Mishna[13] and, arguably, the two most important prayers in Jewish liturgy, the Amida and the Kaddish,[14] with paragraphs focusing on the theme of peace. Furthermore, in the fashioning of these prayers, the rabbis apparently take their cue from God Himself. The divinely authored Priestly Blessing, pronounced daily by the Kohanim over the nation at God's command, culminates with the prayer "May the Lord turn His countenance towards you *and grant you peace*."[15]

Halacha thus mandates that peace, the greatest of God's blessings, must be aggressively pursued by God's judicial agents in this world, even when that peace comes at the expense of truth.[16]

---

10. Rambam, *Mishneh Torah*, Hilchot Sanhedrin 22:4.
11. *Shulchan Aruch*, Choshen Mishpat 12:2.
12. Rambam, *Mishneh Torah*, Hilchot Sanhedrin 22:4.
13. Mishna Uktzin 3:12.
14. Daily siddur.
15. Bamidbar 6:26.
16. The halachically mandated judicial pursuit of peace does have its limits. Once a verdict has been reached, it must be enacted. At that point, the time for compromise in the courtroom has passed. Rambam, *Mishneh Torah*, Hilchot Sanhedrin 22:4; *Shulchan Aruch*, Choshen Mishpat 12:2.

——**D**————————————————————————

Finally, yet another explanation for the phrase *Tzedek tzedek tirdof* is offered
by the rabbis in the same Talmudic passage, based on the recognition that
judges do not bear sole responsibility for the creation of a just society. As
understood by the rabbis, the phrase *Tzedek tzedek tirdof* can be seen as
the last in a series of directives issued by Moshe in Sefer Devarim concerning the essential reciprocal relationship between a society and its judges.

1. Moshe opens his very first farewell address, recorded at the beginning of the book of Devarim, by recalling instructions he had previously
given both to the nation and its judges concerning the establishment of
a just society: *As we left Sinai,* he reminds the people, *I instructed you to
choose appropriate judges.*[17] *And I admonished those judges to apply the
law with justice.*[18]

2. Now, as Moshe returns to the theme of governance at the beginning
of Parshat Shoftim, he again sounds the call for respectful reciprocity:
"Judges and officers shall you set for yourselves in all your gates…. And
they will judge the nation with just judgment."[19] *You, as a people, must do
your part in creating a society built upon the administration of justice, while
those whom you choose as leaders must administer that justice justly.*

3. He then continues by admonishing the judges directly: "You shall not
pervert judgment, you shall not show favoritism and you shall not accept
a bribe, for a bribe will blind the eyes of the wise and make the words of
the righteous twisted."[20]

4. Moshe closes with the declaration *Tzedek tzedek tirdof,* "Justice,
justice shall you pursue, so that you will live and possess the land that the
Lord your God gives to you."[21]

This last sentence, the Talmud suggests, is not directed towards the
judges at all. Instead, with the phrase *Tzedek tzedek tirdof,* Moshe turns
his attention back to the nation by raising the concept of societal judicial
responsibility to a new level. For, at this point, Moshe addresses *potential
litigants.*

---

17. Devarim 1:13.
18. Ibid., 1:16–17.
19. Ibid., 16:18.
20. Ibid., 16:19.
21. Ibid., 16:20.

Tzedek tzedek tirdof, "seek out an exemplary court."[22] *Do not twist the process of jurisprudence to meet your own personal ends. Do not search for a court that is clearly predisposed to your point of view. There is more at stake here than your own personal concerns. Pursue justice; seek out an unbiased, exemplary court. Even as litigants, you play a pivotal role in maintaining the seriousness with which the law is taken and ensuring the proper administration of justice throughout the land.*

—— E ————————————————————————————

Building upon these Talmudic suggestions, numerous other legal interpretations of the phrase *Tzedek tzedek tirdof* are suggested by commentaries across the ages.

It remains, however, for the eighteenth-century German scholar Rabbi Shimshon Raphael Hirsch to remind us not to lose sight of the forest for the trees. For while Hirsch himself quotes a number of the legal Talmudic references cited above, he also interprets Moshe's passionate charge to the nation as *a general directive meant to define the moral character of his people's society*:

> "Justice, justice shall you pursue, so that you will live and possess the land that the Lord your God gives to you."
>
> As the highest unique goal, to be striven for purely for itself, to which all other considerations have to be subordinated, the concept, "Tzedek, Right, Justice," …is to be kept in the mind of the whole nation. To pursue this goal unceasingly and with all devotion is Israel's one task; with that it has done everything to secure its physical and political existence.[23]

A loyal halachist, Rabbi Shimshon Raphael Hirsch would be the first to acknowledge the importance of each legal detail gleaned by the Talmud from the verse *Tzedek tzedek tirdof.* At the same time, however, this visionary leader warns the reader not to overlook the power of Moshe's words as a broad exhortation towards the overall establishment of a just society.

———————————

22. Talmud Bavli Sanhedrin 32b.
23. Rabbi Shimshon Raphael Hirsch, Devarim 16:20.

11. *Tamim tihiyeh im Hashem Elokecha*

———**A**———

The second of the verses before us, *Tamim tihiyeh im Hashem Elokecha*, "Wholehearted shall you be with the Lord your God," appears in the middle of a paragraph in Parshat Shoftim prohibiting the practices of sorcery and divination.

Here the rabbinic divide becomes starker. For, as indicated above, although the rabbis debate the practical significance of the phrase *tzedek, tzedek tirdof*, they are united on one point. This dramatic statement does not constitute a new, unique mitzva. Moshe's eloquent words convey, instead, an expansion on existing law.

When it comes to Moshe's declaration *Tamim tihiyeh im Hashem Elokecha*, however, no such agreement exists. Instead, two fundamentally disparate approaches emerge from rabbinic literature.

———**B**———

At one end of the spectrum stand those authorities, such as the Ramban, who count the imperative *Tamim tihiyeh im Hashem Elokecha* as *an independent positive mitzva*, a separate one of the 613 commandments. This mitzva, these scholars maintain, obligates each Jew to recognize God's sole awareness of and power over future events.

The approach of these authorities is based on consideration of the verse *Tamim tihiyeh im Hashem Elokecha* in context, as a positive iteration of the surrounding prohibitions against sorcery and divination. Through this declaration, the Ramban thus maintains, God commands the nation "to direct their hearts exclusively to Him; to believe that He, alone, is the Doer of all; that He knows the truth regarding the future; and from Him [alone] we should ask about that which is to come, from His prophets and pious ones."[24]

To buttress his approach, the Ramban cites biblical, Midrashic and Talmudic sources. Particularly telling is the parallel this sage draws between the verse before us and the opening imperative in a covenant between God and the patriarch Avraham at the dawn of Jewish history: *Hit'halech l'fanai*

---

24. *Hasagot Haramban* to Rambam's *Sefer Hamitzvot*, positive commandment 8.

SHOFTIM – POETRY OR PRACTICALITY?

v'heyei tamim, "Walk before me and be wholehearted."[25] Here, too, God commands Avraham to remain steadfast in his rejection of the superstitious mores of the surrounding cultures. *Be complete with Me, Avraham; recognize that I, and I alone, guide and control all that you see...*[26]

Puzzled by the Rambam's omission of this obligation from his list of the mitzvot in *Sefer Hamitzvot*, the Ramban posits, "Perhaps the master [the Rambam] perceives this mandate as a general exhortation to perform the commandments and walk in the ways of the Torah...and therefore did not include it in his enumeration."[27]

"As is evident from the words of our sages, however," the Ramban concludes, "the approach we have outlined [viewing this imperative as an independent commandment] is the correct one."[28]

C

At the other end of the spectrum can be found scholars such as Rabbeinu Bachya Ibn Pakuda who openly interpret the verse *Tamim tihiyeh im Hashem Elokecha* in general terms. In his introduction to his famous ethical work *Chovot Halevavot* (Duties of the Heart), Rabbeinu Bachya explains this biblical verse not as a unique mitzva, but as an overarching exhortation on Moshe's part towards uniform ethical behavior throughout the life of each Jew: "And you should know that the intent and purpose of the precepts of the heart is to cultivate a complete harmony between our inner and outward actions in the service of the Lord."[29]

From Rabbeinu Bachya's perspective, the imperative to be *tamim* (wholehearted) is a general one, mandating consistency between a person's thoughts and actions. An individual whose words are at variance with his deeds, Bachya maintains, is not trusted by those around him. Similarly, if

---

25. Bereishit 17:1.
26. *Hasagot Haramban* to Rambam's *Sefer Hamitzvot*, positive commandment 8.
27. In his introduction to *Sefer Hamitzvot*, his enumeration of the commandments, the Rambam explains that his list will only include precepts dealing with a specific rite or action. General, all-embracing principles towards divine obedience will not be listed.
28. *Hasagot Haramban* to Rambam's *Sefer Hamitzvot*, positive commandment 8. It should be noted that the Rambam's failure to list this mitzva does not reflect a philosophical disagreement with the Ramban's points. The Rambam is powerfully strident in his condemnation of superstition, soothsayers and divination (see *Mishneh Torah*, Hilchot Avoda Zara 11:16).
29. Rabbeinu Bachya Ibn Pakuda, *Chovot Halevavot*, introduction.

an individual's service of God is marked by inconsistency and insincerity, if the intentions of his heart are contradicted by his words, if his inner convictions do not match his outward actions, his service of God will not be perfect.

Once again, we are reminded by a great luminary not to allow the details, important as they are, to blind us to the overarching power and passion of Moshe's words. On a global level, Bachya argues, Moshe's proclamation *Tamim tihiyeh* conveys a truth that courses through the entire Torah. An individual must be "wholehearted with God," simply because God will reject insincerity.

Poetry or practicality? Passionate proclamations on the part of an aged leader, or concrete commandments to a people across time?

Moshe's eloquent declarations are both at the same time – text meant to be studied and taught on multiple levels at once. When we recognize this truth, the full beauty of the book of Devarim is revealed…

2 It Was Good Enough for Them!

Context

The following prohibition appears among the laws listed at the beginning of Parshat Shoftim: "And do not erect for yourselves a *matzeiva* (pillar), which the Lord your God hates."[1]

The rabbis connect this ban to an imperative found in the book of Shmot[2] and explain that Jewish ritual worship must take place only upon a *mizbei'ach*, an altar created of earth or many stones. The use of a single-stone pillar, even for the worship of the true God, is expressly prohibited.

Questions

Earlier biblical passages seem to indicate that the use of worship pillars was fully acceptable during the patriarchal period.[3]

Why does a symbol that was once suitable for use in the worship of the Divine now become not only prohibited but actually "hateful" to God?

Approaches

—A—

The Abravanel dismisses the problem entirely by suggesting that two different types of pillars are actually referenced in the text.

The *matzeivot* erected by the patriarchs, the Abravanel maintains, were actually *pillars of testimony*, marking specific locations or events of note. Such pillars are not prohibited, even after the entry of the nation into the land. The *matzeivot* mentioned in Moshe's ban, on the other hand, are *pillars designed for worship*, commonly used by idolaters. These worship

---

1. Devarim 16:22.
2. Shmot 20:21–22.
3. Bereishit 28:18, 28:22, 31:13, 35:4.

pillars were always prohibited, according to the Abravanel, even during the patriarchal era.[4]

———**B**———

The vast majority of authorities, however, reject the Abravanel's distinction and maintain that the ban in Parshat Shoftim does, indeed, prohibit pillars that were previously allowed during the patriarchal period. Rashi's explanation for this shift, based upon the Sifrei, is accepted by most: "And even though it [a *matzeiva*] was pleasing to Him during the days of the patriarchs, He now 'hates' it because they [the Canaanites] made it into an ordinance of idolatrous character."[5]

There is nothing intrinsically objectionable to God, Rashi claims, in the symbol of a single-stone pillar. Once such pillars become normative components in the idolatrous practices of the land, however, they attain a negative overlay that makes them completely prohibited.

———**C**———

An obvious objection to Rashi's approach is raised by a number of authorities, including the Ramban. The Torah itself attests to the use of *mizbechot* (multi-stone altars) by the idolaters who inhabited Canaan.[6] If single-stone pillars are prohibited to the Israelites because of their association with idolatry, these scholars ask, why are *mizbechot* not prohibited, as well?

The Ramban first entertains the possibility that pillars are ultimately forbidden to the Israelites because the idolatrous use of pillars was universal, in contrast to the sporadic use of altars. He then offers his preferred explanation. Every idolatrous temple, the Ramban postulates, actually contained three components: a *mizbei'ach* (a multi-stoned altar for offerings), a *matzeiva* (a single-stone monument at the entrance, upon which the priests stood), and an *asheira* (a tree planted outside the door to point the way for worshippers).

As the Israelites prepare to enter the Land, God strikes a balance. In His desire to distance the nation from the idolatrous practices that He abhors, God expressly prohibits the use of trees and single-stone pillars within the

---

4. Abravanel, Devarim 16:18–22.
5. Rashi, Devarim 16:21.
6. Shmot 34:13; Devarim 12:3.

context of Jewish ritual worship. He continues to allow, however, the use of multi-stone altars necessary for the offerings that He has commanded to the Israelites. The rationale for such an allowance is based on the fact that God found the use of such altars "pleasing," even before the emergence of idolatrous worship onto the world stage.[7]

—— **D** ——————————————————————————————

A deeper distinction between pillars and altars is suggested centuries later by Rabbi Naftali Tzvi Yehuda Berlin, the Netziv, in his commentary on the Torah. While altars were indeed used by the nations of Canaan to facilitate their ritual worship, the Netziv maintains, *pillars were directly venerated as idols.* This fact is reflected in the Mishnaic ruling that prohibits benefit from a stone pillar that has been hewn for the purpose of serving as the base for an idol.[8] Such benefit is circumscribed, the commentaries explain, because the base pillars themselves were worshipped as well as the idols.[9]

Multi-stone altars, which only served as appurtenances to idolatrous practice, the Netziv explains, remain permitted for use within Israelite worship rituals. Single-stone monuments, however, which were directly venerated by the nations of Canaan, become prohibited to the Israelites upon their entry into the land.[10]

—— **E** ——————————————————————————————

Perhaps the most intriguing explanation for the prohibition of previously allowed *matzeivot* is offered by Rabbi Shimshon Raphael Hirsch. Ever true to his rational approach to Jewish thought and law, this towering scholar maintains that the halachic shift in attitude towards single-stone pillars reflects *a fundamental transition in God's expectations of His people.*

A *matzeiva*, a single-stone monument used without any alteration, Hirsch explains, serves as "a memorial to that which God has done for us in nature and history."[11] A *mizbeïach*, a multi-stone altar, in contrast, "is meant to represent the devotion of human activity to God."[12]

---

7. Ramban, Devarim 16:22, Vayikra 1:9 (based on Bereishit 4:4 and 8:21).
8. Mishna Avoda Zara 3:7.
9. Rashi, Talmud Bavli Avoda Zara 47b; Tosafot, ibid.
10. Ha'amek Davar, Devarim 16:22, Shmot 34:13.
11. Rabbi Shimshon Raphael Hirsch, Devarim 16:22.
12. Ibid.

Before Revelation, "no complete individual and national life yet existed, which, by its submission to God's Torah, was meant to be a manifestation of homage to God."[13] The primary responsibility of the patriarchs, therefore, was limited to the recognition of and attestation to God's role in nature and history. Single stone pillars, unaltered products of God's creation, were, therefore, "beloved" to God. Such pillars faithfully represented God's presence and power.

Once Revelation occurs, however, everything changes. "The single-stone pillar is not only included in, and absorbed by, the *mizbei'ach*, but the *matzeiva* actually becomes sinful."[14] God's expectation of the faithful is unalterably transformed. He now rejects any worship that is limited to the recognition of His power and might. Post-Revelation, religious devotion must also express "the moral submission of the whole of the human being to His law, the Torah."[15] Simply worshiping God is no longer enough. Man must now recognize God's will and become a partner in the creation of sanctity through loyal obedience to divine law. The *matzeiva* has been replaced by the *mizbei'ach*. Only a multi-stone altar, built by man, out of material created by God, can properly represent man's Post-Revelation mission to the world.

Seen through the eyes of a master teacher, the shift to a post-*matzeiva* world becomes much more than a technical avoidance of the idolatrous practices of others. Instead, through the powerful use of ritual-related symbols, the Torah underscores the step-by-step development of man's relationship with God. *While it was once enough to worship God, man must now go a step further and partner with the Divine.*

---

13. Ibid.
14. Ibid.
15. Ibid.

3 Rabbinic Infallibility?

Context

A passage critical to the ongoing application of Jewish law is found in Parshat Shoftim:

> If a matter of judgment shall baffle you, between blood and blood, between verdict and verdict, between plague and plague, matters of controversy in your gates, you shall rise up and ascend to the place which the Lord your God shall choose.
>
> And you shall come to the Kohanim, the Levi'im and to the judge who will be in those days, and you shall inquire, and they will tell you the word of judgment.
>
> And you shall do according to the word that they will tell you from that place that the Lord will choose, and you shall be careful to do according to all that they will teach you.
>
> According to the teaching that they will teach you and according to the judgment that they will say to you, shall you do; *you shall not deviate from the word that they will tell you, right or left.*[1]

Commenting on the phrase "you shall not deviate from the word that they will tell you, right or left," the classical Torah commentator Rashi observes: *"Even if they say to you concerning the right that it is left and concerning the left that it is right. How much more so if they say to you that the right is right and that the left is left."*[2]

Questions

Rashi's interpretation of the text is difficult to understand. Would the Torah command us to follow the halachic decisions of the rabbis even when we

---

1. Devarim 17:8–11.
2. Rashi, Devarim 17:11.

know those decisions to be wrong? Does rabbinic decision trump Torah law?

Furthermore, an examination of the Sifrei, the Midrashic source quoted by Rashi as the basis of his position, reveals a striking variation from our text of Rashi. The Sifrei states that the rabbis must be obeyed, "even *if it appears in your eyes* [that the rabbis are telling you that] right is left and that left is right." By omitting the Sifrei's critical phrase "if it appears in your eyes," Rashi seems to expand the Sifrei's requirement to obey the rabbis from cases when you believe that they are wrong to cases when *you are certain that they are wrong.*

Finally, compounding the questions on Rashi is a passage in the Talmud Yerushalmi that clearly contradicts the position of this great scholar: "You might think that if the sages tell you that right is left and that left is right, you must [still] heed them. Therefore, the Torah states, 'you shall not deviate from the word that they will tell you, right or left.' [This text indicates that you should only obey the rabbis] when they tell you that right is right and that left is left – *only if they tell you what you know to be true.*"[3]

Does Rashi go beyond the apparent position of the Sifrei and maintain that the rabbis must be heeded even when we are certain that their decision contravenes Torah law? If he does so maintain, do others agree with him? What justification can be cited for their position?

Approaches

A

Some commentaries, unwilling to accept the possibility that Rashi would obligate compliance to an erroneous rabbinic decree, insist that even Rashi's mandate of obedience only extends to cases where it "appears" that the rabbis are mistaken. In situations of certainty, when the rabbi's decision is clearly flawed, Rashi would agree that their decree should not be obeyed.[4]

Other authorities, including the Siftei Chachamim, explain Rashi's position by proposing what is, in essence, a doctrine of rabbinic infallibility. In situations where you are convinced that the rabbis are wrong, the Siftei Chachamim declares, "do not ascribe the error to them but to

3. Talmud Yerushalmi Horayot 1:1.
4. Nachshoni, *Hagot B'parshiot HaTorah*, vol. 2, p. 773.

yourself. For the Holy One Blessed Be He continually places of his spirit upon the guardians of His holy [Torah], and He will protect them from all error, *that nothing should emerge from their mouths other than the truth.*"[5] (See *Bamidbar*: Beha'alotcha 7a, for discussion concerning the origin and character of rabbinic authority.)

Offering a different rationale, the Abravanel explains that the application of any legal system, even Torah law, will not always yield the truth. The halachic rule, for example, that places the burden of proof in monetary cases upon the claimant fails to address those occasions when a justified petitioner lacks proof of his claims. In order to address such situations, when the letter of the law does not support what they perceive to be true, the rabbis are granted the authority to contravene normative legal principles. To a halachically knowledgeable observer such rabbinic decisions would appear to be fundamentally flawed. The Torah ordains, therefore, that such an observer should not question the rabbis' decision but should, instead, recognize their halachic right to operate beyond the letter of the law.[6]

Each of the above approaches obligates the observer to recognize, in a case of doubt, that the error rests in his own judgment and not in the judgment of the rabbis.

B

Some authorities, however, are willing to take Rashi's apparent acceptance of rabbinic authority even in the case of actual error at face value.

The Ramban serves as a bridge towards this position. On the one hand, this sage opens and closes his remarks on the subject by apparently limiting Rashi's position to situations when "*you think in your heart* that the rabbis are mistaken."[7] On the other hand, the Ramban clearly states that when faced with a situation of apparent rabbinic error, an individual should not say, "How can I possibly eat this forbidden food?" or "How can I possibly execute this innocent man?" Instead, this individual should recognize that the same God Who commanded him to observe the law also commanded him to act in accordance with rabbinic mandate. God gave man the Torah "as taught by them [the rabbis], *even if they are to err.*"[8]

---

5.   Siftei Chachamim, Devarim 17:11.
6.   Abravanel, Devarim 17:8.
7.   Ramban, Devarim 17:11.
8.   Ibid.

Such overarching acceptance of rabbinic authority, the Ramban argues, is essential to the preservation of the uniform character of Jewish law: "The Torah was given to us in written form and it is known that not all opinions will concur on newly arising matters. Disagreements would therefore increase and [were we not to insist upon compliance with rabbinic mandate] the Torah would become many Torahs."[9]

When faced with a conflict between deeply held perceptions of the truth and the health of the continuing halachic process, the Ramban believes the choice to be obvious. *The very survival of the Jewish people depends upon a stable, shared legal tradition.* The decisions of the rabbis, even when flawed, must, therefore, be heeded.

Consistent with this explanation, the Ramban, in his commentary to the Rambam's *Sefer Hamitzvot,* draws a fascinating distinction between two separate situations of perceived rabbinic error. An individual sage who notes that a rabbinic court has erroneously permitted a forbidden action, the Ramban argues, should continue to follow his own dictates and personally act in a more stringent manner. If the court, however, considers the sage's arguments and still retains its original leniency, the sage must then follow the majority rabbinic mandate so that uniform communal practice will be preserved.[10]

Channeling the Ramban's clarion call for consistent halachic practice, the Ba'al Hachinuch is even more emphatic on the issue of actual rabbinic error: "Even if the rabbis err and we perceive their error, we should not disagree with them but, instead, practice according to their faulty decree. *It is better to suffer one error and for the entire community to remain loyal to their wise counsel than for each individual to practice according to his own counsel, and for the Torah to be destroyed.*"[11]

These overarching arguments for communal halachic consistency underlie a well-known Mishnaic narrative concerning a public dispute between the two towering sages Rabban Gamliel (then *nasi* of the Sanhedrin) and Rabbi Yehoshua.

When Rabbi Yehoshua disputed Rabban Gamliel's calculation of the calendar, Rabban Gamliel declared: "I decree that you should appear be-

---

9. Ibid.
10. *Hasagot Haramban* to Rambam's *Sefer Hamitzvot, shoresh* 1.
11. *Sefer Hachinuch,* mitzva 496.

fore me with your staff and your money on the day when, according to your calculation, Yom Kippur falls."[12] (These acts would be considered a desecration of Yom Kippur, the holiest day of the Jewish year.)

After consulting with his colleagues, Rabbi Yehoshua complied with Rabban Gamliel's decree and, on the very day that he reckoned to be Yom Kippur, traveled with his staff and his money to appear before Rabban Gamliel in Yavneh. Upon seeing Rabbi Yehoshua before him, Rabban Gamliel rose, kissed Rabbi Yehoshua on the head and exclaimed, "Come in peace, my master and my disciple – my master in wisdom and my disciple because you have accepted my words!"[13]

Halachic tradition thus records Rabbi Yehoshua's willingness to set aside his own certainty concerning the holiest day of the Jewish year in order to preserve consistent communal practice.

—— C ————————————————————

Finally, a more foundational approach to the issue of rabbinic error can be gleaned from the Rambam's analysis of halachic process, recorded in his introduction to his commentary on the Mishna.

(Note: A longer discussion of these points can be found in our volume on *Shmot*: Parshat Yitro 5. The information contained there is critical, I believe, to a real understanding of the process of Oral Law. For the purposes of our current study, however, I will summarize some of the salient points.)

Halachic process, the Rambam maintains, is built upon the central tenet that after transmitting the written text together with specific oral laws to Moshe, God "steps back" and hands divine law over to man for interpretation and application. As God retreats from active involvement in decision making, He relinquishes His infallible control over the course of the law. The rabbis, using the rules of study transmitted at Sinai, become charged with analysis of the text and with the application of its laws to ever changing times and circumstances. Limited man, prone to error, is now divinely authorized to determine halacha's path, and God Himself agrees to accept the conclusions reached by man as law.[14]

While the authorities of other faith traditions, such as Catholicism's

---

12. Mishna Rosh Hashana 2:9.
13. Ibid.
14. Rambam, *Peirush Hamishnayot*, introduction.

pope, claim to speak in the name of God, halachic authorities speak for themselves. They do not sit and wait for divine inspiration, but instead turn to their books. Armed with the law and with the talent granted to them by God, they attempt to reach divine truth in any given situation. These scholars find reassurance, however, in the knowledge that if they have remained loyal to the process of study in a real attempt to find that truth, God will accept whatever conclusion they reach. In this way, Jewish law continues to address cutting-edge issues in our day, from genetic engineering to space travel to intellectual property, and remains relevant, coherent and consonant with the foundations of the law at Sinai.

In other words, *if they are true to their calling, the rabbis can't be wrong.* It's not that rabbinic authorities are infallible, but that the definition of truth within the halachic process has changed. *Truth is no longer defined by objective fact, but rather by loyalty to the process.* Such loyalty preserves the halachic process itself, and is therefore more important than any one specific decision. Once a rabbinic decision has been reached through appropriate study of the text and faithful application of the law, *by definition, that decision is correct.*

In light of the Rambam's analysis, Rashi's approach to the issue of rabbinic error becomes fully comprehensible. An individual must follow the dictates of the rabbis, even if he is certain that they are objectively flawed. Within the halachic realm, such retrospective objective analysis is immaterial. *If the rabbis have followed the system with loyalty, their decisions are correct,* "even if they tell you that left is right and that right is left."

Points to Ponder

—— **A** ————————————————————————————————

The powerful emphasis placed by the scholars on uniformity of halachic process and the preservation of the halachic system should give us pause.

Together with many of my rabbinic colleagues, I have noted a growing tendency on the part of many, even within the Orthodox community, to try to "remake Jewish law in their own image." In a multitude of areas – including the structure of prayer services, kashrut standards, the role of women in ritual, Sabbath observance, the attitude towards homosexuality and more – authoritative rabbinic dictate is often ignored in favor of what the segments of the community feel is right. Minority opinions are cited and followed, often in the face of more respected views to the contrary, to justify changes in age-old ritual practice and observance.

Don't get me wrong. I firmly believe that halachic decisors need to take communal concerns into account in their deliberations. In each generation, those who chart the course of Jewish law must recognize changing circumstances and the shifting needs of those around them. In our day, the increased secular and religious education of women, changing societal attitudes towards gays, the challenging intrusion of secular culture into our lives through television, the Internet and social media are among the vast constellation of factors that must be considered in the application of Jewish law.

At the same time however, halacha cannot be properly applied unless there is a healthy respect for the process itself. Decisions cannot be agenda driven. Each issue must be considered on its own merit, without predetermined conclusions driving the results. *When the halachic process is viewed simply as a system to be manipulated towards reaching a predetermined goal, rather than as an eternal process that has shown independent value over the long course of Jewish history, the integrity of the system itself, is sorely undermined.*

Dangerous, as well, are potential "unintended consequences" that can often result from manipulation of the law to reach a desired goal. When all aspects of a halachic ruling are not carefully considered, the ancillary outcomes can be unexpectedly damaging.

As a case in point, consider the Conservative movement's decision to permit driving to the synagogue on Shabbat. Based upon a ruling issued in 1950 by three Conservative rabbinic authorities, this decision was ratified by the movement's Committee on Jewish Law and Standards and presented at the subsequent convention of the Rabbinical Assembly. The ruling, couched within a much larger "Program for the Revitalization of the Sabbath," read, in part:

> Refraining from the use of motor vehicles is an important aid in the maintenance of the Sabbath spirit of repose. Such restraint aids, moreover, in keeping the members of the family together on the Sabbath. However, where a family resides beyond reasonable walking distance from the synagogue, the use of a motor vehicle for the purpose of synagogue attendance shall in no wise be construed as a violation of

the Sabbath, but, on the contrary, such attendance shall be deemed an expression of loyalty to our faith.[15]

Even setting aside the significant objections raised by many authorities to the halachic basis of this ruling (some from within the Conservative movement itself),[16] two significant ancillary consequences of the decision must be cited.

Firstly, on a communal level, halfway measures simply do not work.[17] Predictably, once driving became "halachically permissible" within the Conservative community for the purpose of synagogue attendance, the general prohibition against driving for other purposes became almost impossible to defend.

The second consequence of the decision was driven home to me by a phone call received close to thirty years ago from a local Conservative rabbi, shortly after I assumed my current post in Englewood, New Jersey.

"Shmuel," my Conservative colleague complained, "I am jealous of you. You have a synagogue community. Shabbat is felt in the streets of your neighborhood as your congregants walk to and from services every week and to each other's homes on Friday night and Shabbat afternoon.

"I, on the other hand, have a synagogue bereft of community. Our temple is located in Englewood but our parishioners live in Tenafly, Closter, Cresskill and Demarest. No one lives near our synagogue."

I realized then that the Conservative movement's decision to allow driving to synagogue on Shabbat effectively destroyed the insular Conservative community. What sense does it make, after all, to pay a huge premium for a house within walking distance of a synagogue, if you are allowed to drive? What was initially seen, with all good intentions at the time, as a ruling designed to "bring people closer" to the synagogue ultimately resulted in convincing many more to "move away."[18]

---

15. Rabbis Morris Adler, Jacob Agus and Theodore Friedman, "A Responsum on the Sabbath," in *Tradition and Change*, ed. Mordecai Waxman (New York, Burning Bush Press, 1958), pp. 351 ff.

16. David Novak, *Law and Theology in Judaism*, vol. 1 (New York: Ktav, 1974), chapter 3.

17. Centuries ago, the rabbis acknowledged this fundamental truth through their repeated reluctance to enact decrees "subject to varying limits." Talmud Bavli Shabbat 35b; Megilla 18b; Gittin 14a; Bava Batra 21a; Chullin 9a; Chullin 32a.

18. In researching this study, I discovered that the same conclusion that I reached those thirty years ago concerning this ruling of the Conservative movement was openly

For centuries, the delicate balance between preservation and application of Jewish law has maintained us as a people. As experience shows us again and again, the upending of that balance for any predetermined agenda or goal, no matter how well-intentioned, can have very damaging consequences.

── **B** ──

We have clearly argued a strong case for the centrality of rabbinic authority in Jewish thought. A fundamental question, however, remains: How far does such authority extend? Must rabbis be consulted in every arena of life or is their expertise limited to specific areas of halachic application?

This question serves as the focus of an ongoing debate over what is popularly referred to in our time as *da'at Torah* (knowledge of Torah).[19] The issues involved shape personal and communal behavior, and clearly separate different groups within today's Orthodox community.

At one end of the spectrum lie those within the Chareidi (fervently Orthodox) community who maintain that rabbinic scholarship must be consulted not only in matters of Jewish law but concerning all major life issues. *Since halacha is meant to guide every aspect of a Jew's life*, the argument goes, *and since Torah shapes one's entire worldview, the perspective of those steeped in the law should be sought out on all issues.*

An early iteration of the concept of *da'at Torah* in modern times can be found in the writings of Rabbi Yisrael Meir Kagan, one of the most influential Jewish scholars of the late nineteenth and early twentieth centuries, best known as the Chafetz Chaim: "He whose knowledge is truly *da'at Torah* can resolve all queries in human experience, both in the general and in the

──

verbalized in 2003 by Rabbi Ismar Schorsch, then chancellor of the Jewish Theological Seminary, the Conservative movement's flagship institution. At the biennial convention of the Conservative movement in Dallas in 2003, Rabbi Schorsch declared that by sanctioning travel on the Sabbath, the Conservative movement "gave up on the desirability of living close to the synagogue and creating a Shabbos community." Cited in Nacha Cattan, "Conservative Head Calls Sabbath-Driving Rule a 'Mistake'" *Jewish Daily Forward*, November 7, 2003, http://forward.com/articles/6998/conservative-head-calls-sabbath-driving-rule-a/#ixzz37cTyNzJD.

19. I am grateful to Rabbi Anthony Manning for his excellent organization of the sources used in this study, compiled in the source sheet for his series Da'at Torah and Rabbinic Authority, Shiur 1 – Modern Approaches to Da'at Torah, available on his website at www.rabbimanning.com.

specific. There is only one caveat. His *da'at Torah* must be pure, untainted by any outside influence at all."[20]

In even more definitive terms, another towering figure of twentieth-century Chareidi Orthodoxy, Rabbi Avraham Yeshaya Karelitz, the Chazon Ish, argues that those who "divide the Torah into two" by relegating the authority of the rabbis to the area of ritual, as opposed to guidance in everyday life, perpetuate "the viewpoint held by the heretics of old in Germany who drove their brethren to assimilate with the other nations.

"For one to distinguish between instruction regarding ritual and matters of [overall] legislation," the Chazon Ish continues, "constitutes denigration of the sages and places one in the category of those who have no place in the world to come."[21]

More currently, in an oft-reprinted column that first appeared in the New York *Jewish Week*, Rabbi Avi Shafran, the director of public affairs for the flagship American Chareidi organization Agudath Israel, cogently explains the Chareidi approach to *da'at Torah* as follows:

> *Da'at Torah* is not some Jewish equivalent to the Catholic doctrine of papal infallibility. Not only can rabbis make mistakes of judgment, there is an entire tractate of the Talmud, Horiut, predicated on the assumption that they can, that even the Sanhedrin is capable of erring, even in halachic matters.
>
> What *da'at Torah* means, simply put, is that those most imbued with Torah-knowledge and who have internalized a large degree of the perfection of values and refinement of character that the Torah idealizes, are thereby rendered particularly, indeed extraordinarily, qualified to offer an authentic Jewish perspective on matters of import to Jews – just as expert doctors are those most qualified (though still fallible, to be sure) to offer medical advice.[22]

Rabbi Shafran goes on to argue that *da'at Torah* is far from a new concept, as some might argue, but is, instead, the current iteration of the age-old idea of *emunat chachamim* (trust in the judgment of the Torah-wise).[23]

---

20. The Chafetz Chaim's commentary on the Torah with the commentary of Rabbi Chaim Greineman, 1943.
21. Chazon Ish, *Hitorerut* (Bnei Brak, 1988).
22. Avi Shafran, "What Da'at Torah Really Means," New York *Jewish Week*, March 21, 2003.
23. Ibid.

Acceptance of the notion of *da'at Torah* within the Chareidi community is fundamentally uniform, with the phenomenon finding its strongest iteration in Chassidic circles, where the Rebbe is seen as a vessel for the communication of God's will.

At the opposite end of the Orthodox spectrum lie those who find themselves squarely within the Modern Orthodox community, where the concept of *da'at Torah* remains the subject of much lively internal debate and discussion. While clearly acknowledging the centrality of rabbinic authority in halachic matters, Modern Orthodox scholars are more likely to consider the limitation of that authority strictly to areas of clear halachic concern and to validate the expertise of others in extra-halachic matters. The philosophical line these scholars draw is often carefully nuanced, as they acknowledge the inherent wisdom of those steeped in Torah knowledge, yet recognize possible boundaries to their unquestioned authority.

A careful reading of the comments of Rabbi Aharon Lichtenstein, rosh yeshiva of Yeshivat Har Etzion and one of the preeminent spokesmen for the Modern Orthodox and Religious Zionist community today, is well worth the effort. With customary sensitivity and deep intellectual honesty, this scholar outlines the dynamic tension between philosophy and practice that, to his mind, marks the issue of *da'at Torah* in our day:

> This brings us to the familiar shibboleth of *da'at Torah*. This concept is generally in disrepute among varieties of modern Orthodoxy, who have sought to challenge both its historical progeny and its philosophical validity. I must confess that I find myself, in principle, more favorably disposed towards the idea. I readily concede that the concept, in its more overarching permutations, is of relatively recent vintage.... Furthermore, I freely concede that, at times, acknowledged leaders of the Torah world issue pronouncements which anyone with even a trace of modern sensibility finds it difficult to fathom, let alone accept....
>
> Nevertheless, beyond reservations, I find the alternate view, that *gedolei Torah* [Torah sages] are professional experts whose authority and wisdom can ordinarily be regarded as confined to the area of their technical proficiency, simply inconceivable. Our abiding historical faith in the efficacy of Torah as a pervasive ennobling, informing and enriching force dictates adoption of the concept of *da'at Torah* in some form or measure. Still, contrary to the historical course of the idea, I find it less applicable today than heretofore. At a time when many *gedolim*

do not spring organically from the dominant Jewish community to whose apex they rise, but rather distance themselves from it; when the ability to understand and communicate in a shared cultural or even verbal language is, by design, limited – the capacity of even a *gadol* to intuit the sociohistorical dynamics of his ambient setting is almost inevitably affected."[24]

Stronger words are penned by another renowned Religious Zionist scholar and halachist, Rabbi Nachum Rabinovitch, the rosh yeshiva of Yeshivat Birkat Moshe in Ma'ale Adumim, as he expresses his fears over the loss of independent thought in the face of an absolute adherence to the current notion of *da'at Torah*.

> We are not talking about asking advice of those who are experienced and wise in Torah, whose righteousness, Torah knowledge and brilliance provide good guidance and sound advice. It is surely good for any person to seek advice from those who are greater and better than he. But there is a difference between asking advice and taking personal responsibility for one's actions, and relying on others with absolutely no independent thought. There are those who label such childish behavior as '*emunat hachamim* [sic]' while in reality it is a distortion of this great attribute. Instead of acquiring true Torah, those who cling to this distorted '*emunat hakhamim*' distance themselves from the light of Torah and are ultimately incapable of distinguishing between right and wrong.[25]

As is often the case with current critical issues, much of the discussion in the Modern Orthodox community concerning *da'at Torah* centers on the attempt to retrospectively define the position of the late Rabbi Joseph Soloveitchik, the undisputed "Rav" (mentor) of the Modern Orthodox movement.

24. Rabbi Aharon Lichtenstein, "Legitimization of Modernity: Classical and Contemporary," in *Engaging Modernity: Rabbinic Leaders and the Challenge of the Twentieth Century*, ed. Moshe Z. Sokol, The Orthodox Forum (Northvale, NJ: Jason Aronson, 1997), pp. 20–22.
25. Rabbi Nachum Rabinovitch, "What Is Emunat Hakhamim," *Hakirah: The Flatbush Journal of Jewish Law and Thought* 5 (Fall 2007): 45.

On the one hand, in an oft-quoted eulogy for Rabbi Chaim Ozer Grodzinski, the preeminent halachic authority in Vilna during the late eighteenth and early nineteenth centuries, the Rav offers an emphatic defense of *da'at Torah*: "The very same priest whose mind was suffused with the holiness of the Torah of Rabbi Akiva and Rabbi Eliezer, of Abbaye and Rava, of the Rambam and the Ra'avad, of the Beit Yosef and the Rema, could also discern with the Holy Spirit the solution to all current political questions, to all worldly matters, to all ongoing current demands...."[26]

On the other hand, in a speech delivered to the Zionist organization, Mizrachi, in 1962, the Rav vigorously defends the actions of the Zionist pioneers who, against the stated positions of many halachic authorities of their day, paved the way for the return to Zion and the establishment of the State of Israel. Distinguishing between "technical legal matters," handed by God to the authority of the sages, and "historical questions...relating to the destiny of the Eternal People." the Rav declares: "I would like to ask a simple question: what would the yeshivot and Torah scholars rescued from the Holocaust – those burning embers taken from the fire – have done if the Joseph of 5662 [the Zionists] had not trod a path for them in the land of Israel, and had not made possible the transplanting of the Tree of Life of Lithuania and other lands in the Holy Land?"[27]

Overwhelming anecdotal testimony is offered by some of the Rav's most illustrious students of his clear encouragement of independent thought. Rabbi Walter Wurzburger, a well-known Modern Orthodox philosopher and author in his own right, thus maintains:

> But even more important is the Rav's general approach to the nature of rabbinic authority, which in his view was limited to the domain of *pesak halakha*. He respected the right of individuals to form their own opinions and attitudes with respect to matters that were not subject to halakhic legislation. Because of his respect for human autonomy and individuality, he never wanted to impose his particular attitudes upon others or even offer his personal opinions as *Da'at Torah*. On the contrary, when I turned to him for guidance on policy matters, which

26. Rabbi Joseph Soloveitchik, "Eulogy for Rabbi Chaim Ozer Grodzinski," *Ha-Pardes* 14, no. 7 (September 1940): 5–9.
27. Rabbi Joseph B. Soloveitchik, *Chamesh Drashot*, trans. David Telzner (Jerusalem: Machon Tal Orot, 1973), p. 23.

at times also involved halakhic considerations, he frequently replied that I should rely on my own judgment. Similarly, whenever the Rav expounded on his philosophy of halakha, he stressed that these were merely his personal opinions which he was prepared to share with others but which did not possess any kind of authoritative status.[28]

Rabbi Shalom Carmy, professor of philosophy at Yeshiva University and editor of the scholarly Orthodox periodical *Tradition*, sums up the evidence concerning the Rav's attitude towards rabbinic authority as follows:

> There is enough public oral evidence that the Rav did not favor direct rabbinic intervention in political affairs, especially when they lack the requisite expertise to speak with authority. His 1967 ruling that decisions about possible territorial compromise in the land of Israel for the sake of peace should be made by experts in the field, rather than by rabbis, is currently the most discussed example of his outlook. While I am reluctant to rely on private comments, I am sure that many who enjoyed the Rav's company can confirm my recollections of sarcasm on the subject of rabbis whose adherents encouraged them to pontificate on matters of which they were inadequately informed. If his outlook can be inferred from his practice, it is appropriate for *gedolei Torah* who comment on public matters to recognize the complexity of human affairs and the existence of different informed opinions on most contested questions, and to modulate their voices accordingly.[29]

Finally, we return to the words of Rabbi Aharon Lichtenstein, this time as he traces the development of the Rav's attitude in these matters. Rabbi Lichtenstein's testimony is particularly significant, for he speaks not only as a dedicated student of this great sage but also from his unique, personally close vantage point as the Rav's son-in-law.

---

28. Rabbi Walter Wurzburger, "Rav Joseph B. Soloveitchik as a Posek of Post-Modern Orthodoxy," *Tradition* 29, no. 1 (Fall 1994).
29. Rabbi Shalom Carmy, "'The Heart Pained by the Pain of the People': Rabbinic Leadership in Two Discussions by R. Joseph B. Soloveitchik," *Torah u-Madda Journal* 13 (2005): 10.

True, he did not, in the long run, hold aloft the banner of the ideology that is now termed "Da'at Torah," which maintains that every political question has an essentially halakhic character, and is thus susceptible to the obligatory and exclusive decisions of the gedolei Torah. At first he inclined to this view, and even asserted it with enthusiasm [see extracts from his eulogy for Rabbi Chaim Ozer Grodzinski above]....

After a time, he abandoned this view, and in the course of decades he accepted and even sharpened the distinction between matters involving mitzvot (*divrei mitzvah*), which are to be decided by halachic decision-makers, and other matters (*divrei reshut*), in which significant weight is attached to the opinion and authorities of other leaders, or to private judgment. Nevertheless, although he rejected the decisive reach of rabbinic authority in political matters, he was insistent that such matters be determined from a perspective of refined spirituality and in consonance with Torah values. And he fully recognized that he was one of the few who could bring the proper measure of spirituality to bear upon Religious Zionism so as to ensure its standing as a Torah movement.[30]

On the occasion of the Rav's passing in 1982, I spoke in my Englewood synagogue, summarizing my two short years of study with this great sage. "What sets the Rav apart in my mind," I told my congregants, "was that many other rabbinic teachers taught us, '*think like I think*.' The Rav, in contrast, taught us, '*think, like I think*.' He challenged us to think for ourselves."

The depth of the Rav's charge towards independent thought on the part of the students can be seen in the astonishingly wide range of views on all issues possessed by those who continue to identify as his students today. This range ultimately reflects both the strength and the weakness of the more liberal approach to *da'at Torah*. Such an approach on the part of a master teacher like the Rav certainly encourages greater creativity and independence in the application and study of the law. At the same time, however, it encourages an at times confusing proliferation of halachic and philosophical viewpoints, many of which are strongly at odds with each other.

---

30. Rabbi Aharon Lichtenstein, *Leaves of Faith: The World of Jewish Learning* (Jersey City, NJ: Ktav, 2003), vol. 1, pp. 227–228.

How far does rabbinic authority extend? The question will always be front and center as the Orthodox community continues its journey, affecting the formulation of critical decisions ranging from the personal to the communal, for years to come.

4 Kingly Concerns

Context

The Torah opens a review of the laws governing the establishment of a Jewish monarchy with the following two verses:

> When you come to the land that the Lord your God gives to you, and you possess it and settle in it, and you will say: "I will set over myself a king, like all the nations that surround me."
>
> You shall certainly set over yourselves a king whom the Lord your God shall choose; from among your brethren you shall set over yourselves a king; you cannot place over yourselves a foreign man, who is not your brother.[1]

The Talmudic scholars view the appointment of a king as an obligation, one of three positive commandments incumbent on the Israelites upon entry into the land.[2]

Questions

The wording of this mitzva is abundantly strange. Why does the Torah base the appointment of a king on the nation's expressed desire to "set over myself a king, like all the nations that surround me"? If the establishment of a monarchy is a positive biblical commandment, why doesn't the Torah simply say: *When you come to the land, appoint for yourselves a king*? Why would God present a mitzva as developing from the nation's desire to follow the mores of surrounding societies?

The existence of a direct positive commandment to appoint a king also seems to fly in the face of the historical narrative surrounding the selection of Shaul, the first king of Israel. The book of Shmuel clearly records the extreme displeasure with which the prophet Shmuel greeted the nation's

---

1. Devarim 17:14–15.
2. Talmud Bavli Sanhedrin 20b.

request: "Place for us a king, to judge us like all the nations."[3] Even further, when God commands Shmuel to accede to the nation's request – but only after informing them of the laws that will govern a future king's power over them – the prophet clearly uses the opportunity to dissuade the nation from their intended path.[4] If the appointment of the king is a mitzva, why is Shmuel upset with the people's request and why does he attempt to discourage them from fulfilling this positive biblical commandment?

Approaches

——A——

The earliest recorded attempts to address the apparent disconnect between the biblical mitzva to establish a monarchy and Shmuel's reaction to the nation's eventual request are found in the Tosefta, a source from the Mishnaic period. There, three possible approaches are presented.

1. An anonymous position postulates that the nation's request was premature. The time had not yet arrived for the establishment of the monarchy.

2. Rabbi Nehorai maintains that the mitzva to appoint a king is only recorded in the Torah in anticipation of the nation's future murmurings. For this reason, the Torah hinges the mitzva upon the nation's expressed desire to "set over myself a king, like all the nations that surround me."

3. Finally, Rabbi Eliezer the son of Rabbi Yossi argues that the text in the book of Shmuel actually outlines two separate requests that are made of the prophet, one of which was appropriate and one of which was not. The elders first approached Shmuel with the fitting request "Place for us a king, to judge us." The people then inappropriately added: "[That we may be also] like all the other nations." Shmuel was not displeased with the elders' desire to fulfill the mitzva of establishing a monarchy. His upset developed only in response to the people's improper addendum.[5]

——B——

A major philosophical divide separates one of the approaches cited in the Tosefta from the other two. Responses one and three, quoted anonymously

---

3. Shmuel I 8:5.
4. Shmuel I 8:6–18.
5. Tosefta Sanhedrin 4:3.

and in the name of Rabbi Eliezer, do not, in any way, challenge the fundamental character of the biblical mitzva to establish a monarchy. According
to these answers, the concerns that confronted Shmuel were external in
nature. The prophet became upset with the people not because of their basic
request, but because they approached him either prematurely or improperly.
The answer suggested by Rabbi Nehorai, however, *calls the very nature of
the mitzva to establish a monarchy into question.*

Rabbi Nehorai seems to view this mitzva not as a preferred path, but
as a concession to the inevitable. God permits the nation to appoint a king
only because the people themselves will ultimately insist upon doing so.
Were the people willing to rely upon divine rule, without the selection of
a ruler of flesh and blood, there would be no need for the establishment of
a monarchy, with all of its potential for corruption and excess.

Seen through the eyes of Rabbi Nehorai, this mitzva becomes one of
a select group of imperatives *commanded to the people as concessions to
their own limitations.* Among such phenomena that we have already noted
are the Rambam's contention in his *Guide to the Perplexed* that the institution of *korbanot* (ritual offerings) resulted from God's recognition of the
Israelites' inability to suddenly abandon practices in which they had been
steeped (see *Vayikra*: Vayikra 1, *Approaches* A, B); the Midrashic view of
the building of the Mishkan (the wilderness Sanctuary) as God's response
to the sin of the golden calf (see *Shmot*: Teruma 1, *Approaches* A–C); and
the rabbinic belief that the rituals imposed upon a Jewish indentured
servant who desires to remain in his master's service after his release date
are designed to dissuade the servant from his chosen path of continued
servitude (see *Shmot*: Mishpatim 1, *Approaches* I F). We will also see that
the laws governing marriage to an alien woman captured in war can be
similarly interpreted as dissuasive in nature (see Ki Tetzei 1). Concerning
some of these mitzvot, the rabbis openly comment that "The Torah does
not speak [of these obligations] other than to address the *yetzer hara* (the
evil inclination)." *These commandments do not represent preferred paths
but are, instead, paths permitted as concessions to man's own impulses.*[6]

---

6. Talmud Bavli Kiddushin 21b.

—— C ——

Once the battle lines are drawn in the Tosefta concerning the nature of the biblical commandment to appoint a king, later scholars weigh in, each attempting to reconcile the mandate in Devarim with Shmuel's eventual reluctance to allow the nation to proceed. Most of the authorities accept the existence of a positive mitzva to establish a monarchy as a given, and are therefore forced to explain Shmuel's negative reaction to the people's request. A number of answers posed by these scholars also address the puzzling language in the biblical text that appears to base the mitzva upon the people's desire to be like other nations.

The Ramban, for example, separates the Torah's phrase "and you will say: 'I will set over myself a king, like all the nations that surround me'" into two. The first part of the phrase, "and you will say: 'I will set over myself a king...,'" speaks to the requisite process through which the mitzva must be fulfilled. The people must "*say: 'I will set over myself a king'*"; that is, the people must inform the Kohanim, the Levi'im and the judges of their desire to establish a monarchy. Such consultation with the nation's existing leadership is apparently required in order to ensure a smooth, peaceful governmental transition. The second part of the phrase, "...like all the nations that surround me," however, does not speak to the performance of the mitzva at all, but is, instead, *a prophetic foreshadowing of the future*. The nation, the Torah predicts, will ultimately frame their appeal inappropriately when they request of Shmuel, "Place for us a king, to judge us like all the nations." The nation's justified desire for a king will be tainted by their yearning to be "like all the nations."[7]

The Ramban sees similar foreshadowing of the future on other occasions in the text of Devarim. He notes, for example, that in Parshat Va'etchanan, Moshe's warning "When you give birth to children and grandchildren, and you will have been long in the land, and you will grow corrupt..."[8] is not expressed conditionally, but with certainty. Moshe does not state, *if you grow corrupt*. Even as Moshe warns the nation not to sin, the Ramban maintains, the text foreshadows their inevitable future failure.[9]

In his commentary on the book of Bereishit, the Ramban also suggests

---

7. Ramban, Devarim 17:14.
8. Devarim 4:25.
9. Ramban, Devarim 4:25–26.

that the nation sins through a rejection of Shmuel's leadership. While the request for the establishment of a monarchy would have been appropriate at other times, this scholar maintains, the issue should never have been broached while the people were still under the leadership of a brilliant prophet and judge. Shmuel reacts negatively not to the nation's fundamental request, but to their flawed motivation. Even further, the Ramban continues, because of the nation's missteps, God's response to their request is limited. He allows for the appointment of a king, but insists that Shmuel coronate Shaul, from the tribe of Binyamin. Since all enduring royalty is destined to descend from the tribe of Yehuda,[10] Shaul's reign cannot lead to the establishment of a continuing royal line. Even Shaul's son, Yehonatan, will not rule after him.[11]

The Rambam, who codifies the mandate to appoint a king as a positive commandment in his list of mitzvot,[12] agrees with the Ramban's suggestion that the nation's sin ultimately lies in their rejection of Shmuel's leadership. "Their request," the Rambam maintains, "emerged out of a sense of rebelliousness. They did not ask out of a desire to perform a mitzva, but rather because they were rejecting [the leadership of] the prophet Shmuel."[13]

——— **D** ———

Some scholars, through careful reading of the text, determine flaws in other aspects of the nation's request of Shmuel, "Place for us a king, to judge us like all the nations."

Rabbeinu Nissim ben Reuven, for example, points out that the role of a king does not include the task of judging the people. Within the Torah's carefully calibrated system of governmental checks and balances, the fundamental responsibility for jurisprudence lies with the Sanhedrin and other courts. Had the nation requested the appointment of a king without erroneously delineating his function, their request would have been totally appropriate.[14]

The Kli Yakar notes that the nation's request of Shmuel, "Place *for us* a king…," does not match the Torah's mandate, "Place *upon yourselves* a

---

10. Bereishit 49:10.
11. Ramban, Bereishit 49:10.
12. Rambam, *Sefer Hamitzvot*, positive commandment 173.
13. Rambam, *Mishneh Torah*, Hilchot Melachim 1:2.
14. *Derashot HaRan*, drasha 11.

king." The Torah commands the nation to appoint a king *upon themselves*, so that the fear of his power will ensure their participation in the betterment of society. The nation, however, desires a king *for themselves*, a monarch they will be able to control, through political machination, for their own personal gain. When Shmuel reacts negatively to this request, God reassures him by noting that the people's desire for change is evidence of Shmuel's own unimpeachable character as a leader: *The nation wants a change, Shmuel, because of their inability to control you.* God then instructs the prophet to accede to the nation's request for a king but to first debunk their assumptions by informing them of the manifest power that a monarch will wield over their lives.[15]

—— **E** ——

For his part, the Ohr Hachaim perceives a tension between two different models of monarchy in the Devarim text.

The phrase "…and you will say: 'I will set over myself a king, like all the nations that surround me'" mirrors the expected request from the people for a king who, like the kings of other nations, will rely upon his own wisdom, cunning and strength to guide the nation in battle and conquest. With the commandment that follows, however, "You shall certainly set over yourselves a king whom the Lord your God shall choose," God instructs the people to appoint a different type of king, one whose primary motivation will be to determine and obey God's will. Only such a king, unlike the kings of other nations, is acceptable to God. Only such a king will bring honor and glory to the nation.[16]

—— **F** ——

Finally, swimming against an overwhelming tide, the Abravanel leads a small group of commentaries who completely deny the existence of a positive biblical commandment to appoint a king. Basing his position on the Torah's formulation "…and you will say: 'I will set over myself a king, like all the nations that surround me,'" the Abravanel channels the centuries-earlier position of Rabbi Nehorai and maintains that the Torah only *grants the nation permission* to establish a monarchy upon their insistence to do

---

15. Kli Yakar, Devarim 17:15.
16. Ohr Hachaim, Devarim 17:14.

so. The Abravanel goes one step further, however, by insisting that the Talmud's identification of the appointment of a king as a mitzva refers not to the appointment itself, but to the Torah's stipulations guiding that appointment. Once the people decide to establish a monarchy, they are obligated to comply with the requirements outlined in the text. The decision to select a king in the first place, however, is no mitzva at all.

From the perspective of the Abravanel, Shmuel's objection to the nation's request for a king is fully understandable. The prophet regrets the nation's choice and, recognizing the dangers inherent in the establishment of a monarchy, attempts to dissuade them from their intended path. *You have no need for a king of flesh and blood*, Shmuel argues. *The Lord is your King, and His divine authority should suffice.*[17]

Points to Ponder

To king or not to king… Does God desire a Jewish monarchy?

As is true with so many critical issues, regardless of the final decision, the existence of the discussion itself is powerfully significant. In this case, the debate concerning a Jewish monarch reflects the tension between two important philosophical poles: a healthy respect for the importance of a strong government and a deep belief that each individual must be a servant of God and not a servant of other men.

For a nation that has experienced unimaginable persecution at the hands of countless tyrants, the Jewish people have been taught to show surprising loyalty to governmental authority, Jewish and non-Jewish alike. Rabbi Hanina, the deputy High Priest, is quoted in Pirkei Avot as saying: "Pray for the welfare of the government, since but for fear of it, a person would swallow up his fellow alive."[18] Halacha mandates that, upon seeing a Jewish king, an individual should recite the blessing "Blessed art Thou, Lord our God, Who has apportioned of His glory to those who fear Him," and, upon seeing a non-Jewish king, the blessing "Blessed art Thou, Lord our God, Who has given of His glory to flesh and blood" should be recited.[19]

At the same time, Jewish national history, born in the transition from

17. Abravanel, Devarim 17:14.
18. Pirkei Avot 3:2.
19. Talmud Bavli Brachot 58a.

slavery to freedom, is replete with struggles against tyranny. No one understands better than the Jew the overwhelming cruelty and pain that can be
experienced at the hands of corrupt governments. No people has been vic-
timized more than the Jews, by powerful rulers across the face of history.

To king or not to king… Does God desire a Jewish monarchy? The
debate continues to rage. Given what's at stake, it could not be otherwise…

5 Halachic Hide-and-Seek?

Context

Moshe repeats and elaborates upon the obligation, originally outlined in the book of Bamidbar,[1] to establish a minimum of three *arei miklat* (cities of refuge) in Canaan upon the conquest and settlement of the land. These cities, along with three such cities in the Transjordan already designated by Moshe,[2] are to serve as places of safety for individuals found guilty of killing another *b'shogeg* (unintentionally).[3]

Based upon the passages here and in Bamidbar, the Mishnaic scholars record procedures to be observed following an event of murder/manslaughter within the community:

1. An individual who kills another, under any circumstances, should immediately flee to a city of refuge.
2. The court of the city where the event occurred then summons the perpetrator to return and stand trial.
3. A perpetrator who is found by the court to have acted *b'meizid* (with full intent) and to be guilty of the death penalty under the law is handed over to the *go'el hadam*, the blood avenger, for execution. The *go'el hadam* is a close relative of the victim who serves as the agent of the court in carrying out the sentence of execution.
4. A perpetrator who is found to have acted *b'oness*, as a result of coercion or force of circumstance (i.e., as a result of an accident), is set free.
5. A perpetrator who is found guilty of an act that falls into the category of *shogeg*, a specific level of unintentionality, is returned

---

1. Bamidbar 35:9–28.
2. Devarim 4:41–43.
3. Ibid., 19:1–10.

to the city of refuge, where he is to remain until the death of the Kohen Gadol (the High Priest).[4]

6. A perpetrator found liable to exile who fails to flee to a city of refuge or who leaves such a city prematurely becomes liable to death. Rabbi Yossi the Galilean maintains that, under such circumstances, the *goʾel hadam* is obligated to execute the criminal, while others have the right to do so. Rabbi Akiva argues that the *goʾel hadam* is permitted to execute the criminal, while others are forbidden from – but not punished for – doing so.[5] The Rambam codifies the law according to Rabbi Akiva.[6]

7. Clear, direct paths must be established towards the *arei miklat* and two sages are assigned to accompany the convict back to the city after the court hearing, in order to dissuade a *goʾel hadam* from taking action before the city is reached.[7]

Questions

What exactly is *retzicha biʾshgaga*, the level of unintentional killing that warrants exile to an *ir miklat*? Is negligence involved in such an act and, if so, to what degree?

Is physical protection from the blood avenger the sole purpose of a sentence of exile, or are there other dimensions to exile, such as punishment or atonement for the crime?

The Torah mandates that exiles are to be set free with the death of the Kohen Gadol. Why does the Torah use such an arbitrary yardstick in determining the length of a perpetrator's exile? What, if any, philosophical relationship exists between the fate of the Kohen Gadol and the fate of the *rotzeiʾach*?

The inclusion in Torah law of the concept of a *goʾel hadam*, a blood avenger, is deeply unsettling. In all other cases of halachic capital punishment, the court maintains control over the administration of the law. Why in this case does the Torah hand over authority for execution of the perpetrator to the victim's relative? By doing so, the Torah appears to accept and perpetuate the primitive concept of a "familial blood feud." Doesn't

---

4. Mishna Makkot 2:6.
5. Ibid., 2:7.
6. Rambam, *Mishneh Torah*, Hilchot Rotzeiʾach Uʾshmirat Hanefesh 5:10.
7. Mishna Makkot 2:5.

such an approach increase the real potential for escalating violence within Israelite society? The entire thrust of Parshat Shoftim – the establishment of a structured judicial system and the prevention of vigilante justice – would seem to be contradicted by this one halachic decision. The Torah's moral voice, in this area of law, seems strangely silent.

Approaches

——A——————————————————————————————

In order to define *retzicha bi'shgaga*, we must review the general approach of Jewish law to culpability for personal actions and apply that approach specifically to cases of murder/manslaughter.

[Note: A discussion of many of these points can be found in *Vayikra*: Vayikra 3. For the purposes of our current study, however, I will again summarize some of the salient points and elaborate upon others.]

Halachically, responsibility for acts performed falls along a range, based upon the degree of intentionality of an individual's actions. This range is defined by the endpoints of *oness* (pure accident or force) at the bottom and *meizid* (acts performed with full intentionality) at the top. An individual who commits an act as a result of *oness* carries no guilt, while, conversely, an individual who commits an act *b'meizid*, with full premeditation, must be punished to the fullest extent of the law.

Somewhere in the middle of this spectrum of culpability lies the category of *shogeg*, unintentional acts for which the perpetrator, nonetheless, bears a certain degree of responsibility. Although unintended, acts committed *b'shogeg* could have been avoided through greater care and attention. The very existence of this category, and its distinction from the fully blameless category of *oness*, indicates that *not all unintentional acts are "equal" in the eyes of Jewish law.*

In cases of murder/manslaughter, the criterion for *shogeg* is elucidated in a pivotal verse in the parsha before us, as the Torah constructs the paradigm of a woodcutter who, in the act of cutting a tree, mortally wounds a bystander, *b'shogeg*: "And he who will come together with his fellow into the forest to hew trees, and his hand swings the ax to cut the tree, and the iron slips from the tree [alternately, the wood] and finds his fellow and he dies, he [the woodcutter] shall flee to one of these cities and live."[8]

---

8. Devarim 19:5.

The text is not completely clear. What are the details of this crime? At issue is the meaning of the enigmatic phrase *v'nashal habarzel min ha'etz*, "the iron slips from the *etz*." The term *etz* can be defined either as "tree" or as "wood." The text is, therefore, open to interpretation. What exactly causes the death of the bystander?

Two distinct opinions are presented in the Mishna based on the two possible understandings of the term *etz*. Rebbe (Rabbi Yehuda Hanasi) interprets the term *etz* as "tree" and maintains that the Torah refers to a case where the striking ax causes a woodchip to fly off the tree, tragically "finding" and killing the bystander.[9] Rebbe's rabbinic colleagues, however, interpreting the term *etz* as "wood," insist that the Torah refers to a case where the *ax head* slips off its wooden handle, becoming a lethal projectile that strikes and kills the victim.[10]

Rebbe's benchmarks for guilt are clearly much more onerous than those of his colleagues. The woodcutter is guilty, *b'shogeg*, even for lethal damage caused by a flying splinter, a phenomenon that reflects minimal negligence on the part of the woodcutter. Had the ax head killed the victim, Rebbe feels, exile would not have been an adequate sentence. The woodcutter's degree of guilt for failing to keep his equipment in good working order would have placed him too high on the spectrum of intent, somewhere between *shogeg* and *meizid*.[11]

Rebbe's colleagues, on the other hand, adopt a more lenient view. The category of *shogeg*, for which exile is warranted, reflects the case where the ax head causes the damage. Had the wood chip killed the victim, the woodcutter would have been almost blameless, not responsible for indirect events beyond his control. Such a case lies on the spectrum somewhere between *oness* and *shogeg*, and a sentence of exile would have been too severe.

The Rambam and other halachists codify the practical law in favor of the lenient position of Rebbe's colleagues.[12]

9. Talmud Bavli Makkot 7b; Rashi, ibid. Note: the Rambam (*Mishneh Torah*, Hilchot Rotzei'ach U'shmirat Hanefesh 6:15) differs from Rashi and explains Rebbe as referring to a case where the ax head separates from the handle as a result of striking the tree and his colleagues as referring to a case where the ax head separates from the handle before striking the tree. Rabbeinu Chananel (Makkot 7b) cites both the position of Rashi and the position of the Rambam in his commentary.
10. Talmud Bavli Makkot 7b; Rabbeinu Chananel, ibid.
11. Rabbeinu Chananel, ibid.
12. Rambam, ibid.

As we have previously noted, the practical applications of the debate between Rebbe and his colleagues are potentially manifold, even in our day. What, for example, is the level of guilt of the driver of a car that tragically strikes and kills a pedestrian? What would the legal verdict be, according to each of the halachic protagonists, if the accident were the result of brake failure of a recently inspected car? What if the car was neither recently inspected nor properly maintained? What if the driver was talking on a cell phone, otherwise preoccupied, or even inebriated at the time of the accident? Which of these cases would be classified as *shogeg* and which would fall elsewhere on the spectrum of intention?

— **B** ————————————————————————————

Other aspects of the text are also carefully examined by the rabbis to determine details that might affect the outcome of the law. The opening phrase, "And he who will come together with his friend into the forest…," for example, is understood by the rabbis as indicating that the perpetrator is liable to exile only if the incident occurs in a location equally accessible to both the perpetrator and the victim.

If the tragic incident unfolds on the perpetrator's property, however, he is not sentenced to exile in a city of refuge. Under such conditions, the "woodcutter" had no reason to assume that others would be present as he worked. His legal level of responsibility for the safety of potential bystanders would therefore have been dramatically reduced.[13]

— **C** ————————————————————————————

These discussions and others reflect the tremendous care marking the rabbinic efforts to clearly identify those acts of manslaughter falling into the category of *shogeg*. Hanging in the balance, from their perspective, is the issue of precision in the application of the law. Only an individual whose "crime" fits exactly into the appropriate band on the spectrum of culpability should be sentenced to exile to an *ir miklat*.

The rabbinic concerns for precision in this area of law are heightened by their multi-layered view of the ultimate purpose of exile to a city of refuge. For while, as we have seen, such exile provides both *punishment* for the perpetrator's offense and *protection* from execution at the hands of

—————————————
13. Mishna Makkot 2:2.

the blood avenger, another goal is also accomplished through the court's accurate sentencing of the perpetrator. *When the sentence fits the crime, exile serves as atonement.* On numerous occasions, the Talmud discusses whether or not exile can serve as proper atonement for a specific case of manslaughter, at times determining that the offense is too severe to be atoned for by exile and at times determining that the offense is not severe enough to warrant such atonement.[14] These discussions reflect the general halachic attitude that suitable punishment, meted out by an earthly court, actually benefits the perpetrators of specific crimes by enabling atonement that could not be achieved in any other way.[15]

The accurate identification of those actions falling into the category of *shogeg* thus becomes, in the eyes of the halacha, of critical importance.

——— **D** ———

Fascinating, as well, are the rabbinic edicts enacted to establish and maintain the proper character of the exile experience to an *ir miklat*. Under no condition, the rabbis recognize, can the sentence of exile be allowed to become more onerous than intended by Torah law. Building on the text, therefore, the authorities establish numerous laws to legislate the safety and sustenance of those sentenced to such a fate.

The *arei miklat*, the Talmudic authorities maintain, must be neither small towns nor large metropolises, but rather mid-sized cities.[16] If they are too small, Rashi explains, provisions for the inhabitants will become difficult to obtain, while if they are too large, the safety of the *rotzeiach* might become difficult to ensure.[17] These cities must be located in areas where water, marketplaces and lodging are plentiful and readily accessible. If these necessities become scarce, they must be replenished. The populations of the cities must be maintained at a proper balance. At no point should the percentage of convicts in the city's population be allowed to exceed fifty percent.[18] Animal traps, nets and the like may not be set up within the *arei miklat*, lest these items be used by the blood avenger against the *rotzeiach*. So concerned are the rabbis over the welfare of an individual

14. See for example Makkot 2a–b.
15. Rambam, *Mishneh Torah*, Hilchot Teshuva 1:4.
16. Talmud Bavli Makkot 10a.
17. Rashi, Makkot 10a.
18. Talmud Bavli Makkot 10b.

sentenced to exile that, based on the Torah's statement "he shall flee to one of these cities *and live*," they mandate that a perpetrator's spiritual mentor must accompany him into exile. The law, they maintain, must provide the perpetrator with the physical and spiritual ability to "live."[19]

——— E ———————————————————————————————————

In contrast to the logical laws designed to sustain the convict during his exile, the Torah's yardstick for determining the length of each exile period seems strikingly arbitrary. Why does Jewish law base an exile's release upon the death of the Kohen Gadol of his day? What philosophical connection does the Torah draw between the highest and lowest spiritual echelons of Israelite society, between the nation's ritual leader and an individual convicted of accidental or negligent manslaughter?

The Sifrei responds to this question by focusing on the chasm, rather than the connection, between the *rotzei'ach* and the Kohen Gadol. These individuals represent totally antithetical forces. The *rotzei'ach*, through his violent actions, causes the Divine Presence to depart from the land, while the Kohen Gadol, through his ministrations, causes the Divine Presence to rest in the land. Given this essential spiritual conflict, it is not appropriate for the exile to live freely in society during the Kohen Gadol's lifetime. The perpetrator must, therefore, remain in exile until the death of the High Priest.[20]

The Sforno suggests that the Torah bases the termination of exile upon the Kohen Gadol's death in order to transfer decisions to God that are simply too difficult for man to make. An earthly court, this sage argues, cannot properly distinguish between the various levels of intentionality that mark crimes of accidental or negligent manslaughter. On a pure level, these crimes are not all equal. The punishment deserved by each perpetrator will be dependent on a vast array of complex, individualized factors. Had the Torah created a standard length for the period of exile, to be applied in all cases, justice would not have been served. By basing the release of exiles on the death of the Kohen Gadol, the Torah finds a way to create unequal periods of punishment for each of these convicts. Using this yardstick, God will ensure that each convict receives a sentence commensurate with

---

19. Ibid.
20. Sifrei, Bamidbar 35:25.

his deeds, by causing his crime and his subsequent conviction to occur on dates appropriately distant from the death of the Kohen Gadol.[21]

In contrast to both the Sifrei and Sforno, the Talmud philosophically connects the fate of the *rotzei'ach* to the life (and death) of the Kohen Gadol. The High Priest's death releases a perpetrator from exile, the rabbis explain, because the Kohen actually bears a degree of responsibility for the perpetrator's crime. As the spiritual emissary of the nation, the Kohen is required to entreat God to bestow mercy upon his people. The occurrence of violence under a Kohen's watch is evidence of the absence or ineffectiveness of these prayers. The Torah therefore hinges the release of exiles upon the death of the Kohen Gadol, as his death will partially atone for their crimes.[22] A leader, the rabbis remind us, must always be mindful of the responsibility he bears for the quality and character of his people's journey.

Even more telling, perhaps, is a poignant additional link drawn by the rabbis between the exiles and the fate of the High Priests of their day. The Mishna records that the mothers of the High Priests would regularly provide convicts in the *arei miklat* with food and clothing in the hope that the convicts would find their stay comfortable and would, therefore, not pray for the speedy death of the priests.[23] So powerful is the force of prayer, the rabbis maintain, that the heartfelt supplication of a convict in exile can dramatically affect even the High Priest himself.

F

Finally, we turn to what may well be the most vexing problem before us. How can Torah law abide by the concept of a *go'el hadam*, a blood avenger? Given that all other sentences of capital punishment in Jewish law remain under the control of the court, why, in this case, does the law hand over responsibility for the execution to the victim's relative?

In her studies on Parshat Shoftim, Nehama Leibowitz offers a bold solution by suggesting that the Torah's acceptance of the blood avenger's involvement in the proceedings must be viewed as part of God's plan to slowly wean the nation away from the existing mores of the day. Citing the Rambam's approach to *korbanot* in his *Guide to the Perplexed* as precedent

---

21. Sforno, Bamidbar 35:25.
22. Talmud Bavli Makkot 11a.
23. Mishna Makkot 2:6.

(see *Vayikra*: Vayikra 1, *Approaches* II 2 A–B), Leibowitz argues that "the Torah does not demand an immediate and drastic change of life but reforms man through a gradual educational process."[24]

Whereas the Rambam was willing to consider existing societal practice as the basis for the establishment of *korbanot* in Jewish tradition, however, Leibowitz goes a major step further. The court appointment of the blood avenger in cases of murder/manslaughter is not only a concession to existing societal practice. This limited appointment is the first step in a conscious, gradual process designed to ultimately "stamp out the blood feud" entirely from Jewish experience.

Leibowitz quotes the observations of Shmuel David Luzzatto. This scholar insists that any attempt on the part of the Torah to completely deny a family's right to avenge the killing of one of their own would not have been successful. So ingrained were the attitudes of the day that failure on the part a family member to seek such vengeance would have been interpreted as a lack of love for the deceased. *God therefore makes the extraordinary decision to co-opt the problem.* He decrees that the blood avenger be incorporated into the legal process in a controlled, limited way. Prohibited from taking the law into his own hands, the *go'el hadam* can now only act as an agent of the court and is forced to respect its rendered verdict. He must accept the security granted to the convict by the city of refuge and can only act against the convict outside its walls and, even then, only as allowed by the law. Any extralegal action taken against the convict by the *go'el hadam* will be prosecuted to the fullest extent of the law. In this way the blood avenger becomes part of the legal process, creating a paradigm vastly different from the vigilante justice that characterizes surrounding society. And slowly, by denying the blood avenger the right to administer justice, by limiting his avenging powers only to the sphere of execution upon the decision of the court, the Torah will remove the bloodlust from Jewish society and eradicate the very institution of the "blood feud."[25]

Leibowitz suggests that proof of the success of this process can be found in the changing emphasis in Jewish law across the ages. The Torah, when discussing the establishment of the *arei miklat*, repeatedly stresses their role as protection for the perpetrator:

---

24. Leibowitz, *Studies in Devarim*, p. 190.
25. Shadal, Bamidbar 35:12.

...and I shall provide for you a place to which *he shall flee*.[26]

For the people of Israel and for the convert and for the resident in their midst these six cities shall be a refuge; for anyone who kills a person *bi'shgaga* to *flee* there.[27]

...*he shall flee* to one of these cities and live. Lest the blood avenger pursue...[28]

By the time we reach the era of the Mishna, however, the picture changes. The legal text no longer speaks of a perpetrator's *flight* to the *arei miklat*. Instead, the Mishna speaks of the perpetrator's journey as *exile*: "These are those *who are exiled*..."[29]

In Leibowitz's view, this shift of emphasis in the halachic text is indicative of a much larger shift in reality. By the time of the Mishna, God's plan to eradicate the institution of the blood feud from the psyche of the Jewish nation has succeeded:

> The cities of refuge were no longer needed as a protection against the angry pursuer since the blood avenger no longer pursued his victim. This instinct of personal vendetta had been blunted. No longer was it so deeply felt that the son who did not avenge his father's death was shirking his duty. The city of refuge remained not as an asylum but as a punishment, an exile that atoned for the iniquity.[30]

In carefully identified cases of unintentional manslaughter, when capital punishment would be too onerous for the crime and full release too lenient, the *arei miklat* emerge as the appropriate measure of punishment/atonement.

---

26. Shmot 21:13.
27. Bamidbar 35:15.
28. Devarim 19:5.
29. Mishna Makkot 2:1.
30. Leibowitz, *Studies in Devarim*, p. 193.

Ki Tetzei

CHAPTER 21:10–25:19

כי תצא

פרק כא:י-כה:יט

Parsha Summary

Mitzvot, mitzvot, mitzvot…

A burst of mitzvot characterizes Parshat Ki Tetzei, as Moshe conveys to the nation the details of ongoing observance that will characterize their relationship with God. This parsha contains the single greatest number of mitzvot of any parsha in the Torah – a total, according to the Rambam, of seventy-two.

After outlining the complex laws concerning an eishet yefat to'ar *(a beautiful woman captured in battle)*, specific rules concerning inheritance, and the decrees that will govern the puzzling, tragic case of the ben sorer u'moreh *(the rebellious son)*, the text touches upon a vast array of subjects. Included are edicts concerning lost and found objects; specific chukim *(laws for which no logical reason is clearly evident)*; defamation of character; forbidden and restricted marriages; preservation of the sanctity of the camp; vows; divorce; proper treatment of workers, debtors, orphans and widows; exemptions from armed service; corporal punishment; honesty in business dealings; and more.

The parsha closes with the admonition to remember the villainous actions of Amalek, the archenemy of the Jewish nation. God exhorts the people to eventually "eradicate the memory of Amalek from under the heaven."[1]

---

1. Devarim 25:19.

1 Beautiful Dreams?

Context

Parshat Ki Tetzei, the parsha with the greatest number of recorded mitzvot, opens with a set of instructions concerning the treatment of an *eishet yefat toʾar*, a beautiful woman who is captured in battle:

> When you will go out to war against your enemies, and the Lord your God will deliver them to your hand, and you will capture his captives.
>
> And you will see among the captives an *eishet yefat toʾar*, a beautiful woman, and you will desire her and you would take her as a wife.
>
> And you shall bring her into the midst of your home and she shall shave her head[2] and let her nails grow; and she shall remove from herself her garment of captivity; and she shall remain in your home; and she shall weep for her father and for her mother for a full month.
>
> And after that you may come to her and live with her and she shall be a wife to you.
>
> And it will be that if you do not desire her, then you shall let her go where she will. You may not sell her for money nor may you enslave her, because you have afflicted her.[3]

Questions

How are we to understand the Torah-mandated treatment of an *eishet yefat toʾar*?

---

2. We are following the generally accepted viewpoints in a series of Talmudic debates concerning the procedures to be followed in the treatment of an *eishet yefat toʾar* (see Talmud Bavli Yevamot 48a–b).
3. Devarim 21:10–14.

Why must this captive woman be subjected to such seemingly demeaning rituals?

Why, in addition, is this unfortunate woman ultimately granted no real control over her own fate?

Finally, why does the Torah allow a soldier to marry an alien woman captured in battle, even after all these rituals are carried out?

Approaches

[Note: Before continuing with this study, I recommend that the reader review our prior discussions concerning the Canaanite slave and the Torah's attitude towards war (see *Shmot*: Mishpatim 1, *Approaches* II A–E and *Bamidbar*: Matot-Masei 2). These studies provide a useful backdrop to our current discussion.]

—— **A** ——

The vast majority of scholars agree that, upon confronting this difficult narrative, we have once again entered an arena in the Torah where God mandates law as a *concession to man's frailty* (see Shoftim 4, *Approaches* B; Shoftim 5, *Approaches* F; *Shmot*: Teruma 1, *Approaches* A–C; *Vayikra*: Vayikra 1, *Approaches* A–C).

Had the Torah not allowed the Israelite soldier to wed this woman legally, the rabbis of the Talmud maintain, he would have been driven by his desires to initiate an illicit relationship with her, without permission of the law: "The Torah does not speak [of these obligations] other than to address the *yetzer hara* (the evil inclination). It is preferable that Israel should consume the meat of [animals] that are about to die than the meat of animals that are already dead."[4] *It is preferable for the Israelite soldier to wed the eishet yefat to'ar in a legally sanctioned manner than to continue his relationship with her without the law's consent.*"[5]

—— **B** ——

In the case of an *eishet yefat to'ar*, however, the Torah goes a significant step further. *Instead of passively conceding to man's weaknesses, the Torah actively uses the law as a means of dissuasion.* According to the overwhelming pre-

---

4. Talmud Bavli Kiddushin 21b.
5. Rashi, Devarim 21:11.

ponderance of rabbinic thought, the divinely ordained laws concerning the treatment of a captive woman are calculated to dissuade the soldier from following his intended path.[6]

Recognizing the power of the lust that drives the soldier towards his beautiful captive, the Torah deliberately constructs a course of action designed to cool the warrior's ardor and allow his calmer reason to prevail. The steps mandated in the text – the shaving of the captive woman's hair; the growing of her nails; the removal of her (attractive) clothing; even her placement in the warrior's home, where the soldier will encounter his captive over and over again in her disheveled state – are all designed to make this woman unattractive to her captor. As the soldier observes the *eishet yefat to'ar* stripped of her external beauty, he will hopefully come to see her for who she is, an unknown woman from an alien culture, unsuitable for his choice as a life partner.[7]

The Torah's granting of a period of mourning to the captive can also be seen as another significant step in this process. Numerous rationales are offered by the scholars for the granting of this license to grieve. One opinion in the Talmud views this period as an opportunity for the captive to mourn the loss of her past idolatrous beliefs and practices.[8] Some scholars, including the Rambam in his *Guide to the Perplexed*, interpret this allowance as a gesture of compassion on the Torah's part, affording the captive the limited spiritual solace that such bereavement might provide.[9] Many other authorities, however, maintain that the acts involved in personal mourning will distance the captive further from her captor by making her even more unattractive to the beholder.[10]

Finally, even the seemingly unconnected textual passages that follow the *eishet yefat to'ar* narrative are viewed by Midrashic authorities as additional warnings to the Israelite soldier, calculated to alert him to the real dangers of following his intended path. Immediately after outlining the laws guiding the treatment of the *eishet yefat to'ar*, the Torah turns its

---

6. Sifrei, Devarim 21:10–13; Talmud Bavli Yevamot 48a; Rashi, Devarim 21:13; Rashbam, Devarim 21:13 and numerous other sources.
7. Sifrei, Devarim 21: 10–13; Talmud Bavli Yevamot 48a; Rashi, Devarim 21:13; Rashbam, Devarim 21:13 and numerous other sources.
8. Talmud Bavli Yevamot 48b.
9. Rambam, *Moreh Nevuchim* 3:41.
10. Sifrei, Devarim 21:10–13; Rashi, Devarim 21:13.

attention to two other topics: the rights that must be granted to a firstborn son, even if he is the product of a "hated wife," and the laws governing the tragic case of a *ben sorer u'moreh*, a rebellious son.

The positioning of these themes in the text following the narrative concerning the treatment of the *eishet yefat to'ar*, the Midrash Tanchuma explains, is far from accidental. A union based solely on lust, without the benefit of shared backgrounds and values, is destined to produce a tension-filled, disharmonious home marked by "hated" wives and "rebellious children."[11] Any transient benefits to be gained from a relationship with a beautiful captive, the Torah warns, will soon give way to a life of enduring pain and sorrow.

—— C ——

The *eishet yefat to'ar* narrative thus emerges as a parallel to another passage in the book of Shmot that we have previously studied, detailing the treatment of an *eved Ivri* (an Israelite indentured servant) who desires to remain in service past his release date. There, the rabbis also view the rituals prescribed as dissuasive in nature, designed to convince the servant to choose freedom over continued servitude (see *Shmot*: Mishpatim 1, *Approaches* F).

In each of these cases, the Torah confronts an individual determined to travel along a self-destructive path. Yet, in each of these cases, the Torah recognizes that a proper path cannot be mandated. Were the Torah to force the indentured servant out the door, he would soon end up as a servant to another household, or worse. Were the Torah to prohibit the Israelite soldier's marriage to the *eishet yefat to'ar*, he would continue the relationship illicitly or move to another, equally disastrous relationship with a different unsuitable partner.

The Torah, therefore, addresses these situations in a manner that is strikingly out of character for the text. God does not prohibit the undesirable behavior outright. He instead mandates a last-ditch effort to change the individual's perspective. Hopefully, the servant or soldier, as a result of the rituals prescribed, will come to recognize the error of his ways. *The life choices that lie at the core of each of these cases cannot be mandated; they can only be made by the individuals themselves.*

---

11. Midrash Tanchuma Ki Tetzei 1; Rashi, Devarim 21:11.

— **D** —

One critical component, however, obviously sets these two narratives apart from each other.

The choice to be made by the *eved Ivri* between freedom and servitude is primarily self-directed, chiefly affecting the *eved* himself. While his decision, like all life decisions, will impinge upon the lives of others, the path the *eved* chooses will shape his own life, above all.

The choice to be made by the soldier, in contrast, has a second direct target. The future of the captive woman hangs in the balance. Will she be freed to return to her home or will she be forced to remain in a life of captivity, the wife of a stranger in a strange land and household? If we view the proceedings from the perspective of the *eishet yefat to'ar* herself, the morality of the Torah's approach becomes difficult to understand. How can the Torah allow this woman to be treated so cavalierly, without affording her control over her own life and destiny?

— **E** —

We have noted at length the hesitation with which we confront these and similar issues of Torah morality. Numerous obstacles emerge when we try to analyze Torah ethics from our "modern" perspective.

First of all, we have no right to expect that the morality of the Torah will automatically correlate to the transient mores of our day. Societies and their ethical structures have risen and fallen, each laying claim to permanence in their day, while Torah law has outlasted them all.

Secondly, as we have also noted, the relationship between the eternal nature of Torah law and the temporal context of the particular time and world into which the Torah was given is not always clear.

Nonetheless, such obstacles should not stop us from struggling with the text in an effort to glean the enduring lessons that might emerge.

With these concerns and caveats in mind, we return to our questions concerning the morality of the Torah's treatment of the *eishet yefat to'ar*.[12]

---

12. The following analysis is based on the positions of Rashi, the Ramban and others who, adhering to the straightforward meaning of the text, maintain that the Torah prohibits any relationship at all with the *eishet yefat to'ar* until after the rituals prescribed in the Torah are performed. (See Tosafot, Kiddushin 22a, for a discussion of other points of view.)

—— F ————————————————————————————

One short Talmudic comment puts this entire biblical narrative into perspective. Commenting on the phrase "and you shall bring her into the midst of your home...," the Talmud states, "You may not molest her on the battlefield."[13]

The world of war is an abnormal world. On the battlefield, passions and energies are unleashed, resulting in excesses that would not naturally arise anywhere else. As the bloodlust rises in the soldier's heart, as his own mortality hangs by a thread, he becomes capable of acts that would be unthinkable to him in any other setting.

Against this backdrop of unfettered violence, the victimization of women in warfare has been tragically commonplace since the beginning of time. Whether perceived as an opportunity to heap further attack and humiliation upon the enemy, as deserved benefit from the "spoils of war," or simply as a means to prove a soldier's masculinity, the rape of women noncombatants has accompanied warfare in virtually every known historical era to this day. No army is totally immune from the possibility of such horrific excesses. As recently as 2013, the United Nations Security Council found it necessary to adopt two resolutions: one calling for a complete and immediate end to all acts of sexual violence by all parties in armed conflict and another supporting abortion rights for girls and women raped in wars.

—— G ————————————————————————————

Facing the tragic reality of "war rape," the Torah's approach, as understood by the rabbis, is clear: "And you shall bring her into the midst of your home.... You may not molest her on the battlefield."

Remove the potential victim from the place of heightened danger. Leave the battlefield and its warped sense of reality behind. Take the captive home, thereby gaining the benefit of a calmer place and time. Perform the acts mandated by the Torah so that you will no longer see her solely as an object of your desire, but as the person she is – a frightened, shattered woman, torn from her home and people, whose alien mores render her unsuitable for your choice as a life partner.

And, after everything calms down, the choice will be yours.

If you come to your senses, then this woman is to be set completely free

———————————

13. Talmud Bavli Kiddushin 22a.

and allowed to return to her people. And if, in spite of all that has transpired, you obstinately refuse to see the error of your ways, she must nonetheless be treated with respect and dignity. She is to become your wife, with all rights and privileges that role provides.

—— H ——

In summary, faced with the horrors that inevitably accompany the tragedy of war, the Torah slows things down in an attempt to control an essentially uncontrollable situation.

The *eishet yefat to'ar* cannot be totally redeemed by fiat. Were the law to completely deny the soldier the possibility of a relationship with his captive, he would be driven to take matters into his own hands on the battlefield, with the horrific results seen over the course of human history. The choice must made be available to him; but only, the Torah maintains, after an opportunity for clearer perspective has been gained.

And, whatever choice he makes, the *eishet yefat to'ar* will be treated with as much respect as the situation allows. She will either be granted her complete freedom or she will become a respected member of an Israelite household. While the latter path will not be her choice, it remains the best option available to her, under the difficult circumstances.

When we contrast the treatment of the *eishet yefat to'ar* to the treatment of women during war until this day, we once again confront the wisdom of Torah law. Consistently, the Torah does not simply preach morality, but devises the best possible path for the application of that morality in the real, often cruel world.

Points to Ponder

Before the reader accuses us of engaging in apologetics in this study, arguing that the most humane path the Torah could have chosen would have been to allow freedom of choice to the *eishet yefat to'ar*, no matter the circumstances, consider not only the reality of the time into which Torah was given, but also the reality of the world in which we now live. The UN resolutions quoted in our study are proof positive that the horrific mistreatment of women during warfare continues to this day. In spite of studies, resolutions, proclamations and public protestations, in conflict after conflict across the globe, reports of atrocities on the battlefield and beyond continue to emerge unabated.

While some particulars of the narrative of the *eishet yefat to'ar* may speak to the temporal world into which the Torah was given, the general message of the text remains as relevant as today's headlines. The preaching of morality on the world stage, often cynically by the worst perpetrators themselves, may provide the illusion of progress but, in fact, accomplishes little. Only if realistic, practical paths towards behavioral change are forged will future victims be spared.

Once again, the Torah teaches through example that we are obligated not only to proclaim our moral vision, but to find a way to implement it.

Not by coincidence, the two Torah portions compared in our study – the passage dealing with *eved Ivri* (the Israelite indentured servant) and the passage concerning the *eishet yefat to'ar* – share a common textual role. They both open very similar parshiot in the text.

Eved Ivri is the first subject discussed in Parshat Mishpatim in the book of Shmot, a parsha that conveys, in staccato fashion, a litany of interpersonal laws that form the foundation of Jewish societal responsibility. The treatment of an *eishet yefat to'ar* opens Parshat Ki Tetzei, a parsha that conveys, again in staccato fashion, the greatest number of mitzvot of any parsha in the text.

Two suggestions can perhaps be offered to explain this textual phenomenon.

Firstly, the measure of any society can be clearly gauged by the quality of the care that it provides for the least fortunate within its ranks. The Torah, therefore, opens its lists of mitzvot in the parshiot of Mishpatim and Ki Tetzei with edicts concerning the treatment of individuals whose very existence is dependent upon the compassion of others. *How you treat the indentured servant in your charge and the captive women in your care*, God declares to the nation, *will go a long way in showing Me who you really are...*

Secondly, as discussed in our study, the narratives concerning *eved Ivri* and *eishet yefat to'ar* both address life choices that cannot be mandated but must, instead, be chosen by the individuals themselves. As God prepares to transmit the dual lists of commandments found in the parshiot of Mishpatim and Ki Tetzei, He therefore first reminds the nation each time: *My mitzvot can only go so far. Many of the critical choices that will shape your lives cannot be mandated; they must be freely chosen by you. Choose well and wisely, and My commandments will then find their home, further enriching lives that you have already determined will be lived well.*

2 One for the Books?

Context

A devastating halachic scenario of familial and communal tragedy is presented in Parshat Ki Tetzei:

> And if a man shall have a *ben sorer u'moreh*, a disobedient and rebellious son, who does not listen to the voice of his father and to the voice of his mother, and they discipline him, and he does not listen to them, then his father and his mother shall lay hold of him and they shall take him out to the elders of his city and to the gate of his place.
>
> And they shall say to the elders of his city: "This is our son, disobedient and rebellious; he does not listen to our voice; he is a glutton and a drunkard."
>
> And all the men of his city should pelt him with stones and he shall die; and you shall remove the evil from your midst; and all Israel shall hear and they shall fear.[1]

Questions

We cannot help but be stunned as we consider the picture painted by the Torah in the passage dealing with the *ben sorer u'moreh*.

What exactly are the sins of this "disobedient and rebellious" son? What crimes could this young man have committed that warrant such severe punishment? To put it mildly, execution seems a bit severe for someone who fails "to listen to the voice" of his parents. Clearly, there must be more here than meets the eye.

Can the Torah truly expect parents to take an active role in the execution of their own child?

---

1. Devarim 21:18–21.

What legal protections are provided to the accused? The text seems to mandate no judicial process in the case of *ben sorer u'moreh* at all.

Approaches

—— A ——

We can gain a degree of solace in the knowledge that we are not alone in our concerns over this difficult passage. A series of striking comments by the Talmudic scholars clearly mirrors their dismay as they face the ramifications of the *ben sorer u'moreh* narrative.

Given the complexities before us, we will approach this study a bit differently than usual. We will first list a series of rabbinic observations on the passage of *ben sorer u'moreh*, without comment. We will then use these statements as a guide in piecing together possible approaches to what will certainly remain, even after all of our efforts, one of the most puzzling and difficult passages in the entire Torah.

1. Rabbi Kruspedai maintains in the name of Rabbi Shabtai that a young man can only become a *ben sorer u'moreh* during the three months following the onset of puberty.[2]

2. Based on the verse "This is our son, disobedient and rebellious; he does not listen to our voice; he is a glutton and a drunkard," the Mishna and the Tosefta, as elaborated upon by the Gemara, explains that a young man can only become a *ben sorer u'moreh* through three specific steps: the theft of funds from his father, the purchase with those funds of a particular measure (or more) of meat and fine wine at a cheap price, and the consumption of those items while on someone else's property, in the company of other rebels.[3] The Talmud further requires that the meat be consumed half-cooked and the wine half-diluted, in the manner of thieves.[4] These particulars are required by the rabbis for the conviction of a *ben sorer u'moreh* because, acting together, they shape an environment that encourages further sin on his part.[5]

---

2. Talmud Bavli Sanhedrin 69a.
3. Mishna Sanhedrin 8:2–3; Tosefta, Sanhedrin 11; Talmud Bavli Sanhedrin. Although other opinions on specific details are offered both in the Mishna and Gemara, we have chosen those opinions accepted by the majority of later halachic authorities.
4. Talmud Bavli Sanhedrin 70a.
5. Ibid., 71a.

3. From the verse "and they discipline him, and he does not listen to them," and other sources, the rabbis glean that a three-step judicial process is also required in order to fully convict a *ben sorer u'moreh.*

Upon discerning the life path upon which their son is traveling, the parents must warn him of the potential consequences of his actions in the presence of two witnesses. If, in spite of this warning, the young man again commits the crimes described in the previous paragraph, he is brought before a court of three judges and, upon their decision, he receives lashes. If, in spite of that punishment, the young man again commits these crimes, he is brought before a court of twenty-three judges for judgment as a capital offender.[6]

4. The Mishna maintains that a *ben sorer u'moreh* is not judged on the basis of his current actions but rather on the basis of where those actions will inevitably lead. "Better that he should die while still 'innocent' than that he should die once he has become guilty."[7]

Rabbi Yossi the Galilean further explains that the Torah would never mandate the execution of an individual who simply stole and ate a specific measurement of meat and wine. Instead, this sage insists, the Torah foresees the inevitable outcomes of the rebellious son's current attitude. Left unchecked, this young man will ultimately deplete his father's resources, find himself unable to maintain his self-destructive habits, and turn to a life of violent crime. He is executed in order to prevent him from traveling along this path.[8]

5. The Mishna maintains that both parents must agree to bring the *ben sorer u'moreh* to court (as the Torah specifies the plural "they will grasp him").[9]

6. Rabbi Yehuda further insists that, in order for the laws of *ben sorer u'moreh* to go into effect, the young man's mother and father must be equal in voice, appearance and height (a fundamental impossibility).[10]

7. An opinion from the Mishnaic period cited in the Talmud and attributed to Rabbi Yehuda and/or Rabbi Shimon declares: "There never was, nor will there ever be a *ben sorer u'moreh.* Why then was [this law] written?

6. Mishna Sanhedrin 8:4; Talmud Bavli Sanhedrin 71b.
7. Mishna Sanhedrin 8:5.
8. Talmud Bavli Sanhedrin 72a.
9. Mishna Sanhedrin 8:4.
10. Ibid., as explained by Talmud Bavli Sanhedrin 71a.

To enable us to expound upon the passage and to receive reward for doing so." Rabbi Yonatan adamantly disagrees with this contention and claims: "I, myself, saw [a *ben sorer u'moreh*] *a*nd I sat upon his grave."[11]

——**B**——

Clear patterns emerge as we consider the observations of the rabbis on the *ben sorer u'moreh* narrative. The Talmudic scholars, unwilling to accept the possibility that the Torah would punish an individual so severely without due cause, search this text and beyond in order to both quantify the transgressions of the "rebellious son" and to establish a judicial framework for his sentencing and execution. The scholars apparently recognize, however, that their efforts fall short of adequately explaining this passage. They therefore make two startling claims.

The first of these contentions is suggested in the Mishna, elaborated upon by Rabbi Yossi the Galilean and apparently accepted with unanimity. Unable to correlate the *ben sorer u'moreh*'s current punishment with his crime, the rabbis conclude that the *ben sorer u'moreh is punished not for something he has done, but for something he is going to do.*

The second assertion is arrived at gradually, as the Talmudic scholars develop a series of nearly, if not completely, impossible prerequisites for the conviction of a *ben sorer u'moreh*. Ultimately, however, the logical conclusion of these prerequisites is verbalized. Unwilling to accept, even with all of the rabbinic caveats, the possibility of an actual *ben sorer u'moreh* event, Rabbi Yehuda and/or Rabbi Shimon contend that *an episode of* ben sorer u'moreh *has never occurred, nor will one ever occur. The textual narrative on this topic is theoretical and is only included in the Torah to grant reward for its study.*

This conclusion is disputed by Rabbi Yonatan in the Talmud and remains a source of contention in rabbinic literature across the ages. Some authorities, such as the Rambam[12] record the *ben sorer u'moreh* narrative as a practical possibility, while others maintain that such an event could never occur.

---

11. Talmud Bavli Sanhedrin 71a.
12. Rambam, *Mishneh Torah*, Hilchot Mamrim; *Moreh Nevuchim* 3:33, 41.

— **C** —

Each of these striking claims appears to openly contradict normative halachic principles.

As early as the patriarchal period, the Torah, according to the rabbis, makes it clear that an individual can only be punished for crimes already committed, and not for future sins. The text relates that Hagar, Avraham's concubine and the mother of his son Yishmael, is exiled from the patriarch's home. Finding herself lost in the wilderness, she despairingly casts Yishmael under a tree and sits at a distance, in order to avoid witnessing the death of her child. Suddenly a heavenly angel calls to her, saying: "Fear not, Hagar, for God has heard the cry of the lad, there where he is."[13]

Commenting on the angel's strange remark, "there where he is," the Talmud quotes the declaration of the Mishnaic sage Rabbi Yitzchak: "*An individual is only judged according to his deeds at the time, as it states in the text, 'God has heard the cry of the lad, there where he is.'*"[14]

The Midrash, elaborating on this point, portrays a dramatic heavenly dispute unfolding over Yishmael's fate. Discerning God's intention to spare Hagar's son, the angels object: *Master of the Universe, a man who is destined to torment Your sons with thirst*[15] – *You will now provide with water?* God responds: *Is he now guilty or innocent? I only judge an individual as he is, at this moment.*[16]

God, armed with certainty of the future, refuses to take that future into account in the judgment of an individual who stands before Him. How, then, can the rabbis suggest that an earthly court judge a *ben sorer u'moreh* not on the basis of what he has done, but on the basis of what he is going to do? How can fair justice be meted out over events that have not yet occurred?

— **D** —

Even more troubling is the citation quoted in the name of Rabbi Yehuda and/or Rabbi Shimon: "There never was, nor will there ever be, a *ben sorer u'moreh.*"

---

13. Bereishit 21:17.
14. Talmud Bavli Rosh Hashana 16b.
15. Rashi traces this accusation to an event rooted at the time of Babylonian conquest of Judea and referenced in Yeshayahu 21:13–14.
16. Midrash Rabba Bereishit Vayeira 53.

While not unanimously agreed upon, the very suggestion that the Torah would mandate halacha that was never meant to be practiced seems to fly in the face of all that we know about Jewish law. Halacha is not a theoretical construct, but a practical blueprint for daily life. While philosophical concepts are certainly transmitted through the mitzvot, these ideas are meant to be conveyed through concrete observance of the law and not solely through its study.

How, then, could some scholars suggest that, in this exceptional case, Torah mandates law that is never meant to be observed, only studied?

— **E** ————————————————————————————————

We are clearly faced with a situation where "the questions are better than the answers." Nonetheless, we will suggest an approach to the difficult narrative of the *ben sorer u'moreh*.

As background, I direct the reader's attention to our analysis of another exceptional case in the Torah, the ritual trial of the Sota, a married woman suspected by her husband of adultery (see *Bamidbar*: Naso 2). There we confronted a pattern similar to the one we now witness unfolding in the case of the *ben sorer u'moreh*. As the rabbis analyzed the Sota narrative, they detected safeguards within the text, ensuring a degree of judicial process in what, at first, seemed to be a totally arbitrary "trial by fire." Finally, however, even after the elucidation of these legal steps, most authorities felt forced to accept the stark conclusion that, in the case of Sota, *God breaks His own rules*. He miraculously intervenes in a judicial process that, in all other cases, He has handed over to man.

We suggested that God takes this dramatic step in order to preserve the all-important phenomenon of *shalom bayit*, peace within the home. At the center of the case of Sota lies a family in profound distress, a family that has lost the single most essential component in a relationship: the component of trust. In the face of this devastating development, everything is set aside. So pivotal is the family unit, so central to Jewish thought and practice, that the wheels of justice grind to a halt. All eyes focus on this one family until the corrosive doubt within has been addressed. To address this doubt, to preserve *shalom bayit*, God publicly steps in to adjudicate the case; thereby breaking His own rules as He enters an arena that He has reserved for man.

Perhaps in the case of a *ben sorer u'moreh*, for the same reasons, *God is once again forced to break His own rules*.

Through the *ben sorer u'moreh* narrative we once more confront a family in crisis. In this case, however, the crisis strikes deeper and is even more profound. At risk is this family's legacy and, by extension, the legacy of the nation. The rebellious son does not "act out" in a vacuum. While this young man's spiritual decline most directly and tragically affects his nuclear family unit, his public example will inevitably create instability in other families, as well. Such a threat to the *mesora*, the transmission of Jewish heritage from parent to child, cannot remain unanswered. Steps are therefore instituted to check this young man's downward spiral: official warnings, preliminary punishment, courtroom proceedings. If, however, the rebellious son remains unrepentant in spite of all these attempts, and if his continued transgressions unfold in a way that will ultimately lead to greater sin, the first of God's own rules must be broken. Torah law can afford to judge other sinners by who they are at that moment. The rebellious son, however, must be judged by who he will become, by the acts that he will inevitably perform. The cycle must be stopped forcefully, immediately and publicly.

And still...the rabbis argue. In spite of what is at stake, can the Torah truly expect us to fulfill the mandates described in the *ben sorer u'moreh* narrative? Would the Torah actually command the joining of parents and community in the execution of this young man?

Some authorities will follow the lead of Rabbi Yonatan and respond with a resounding yes. Confronted with the danger that the *ben sorer u'moreh* represents, they maintain, *the Torah expects us to respond full force.* To be sure, safeguards will be put in place, warnings will be issued, preliminary punishment will be meted out and an overall process of jurisprudence will be followed. But when all is said and done, if the "rebellious son" remains set on his path, we will have no choice but to react with severity.

Other scholars will follow the lead of Rabbi Yehuda and/or Rabbi Shimon. *There are limits to what God will expect from us*, they will maintain. *Parents cannot be ordered to serve their child up for capital punishment. A* beit din *cannot be expected to sentence a young man to death for what he might do in the future. The lessons involved in this area, however, are so critically important that they must be dramatically taught. And, consequently, another of God's rules must be broken...*

In the case of *ben sorer u'moreh*, these authorities declare, the halacha will relinquish its role as a practical guide and become solely a theoretical teaching tool. So critical is the phenomenon of parent-child transmission to the survival of Jewish tradition that God will apply the concrete language of the law to the painting of a theoretical picture. In this way, theory will enter the realm of practicality, as "what could be" becomes frighteningly real: *Gaze upon the tragedy that can unfold if you are not careful. Parent your children; teach together with consistency; watch for warning signs; show extra care during the transition from childhood to adolescence; intervene before it's too late; turn to others for help; do not let it come to this.*

And if these lessons are learned well, the case of *ben sorer u'moreh* will remain forever theoretical. Such tragedy will never darken the nation's experience, until the end of time.

Points to Ponder

My rabbinic colleagues and I have noticed a troubling phenomenon within our communities, the evidence of which is anecdotal, but nonetheless compelling:

Increasingly, parents do not want to parent their children. They want, instead, to be their children's friends.

This phenomenon is reflected, for example, in the striking disappearance of many teenagers from our synagogues on Shabbat morning. When parents are questioned concerning their children's absence, they typically respond: *Rabbi, you have to understand. Our kids are simply over-programmed. Between school, homework, clubs and sports, they get home so late and are up until all hours of the night. We just don't have the heart to wake them up and insist that they attend shul services on Shabbat mornings.*

Embedded in such answers are, of course, numerous red flags. Most immediately, a serious question of priorities can be raised. By placing all other concerns above synagogue attendance, these parents are sending the powerful message to their children that active synagogue affiliation is simply not that important. These same parents, years later, may well find themselves wondering why their college-age children are not affiliating with the Jewish communities on campus, why they are attending parties on Friday nights, rather than participating in campus synagogue services.

Even more significant, however, is these parents' abdication of their parental responsibilities. I often tell my congregants that my father, of blessed memory, did not wake me up on Shabbat mornings during my teenage years and softly ask me: *Honey, do you feel like attending shul today, or are you too tired*? It was not a matter of choice. Whether I liked it or not, I was going…

Don't get me wrong. I am not completely "passing the buck." Clearly, synagogues must bear the responsibility of creating innovative programs designed to attract and engage these young men and women. If parents don't do their part, however, the synagogue does not stand a chance. How many healthy teenagers, given the choice between a warm bed and synagogue services on a cold Shabbat morning, will turn down the bed? As difficult as it may be, parents must do their best to educate and not simply accept existing behaviors.

Moving to a different arena, teachers and administrators in Jewish schools often speak of dramatic changes in parental attitudes over the years. In the past, if a teacher and a student experienced a "disagreement," if there was an issue between a child and the school administration, parents generally took great pains to be overtly supportive of the teacher and the school. Right or wrong, these parents felt, their children needed to learn respect for authority. At most, if they felt the need to inquire about a perceived injustice to their child, parents did do so respectfully, often without their child's initial knowledge. Today, however, from the parents' perspective, *the student is invariably right*. Parents have a difficult time believing that their son or daughter could possibly ever be at fault, and an even more difficult time watching that child struggle with disappointment and difficulty. Children in hand, parents often respond with righteous indignation, openly challenging teachers and administrators alike on behalf of their young charges.

Most devastating of all, however, is the apparent excision of the word *no* from the lexicon of many parents today. So anxious are these parents for their children to be "happy," so intent are they to be "liked" by their children, that they fail to create limits or boundaries in their children's lives. *The more I give to my child, and the less I deny*, the reasoning goes, *the happier my child will be and the more he/she will love me*. As a result, children often enter their adult lives with an inflated sense of their own centrality and little sense of responsibility.

The *ben sorer u'moreh* narrative could well have been included in the Torah specifically for times such as ours, serving as a stark reminder of the responsibilities of parenthood and of the consequences of their avoidance.

Our children have enough friends. They need us to be their parents.

3 Finders [Not] Keepers

According to the Rambam's count in his *Sefer Hamitzvot*, Parshat Ki Tetzei contains no fewer than seventy-two individual mitzvot.

A full analysis of these edicts leads to an appreciation of the essential interplay between the Written and Oral Law in the application of halacha to daily life.

This study selects one area of law from this rich parsha to serve as a paradigm of this process.

Context

The Torah elaborates on an obligation first mentioned in the book of Shmot,[1] the mitzva of *hashavat aveida*, returning lost property:

> You shall not see your brother's ox or his sheep go astray and hide yourself from them; you shall surely return them to your brother.
>
> If your brother is not near to you or you do not know him, then you shall bring it into your home and it shall be with you until your brother inquires after it, and you return it to him.
>
> And so shall you do for his donkey, and so shall you do for his garment, and so shall you do for any lost item of your brother that may become lost and you shall find it; you may not hide yourself.[2]

Questions

While, in theory, the mitzva of *hashavat aveida* is clearly moral and appropriate, a number of significant issues concerning the practical application of this law immediately emerge:

Under what conditions must a lost item be returned?

Is the finder of a lost object required to search for its owner?

---

1. Shmot 23:4.
2. Devarim 22:1–3.

How can the finder of a lost item determine and verify the identity of the item's owner?

What is the finder's obligation towards the maintenance and care of the lost object? What is the extent of the financial obligations that he is required to incur in the course of this care?

How long must the finder maintain the lost item in his care?

What happens to lost objects that remain unclaimed?

Approaches

— A —

The short Torah passage concerning the mitzva of *hashavat aveida* does not address these and other critical issues directly. That task is reserved for the Oral Law.

As a first step in their application of this law, the rabbis make a critical distinction between two types of lost objects: those that possess a *siman* (an identifiable mark or sign) and those that possess no such sign. A *siman*, the rabbis explain, can either be a sign on the object itself or an external identifying feature. For example, number (as in the exact number in a group of lost items), weight, and the exact placement and location of the item(s), can, at times, serve as identifying signs.[3]

As a general rule, the Mishna maintains, *items possessing a* siman *must be returned to their original owners, while items possessing no such sign become the property of the finder.* This rule is derived from the Torah's statement "and so shall you do for his garment," indicating that only items that are identifiable, like garments, must be returned to their original owners.[4]

— B —

At first glance, this rule would seem to be the product of practicality. Only an item with an identifiable sign can be reliably claimed by its original owner. The individual's knowledge of the *siman* serves as proof of his ownership.

Further study, however, reveals that the role of a *siman* is not simply

---

3. Talmud Bavli Bava Metzia 22b, 23b.
4. Mishna Bava Metzia 2:5.

practical in nature. The function of a *siman* actually strikes much deeper, to the very core of ownership in Jewish thought.

In order to understand a *siman's* role, two essential halachic concepts must be clearly defined:

1. *Hefker*: a legal state of "ownerlessness." An item that is totally *hefker* has no owner and is available for possession by anyone.

2. *Ye'ush*: loss of hope. Classically, an item enters a state of ownerlessness when its owner consciously decides to relinquish his possession of the item. Such a state is also automatically achieved, however, when an owner is *meya'esh* – if, due to specific circumstances, he loses hope over his continued possession of the item.

If an individual loses an item that possesses a *siman*, the rabbis posit, he will retain hope over its eventual return. *Because my item is identifiable by me*, he reasons, *it will eventually be returned to me.* An item with a *siman*, therefore, legally remains in the possession of the original owner and must be returned to him by any finder.

If, in contrast, an individual becomes aware that he has lost an item that does not possess an identifiable mark, he will automatically experience *ye'ush*. Recognizing that he has no way of claiming his property, he will lose hope over its return. Such loss of hope effectively severs his ownership over the item and it immediately becomes *hefker*. When a finder encounters such an object, therefore, that object is ownerless and may legally be retained by the finder.[5]

The rabbis thus explain the mitzva of *hashavat aveida* on the basis of the most fundamental laws of ownership. If you find an item that is still "owned" (as indicated by the presence of a *siman*), that item cannot become yours and you must return it to its original owner. If you find an ownerless item (as indicated by the absence of a *siman*), you may acquire that item immediately.

— C —

Having established a clear formula delineating between a finder's obligation to return and his right to retain a lost object, the Talmud, in typical fashion, explores the parameters of this formula and the various circumstances that might create exceptions to the rule. A review of some of these deliberations provides a fascinating insight into the workings of the rabbinic mind. Above

---

5. Talmud Bavli Bava Metzia 21b.

all, the great care shown by the scholars in their efforts to "get it right" – to properly protect the ownership rights of all involved – remains strikingly clear across the ages.

Perhaps the best-known complication concerning the above rules rises out of a situation known in the Talmud as *ye'ush she'lo mi'da'at*, literally "loss of hope without knowledge."

The rabbis posit the following question: What is the ruling if an object without a *siman* is found before the owner becomes aware of his loss? At the time of the object's finding the owner is unaware that he has lost an object; he has experienced no *ye'ush*; and the object has, consequently, not yet become *hefker*. The finder has, therefore, found an object that is technically still "owned."

Can we apply, the rabbis ask, "retroactive *ye'ush*"? Can we reason that since the original owner will eventually discover his loss and lose hope, the situation can be considered as if loss of hope has already occurred by the time of the object's finding? Or are we forced to be absolutely concrete in our ruling and maintain that since *ye'ush* did not actually occur by the time the object was found, the item was still "owned" when it entered the finder's hand and must, therefore, somehow be returned to the original owner? This issue becomes the focus of a famous debate between the two towering Talmudic scholars Rava and Abbaye.

Rava maintains that retroactive *ye'ush* is acceptable. Since the item has no identifying signs, Rava reasons, when the owner discovers his loss, he will certainly lose hope over the item's return. Given the inevitable nature of the owner's ultimate *ye'ush*, we can consider the loss of hope to have already occurred by the time of the item's finding. The item is therefore legally ownerless when found and may be kept by the finder.

Abbaye adamantly disagrees. A strict constructionist in this matter, Abbaye maintains that the facts are the facts. Since the original owner is yet unaware of his loss at the time of the object's finding, no *ye'ush* has yet occurred. The original owner's possession of the item, therefore, has not been severed. The object is consequently an "owned" object at the time of its finding and must be returned.

Following a wide-ranging debate over several pages of the Talmud, the law is decided in Abbaye's favor. *An object without a* siman *can only be retained by the finder,* the Talmud decides, *if the original owner was aware of the loss and therefore lost hope by the time of the object's finding.*

The Talmudic decision in this matter, however, creates its own set of problems. Putting aside the practical question of how an item's original owner can be recognized without the presentation of an identifying sign, how is the finder to know, in any specific case, whether or not the original owner is aware of the object's loss at the time that it is found? The ruling in favor of Abbaye would seem to indicate that, on a practical level, we can never assume that *ye'ush* has occurred and that all items, whether or not they have a *siman*, must somehow be returned to their original owner. The practical difficulties created by this approach are overwhelming.

The Talmud carves out solutions to this problem by identifying cases where we can safely assume the original owner's awareness of the loss by the time of the object's finding. If money is found scattered in a public thoroughfare, for example, it may be kept by the finder. Since an individual carrying money regularly checks his pocket to "make sure that it is still there," we assume that the original owner quickly becomes aware of his loss. Furthermore, as money inherently has no identifying sign, he also immediately loses hope over its retrieval. Money found under these circumstances, therefore, can always be viewed as ownerless and may be retained by the finder.[6] Similarly, heavy or bulky carried items that possess no identifying features may be kept by their finders because we assume that the original owners also immediately become aware of their loss.[7] Numerous other similar cases are identified by the Talmud, making Abbaye's rejection of retroactive *ye'ush* easier to live with on a practical level.

Additional exceptions to the general rules of *hashavat aveida* are noted, as well. Items that disappear during a natural calamity, such as a tidal wave, for example, may be retained by their finders, even if the items have identifying marks. This ruling is derived by the rabbis from the textual verse "and so shall you do for any lost item of your brother that may become lost *and you shall find it*." Individuals are obligated to return only those items that are "lost" to the original owners but still accessible ("found") to all others. Items that are, for a period of time, "lost" to the entire world are excluded from the obligation of *hashavat aveida* and need not be returned.[8]

---

6. Ibid.
7. Ibid.
8. Ibid.

—— D ——

Once the obligation to return an object has been determined, what obligations are placed upon the finder towards discovering and verifying the identity of the original owner?

The rabbis begin to answer this question with the first sentence of the first Mishna in the Talmudic chapter of Eilu Metziot, the chapter that deals with the laws of returning lost objects: "These are the found items that may be kept [by their finders] and *these [are the items] that must be publicly announced...*"[9]

The finder of a lost object that must be returned, the rabbis imply, *is obligated to publicly announce the fact that he has found a lost object.* Numerous practical questions, however, remain.

What are the parameters of this obligation to "announce" the finding of lost objects? How and where should these announcements be made? For how long does this obligation of publication continue? What, exactly, should the finder announce? If he reveals too many facts, he will he be unable to properly verify the owner's identity. If he is too vague, the owner may not realize that he should step forward. Finally, what happens to objects that remain unclaimed?

—— E ——

As might be expected, the answers to these questions become the subject of discussion and debate in the Mishna and Gemara.

Further on in the chapter of Eilu Metziot, for example, the Mishna records a fundamental dispute between Rabbi Meir and Rabbi Yehuda concerning the reasonable requirements that halacha can place upon the finder towards determining the object's original owner.

Rabbi Meir maintains that *the finder's responsibility is limited to alerting those living within the area where the object was found.* The finder need not be concerned, according to Rabbi Meir, about the possibility that the item was lost by a visitor or a traveler from outside the area. The finder's obligation to announce his find is halachically satisfied, therefore, once "the neighbors have become aware."[10]

Rabbi Yehuda adamantly disagrees and argues that the finder must,

---

9. Mishna Bava Metzia 2:1.
10. Ibid., 2:6.

indeed, be concerned that the ownership of the item might trace to an individual from outside the neighborhood where the object was found. Rabbi Yehuda, therefore, maintains that *the finder must announce his find in the one location where the greatest number of Jews from the greatest number of communities converge: Jerusalem during the Shalosh Regalim* (pilgrimage festivals). Furthermore, the finder cannot assume that the owner will definitely be present at any one of the pilgrimage festivals, as illness or other circumstances may prevent his attendance. The finder must therefore announce his find over three subsequent festivals and for an additional seven days after the last of these occasions: three days to allow the owner to return home and determine if he has actually lost the item, three days to allow for the owner's return to Jerusalem, and one day to allow for the owner and finder to meet.[11]

The Gemara relates that in this case, halacha and history tragically converge in the ultimate determination of the law. Originally, the ruling was decided in favor of Rabbi Yehuda and finders of objects were actually required to announce their finds in Jerusalem over the course of three pilgrimage festivals and for seven days thereafter. A source from the Mishnaic period actually identifies a "claimant's stone" in Jerusalem to which finders and owners of lost objects converged in order to respectively return and reclaim the items. Upon the destruction of the Temple, the rabbis decreed that lost objects should be announced in synagogues and houses of study, natural locations of communal convergence in the absence of the Temple. Eventually, however, even that requirement was suspended due to confiscation by non-Jewish government officials of all lost items in the name of the king.

At that point, given little choice, the rabbis decreed that finders could satisfy their obligation of announcement by simply informing their neighbors and acquaintances of their finds.[12] The Rambam codifies this sequence of events, as well.[13] Centuries later, however, based on further twists and turns in the fate of the Jewish nation, Rabbi Yosef Caro records the reinstatement of the obligation to announce lost items in synagogues and houses of study in cases where fear of confiscation does not exist.[14] The

---

11. Ibid.
12. Talmud Bava Metzia 28b.
13. Rambam, *Mishneh Torah*, Hilchot Gezeila V'aveida 13:8.
14. *Shulchan Aruch*, Choshen Mishpat 267:3.

sixteenth-century scholar Rabbi Yehoshua Falk, in his commentary to Caro's *Shulchan Aruch*, notes the custom prevalent in his day to announce lost and stolen items in the synagogues during the time of communal prayers. He chastises, however, those who interrupt the prayers for this purpose and instructs the community to limit such announcements to points between or after specific prayer services.[15]

Clearly, to the rabbinic mind, the obligation to announce lost items in public places of assembly, where the greatest number of community members can hear, was never actually overturned. This practice, temporarily set aside due to tragedy and persecution, should be resumed whenever and wherever possible. Upon the rebuilding of the Temple, the halacha might well revert to Rabbi Yehuda's initial decree and the obligation upon the finder of a lost object to announce his find in Jerusalem on three pilgrimage festivals and seven days thereafter would, once again, be reinstated. In addition, we can assume that the creation of additional venues for announcement to the general Jewish community, through media such as the Internet, greatly expands the finders' opportunity and obligation to determine the rightful owners of objects that must be returned.

—— **F** ————————————————————————————

Rabbinic debate emerges in the Talmud, as well, concerning the content of the announcement to be made by the finder. Of great concern to the scholars is the task of ensuring that the object be returned only to the rightful owner and not to an imposter.

Rav Yehuda maintains that the finder should simply announce that he has found "an object." To claim the item, the owner will then be required to identify both the nature of the object itself as well as any identifying signs this specific object may have. Rav Nachman demurs, arguing that such an announcement is too broad and may not alert the owner to his loss. Instead, this scholar argues, the finder should announce the nature of the object and the owner should provide its identifying signs.[16] The Rambam and the *Shulchan Aruch* rule according to Rav Nachman, obligating the finder to announce the item's character. The owner, for his part, must provide

---

15. *Me'irat Einayim*, Choshen Mishpat 267:4.
16. Talmud Bavli Bava Metzia 28b.

adequate detailed information to prove his ownership and thus deny the claims of all others.[17]

── G ────────────────────────────────────

While all authorities agree that the finder of a lost object is obligated to protect and sustain that object for as long as it remains in his care, the level of that responsibility becomes the subject of debate.

As background to this discussion, we must first note that Jewish law establishes four levels of *shemira*, guardianship of an object, with accompanying specific levels of responsibility.

1. *Shomer chinam (unpaid bailee)*. Since an unpaid bailee receives no benefit from his task, and all benefit therefore flows to the object's owner, the *shomer chinam* stands at the lowest level of responsibility. He is obligated to pay for damages only in cases of his own negligence.

2. *Shomer sachar (paid bailee)*. Since a *shomer sachar* is paid for his efforts, with benefit therefore flowing both to the owner and to the bailee, the *shomer sachar*'s responsibility is raised one step. He is obligated to pay for damages in cases of loss and theft as well as negligence.

3. *Socher (renter)*. This case is, according to most halachic decisors, judged to be similar to that of a paid bailee. In a rental agreement, benefit once again flows both to the owner and to the renter. The renter is, therefore, obligated to pay for damages in cases of loss, theft and negligence.

4. *Sho'el (borrower)*. As all benefit flows in this case to the borrower, with the owner receiving no benefit at all, the borrower finds himself at the highest level of responsibility. He is obligated to pay for damages not only in cases of loss, theft and negligence, but also in cases where the object becomes damaged through total accident or force of circumstance. The only situation in which the *sho'el* is exempt from payment is when the item self-destructs as a result of its inability to perform the task for which it was borrowed.[18]

Into which formal category of guardianship, ask the rabbis, do the responsibilities of the finder of a lost object fall, as he cares for the owner's item?

─────────────────

17. Rambam, *Mishneh Torah*, Hilchot Gezeila V'aveida 13:2–3; *Shulchan Aruch*, Choshen Mishpat 267:4–5.
18. Mishna Bava Metzia 7:8; Shevuot 8:1.

Two distinct positions are offered in the Talmud. Rabba maintains that, as the finder receives no monetary remuneration for his efforts, he is to be defined as an unpaid bailee and is responsible for damage to the item only in the case of his own negligence. Rav Yosef, in contrast, identifies a type of benefit that does accrue to the finder. During the times when the finder actively cares for the item, Rav Yosef explains, he is involved in the performance of a mitzva. A general rule within Jewish law mandates that an individual actively involved in the performance of one mitzva is exempt from performance of other mitzvot.[19] There will therefore be occasions, Rav Yosef argues, when the finder, occupied with the object's care, will be temporarily exempt from obligations such as providing immediate care to the poor. On those occasions, the finder will benefit concretely from his task as the object's guardian. The finder must therefore be categorized as a *shomer sachar*, a paid bailee, and will be responsible in cases of loss and theft, as well as in cases of his own negligence.[20]

The Rambam and Rabbi Yosef Caro in the *Shulchan Aruch* both codify the law in agreement with Rav Yosef, maintaining that the finder is obligated to the higher level of responsibility incumbent on a paid bailee.[21] Numerous other authorities, however, offer arguments to the contrary, including that the ruling should not be determined on the basis of those rare occasions where the finder might benefit from his involvement with the lost object. These scholars, therefore, codify the law in agreement with Rabba, who views the finder of a lost object as an unpaid bailee.[22]

In a striking decision, Rabbi Moshe Isserles rules that due to this dispute, the categorization of the finder's exact level of responsibility remains uncertain. In a case of loss or theft of the item, therefore, the owner cannot claim payment from the finder. If, however, the owner does somehow secure payment for the item, the finder cannot then retrieve those funds. *In such cases of legal uncertainty, money remains in the possession of the*

---

19. Talmud Bavli Succa 25a.
20. Ibid., Bava Kama 56b; Bava Metzia 29a.
21. Rambam, *Mishneh Torah*, Hilchot Gezeila V'aveida 13:10; *Shulchan Aruch*, Choshen Mishpat 267:16.
22. See *Me'irat Einayim*, Choshen Mishpat 267:16–17 and *Siftei Kohen* 267:14 for a discussion of these issues.

holder. The law cannot move the funds from one party to the other, in either direction.[23]

———— **H** ————————————————————————————

Concerns surrounding the extent of the finder's responsibility are, of course, further complicated when concrete expenditures of time and/or funds are required for the found object's maintenance.

In response to this issue, the Mishna offers the following formula: "Anything that works and eats, should work and eat; and something that does not work but eats should be sold."[24] *An animal that both produces and consumes should be sustained from what it produces. An animal that does not produce but consumes should be sold and the money should be returned to the original owner.*

This rule reflects the balance that must be struck between two opposing considerations. Where possible, the lost animal itself must be returned to its owner. As Rashi explains, the owner would prefer to regain an animal that he already knows and has trained to meet his needs.[25] Nonetheless, the finder of the object cannot be expected to invest his own funds in its maintenance.

Even if no financial obligation is incurred in the animal's maintenance, however, the very act of caring for the animal over an extended period will potentially place an unfair burden on the finder. The Gemara, therefore, immediately refines the Mishnaic ruling by establishing a twelve-month cap on the finder's obligation to keep the animal itself. After that time, the finder may sell even an animal that is sustained by its own produce. The funds garnered from the sale are kept in trust by the finder, for eventual return to the owner. Further refinements then follow, with the Talmudic scholars delineating even shorter periods of obligation for specific animals, based upon the level of care required.[26]

Another fascinating Mishnaic dispute develops concerning the funds received by the finder in trust for the owner upon the sale of the animal. Rabbi Tarfon maintains that this money may be used and invested by the finder. The lost object no longer exists, this sage reasons, and the incum-

———————————

23. *Hagahot HaRema, Shulchan Aruch*, Choshen Mishpat 267:16.
24. Mishna Bava Metzia 2:7.
25. Rashi, Bava Metzia 28b.
26. Talmud Bavli Bava Metzia 28b.

bency upon the finder has been translated into value. That value can be obtained from any funds that the finder may possess. The actual money gained from the sale, therefore, need not be preserved. Rabbi Akiva, in contrast, forbids the use of the funds gained by the object's sale. This great sage apparently views the funds received as physical replacement for the lost item and therefore prohibited from use by the finder.[27]

Additional minimal responsibilities are placed upon the finders of specific lost objects in order to ensure the proper preservation of the items they have found. Scrolls, for example, must be periodically read or simply rolled; garments must be aired; silver and copper utensils must be periodically removed from storage and lightly used, etc.[28]

In short, the laws of *hashavat aveida* obligate the finders of lost objects that must be returned to exert reasonable effort towards the return of the actual object or, if that becomes too onerous, the value of the object to the original owner. This obligation remains in force until the appearance of the owner or, if the owner fails to appear, until the appearance of the prophet Eliyahu, the harbinger of redemption.[29]

— I —

Our analysis of the mitzva of *hashavat aveida* is far from complete. Numerous other issues – ranging from the right to seek payment for caring for and/or returning a lost item to a consideration of the exemptions from the mitzva – are discussed in Talmudic and later rabbinic literature, as the scholars struggle to analyze the parameters of this obligation and apply them to our daily lives.

We will close, however, with one final, critical observation. The rabbis do not limit their understanding of the mitzva of *hashavat aveida* to the classical case of returning a physical item to its original owners. From the perspective of the rabbis, this mitzva is vastly more expansive. *We are obligated under the rubric of* hashavat aveida *to "restore" to our fellow any loss of any type that he may be experiencing or about to experience.*

The mitzva of *hashavat aveida* thus includes the obligation to actively prevent a loss that one witnesses occurring to his fellow's property.[30] This

27. Mishna Bava Metzia 2:7.
28. Ibid., 2:8.
29. Rambam, *Mishneh Torah*, Hilchot Gezeila V'aveida 13:10.
30. Talmud Bavli Bava Metzia 31a.

obligation extends, according to many authorities, to situations such as testifying in court on a monetary manner concerning which an individual has knowledge, even if he has not been summoned by the litigant;[31] alerting an individual to an erroneous judgment in a case where the verdict can be reversed;[32] "restoring health" to a sick individual if one is a doctor or otherwise expert in medical matters;[33] and much more.

Granted the opportunity to restore any losses to your fellow, the Torah proclaims, "...you shall surely return them to your brother."

Points to Ponder

Our study has shown that the relationship between the two essential components of the halachic process – Torah She'bi'chtav and Torah She'b'al Peh (the Written and Oral Laws) – is broader, deeper and much more intricate than is commonly understood. Through an amalgam of received oral tradition, edicts determined through analysis of existing law, and decrees enacted by the rabbis, the Torah She'b'al Peh analyzes, elucidates, explains, applies and breathes continuing life into an eternal tradition (see *Shmot*: Yitro 5, for an analysis of the structure and process of the Oral Law).

We began our study with three sentences of Torah text in the book of Devarim. Over nine pages later, we have barely scratched the surface of the philosophical and legal application of those three sentences. The exercise, however, has provided us with a glimpse into the process by which the Oral Law enables God's word to span the centuries and speak to us in practical terms, every day of our lives.

---

31. *She'eilot U'tshuvot Mishkenot Yaakov*, Choshen Mishpat 8.
32. *She'eilot U'tshuvot HaRosh* 99:6.
33. Rambam, *Peirush Hamishnayot*, Nedarim 4:4.

4 Mandated Memory

Context

With the final three sentences of Parshat Ki Tetzei, the Torah turns its attention to the mitzva of remembering the crimes of the nation of Amalek, the archenemy of the Jewish people.

> *Zachor*, remember that which Amalek did to you, on the way as you left Egypt.
>
> *Asher korcha ba'derech*, how he happened upon you on the way, *va'yezaneiv becha kol hanecheshalim acharecha*, and he struck those who were hindmost among you, all the weakest at your rear, *v'ata ayeif v'yageia v'lo yarei Elokim*, and you were faint and weary, and [he] feared not God.
>
> And it will be when the Lord your God gives you rest from all your enemies round about, in the land the Lord your God gives you as an inheritance to possess it, *timcheh et zecher Amalek mi'tachat hashamayim*, you shall erase the memory of Amalek from under the heaven – *lo tishkach*, you shall not forget![1]

The rabbis eventually ordain a special reading of this passage each year on the Shabbat before the festival of Purim, a Shabbat that consequently becomes known as Shabbat Zachor, the Shabbat of remembrance. This reading is ordained in order to ensure the yearly fulfillment of the positive biblical mitzva conveyed by the passage itself: the mitzva to remember the crimes of Amalek.[2] The Shabbat before Purim is chosen for the fulfillment of this mitzva because Haman, the villain of the Purim story, was a descendent of Agag, the last king of Amalek.[3]

---

1. Devarim 25:17–19.
2. Mishna Megilla 3:4; Tosafot, Brachot 13a; *Shulchan Aruch*, Orach Chayim 785:7.
3. Megillat Esther 3:1.

Questions

No other nation is singled out by the Torah for enduring enmity as is the nation of Amalek.

Why must an eternal battle be waged against this nation? What was the exact nature of its crimes? The Egyptians enslaved and tormented the Israelites for centuries; the Canaanites and Emorites attacked the nation during its wilderness travels; the Moabites and Midianites conspired to spiritually destroy them; the Edomites refused to allow them to pass through their land and denied them water to drink. Yet, while these nations are chastised – and in some cases ostracized – by the Torah, none of them earn the enduring enmity that is reserved for Amalek. What aspects of Amalek's crimes warrant this treatment?

Furthermore, whatever Amalek's crimes may be, how can the Torah mandate perpetual hostility towards this nation? Does the Torah accept the concept of collective guilt? Are descendents to be blamed for crimes committed by their forefathers centuries earlier? What are the practical ramifications of the mandate to erase the memory of Amalek across the ages?

Finally, the mitzva of remembering the crimes of Amalek, as outlined in the text, seems to be inherently contradictory. The Torah enjoins us to remember, and yet, the ultimate goal of remembering is to reach the point when we will "erase the memory of Amalek from under the heaven." *It seems as if the Torah is commanding us to remember, in order to forget?* The Torah then deepens the mystery by closing the passage with the admonition: "You shall not forget!" On a practical level, how are we meant to understand this mitzva?

Approaches

—— A ——————————————————————————————————

The Torah's terse description of Amalek's original attack upon the Israelites conveys volumes concerning the nature of the evil that this nation represents.

1. *Asher korcha ba'derech*, "how he happened upon you on the way…"

To underscore the unique nature of Amalek's attack, the Torah utilizes an unusual verb, *korcha*, that is not conjugated in this form anywhere else in the Torah.

According to the *pshat*, the straightforward meaning of the text, the verb *korcha* is derived from the word *mikreh* (happenstance). The central feature of Amalek's sin, the Torah informs us, was *the casual nature of their attack upon the Israelites.* The Israelites did not threaten Amalek in any way; they were not passing through their land; these nations were not engaged in physical or philosophical conflict. They simply "happened" to meet each other on the way. Amalek's attack was entirely unprovoked, motivated by the "pure joy of massacre."[4]

The connection between Amalek and Haman, the villain of the Purim story, now becomes clearer as well. Haman is not simply the biological descendent of the nation of Amalek, but the philosophical descendent of that nation, as well. Faced with one individual's stubborn unwillingness to bow down before him, a "normal villain" would be satisfied with vengeance wrought upon the perpetrator alone. It takes an Amalekite, like Haman, to use the opportunity to spitefully attack not only that individual but his entire people.[5] Unreasonable, reasonless hatred is the mark of Amalek – a mark clearly reflected in Haman's reactions.

A Midrashic interpretation, quoted by Rashi, adds another layer of significance to the verb describing Amalek's crimes. The Midrashic scholars discern the term *kar* (cold) embedded in the verb *korcha. When you left Egypt,* God informs the Israelites, *you were "boiling hot" to the touch. No nation, upon hearing of the miracles wrought on your behalf during the Exodus, would dare attack you…until Amalek attacked. And then, just as an individual who enters a hot tub cools the water for those who follow, Amalek's brazen attack upon you "cooled" your image and rendered you vulnerable to attack from other sources, as well.*[6]

2. *Va'yezaneiv becha kol hanecheshalim acharecha…*, "and he struck those who were hindmost among you, all the weakest at your rear…"

Once again, the Torah underscores the extraordinary nature of Amalek's crimes through the unique conjugation of a verb, *va'yezaneiv*, found in this form nowhere else in the Torah text.[7]

Derived from the noun *zanav* (tail), the verb *va'yezaneiv* underscores the despicable, cowardly nature of Amalek's attack. Amalek fails to attack

4. Rabbi Shimshon Raphael Hirsch, Devarim 25:18.
5. Megillat Esther 3:6.
6. Midrash Tanchuma Ki Teitzei 9; Rashi, Devarim 25:18.
7. This verb is found in the book of Yehoshua 10:19.

the Israelites head-on, but deliberately targets the hindmost section of the Israelite column: the sector containing, as the Torah testifies, *kol hanecheshalim acharecha*, "all the weakest at your rear." The weakness of others does not move the nation of Amalek to compassion and sympathy, as it would any human being imbued with the spirit of God. Instead, discerned weakness and vulnerability only awakens the bloodlust and scorn embedded in Amalek's heart.

3. *V'ata ayeif v'yageia v'lo yarei Elokim*, "and you were faint and weary, and [he] feared not God."

We have translated the final notes on Amalek's attack according to the interpretation of the vast majority of scholars from Midrashic times onward. These closing comments, the authorities maintain, can only be understood if we divide the text into two sections, each referring to a different subject. The phrase "and you were faint and weary" refers to the Israelites, while the phrase "and [he] feared not God" refers to Amalek.[8]

In summary, the Torah thus declares, Amalek attacked you at the point when you were, as a whole, weakened from the journey. This brazen assault and its despicable characteristics showed a total lack of any God awareness on Amalek's part.

Some scholars,[9] however, suggest a different, bold approach to these closing notes – an approach that is also based on a Midrashic source.[10] Noting that the text literally reads, "and you were faint and weary, and feared not God," these commentaries insist that the entire textual description, including the statement "and feared not God," applies to the Israelites. The Torah informs us of the true source of the nation's vulnerability to Amalek's attack. Not only were the people physically weary but, at this moment, they were also "bereft of mitzvot."[11] A related tradition, found in many sources, connects Amalek's attack to the event recorded immediately prior in the book of Shmot. There, the Torah describes that, at a location known as Refidim, the Israelites complain to Moshe over a lack of water. These protests, according to Moshe, ultimately descend into an overall test of God, as the nation asks, "Is the Lord in our midst or not?"[12] The spiritual weakness

8. Sifrei, Devarim 25:18; Rashi, Devarim 25:18 and many others.
9. Chizkuni, Devarim 25:18.
10. Mechilta, Shmot 17:8.
11. Ibid.
12. Shmot 17:7.

demonstrated by the people during this event ultimately leaves them open to the assault by Amalek that immediately follows.[13]

—— **B** ——

A clear picture thus emerges from the Torah's brief description of the crimes for which the nation of Amalek is singled out. This is a people filled with spite and hatred – a nation that attacks without warning or cause, that preys upon the physically and spiritually weak, that revels in violence, and that represents the antithesis of all the Torah stands for. Good cannot triumph while Amalek exists.

—— **C** ——

While the Torah makes a cogent case for opposition to Amalek, however, the permanent character of this mandated hostility gives us pause. What are the practical ramifications of the commandment to erase the memory of Amalek in our day? Do the descendents of an ancient people bear continuing responsibility for crimes committed by their ancestors centuries ago?

A broader analysis of these issues can be found in our earlier study concerning the approach of Jewish law to war (see *Bamidbar*: Matot-Masei 2). For the purposes of this study, however, we will summarize some of the salient points that apply specifically to the laws surrounding Amalek.

1. The questions we raise are not new. An early Midrashic source reflects the ambivalence felt by the rabbis as they consider the Torah's approach towards Amalek. The Talmud suggests that Shaul, the first king of Israel, engages God in poignant debate after receiving the divine command to utterly destroy the nation of Amalek and all of its wealth.

When Shaul raises concerns over the morality of killing countless souls – men, women, children and animals – God refuses to address the issues directly and commands the king "not to be overly righteous."[14] Through this Midrashic medium, the rabbis perhaps give voice to their own concerns and conclude that, while the answers to the issues raised will forever remain elusive, God's will must be obeyed.

2. Some authorities, over time, increasingly perceive Amalek as a

---

13. Rashi, Shmot 17:8; Midrash Tanchuma Yitro 3.
14. Talmud Bavli Yoma 22b.

conceptual rather than as a physical entity.[15] The evil represented by this ancient nation, these authorities maintain, continues to exist and must be eradicated if good is to triumph. An argument might be made that this transition to the conceptual is reinforced by the text itself when it speaks of the obligation to eradicate the "memory of Amalek," without reiterating the requirement to physically destroy the nation.

3. Most scholars, in contrast, continue to interpret the Torah's commandment concerning Amalek in concrete terms. The physical obligation to destroy the Amalekite people, these authorities maintain, continues over time.[16]

The practical application of this law, however, runs into a serious roadblock. How does one identify an Amalekite?

Complicating this question is a conclusion reached in the Mishna allowing the acceptance of a convert of Ammonite descent into the Jewish community, in spite of the biblical injunction "An Ammonite or a Moabite may not enter the congregation of the Lord, even their tenth generation... to eternity."[17]

This allowance is made, the Mishna explains, because of the actions of the ancient Assyrian king Sancheriv (sixth century BCE), who, upon embarking on a campaign of conquest in the ancient Middle East, completely subdues his enemies by exiling them from their homelands and scattering them across the face of his empire. Tragically, Jewish history is indelibly altered when the Kingdom of Israel is conquered[18] and treated in this fashion by Sancheriv.[19] As a result, ten tribes of Israel assimilate into surrounding cultures and disappear from the historical stage.

Like the "Ten Lost Tribes" of Israel, the Mishna claims, other ancient biblical nations, including the Ammonites and the Moabites, were scattered by Sancheriv, resulting in the loss of their independent identities. Even someone claiming to be of Ammonite descent, therefore, is not treated as such and may become a full-fledged member of the Jewish people.

The Rambam codifies the Mishna's conclusion in broad terms: "When Sancheriv, the King of Assyria, rose, he confused all the nations and com-

---

15. Rabbi Shimshon Raphael Hirsch, Shmot 17:14, Devarim 25:18.
16. Rambam, *Mishneh Torah*, Hilchot Melachim 5:5; *Sefer Hachinuch*, mitzva 558.
17. Devarim 23:4.
18. Melachim II 17.
19. Ibid., 18:11–12.

mingled them with one another and exiled them from their places.... Therefore, a convert who comes in our time, in all places, whether he [claims to]
be Egyptian, Ammonite, Cushite or of any other nationality, both men and
women, are immediately permitted to join the congregation."[20]

Centuries later, the concept of commingled nations again becomes part
of the halachic discourse when a number of halachists revisit the biblical
commandment to blot out the nation of Amalek.[21] Rabbi Yosef Babad
mirrors the position of many when he emphatically states in the *Minchat
Chinuch*, his renowned commentary to the *Sefer Hachinuch*, "And today we
are no longer commanded in this [commandment to blot out the remembrance of Amalek] because Sancheriv has already risen and confused the
whole world."[22] Due to Sancheriv's policies of conquest, these authorities
maintain, *after the sixth century, the archenemy of the Jewish nation is no
longer recognizable.*

4. A fascinating "blended" position is offered by Rabbi Joseph Soloveitchik, the Rav, based upon a subtle discrepancy in the rulings of the
Rambam.

The Rav notes that the Rambam clearly states in his codification of the
law that the obligation to destroy the seven Canaanite nations no longer
applies because "their memory has long since perished." Strikingly, however, the Rambam makes no such allowance concerning the obligation to
destroy the nation of Amalek.

Why, asks the Rav, does the Rambam assume that Amalek survives
while the memory of other ancient nations "perishes"?

To explain this legal disparity, the Rav suggests that *two distinct commandments concerning Amalek emerge from the Torah text reflecting two
different categories of Amalek.*

The verse "You shall blot out the remembrance of Amalek" mandates
the destruction of each individual genealogical descendent of Amalek. This
commandment loses its force when Sancheriv's method of conquest robs
the ancient nations of their independent identities.

The verse "the Lord will have war with Amalek from generation to generation" establishes the obligation to obliterate any nation across the face

---

20. Rambam, *Mishneh Torah*, Hilchot Issurei Biah 12:25.
21. Chaim Palagi, *Einei Kol Chai*, Sanhedrin 96b.
22. *Minchat Chinuch*, mitzva 604.

of history that seeks to destroy the Jewish people. This second commandment, which defines Amalek in broad conceptual rather than biological terms, remains unaffected by Sancheriv's actions. "There still exists," the Rav maintains, "a category of Amalek [as a people] even now after the peoples have been intermingled [and there are no longer individual Amalekites]."

The Rav explains that within the context of this commandment, Hitler and the Nazis were the Amalekites of the 1930s and '40s, while "the mobs of Nasser and the mufti" were the Amalekites of the 1950s and '60s. We can safely assume that the Rav would similarly identify the members of Hamas, Hezbollah, Al Qaeda, the Iranian Revolutionary Guard and others as the Amalekites in our day.

The Rav thus agrees that the concept of obligatory warfare based on genetic national identity becomes moot after Sancheriv's conquests. He maintains, however, that a second type of national identity emerges from the Torah's commandments concerning Amalek – an identity determined by behavior rather than bloodline. *This national identity remains intact to this day, obligating the Jewish people in each generation to ongoing struggle against the Amalekites of their day.*

—— **D** ——————————————————————————————

Finally, we turn our attention to the character of the mitzva concerning Amalek. As noted earlier, a fundamental inconsistency seems to emerge from the text.

The Torah clearly commands us to "remember that which Amalek did to you…" The text then explains, however, that the goal of this remembrance is to reach the point when we will successfully "erase the memory of Amalek from under the heaven." *The Torah seems to be commanding us to remember, in order to forget.* Deepening the mystery, the text then closes with the admonition "You shall not forget!" On a practical level, how are we to understand this mitzva?

The key to understanding the mitzva of *zachor* lies in recognizing that the Torah clearly distinguishes between two distinct phenomena: "*forgetting*" and "*erasing*."

When something is *forgotten*, that condition still exists. We have simply sublimated our awareness of the issues involved. In contrast, when something is *erased*, that condition is obliterated. We have successfully confronted the issues involved and dealt with them.

Once this distinction is noted, the Torah's approach to Amalek becomes abundantly clear and profoundly relevant: "*Zachor*, remember, that which Amalek did to you..." *Keep this memory alive, for if you "forget," the challenges and horrors of Amalek will resurface over and over again.*

Timcheh et zecher Amalek mi'tachat hashamayim, "you shall erase the memory of Amalek from under the heaven..." *Remember, until you have convinced the world to erase, to eradicate, Amalek in all of its forms from its midst. Remind the world of the lesson that you have learned through bitter experience – that for good to triumph, evil must be destroyed. Speak out and oppose evil, wherever it may exist.*

Lo tishkach, "you shall not forget!" *Do not take the easy way out. Do not succumb to temptation. Do not forget until you have succeeded in the eradication of Amalek. And if the world fails to listen, continue to remember and remind them, until the end of days.*

E

How prescient the commandment to remember the crimes of Amalek seems today as we consider our world, seventy years after the Holocaust.

The rising tide of anti-Semitism throughout Europe, even in countries almost bereft of Jews; anti-Zionism and the devastating double standard applied against Israel by the world community; countless atrocities committed against ethnic, racial and religious minorities in countries across the globe – all these and other phenomena give lie to the public proclamations, resolutions and commitments for a better world that followed the close of World War II.

The world grows tired of hearing about the horrors of the Shoah. In the presence of a dwindling community of survivors, there are already those who loudly deny that the Holocaust ever occurred.

Such a world is doomed to see horrors recur. We are, therefore, obligated to change the world by insisting that its inhabitants "remember." And when, with God's help, we finally do succeed in fully "erasing the memory of Amalek from beneath the heavens," there will no longer be a need to "remember."

Points to Ponder

The discerning reader might have noticed that we "dodged" a particularly difficult question in our study.

We noted that, according to many authorities, the commandment to destroy "genetic Amalekites" cannot be fulfilled today. We failed to answer, however, how God could issue such a commandment. Is the Torah preaching the mantra of collective guilt? Are descendents to be blamed for crimes committed by forefathers centuries earlier? How do we relate to the fact that, according to most authorities, if we could definitively identify a genetic Amalekite today, we would be obligated to summarily execute him or her?

We have stated many times before that questions like these are based on the erroneous assumption that Torah morality must always correlate to the temporal mores of our day. We may never fully comprehend the philosophical underpinnings of the commandment to eradicate the nation of Amalek. The rabbis clearly made this point in the Midrash positing Shaul's struggle with God's decree (see study).

Nonetheless, a glimmer of understanding of these difficult issues might emerge from our own unfortunate experience.

As the State of Israel continues its arduous search for peace with its neighbors, one fact, ignored by the world, becomes clearer each day. As long as the Palestinians and so much of the Arab world continue to educate their children towards violence, martyrdom and hatred of Jews, no peace will ever take root. In classrooms and mosques, in textbooks and over the airwaves, young Palestinians are bombarded with images portraying Jews as subhuman enemies, worthy only of destruction.

Can a child from such a culture be "blamed" when he reaches adulthood and acts in consonance with these images? Is a suicide bomber, raised since childhood in a seething cauldron of hatred, fully responsible for his actions? Was the ordinary German, pummeled by Nazi propaganda, guilty when he turned a blind eye towards genocide?

Certainly, in the heat of battle, such delicate debates concerning "personal fault" have no place. The evil must be confronted and eliminated without hesitation.

In the quiet moments that follow, however, blame must be assessed, certainly upon the perpetrators, but also upon the guilty society, as well. A society that educates its young towards hatred, violence and murder must share responsibility, as a whole, for their crimes. In Amalek, the Torah confronts such a society and the resulting mandate is abundantly clear.

Ki Tavo

CHAPTER 26:1–29:8

כי תבוא

פרק כו:א-כט:ח

Parsha Summary

Agricultural offerings, ritual pageantry, blessings and curses…

 After detailing the laws and verbal formulas associated with the first fruit offering in the Temple and the ma'aser *(tithing) obligations, Moshe outlines a series of rituals that are to be performed immediately upon the nation's entry into the land. Central to these rituals will be the public recitation of twelve curses and blessings on the mountains of Gerizim and Eival, first mentioned in Parshat Re'eh. Moshe's description of this pageant serves as the textual segue into the major theme of Parshat Ki Tavo, the rewards and punishments to be experienced by the nation, based upon their future behavior.*

 Moshe outlines the divine blessings that will be bestowed upon the nation in return for their loyalty to God's law. Opening with the promise "Blessed will you be in the city and blessed will you be in the field," he describes a world in which "the Lord will open for you His storehouse of goodness" and in which "you will only be above and you will not be below."

 In contrast, if the nation fails to heed God's voice and to observe His commandments, Moshe warns, "all these curses will come upon you and overtake you." This warning introduces the second of the two tochachot, *sections of rebuke, found in the Torah text. Longer and more detailed than the first* tochacha – *recorded in Parshat Bechukotai at the close of the book of Vayikra – the* tochacha *of Ki Tavo catalogues a dire, unremitting and ultimately prescient list of the tragedies that will befall the nation in the event of their disloyalty to God and His law.*

 Moshe closes Parshat Ki Tavo by reminding the nation of the miracles they have experienced. He again encourages them to adhere to their covenant with God and to observe His laws, "so that you will succeed in all that you do."

1 A Strange Choice

Context

Parshat Ki Tavo opens with a description of *hava'at bikkurim*, the bringing of the first fruits of the season to the Temple, a yearly ritual to be observed after the conquest and settlement of Canaan. As part of this ritual, the Torah delineates the *vidui bikkurim*, the formula to be recited by the farmer upon the bringing of these fruits:

> An Aramean sought to destroy my forefather, and he descended to Egypt and dwelt there, few in number, and he became there a nation, great, strong and numerous.
>
> And the Egyptians mistreated us and afflicted us, and they placed upon us hard work.
>
> And we cried out to the Lord, the God of our fathers, and the Lord heard our cries, and He saw our affliction and our travail and our oppression.
>
> And the Lord took us out of Egypt with a strong hand and an outstretched arm and with great awesomeness and with signs and with wonders.
>
> And He brought us to this place, and He gave us this land, a land flowing with milk and honey.
>
> And now behold, I have brought the first of the fruits of the ground that You have given to me, O Lord![1]

A rabbinic decision made centuries after the writing of the Torah catapults this passage into another position of prominence in Jewish liturgy.

When the sages decide to formalize the Haggada, the text used as a guide for the fulfillment of the obligations of the Passover Seder, they select one biblical passage to be studied as the centerpiece of the

---

1. Devarim 26:5–10.

mitzva of *sippur Yetziat Mitzraim*, retelling the Exodus story on the Seder night. The biblical section they choose is the *vidui bikkurim*.[2]

Questions

The selection of the *vidui bikkurim* as the centerpiece of the mitzva of *sippur Yetziat Mitzraim* seems abundantly strange.

Given the host of primary sources in the Torah concerning the Passover story, sources from the book of Shmot that record the details of the Exodus as they unfold, why do the rabbis deliberately choose a secondary textual source that refers to these events only in retrospect? The *vidui bikkurim* is designed, after all, to be recited by Israelite farmers only after the land of Canaan is conquered and settled, long after the events surrounding the Exodus have occurred.

To complicate matters further, the *vidui bikkurim* is clearly associated in the Torah with a festival other than Pesach. The first fruits are to be brought to the Temple each year on the holiday of Shavuot. Why designate a passage associated with Shavuot as the centerpiece of the Pesach ritual?

Finally, even if we move past our questions concerning the rabbinic choice of text, another problem emerges: in practice, we actually fail to fulfill the rabbinic mandate. The Mishna designates the *vidui bikkurim* for inclusion at the Seder with the following clear instruction: "And one studies from [the phrase] *Arami oved avi* until he finishes the entire textual passage."[3] We, however, stop short of finishing the passage. While the portions of the *vidui* that chronicle the descent into and the Exodus from Egypt are included in the Haggada, the final statement of the passage, referring to entry into the land of Canaan, is glaringly omitted.[4] If the Talmud instructs us to complete the recitation of the *vidui* on the Seder night, why do we deliberately stop short of fulfilling that goal?

Approaches

—A—

Rabbi Joseph B. Soloveitchik suggests that by incorporating the *vidui bikkurim* into the Seder service, the rabbis underscore the thematic connec-

---

2. Mishna Pesachim 10:4.
3. Ibid.
4. Passover Haggada.

tion between two seemingly distinct ritual obligations: *hava'at bikkurim*, the bringing of the first fruits on Shavuot, and *sippur Yetziat Mitzraim*, the retelling of the Exodus story on the Seder night.

These rituals, the Rav suggests, as different as they may seem, are both fundamentally acts of *hakarat hatov*, the expressing of thanks, to the Almighty. In each case, the recitation of historical events is calculated to awaken within the participant a heightened awareness of and gratitude for God's guiding hand in the course of human events.[5]

The Maggid section of the Haggada, the section of the Seder within which the Exodus story is retold, climaxes with the statement "Therefore we are obligated to thank and praise...exalt and revere Him Who performed all those miracles for our fathers and for us."[6] Similarly, the farmer's introduction to the *vidui bikkurim*, "I say today before the Lord,"[7] is rendered by the interpretive Aramaic translation Targum Yonatan ben Uziel as "I will give gratitude and praise this day to the Lord."[8] Neither of these rituals is to be perceived as sterile storytelling; rather, each is to be seen as a mitzva of *hakarat hatov*. In each case, if we retell the historical tales but are not moved to thanks, we have not performed the mitzva at all.

In the Rav's view, the impetus for the rabbinic decision to study the text of the *vidui bikkurim* on the Seder night is abundantly clear. This text serves to remind us that "the essence of the Seder, and hence that of Sippur Yetziat Mitzrayim, is the expression of gratitude to the Almighty on the great liberation and miracles that he wrought for us in Egypt."[9]

— **B** —————————————————————————————

The Rav weighs in, as well, concerning the omission from our Haggada of the verse of the *vidui* discussing entry into the Land of Israel. Two of the answers the Rav proposes demonstrate this great sage's renowned intellectual honesty, reflected in his willingness to consider widely disparate solutions to a single problem.

On a technical level, the Rav proposes, we should recognize that we

---

5. Rabbi Joseph B. Soloveitchik, "The Nine Aspects of the Haggada," in *The Yeshiva University Haggada*, ed. Steven F. Cohen and Kenneth Brander (Jerusalem: Koren, 1984).
6. Passover Haggada.
7. Devarim 26:3.
8. Targum Yonatan ben Uziel, Devarim 26:3.
9. Soloveitchik, "The Nine Aspects of the Haggada."

may be using an edited version of the Haggada: "It is possible to suggest that during the time the Temple still stood, the text of the Haggada did include the last verses relating to the entry into the Land of Israel. Upon the destruction of the Temple and the subsequent exile, ChaZa"L [the rabbis of blessed memory] amended the text in order to conform to the new reality in which Am Yisrael [the nation of Israel] found itself."[10]

With this suggestion the Rav reminds us that the Haggada not only chronicles Jewish history, but also mirrors the flow of that history structurally. Additions and emendations to the Seder service were made across the ages, often as a result of the changing circumstances of the Jewish people.

This phenomenon, of course, is not isolated to the Seder service, but is characteristic of many other Jewish texts and rituals. Jewish experience is often reflected in the details of the nation's liturgy and observance. Consider, as one example, the Haftara, a portion from the books of the Prophets, recited after the reading of the Torah on Shabbat and festival mornings and on fast days. According to many authorities, the recitation of these prophetic passages traces to a time when alien rulers prohibited the public study of Torah text within the Jewish community. Responding to this tragic challenge, the rabbis instituted the recitation of a prophetic text related to the theme(s) of the prohibited designated Torah portion.[11] Once the practice of reading Haftarot was established, it remained in force even after the ban on study of Torah was lifted.

— C —

Moving in an entirely different direction, the Rav also offers a striking philosophical theory as to why the verse concerning entry into the Land of Israel is omitted from the Seder service:

Although the Jewish people did enter the Land of Israel subsequent to the Exodus from Egypt this was not the primary goal of Yetziat Mitzrayim, the Exodus from Egypt. *It [the land] was their destination but not their destiny* [my italics]. The direct goal of Yetziat Mitzrayim was the revelation at Sinai. The goal was the transformation of a subjugated people into "a nation of priests and a holy nation." It was not

---

10. Ibid.
11. Abudarham, *Seder Tefillot shel Shabbat* 63.

just to grant them political and economic freedom, but also to create a sacred people.[12]

Textual proof that the Sinaitic Revelation, and not entry into Canaan, was the primary goal of the Exodus can be found, according to the Rav, in God's first response to Moshe's objections at the burning bush. When Moshe questions his own worthiness for leadership, God responds: "And this shall be unto you the sign that I have sent you: when you have brought forth the people out of Egypt, they will serve God upon this mountain" (Shmot 3:12). *I am not choosing you, Moshe, to be a politician or a diplomat but to serve as a Rebbe, a spiritual mentor, to this people. Together we will fashion them into a holy nation. That is the purpose of your ascension to leadership and that will be the ultimate goal of your mission.*

From the Rav's perspective, the Haggada omits the verse in the *vidui bikkurim* concerning entry into the land in order to remind the reader that the Land of Israel must be seen as one component of a much greater whole. The Jewish nation, born and forged at Sinai, is wholly defined by its relationship to God. That relationship, built upon the study, observance and living of divine law, reaches its fullness only when the nation exists as a free, independent people on its land.

— **D** ———

Another answer can be offered to our initial question concerning the selection of the *vidui bikkurim* as the textual centerpiece for the mitzva of *sippur Yetziat Mitzraim*. Careful study of this biblical formula reveals an easily missed yet powerfully profound internal textual transition.

The farmer begins his proclamation in the third person: "…An Aramean tried to destroy my father, and *he descended* to Egypt and dwelt there, few in number, and *he became* there a nation, great, strong and numerous."

When, however, the farmer begins to discuss the birthing pangs of the Jewish nation in the cauldron of Egyptian slavery, a remarkable change occurs. Suddenly this man, speaking centuries after the Exodus, begins to speak of these historical events *in the first person*:

---

12. Soloveitchik, "The Nine Aspects of the Haggada."

And the Egyptians mistreated us and afflicted us, and they placed upon us hard work.

And we cried out to the Lord, the God of our fathers, and the Lord heard our cries, and He saw our affliction and our travail and our oppression.

And the Lord took us out of Egypt with a strong hand and an outstretched arm and with great awesomeness and with signs and with wonders.

And he brought us to this place, and he gave us this land, a land flowing with milk and honey.

As the *vidui* progresses, the farmer is transformed from an observer to a personal participant. He no longer objectively reports on events that happened to others; he now describes events as if they happened to him. Past, present and future merge for the Jew, once the Jewish nation is born. *An event that happens to any Jew at any time happens to all Jews at all times.*

The rabbis, therefore, could not have chosen a more appropriate textual centerpiece for the mitzva of *sippur Yetziat Mitzraim*. The purpose of the storytelling on the Seder night is summed up in the Haggada with the following statement: *B'chol dor va'dor chayav adam lirot et atzmo k'ilui hu yatza mi'Mitzraim*, "In each generation, a person must see himself/herself as if he/she came out of Egypt…"

No other passage of biblical text aids us more directly in the fulfillment of this mitzva then the passage of *vidui bikkurim*. As we channel the words of that long-ago farmer, bringing his first fruits to the Temple, we join him in his temporal journey as well. Together we become one with our forefathers in the land of Egypt, experiencing the Exodus as if it happened to us.

Points to Ponder

Our observations concerning the *vidui bikkurim* passage provide us with the opportunity to revisit the mitzva of *sippur Yetziat Mitzraim*, one of the central mitzvot of the Seder night. While a full analysis of this mitzva is well beyond the scope of our discussion, I hope that this summary will increase our understanding of one of the most beautiful and foundational experiences of the Jewish calendar year.

The Mishnaic scholars outline a three-step response to the Ma Nishtana, the introductory questions that launch the retelling of the Exodus story. This response becomes the blueprint for the Maggid section of our Haggada text and provides a powerful insight into the rabbinic vision of the Seder night.

I. *Matchil b'genut u'mesayeim b'shevach*

—— **A** ——————————————————————————————————————

The first step of the mitzva of *sippur Yetziat Mitzraim*, the rabbis explain, consists of "opening with shame and closing with praise."[13]

Rav and Shmuel, the two towering scholars who play a major role in the transition from the Mishnaic period to the period of the Gemara, each offer a possible path towards the fulfilling of the Mishna's initial mandate. Rav argues for a global approach to the narrative and maintains that the retelling of the Exodus story should begin earlier, with a statement reflecting the negative origins of the Jewish people: "In the beginning, our fathers were idol worshipers." Shmuel, in contrast, argues for a narrower approach. This scholar maintains that the narrative should be limited to the Exodus itself and thus open with the negative statement "We were once slaves to Pharaoh in Egypt."

Apparently adopting the position of some later scholars who interpret Rav and Shmuel's suggestions as complementary, our Haggada incorporates the positions of both of these authorities. As a direct answer to the Ma Nishtana, the text offers, "We were once slaves to Pharaoh in Egypt, but the Lord our God brought us out of there." Later, in the form of further context to the story, the Haggada proclaims, "In the beginning our fathers were idol worshipers and now God has brought us near to serve Him."

—— **B** ——————————————————————————————————————

What is the thrust of the Mishna's initial instruction to open with shame and close with praise? Isn't it abundantly obvious that any retelling of the Exodus story will begin with "shame" and proceed to "praise"? The historical transition from the negative to the positive is, after all, the whole point of the Exodus from Egypt.

—— **C** ——————————————————————————————————————

These questions can be answered if we accept a postulate presented in our study. From the rabbinic perspective, the biblical mitzva of *sippur Yetziat*

---

13. Mishna Pesachim 10:4.

Mitzraim does not simply obligate the retelling of a historical story. *Instead, specifically on the holiday of Pesach, as the Jewish nation celebrates the first footfalls of its national journey, the Torah enjoins each individual Jew to reconnect with his or her role as a participant in that journey.* Charged with the quantification of this mitzva, the rabbis delineate a three-step process carefully designed to move each participant in the Seder along a personal path towards the recognition of his/her own place in history. As designed by the rabbis, the three stages of the personal Seder night journey are *historical awareness, historical personalization/participation, and historical perpetuation.*

The first, essential step of the Maggid mandated by the rabbis is the step of *historical awareness.* At this stage, the rabbis address the fundamental question "How does the Jew view history?" Their answer is powerful and succinct: *Matchil b'genut u'mesayeim b'shevach,* "we open with shame and close with praise."

This rabbinic observation does not refer to the Exodus story alone. It is, instead, a global statement referring to Jewish history as a whole. That is why the Haggada is not content with the inclusion of Shmuel's "we were once slaves…" The story must hearken back to the dawn of Jewish history, to Rav's "in the beginning our fathers were idol worshipers…" The Jewish journey in its entirety, the rabbis maintain, is structured and purposeful. The path along which we travel is not haphazard, but moves from a fixed point to a fixed goal, from humble beginnings to a glorious end.

This first stage of Maggid thus captures the central contribution that, according to Rabbi Joseph Soloveitchik, Judaism offers towards man's understanding of history: the concept of a *destiny-driven history* (see *Bamidbar*: Bamidbar 2a, *Approaches* B):

> While universal (non-Jewish) history is governed by causality, by what preceded, covenantal (Jewish) history is shaped by destiny, by a goal set in the future…. Jewish history is pulled, as by a magnet, towards a glorious destiny; it is not pushed by antecedent causes. This is the meaning of the Patriarchic Covenant; it is a goal projected, a purpose pursued, a destination to be reached.[14]

---

14. Abraham R. Besdin, *Reflections of the Rav*, vol. 2, *Man of Faith in the Modern World* (Hoboken, NJ: Ktav Publishing House, 1989), p. 70.

Centuries earlier, the Maharal ingeniously conveys this same idea by reinterpreting the very title afforded to the entire Pesach evening ritual: *Seder*
(order). The evening is called the Seder, this Sage insists, not only because
of the ordered, ritualized structure of the proceedings. Instead, the title
testifies, on this night of history, to the existence of *historical seder* – to the
fact that there is "order" to Jewish history itself.[15]

*Each participant's Seder journey must begin with the attainment of "his-
torical awareness," with the realization that there is a pattern and purpose to
Jewish history. We are traveling from* genut *to* shevach: *from humble beginnings to a glorious future.*

Not by accident, this section of Maggid closes with *V'hi she'amda*, "And
this has stood," delineating God's protection of the Jewish nation from its
enemies, over and over again, across time.

II. *V'doresh mei'Arami oved avi ad she'yigmor kol haparasha kula*

——A————————————————————————————

In this second stage of Maggid, the Mishna mandates: "And one studies the
passage beginning with the words 'An Aramean tried to destroy my father…'
until he finishes the entire passage."[16] In fulfillment of this mandate, the
paragraph of *vidui bikkurim* is recited, dissected and analyzed through the
prism of the Oral Law.

——B————————————————————————————

Our study defended the choice of the *vidui bikkurim* as the central biblical
text for this portion of Maggid. As we noted, no other Torah passage can
aid us more directly in fulfilling the challenge of this section, which, as
our study explained, is the task of *historical personalization/participation*.
The way in which this text is presented in the Haggada, however, seems
abundantly strange. The *vidui* is quoted, dissected and analyzed in what
can best be described as a ritualized exercise in Torah study. While the
study of Torah text is always appropriate, why is this formalized, somewhat
stilted biblical analysis so critical to the mitzva of *sippur Yetziat Mitzraim*?

———————————

15. Chidushei Harim, quoting the Maharal, *Haggada Ma'ayana shel Torah.*
16. Ibid.

The story can clearly be told without the far-ranging rabbinical exegesis contained in our Haggada.

—— C ——————————————————————————————————————

The answer to these questions lies in appreciating the conscious rabbinic decision to teach the critical lesson of *historical personalization/participation* not only through the selection of the *vidui* text, but also through its mode of presentation in the Haggada. The rabbis recognize that no other single act in Jewish experience injects the participant more personally into the flow of Jewish history than the act of Torah study. The challenge of personalizing history is therefore met in this section of the Haggada, both through the text chosen to be studied and *through the very act of Torah study itself.*

A number of years ago, an acquaintance who became Jewishly observant later in life shared with me the following observation:

> Do you know what I find most amazing about the experience of Talmud study? It is that when I study Talmud, the boundaries of time fall away. I sit at my study table and the Tannaim of the Mishna – Rabbi Akiva, Rabbi Meir and their colleagues (32 BCE–200 CE) – speak to me. Suddenly, the Amoraim of the Gemara – Rav Papa, Rav Huna and their contemporaries (200–500 CE) – enter the discussion. Then Rashi (1040–1105) chimes in to explain a difficulty. Strikingly, Rashi's descendents and their colleagues (the Tosafists, 1105–1290 CE) object to Rashi's comments. Other voices emerge from multiple eras. And, in my struggle to understand, I become part of the conversation, as well – a conversation that stretches from the dawn of our history and that will continue to the end of time.[17]

During the second stage of Maggid, we thus move beyond historical awareness to personalization in multiple dimensions at once. *Both the chosen text of this section and the very act of shared Torah study inject us into the historical flow of our people, enabling us to become personal participants in the unfolding drama.*

---

17. Rabbi Joseph Soloveitchik's eloquently expressed similar sentiments can be found in Besdin, *Reflections of the Rav*, vol. 2, *Man of Faith in the Modern World*, pp. 21–23.

III. *Rabban Gamliel haya omer, kol she'lo amar shelosha devarim eilu b'Pesach lo yatza yedei chovato*

—**A**———————————————————————————————————

The final, third stage of the Maggid opens with a declaration in the name of the Mishnaic sage Rabban Gamliel: "Anyone who has not said [spoken of] these words on Pesach has not fulfilled his obligation: Pesach (the Paschal Lamb), matza (unleavened bread), and *marror* (bitter herbs)."[18] The text continues with Rabban Gamliel's elucidation of these three symbols.

—**B**———————————————————————————————————

Rabban Gamliel states that a failure to "say" the symbols of the Seder – Pesach, matza and *marror* – prevents the participant from "fulfilling his obligation." To what obligation does Rabban Gamliel refer? Some authorities maintain that Rabban Gamliel refers to the obligations incorporated in the symbols themselves.[19] According to this approach, for example, Rabban Gamliel maintains that an individual who consumes matza during the Seder but fails to discuss the significance of this act has not properly fulfilled the mitzva of *achilat matza*, the mitzva of consuming matza on the Seder night. Many other sages, however, disagree and maintain that Rabban Gamliel refers to the mitzva of *sippur Yetziat Mitzraim*.[20] According to this view, Rabban Gamliel argues that an individual cannot properly fulfill the obligation to retell the Exodus story on the Seder night without verbally mentioning the Paschal Lamb, the unleavened bread and the bitter herbs in the process.

This second position seems abundantly strange. Isn't Rabban Gamliel turning the medium into the message? Logically, the symbols of the Seder night are tools designed to aid in the reexperiencing of the Exodus story. Why would Rabban Gamliel transform them into essential features of the narrative itself? Surely, the story of the Exodus can be told without a verbal mention of these three symbols.

---

18. Ibid., 10:5.
19. Commentary of Abudarham and Maharsha as explained in Rabbi Shlomo Wahrman, *Sefer Orot HaPesach* (North Bergen, NJ: independently published, 1992), chapter 54.
20. Rambam, *Mishneh Torah*, Hilchot Chametz U'matza 7:5.

——— C ———————————————————————————————

Rabban Gamliel's position becomes clear when we recognize that the most elusive and important step of Maggid remains the step of *historical perpetuation*. Within this context, Rabban Gamliel reminds us that *concrete mitzvot* are essential to the perpetuation of Jewish tradition.

Ideas, concepts and values, as important as they are to any faith tradition, are individual and varied. An individual's understanding of Jewish tradition is bound to be different from that of his ancestors and different, as well, from that of his children and grandchildren. Religious perspective is, after all, greatly shaped by a person's personality, environment and experience.

The tefillin that an individual puts on each morning, however, are the same as those that were worn by his great-great-grandfather and the same as those that will be worn, please God, one day by his great-great-grandsons. Concrete, physical, symbolic mitzvot are critical to the uniform transmission of Jewish tradition, thought and law. Without such mitzvot, the Jewish nation would have long ago faded into oblivion.

Rabban Gamliel confronts a chilling challenge as he arrives at the third and final step of the mitzva of Sippur Yetziat Mitzraim:

We have arrived at an awareness of, and have achieved a sense of personal participation in, the flow of Jewish history. Our task, however, is far from complete. Not by accident, the very formulation of the mitzva of sippur Yetziat Mitzraim *emerges, in part, from the biblical statement:* V'higadeta l'vincha,[21] *"and you shall speak to your child."*[22]

To become full participants in history, on this night of history, we must ensure the future participation of our progeny. I therefore insist that we have not accomplished the mitzva of sippur Yetziat Mitzraim *unless the narrative includes a discussion of the concrete mitzvot of the Seder evening. While these are independent mitzvot, they are also critical components of the narrative itself. These mitzvot, and mitzvot like them, will guarantee the perpetuation of Jewish history. They must therefore be spoken of as we journey towards a full understanding of our personal place in history.*

Thus, with Rabban Gamliel's assistance, we arrive at the third and final stage of the Maggid: the stage of *historical perpetuation*. We recognize that

---

21. Shmot 13:8.
22. Rambam, *Mishneh Torah*, Hilchot Chametz U'matza 7:1.

to become full participants in our nation's journey, we must actively enable that journey to continue. Only upon reaching that realization and making that commitment do we fully rise to the challenge of the Seder night.

Once again, this section of the Maggid closes with a paragraph reflecting our accomplishment. Having coursed through the stages of historical awareness, personalization and perpetuation, we can now fully state: *B'chol dor va'dor chayav adam lirot et atzmo k'ilu hu yatza mi'Mitzraim*, "In each generation, a person must see himself/herself as if he/she came out of Egypt." The Haggada then automatically moves to the section of Hallel (praise) that precedes the meal, as the Seder participants express gratitude to God for the gifts that He has bestowed upon them and upon the entire Jewish people.

And thus we complete our personal Seder-night journey, mandated by the rabbis centuries ago. A journey designed to help each of us realize, on the night that celebrates Jewish history, our own personal, active and essential role in the story of our people.

2 Etched in Stone

Context

Upon concluding the long list of mitzvot recorded in Sefer Devarim, Moshe turns the people's attention to a unique ceremony designed to take place immediately upon their entry into the land.

> And it will be on the day that you cross the Jordan into the land that the Lord your God gives to you, and you shall set up great stones for yourselves and you shall coat them with plaster.
>
> And you shall inscribe upon them all the words of this law, when you cross over, so that you may come into the land that the Lord your God gives to you, a land flowing with milk and honey, as the Lord, the God of your fathers, has promised you.
>
> And it shall be when you have passed over the Jordan, *you shall erect these stones, of which I command you today, on Mount Eival,* and you shall coat them with plaster.
>
> And there you shall build an altar to the Lord your God…
>
> And you shall inscribe upon the stones all the words of this Torah, well explained.[1]

The book of Yehoshua relates that, after Moshe's death, as the nation miraculously crosses the Jordan under Yehoshua's leadership, God commands that twelve stones be taken from the riverbed and carried to "the lodging place where you shall lodge this night." Yehoshua complies and, in addition, replaces these stones with twelve others to remain in the riverbed.[2] The twelve stones taken from the Jordan are erected by Yehoshua at Gilgal, the location of the nation's first formal encampment in the land.[3]

A few chapters later, however, the text records that Yehoshua builds

---

1. Devarim 27:2–5.
2. Yehoshua 4:2–9.
3. Ibid., 4:20.

an altar on Mount Eival, in accordance with Moshe's earlier instructions. After offering *korbanot*, Yehoshua proceeds to "inscribe there upon the stones, the repetition of Moshe's Torah that he [Moshe] had written in the presence of the children of Israel."[4]

Questions

A series of questions emerge as we consider Moshe's initial instructions concerning the stone monument to be erected on Mount Eival and the events later recorded in the book of Yehoshua as the nation enters the land.

What is the significance of the shrine to be erected on Mount Eival? Why is the building of this monument so important that it is divinely chosen to be the first act performed by the nation upon entry into the land?

What exact text is meant to be inscribed on the stones?

Moshe states: "And it shall be on the day that you cross the Jordan into the land that the Lord your God gives to you, and you shall set up great stones for yourselves and you shall coat them with plaster. And you shall inscribe…" He then reiterates: "And it shall be when you have passed over the Jordan, you shall erect these stones, of which I command you today, on Mount Eival, and you shall coat them with plaster… And you shall inscribe…" Why does Moshe repeat the same commandment twice within the span of a few sentences?

What is the meaning of God's instruction that the inscription on the stones must be "well explained?"

Are the stones that God commands Yehoshua to remove from the Jordan's riverbed synonymous with the ones of which God spoke in His initial instructions to Moshe? If so, why does Yehoshua erect these stones at Gilgal and not directly at Mount Eival, as God had originally specified?

What is the character of the stones that Yehoshua does eventually erect at Mount Eival? Are they the same set that he had originally erected at Gilgal, or are they a new array?

Finally, why does Yehoshua decide to replace the twelve stones that he takes from the Jordan riverbed with twelve others?

---

4. Ibid., 8:30–32.

Approaches

——A——————————————————————————————————————

We open our discussion by analyzing, through the eyes of the scholars, the chain of events that actually unfolds upon the Israelites' entry into the land. This analysis will inexorably lead us back to Moshe's initial instructions to the nation before his death.

The subject of our discussion becomes even more tantalizing in light of archaeological findings on Mount Eival that, according to Haifa University professor Adam Zertal, are those of a solitary altar dating to the time of the Israelite conquest of the land.[5]

An early Talmudic source maintains that two sets of stones are referred to in the Yehoshua narrative: one set erected by Yehoshua in the Jordan and one erected by this leader in Gilgal.[6] Commenting on the Talmud's failure to mention a third set of stones erected on Mount Eival, Rashi quotes a Mishnaic tradition,[7] elaborated upon by the Gemara,[8] that the stones used at Gilgal and Eival were *one and the same*.

Although the book of Yehoshua mentions the placement of the stones at Gilgal before their placement at Eival, the Mishna explains, the sequence actually unfolds in reverse order. On the day of the nation's entry into the land, the Israelites immediately travel the lengthy distance to the mountains of Gerizim and Eival, carrying with them the stones from the Jordan's riverbed. Upon arriving at their destination, the people participate in a series of powerful, divinely ordained rituals. The blessings and curses designated for public recitation on the mountains of Gerizim and Eival[9] are presented, the stones removed from the Jordan are constructed into an altar on Mount Eival and plastered over, passages of text are inscribed on the stone altar, offerings are brought, the altar is disassembled and the stones are transported to Gilgal, where they remain.[10]

---

5. Adam Zertal, "Has Joshua's Altar Been Found on Mount Ebal?" *Biblical Archaeological Review* 11, no. 1 (January–February 1985): 26–44.
6. Talmud Bavli Sota 35b.
7. Mishna Sota 7:5.
8. Rashi, Talmud Bavli Sota 35b.
9. Devarim 27:11–26.
10. Talmud Bavli Sota 36a.

——— **B** ———————————————————————————————

A striking puzzle emerges, however, when we compare Rashi's commentary on the Talmud to his commentary on the book of Devarim. In his explanation of Moshe's instructions in Devarim concerning the stone monument, Rashi declares: "There were, thus, *three sets of stones*: twelve stones [erected in] the Jordan, the same number [erected at] Gilgal and the same number [erected on] Mount Eival, as it states in the tractate of Sota."[11]

Not only does Rashi apparently contradict his own contention identifying the stones of Eival and Gilgal as one and the same, but he also quotes the Talmudic discussion as proof of the existence of three separate sets of stones in Joshua's time. As explained above, however, *the Talmud identifies only two sets of stones associated with Joshua's actions.*

The riddle of these conflicting comments is noted by scholars from Rashi's time onward. Some authorities, such as the Maharal, offer potential solutions. In his commentary on Rashi, the *Gur Aryeh*, the Maharal suggests that Rashi's observations on Devarim actually reference three acts of stone construction, as opposed to three separate sets of stones. Two of these acts of construction, at Eival and Gilgal, utilize the same stones.[12] Many other authorities, however, find the Maharal's answer, as well as other suggested answers, unsatisfactory. These scholars are forced to remain with unanswered questions concerning Rashi's commentary.

——— **C** ———————————————————————————————

The motivation for Yehoshua's decision, as the nation crosses the Jordan, to replace the twelve stones taken from the riverbed with twelve others is debated by the scholars. Some authorities maintain that this action is utilitarian in nature. Having removed twelve stones from under the "standing site" of the Kohanim, Yehoshua replaces these stones to ensure that the priests, who are commanded to remain in place until the nation miraculously crosses the Jordan, will not sink into the riverbed mud.[13] Other authorities disagree, maintaining that the stones placed in the riverbed are meant to serve as a lasting monument, marking the place where the waters of the Jordan miraculously stood and allowed the Israelites to cross.[14]

—————————————

11. Rashi, Devarim 7:2.
12. Gur Aryeh.
13. Quoted in Nachshoni, *Hagot B'parshiot HaTorah*, vol. 2, p. 808.
14. Ralbag, Yehoshua 4:9; Aggadot HaMaharsha, Sota 35b.

In a startling move, Rashi traces the origin of Yehoshua's riverbed monument to Moshe's original instructions to the nation in Devarim. According to Rashi, Moshe's opening statement "And it shall be on the day that you cross the Jordan into the land that the Lord your God gives to you, and you shall set up great stones for yourselves and you shall coat them with plaster," refers not to the stones eventually erected on Mount Eival, but to *the twelve replacement stones* placed by Yehoshua in the Jordan. Only after referencing this riverbed monument does Moshe then delineate the commandment to erect the monument on Mount Eival. By insisting that Moshe speaks of two different monuments in his instructions to the nation, *Rashi solves the apparent redundancy in Moshe's words.*[15]

Rashi's contention that the riverbed monument is part of God's original intent seems to be contradicted by the absence of any divine commandment concerning the placement of twelve stones in the Jordan as the events unfold. At face value, this act seems to emerge as a product of Yehoshua's own initiative. Addressing this omission, the Radak suggests, "Even though we do not see God commanding Yehoshua concerning these stones, once [Yehoshua] places them, we can deduce that he did so at God's command."[16]

Another difficulty arises, however, concerning Rashi's suggestion that Moshe references the riverbed monument in his initial directive to the people. As Moshe speaks of these stones, he states, "And you shall inscribe upon them all the words of this law, when you cross over..." Nowhere, however, in the book of Yehoshua is there any indication that the stones erected by Yehoshua in the Jordan were inscribed at all.

— **D** —————————————————————————

Most authorities maintain, therefore, that Yehoshua's riverbed monument is not commanded by God in the Torah at all.

Faced with the resultant apparent redundancy in Moshe's words (see above), the Abravanel offers a creative solution. Moshe, this sage maintains, does not simply outline the first rituals to be observed by the Israelites upon entry into the land. Instead, step by step, this great leader explains how these rituals are divinely calculated to perform an all-important goal:

---

15. Rashi, Devarim 27:2.
16. Radak, Yehoshua 4:9.

to transform the nation's natural desire for personal glory into a powerful statement of submission to God's will.

Noting the common practice of nations to memorialize their conquests through the erection of stone monuments, Moshe opens his remarks to the people in *narrative, as opposed to imperative, terms*: "And it will be on the day that you cross the Jordan into the land that the Lord your God gives to you, and you shall set up great stones for yourselves and you shall coat them with plaster. And you shall inscribe upon them all the words of this law, when you cross over." *When you enter the land, you will naturally, of your own volition, desire to erect a monument to mark your entry. And you will plan to inscribe on this monument the glorious story of your achievements through the Exodus, Revelation, desert travels and conquests in the Transjordan.*

Changing his tone to the imperative, however, Moshe then continues: "And it shall be when you have passed over the Jordan, you shall erect these stones, of which I command you today, on Mount Eival, and you shall coat them with plaster. And there you shall build an altar to the Lord your God…. And you shall inscribe upon the stones all the words of this Torah, well explained." *God directs you to transform your natural desire for personal glory into a public acknowledgment of God's power, your dependence upon Him, and your submission to His will. The very monument that you planned to erect as a testament to your own achievements must be turned into an altar for His worship on Mount Eival, upon which you will inscribe His law.*

Specifically as they enter the land, at a time when other nations would celebrate their own glorious achievements, the Israelites are commanded to publicly acknowledge that their partnership with the divine is the source of all their past, current and future accomplishments.[17]

——— **E** ———————————————————————————

Other far-ranging possibilities are considered by the scholars as they struggle to explain the apparent redundancy in Moshe's words.

The Malbim, for example, postulates that God actually commands the nation to inscribe the same monument stones twice.

The first inscription, engraved as the nation crosses the Jordan, is executed without any expertise and is almost immediately plastered over. The

17. Abravanel, Devarim 27:1–8.

second inscription, in contrast, is carefully etched by professional scribes into the plaster covering the first, as the nation assembles at Mount Eival.

Each of these inscriptions, the Malbim explains, served a unique purpose. The outer writing, professionally executed, was designed to be readily accessible and comprehensible to the surrounding nations. The hidden, protected, original inscription was fashioned to serve as a proof text at the "end of days," to counter potential arguments that the exposed text had been corrupted across the ages due to its accessibility.[18]

F

As the scholars continue to delve into the significance of the entire monument ritual, the question of the text inscribed on the stones takes on pivotal significance.

Basing his opinion on Moshe's statement "And you shall inscribe upon them all the words of this law, when you cross over, so that you may come into the land that the Lord your God gives to you…," the Ramban maintains that *the entire Torah* was to be inscribed on the stones. Only the inclusion of the complete text would fully demonstrate to all that the Israelites had entered the land solely "for the sake of the Torah."[19]

Other authorities take a more practical approach, maintaining that only portions of the biblical text were recorded on the stones. Offering a position later quoted by the Chizkuni, the Ibn Ezra and others, Rav Saadia Gaon argues that the inscribed text was limited to a listing of the Torah's 613 commandments. Later scholars offer additional theories, identifying passages such as portions of the Shma[20] and the prohibition against idolatry[21] as possible texts included in the inscription on the stones.

Whatever the original text carved on these stones, God's message to the Israelites through the powerful rituals to be performed immediately upon their entry into the land seems abundantly clear: *Your entry into, and successful conquest, settlement and retention of the land will be forever dependent upon your continued study and observance of My law.*

---

18. Malbim, Devarim 27:1–8.
19. Ramban, Devarim 27:3.
20. *Haktav V'hakabala*, Devarim 27:8.
21. Rabbi David Tzvi Hoffman, quoted in Nachshoni, *Hagot B'parshiot HaTorah*, vol. 2, p. 809.

— G —

The Talmud, however, makes a startling claim, based upon Moshe's closing phrase, "explained well."

"And they inscribed upon it [the altar] the entire Torah *in seventy languages*, as it states in the text: 'explained well.'"[22]

Mirroring the Talmudic tradition that postulates the existence of seventy Gentile nations in the world at the time of the giving of the Torah, the Mishnaic tradition opens the door to a greater contemplation of the monument's purpose. To the rabbinic mind, the messages of the monument were not only directed internally towards the Israelites, but *outwardly towards the nations of the world, as well.*

One possible worldwide message emerges from a technical Talmudic debate between Rabbi Yehuda and Rabbi Shimon concerning the method of inscription on the monument. This debate quickly widens into a discussion of the guilt incumbent upon the nations of the world for their failure to learn and accept Torah. The existence of a permanent engraved text of the Torah or portions thereof, these scholars maintain, removes any possible excuse for that failure.[23] Later scholars, including Rabbi Levi Yitzchak of Berditchev, view the monument's inscription as continuing testimony to the world concerning the Jewish nation's right to the Land of Israel. *Only the people who accept the law reflected on My stones*, the monument silently testifies, *will merit possession of this holiest of lands.*[24]

Other universal lessons are identified by the authorities as they continue to uncover meaning for the non-Jewish world in this ancient seventy-language monument.

Glimpsed through the mists of history, fashioned by the hands of the Israelites at the moment of their entry into their land, a series of stones and the messages upon them continue to speak to us and to the world around us, to this day.

Points to Ponder

The rituals to be performed immediately upon the Israelites' entry into the land acquire greater significance when viewed against an overarching truth

---

22. Mishna Sota 7:5.
23. Talmud Bavli Sota 35b.
24. *Kedushat Levi al HaTorah*, Ki Tavo, Devarim 27:3.

that we have encountered before in our studies: *Sanctity in this world is established by man, acting in partnership with God.*

Our point can best be made by raising a seemingly simple question. At what historical juncture does the Land of Israel become holy?

Logic would dictate that God sanctifies the land from time immemorial, that by the time the patriarch Avraham travels at God's behest from Charan to Canaan, he is already traveling to a sanctified, holy place.

According to rabbinic thought, however, such is not the case. The rabbis, in fact, identify two historical "sanctifications" pertaining to the Land of Israel.

1. *Kedusha rishona*, the first sanctification, dates to the nation's entry into and conquest of the land under the leadership of Yehoshua.

2. *Kedusha shnia*, the second sanctification, is established centuries later when a small contingent of Jews returns from the Babylonian exile to rebuild the Temple under the leadership of Ezra and Nechemia.

The very fact that the rabbis posit these two historical moments of sanctification indicates that *they are unwilling to accept a process of sanctification of the Land of Israel that does not involve the Jewish nation.* Until the Israelites become a nation and actively establish a relationship with their land, the Land of Israel is like any other land on the globe, bereft of unique sanctity or holiness. As we have already noted in numerous other contexts, *sanctity cannot take root in the world without man's involvement in partnership with God* (see *Shmot*: Shmot 3, *Approaches* D, E; Yitro 2, *Approaches* C, D; Teruma 2, *Approaches* C).

Even more telling, however, is the majority rabbinic view concerning the lasting effect of these two investitures of sanctity. The first sanctification of the Land of Israel, the rabbis maintain, establishes temporal holiness for that time, *but does not establish lasting holiness for the future.* With the exception of Jerusalem, the land loses its sanctity upon the nation's exile to Babylon. The second sanctification of the Land of Israel, in contrast, establishes both temporal holiness for that time *and lasting holiness for the future, throughout the land.*[25]

This conclusion seems powerfully counterintuitive. The first sanctification unfolds convincingly, as a triumphant Israelite nation, aided by God's miraculous intervention, sweeps into the land, conquering their enemies

---

25. Rambam, *Mishneh Torah*, Hilchot Terumot 1:5; Hilchot Beit Habechira 6:15.

before them. The second sanctification is much humbler and quieter. A small percentage of the exiled Jewish population of Babylon returns to its homeland and struggles to reestablish its presence in the land.

Why, then, is the second sanctification of the Land of Israel, at the time of Ezra and Nechemia, more effective than the first?

An intriguing answer is provided by Rabbi Joseph Soloveitchik. The first sanctification of Israel, the Rav explains, begins at the spiritual periphery of the land and only eventually, centuries later, works its way to Jerusalem, the land's spiritual heart. The second sanctification, however, strikes to Jerusalem first and then works its way outward, allowing the lasting holiness of Jerusalem to invest the rest of the land.[26]

Expanding on the Rav's observation, we can also note the primarily spiritual nature of Ezra and Nechemia's entry into the land as they move to immediately rebuild the Temple. This approach stands in stark contrast to the necessary physical character of Yehoshua's conquests. Telling, as well, is the personal sacrifice of the Jews returning to Israel under Ezra and Nechamia, as they turn their backs on the ease and comfort of Babylon in order to return to and rebuild a devastated land.

For these and other reasons, the second sanctification of Israel outlasts the first.

Nonetheless, the first entry of the nation into the land requires a spiritual component to establish even its temporal effectiveness. Perhaps that reality underlies the divinely mandated rituals that unfold on Mount Eival. As the first acts performed upon the nation's entry into the land, before the physical business of conquest begins, these powerful ceremonies drive home to the Israelites the true nature of their current adventure. *They are not simply coming home. In partnership with God, they are investing their homeland with sanctity.*

---

26. Pinchas Peli, *On Repentance: The Thought and Oral Discourses of Rabbi Joseph Dov Soloveitchik* (Northvale, NJ: Jason Aronson, 1996), pp. 314–316.

3 Which of These Does Not Belong?

Context

As Moshe continues his discussion of the rituals divinely mandated for performance immediately upon the nation's entry into the land, he elaborates on a powerful ceremony first mentioned in Parshat Re'eh: the public blessings and curses to be pronounced at Mount Gerizim and Mount Eival.

Moshe delineates twelve curses that are to be included in this ceremony, with the understanding that twelve corresponding blessings are to be recited, as well.[1] Each curse is presented as resulting from a specific, easily identifiable sin, such as idolatry, perversion of justice, incest, the taking of bribes, etc....with one exception. The last in the litany of curses reads: "Accursed is he who will not uphold the words of this Torah, to perform them."[2]

Questions

The final curse in the list seems clearly out of place. What specific sin is reflected in a failure to "uphold the words of this Torah, to perform them"?

After delineating a litany of clear, detailed sins, why does the Torah cap the list with such a vague, general statement?

Approaches

—A—

Two very different approaches emerge in rabbinic literature as the scholars struggle to understand this final curse in the litany at Gerizim and Eival. Reaching across the centuries, they interpret it in ways that are uncannily relevant to the challenges of our time.

---

1. Talmud Bavli Sota 37b.
2. Devarim 27:11–26.

At one end of the spectrum lie those authorities who attempt to identify *a specific act or omission* that would fall under the rubric of failing to
uphold the Torah.

The Talmud Yerushalmi, for example, quotes a series of scholars who
interpret this phrase as referring to individuals who possess the power to
sustain the honor and authority of the Torah but fail to do so. Included
in this category, the rabbis maintain, are individuals who have the means
to enable others to study, as well as those who can effectively defend the
Torah against its detractors.

In a dramatic application of this approach, Rav Huna and Rav Yehuda
quote Shmuel, who identifies this verse as the catalyst for a powerful historical event. During the reign of the righteous Judean king Yoshiyahu, the
Temple is renovated under the direction of the High Priest, Chilkiyahu.
In the course of this renovation, a Torah scroll is found and read before
the king, who experiences a deep emotional reaction to what he hears.[3]
Shmuel maintains that it is the verse "Accursed is he who will not uphold
the words of this Torah, to perform them" that causes Yoshiyahu to "rend
his garments"[4] and exclaim, *It is my responsibility to uphold!*[5] Fearful of
divine retribution over the rampant corruption in Judea, and newly sensitive to his own responsibility to address the situation, Yoshiyahu launches a
major religious reformation across the length and breadth of his kingdom.[6]

Centuries later, the rosh yeshiva of the Yeshiva of Volozhin, Rabbi
Naftali Tzvi Yehuda Berlin (the Netziv), quotes and tellingly applies the
Yerushalmi's observations concerning each individual's obligation to sustain,
when possible, the Torah's honor and authority.

This towering nineteenth-century Talmudist, whose scholarship and
personal love for his students transformed his yeshiva into the largest of its
time, sees the biblical imperative to "uphold the words of [the] Torah" as
mandating communal support for those engaged in Torah study. Individuals capable of providing such support, Rabbi Berlin argues, are obligated to
enable Torah scholars to "be free to fight the war of Torah study, that they
may be strengthened through the Torah of the Lord."[7]

---

3. Melachim II 22:3–11.
4. Ibid., 22:11.
5. Talmud Yerushalmi Sota 7:4.
6. Melachim II 23:1–31.
7. *Haamek Davar*, Devarim 27:26.

The Netziv's observations hardly break new ground. As we have noted before, the concept of community-supported yeshivot and *kollelim* (institutions of all-day high-level Torah study for the married man) has a long and proud tradition within Jewish history (see *Bereishit*: Toldot 3, *Points to Ponder*). Nonetheless, the Netziv's emphasis on this issue does reflect his own pivotal position in the growing yeshiva movement of his time and foreshadows the proliferation of communally supported institutions of higher Torah study in Europe, America and Israel in the years that follow. The efforts of this great sage, his contemporaries, and countless leading scholars in the decades that follow ensure the survival and dynamic growth of Torah study during the turbulent years prior to and after the Holocaust. Largely due to their efforts, the amount of Torah being studied in Israel, America and across the globe has, a short eighty years after the Holocaust, reached heights unattained since the days of the Babylonian academies. At the same time, this monumental growth has ignited an increasingly bitter debate in Israel and elsewhere over the appropriate level of communal support for full-time Torah study and over the potential familial and communal obligations of the students themselves. (See *Bereishit*: Toldot 3, *Approaches* C, *Points to Ponder* and *Shmot*: Beshalach 4, *Approaches* D, *Points to Ponder*, for a discussion of this critical issue.)

———— **B** ————

At the other end of the spectrum lie those scholars who see no need to re-define the last curse at Gerizim and Eival in specific terms. These scholars are, instead, willing to accept the broad, general tone of the declaration, "Accursed is he who will not uphold the words of this Torah, to perform them," at face value.

Leading this group, Rashi builds on a Talmudic discussion[8] and insists that with this final admonition to "uphold the words of [the] Torah, to perform them," God includes the *obligation to observe the entire Torah* in the pact enacted upon the Israelites' entry into the land. With their public acceptance of this admonition, Rashi continues, the nation accepts this full observance "with an imprecation and an oath."[9]

While Rashi's broad approach would appear to be in line with the text

---

8. Talmud Bavli Shevuot 36a.
9. Rashi, Devarim 27:26.

of this curse, a serious problem emerges. If God closes the litany of curses at Gerizim and Eival with an overarching warning to observe the entire Torah on pain of divine sanction, why are all the previous curses detailing specific sins necessary? A simple issuance of this last warning should have been sufficient.

In a brilliant stroke, the Ramban answers this question by suggesting that the last warning at Gerizim and Eival does not deal with the issue of *observing* the mitzvot, but with the issue of *accepting* them:

> In my opinion, this acceptance requires that an individual acknowledge the mitzvot in his heart and consider them to be the truth, that he believe that one who observes them will receive reward and goodness and that if someone denies any of them or considers any of them annulled forever he will be cursed.... This verse is thus a ban on those who rebel [against Torah authority] and who deny [its legitimacy].[10]

According to the Ramban, while the first eleven curses pronounced at Gerizim and Eival are directed against those who commit a specific transgression, the final admonition of the ceremony is totally different. The last warning at Gerizim and Eival, the Ramban notes, does not state "Accursed is *he who will not perform* the words of this Torah." Such a statement would have had the onerous effect of including in this overarching curse any individual who, through weakness or negligence, slips in the performance of even a single mitzva. This general warning instead addresses belief rather than action, condemning those who *fail to accept the validity of the entire Torah*.

Centuries later, the Ramban's approach to the text finds particular resonance in the observations of two towering nineteenth-century scholars who battle for orthodoxy in the face of the developing reform movement and its philosophy of selective observance.

Rabbi Shimshon Raphael Hirsch, the powerful German scholar whose intellectual contributions pave the way for the development of a relationship between Orthodoxy and the modern world, maintains that the last curse at Gerizim and Eival condemns anyone who deliberately "deprives one single word of God's Torah of its validity or binding power, who

---

10. Ramban, Devarim 27:26.

persuades himself or lets himself be persuaded that it no longer need be kept, has lost its meaning and importance…"

Similarly, the Malbim, who earns the enduring enmity of many influential reformers by refusing to compromise on any aspect of traditional observance or belief, and who pays a dear personal price for this resoluteness throughout his rabbinic career, declares: "According to the straightforward meaning of the text, this curse is directed towards those who say that only the spirit and ideals of the Torah are eternal, who argue that the practical mitzvot directed towards man's actions can no longer be relevant because of societal mores and norms that shift over time and place."[11]

With powerful prescience, the Torah thus addresses a threat that will gather strength over two thousand years later, with the advent and growth of the nontraditional denominations of Judaism. Facing the nascent challenge in their day, Rabbi Shimshon Raphael Hirsch and the Malbim respond to the proponents of selective Jewish observance by channeling God's own words, delivered with the first footfalls of the nation into its land: "Accursed is he who will not uphold the words of this Torah, to perform them."

Points to Ponder

A number of years ago, I shocked the members of my congregation on Kol Nidre night by opening my remarks with the topic of *shaatnez*, the biblical prohibition against wearing clothing made of a combination of wool and linen. The response of those present was immediate and visceral, clearly evidenced in the expressions on their faces: *This is what the rabbi chooses to speak to us about on the holiest night of the year? Aren't there more important issues to address? Why has he chosen to speak about an esoteric mitzva that so many of us hardly pay attention to?*

That was precisely the reaction that I expected to see, and it opened the door for the message that I really wanted to deliver: It's one thing when we fail to observe a mitzva. It's quite another when we try to rationalize that mitzva away.

None of us is perfect. We will all stumble in our Torah observance periodically. That, after all, is why we need Yom Kippur. The moment, however, that we dismiss a mitzva as irrelevant to our lives, the moment

---

11. Malbim, Devarim 27:26.

that we begin to pick and choose between the observances that we find meaningful and those that we don't, that's the moment we become guilty of failing to "uphold the words of [the] Torah."

The Torah is a package deal and we are bound by all of its mitzvot. *Loyalty to this principle demonstrates our willingness to adhere to God's will, rather than our own.*

4 Because We Want To...

Context

The Torah abruptly interrupts the Ki Tavo *tochacha* – the lengthy description of potential penalties for collective national failure – in order to address a critical issue: *What sins will be grievous enough to bring about the terrible curses of the* tochacha?

A three-sentence answer is proposed:

And all these curses will come upon you and pursue you and overtake you, until you are destroyed, because you have not listened to the voice of the Lord your God, to observe the commandments and His statutes that He has commanded you.

They [these punishments] will be a sign and a wonder in you and in your offspring, forever.

Because you did not serve the Lord your God *b'simcha*, with joy, and goodness of heart, *mei'rov kol*, through abundance of everything.[1]

Questions

The Torah's response to its own implicit query is problematic on a number of counts.

First of all, the text seems unclear, even contradictory. Will the nation be punished in the future *for a failure to serve God entirely*, as indicated by the first sentence of the passage, or *for a failure to serve God b'simcha, with joy*, as indicated in the last sentence?

If the latter is true, doesn't God's justice seems unduly harsh, to say the least? Can it be that the harrowing penalties of the *tochacha* will befall a people who fulfill God's will completely, yet fail to do so "with joy"?

Why does the Torah interrupt its examination of the possible causes

---

1. Devarim 28:45–47.

of the *tochacha* with the interjection "They [these punishments] will be a sign and a wonder in you and in your offspring, forever"?

Finally, what is the meaning of the linkage drawn in the text between the nation's sin and the passage's closing phrase *mei'rov kol*, "through abundance of everything"?

Approaches

—— A ——————————————————————————

Before addressing the flow of this three-sentence passage as a whole, we turn to its most problematic components.

Confronting the phrase "Because you did not serve the Lord your God *b'simcha*, with joy, and goodness of heart," numerous authorities raise the obvious question: Can it be that God would visit the severe punishments of the *tochacha* upon a people whose only sin is the absence of joy?

Unwilling to accept this possibility, authorities as disparate as Rabbi Menachem Mendel Morgensztern of Kotzk (the first Kotzker Rebbe), the Chatam Sofer and Rabbi Baruch Halevi Epstein suggest a rereading of the text. This phrase, these scholars contend, should not be read "because you did not serve the Lord your God with joy" but, instead, *"because with joy [i.e., joyfully] you did not serve the Lord your God."* The nation will be punished *not for the absence of joy in their fulfillment of God's law but for the presence of joy in their defiance of that law.*[2]

Other scholars, in contrast, fully embrace the possibility that the nation could be severely punished for the absence of "joy" in their observance of God's law.

Rabbeinu Bachya ben Asher, for example, explains that "joy in the performance of a mitzva is a mitzva unto itself, meriting its own distinct reward."[3] An individual who fulfills God's will grudgingly, therefore, transgresses a fundamental commandment and becomes liable for punishment.[4]

Centuries later, Rabbi Chaim of Volozhin, the founder of the first great Lithuanian yeshiva, further expounds upon the essential nature of joy in the performance of mitzvot. Service performed grudgingly at another's

---

2. Kotzker Rebbe, quoted in Aharon Yaakov Greenberg, *Iturei Torah* (Tel Aviv: Yavneh, 1972), Devarim 28:47; *Tosefet Bracha*, Devarim 28:47.
3. Rabbeinu Bachya ben Asher, Devarim 28:47.
4. Ibid.

behest, this scholar argues, carries the character of "the service of slaves" executed to satisfy the whim of a hated taskmaster. An individual who observes God's will reluctantly, therefore, treats God as an "enemy" and will ultimately pay a heavy price.[5]

Rabbi Shmuel Bornstein, the second Rebbe of the Sochatchover dynasty, argues that the presence of joy and personal gratification in any societal enterprise is critical to the success and continuity of the enterprise itself. Absent *simcha*, all communal endeavors run the risk of descending into dissension, rivalry and strife. Only a generation lacking joy in their service of God could have evidenced the baseless hatred that, according to Talmudic testimony,[6] caused the destruction of the Second Temple. To this day, Rabbi Bornstein adds, the act of "gladdening" a bride and groom at their wedding remains a critical mitzva. All effort must be made to ensure that this couple's initial step towards the creation of a Jewish home and the perpetuation of the Jewish nation will be rooted in sustaining *simcha*.[7]

— **B** —

Moving to the close of the passage, numerous scholars struggle with the Torah's puzzling contention that the people will be punished for sinning *mei'rov kol*, "through abundance of everything." What connection between abundance and sin, these authorities ask, does the Torah implicitly draw in this statement?

Following Rashi's lead, some scholars reinterpret the words *mei'rov kol* to mean "*while you yet possessed* an abundance of everything."[8] The nation, these authorities contend, will be condemned for its lack of *hakarat hatov* (appreciation) for the gifts bestowed upon them by God during times of plenty. This sentiment is reflected in Rabbi Natan's famous maxim in Pirkei Avot, "He who neglects the Torah in wealth shall, in the end, neglect it in poverty."[9]

A literal interpretation of the phrase *mei'rov kol*, however, projecting abundance not only as the backdrop for sin *but as a catalyst for sin*, can be

---

5.   Greenberg, *Iturei Torah*, vol. 6, p. 167.
6.   Talmud Bavli Yoma 9b.
7.   Shem Mishmuel.
8.   Rashi, Devarim 28:47. Note the Siftei Chachamim's defense of Rashi's reinterpretation of the text on technical, grammatical grounds.
9.   Pirkei Avot 4:11.

defended on the basis of numerous warnings in the Torah. The powerful caution recorded in Parshat Ekev serves as a prime example:

> Be careful lest you forget the Lord your God by not observing His commandments, His laws and His statutes, which I command you today. Lest you eat and be satisfied, and build good homes and settle down. And your cattle and your sheep will increase, and silver and gold will increase for you, and all that you have will increase. And your hearts will become haughty and you will forget the Lord your God Who took you out of the land of Egypt, from the house of slavery.[10]

Material wealth, the Torah warns, can blind the people to the limitations of their own power, causing them to forget their ultimate dependence upon God. The nation could easily be led to sin, "through abundance of everything."

—— C ——

Adopting an alternate approach, the Meshech Chochma ingeniously interprets the entire sentence as a cohesive whole: "Because you did not serve the Lord your God with joy, and goodness of heart, through abundance of everything."

The nation will fail to serve God, this scholar maintains, specifically because of *the inappropriate "joy and goodness of heart"* that they will experience in response to "an abundance of everything." Quoting the prophet Hoshea, the Meshech Chochma explains that the Jew is enjoined from sharing in "the exultation of [other] nations."[11]

In contrast to those who celebrate physical abundance itself, the Jew is meant to celebrate what that abundance reflects: the clear favor that he has found in God's eyes. By failing to identify the bounty they receive as a God-given gift, by celebrating abundance rather than its source, the nation will set the stage for their own tragic descent into sin.[12]

---

10. Devarim 8:11–14.
11. Hoshea 9:1.
12. Meshech Chochma, Devarim 28:47.

294   UNLOCKING THE TORAH TEXT

— **D** —————————————————————————————————

The sixteenth-century scholar Rabbi Moshe Alshich addresses the apparent internal contradiction in the short three-sentence passage. Will the people be punished, asks the Alshich, for failing to observe God's law *entirely*, as the first sentence of the passage suggests, or will they be punished for failing to observe God's law *with joy*, as the last sentence suggests?

To resolve this contradiction the Alshich maintains that throughout the *tochacha* the Torah actually references two distinct populations. The first of these groups, those who "have not listened to the voice of the Lord" and have thus turned their backs on the commandments completely, will merit total destruction. The second group, however, those whose sin is limited to a failure to serve God with *simcha*, will be punished less severely.[13]

— **E** —————————————————————————————————

A final, global approach to the entire passage before us might be suggested. In three sentences, step by step, God conveys a unified, powerful message to the nation.

When you do something because you have to, and not because you want to, you will ultimately fail.

1. First God identifies the ultimate failure that will give rise to the horrors of the *tochacha*: "…because you have not listened to the voice of the Lord your God, to observe the commandments and His statutes that He has commanded you." *Your global failure to observe My law will condemn you to severe punishment.*

2. In the final sentence of the passage, however, God backs up and notes the origins of that failure. "Because you did not serve the Lord your God *b'simcha*, with joy, and goodness of heart, *mei'rov kol*, through abundance of everything." *You will not abruptly abandon the observance of My law. Instead the roots of your failure will trace to an earlier time when you observed the law, but without passion or joy. Tragic consequences will result from this fatal flaw. Success in our shared enterprise can only be achieved if you invest yourselves in the process, if you derive personal significance, meaning and gratification from our relationship. Your failure to find the* simcha *inherent in the observance of the divine law will inexorably lead to total abdication of that law.*

—————————
13. Torat Moshe, Devarim 28:47.

3. In the midst of this discussion of cause and effect in the development of communal sin, the Torah outlines the true extent of the tragedy through a striking interjection: "They [these punishments] will be a sign and a wonder in you and in your offspring, forever." *The clearest arena of your failure will be the arena of intergenerational transmission. If your observance is absent passion, meaning and significance, you may yet go through the motions. Your children, however, will not. That which you perform grudgingly, they will abandon entirely. Consequently, these punishments will truly become* "a sign and a wonder in you and in your offspring, forever."

Points to Ponder

I believe that one of the greatest failings in today's modern Orthodox community is the absence of *simcha* in the performance of mitzvot.

While we proclaim loyalty to the laws of the Torah, our actual ritual observance is often pro forma, habitual, even grudging, with little passion or meaning marking the proceedings.

The signs of this phenomenon in our communities are ubiquitous, and include:

- the half-empty sanctuaries on Shabbat morning until midpoint in the prayer services when the pews finally begin to fill
- the absence of positive Shabbat-related activities in many homes, e.g. zemirot (Shabbat songs), Torah discussion and study, special Sabbath dress and decorum, as the letter of the Sabbath law is observed while its spirit is ignored
- the emptiness of the prayer experience on Shabbat and throughout the week, at services marked by the participants' lack of emotional involvement and by side conversations that often drown out the prayers themselves
- the advent of shortcuts to make religious life "easier" – professionally prepared Purim baskets, catered Shabbat meals, Pesach vacations – taking the place of the family-focused preparations and observances that traditionally involved the entire family in the celebration of these occasions

Sadly, the unintended intergenerational consequences of this phenomenon are evident, as well:

- the diminishing participation of community teenagers in any form of worship on Shabbat morning
- the graduates of Modern Orthodox high schools who abandon Shabbat and *kashrut* observance within a few years of their graduation
- the growing number of young men and women who become totally disenfranchised from Jewish observance shortly after arriving at the college campus
- the development of "half-Shabbat" – observing some Shabbat laws yet ignoring others, particularly the prohibition of texting friends on Shabbat
- The vexing problem of alcohol and drug abuse within the observant high school community as our children search for fulfillment elsewhere

The message of the *tochacha* is frighteningly clear. Absent passion in our religious observance, the transmission of any tradition to our children will become increasingly difficult. A religion that does not speak to their hearts may, tragically, be abandoned.

To address the problem, we cannot start with our children, but rather with ourselves. Only if we find *simcha shel mitzva* – the joy inherent in the performance of the mitzvot – in our own lives can we hope to foster such *simcha* in theirs. Only if we search for personal meaning in our observance of God's law do we stand a chance of passing that observance on to the next generation.

5 Cause and Effect Confusion?

Context

Two similar verses are found in the *tochacha* of Ki Tavo, the lengthy list of potential penalties for collective national failure:

> The Lord will bring you and your king, whom you have set up over yourselves, to a nation you never knew, neither you nor your fathers, *v'avadeta sham* (and there you will serve) other gods, of wood and stone.[1]
>
> And the Lord will scatter you among all the peoples from one end of the earth to the other end of the earth, *v'avadeta sham* (and there you will serve) other gods whom you did not know, neither you nor your fathers, [gods] of wood and stone.[2]

Questions

The second half of each of these sentences, stating that the nation will "serve other gods," hardly seems to belong in the lengthy list of penalties outlined in the *tochacha*. Idolatry and apostasy are, after all, each *causes* for punishment rather than *punishments* themselves.

Why are these apparent *accusations* of sin abruptly leveled here, in the midst of the Torah's description of the *consequences* of sin? If the Torah intended to cite idolatry as a reason for the nation's decline, why not include that citation much earlier in the text, at the start of the *tochacha*, in a description of the "causes" of failure rather than in a description of its "effects"?

---

1. Devarim 28:36.
2. Ibid., 28:64.

Approaches

─── A ───

An early approach towards reconciling these Torah passages contextually is found in Targum Onkelos, the seminal Aramaic translation of the Torah penned during the Mishnaic period. Implicitly recognizing that a straightforward mention of idolatry would be out of place at either of these points in the text, Onkelos, a righteous Roman convert to Judaism, interpretively translates each of these phrases as an additional threat of divine retribution: "and there you will serve other gods whom you did not know…," *and there you will serve nations who serve gods whom you did not know…*

Onkelos apparently finds latitude for his approach in the inherent ambiguity embedded in the Hebrew word *v'avadeta*. Dependent upon the context, this term can either mean "you shall worship" or "you shall serve." Faced with the contextual problem raised by the mention of idolatry in the *tochacha's* list of punishments, Onkelos translates the phrase to mean "*you shall be subject to those who worship other gods.*"

Three towering biblical scholars, separated by centuries, choose, each in their own way, to follow Onkelos's approach in their interpretations of the text.

Commenting on the second of the two verses, Rabbi Saadia Gaon, arguably the greatest scholar of the Geonic period (late sixth–eleventh centuries), simply states: "[This phrase implies] the concept of subjugation and servitude."[3]

In the eleventh century, Rashi places a practical spin on Onkelos's theme by explaining this same passage to mean: "You will be required to pay taxes and tribute to the priests of idolatry."[4]

Finally, the nineteenth-century scholar Rabbi Shimshon Raphael Hirsch, in explaining both verses, waxes philosophical:

> The context teaches that here it is not speaking of actual idolatry, but is rather a description of the general fate that will befall Israel in exile. The nations to whom Israel would be subject are themselves under

─────────────────────

3. Saadia Gaon, Devarim 28:64.
4. Rashi, Devarim 28:64.

the mastery of the heathen gods and form their whole way of life and behavior under their influence.

So that in truth Israel is subject to the pagan worship of the gods.... All the bitterness of the future centuries of exile is rooted in the fact that *Israel's fate became dependent on men before whose eyes the light of monotheistic Truth did not shine and did not bring them to humaneness by its penetrating education.*[5]

According to Rav Hirsch, the very dependence of the Jewish nation on alien cultures subjugates them to the cruel and immoral belief systems – to "the gods" of those cultures.

— **B** —————————————————————

A totally different approach to these passages is suggested by Rabbi Don Yitzchak Abravanel, the last great figure of Spanish Jewry.

The Abravanel openly rejects Onkelos's suggestion that the repeated phrase "and there you will serve other gods" references the nation's future subjugation to idolaters. Adhering instead to the literal interpretation of the text, the Abravanel insists that the Torah does include the practice of idolatry in its litany of *tochacha* punishments.

By way of explanation for this phenomenon, this great sage, whose personal life trajectory takes him from the Spanish royal palace to exile from Spain in 1492, offers an explanation in which we can glimpse the pain and anguish that he must have experienced and witnessed. *Apostasy, the Abravanel maintains, can sometimes be viewed as a punishment*: "The intent of this verse is not that they [the Israelites] will become subject to those who worship other gods, as Onkelos and Rashi suggest. Instead the concept here is that after their exile, many will abandon their faith due to the torments and persecutions that they will be unable to bear."[6]

An even clearer exposition on this theme can be found in the Abravanel's comments on the earlier, similar verse in Parshat Va'etchanan, "And there you will serve other gods, the handiwork of man, of wood and stone, that do not see, and do not hear, and do not taste, and do not smell"[7]:

---

5. Rabbi Shimshon Raphael Hirsch, Devarim 38:36, 38:64.
6. Abravanel, Devarim 28.
7. Devarim 4:28.

> Due to overwhelming persecution in the lands of their dispersion, many of them will leave the community of their faith and embrace idolatrous worship...not because they will believe in these idols.... They will worship them only in order to escape death...
>
> The idolatry referred to here is thus not in the sense of sin, but rather as part of the punishment inflicted on them, *for this will be the greatest of the tragedies, that in spite of their internal recognition of and belief in God, they will be forced against their will to serve idols...* (Italics mine)"[8]

From the vantage point of history, the Abravanel's words can be seen as frighteningly prescient, ironically concerning his own community. No chapter of the Jewish journey is fraught with greater pain, anguish and controversy then that of the Conversos, three groups of Jewish converts to Christianity and their descendents in the Iberian Peninsula. The first group converted in the wake of the massacres in Spain in 1391; the second, also in Spain, following the decree of Ferdinand and Isabella in 1492, expelling all Jews who refused to accept Christianity; the third group, in Portugal, by force and royal fiat in 1497. While many Conversos embraced their new Christian identity fully, others became Crypto-Jews (more famously known as Marranos, a pejorative term), practicing Judaism secretly while publicly professing allegiance to the Catholic faith.

The years that followed their conversions failed to provide the Conversos with the safety and security they might have hoped for. Even those who considered themselves "New Christians" were met with suspicion, ostracism and persecution from the general Christian population, while the Crypto-Jews lived in constant fear for their lives. The rising Spanish Inquisition specifically targeted the Conversos, in an attempt to root out "heresy" from their midst. Thousands were tortured, imprisoned and executed in Spain, Portugal and their colonies throughout the world.

Heaping insult upon injury, those Crypto-Jews who eventually fled in the face of the continuing persecution faced obstacles in their attempts to rejoin the Jewish community. At the core of the issues lay the question of the Crypto-Jews' failure to obey the overarching halachic principle

---

8. Abravanel, Devarim 4:25–30.

mandating the choice of martyrdom over apostasy during times of public persecution.[9]

Numerous authorities attempted to reconcile this severe ruling with the sad fate of the Crypto-Jews by adopting lenient halachic positions.[10] Some based their decisions on an earlier decision of the Rambam that although individuals who choose apostasy over martyrdom "annul the positive precept of sanctifying God's name and transgress the negative commandment of desecrating God's name," they are, nonetheless, exempt from punishment because of the coercion they faced.[11] Many of these scholars distinguished between those Conversos who fled the lands of persecution when possible, in order to practice their religion freely, and those who remained behind because of material or other practical considerations.[12]

With the passage of time, the situation of the Conversos became increasingly complex. Many descendents of the original Crypto-Jews who remained in their native lands began to forget Jewish tradition and assimilated into the general culture, some retaining vestiges of Jewish practice without any knowledge of their own Jewish origins. Those Crypto-Jews who continued to escape across the centuries faced increased doubts and debates over issues of their personal status.

To this day, the sad saga of the Conversos continues to reverberate through the Jewish world, in the debate over the percentage of natives of the Iberian Peninsula who can trace part of their ancestry to Jewish origins, in unexpected personal discoveries of Jewish ancestry by the descendents of Crypto-Jews, even in the discovery of communities of knowing and unknowing Crypto-Jews.

While the exact number of souls lost to the Jewish people during this tragic process will never be known, there is no question that the story of the Conversos proves the Abravanel's point: *Within the turbulent history of the Jewish people, apostasy itself can be a punishment.*

— C —

Following a similar path, another Spanish scholar, a contemporary of the Abravanel, openly notes a connection between the *tochacha* and his own

---

9. Rambam, *Mishneh Torah*, Hilchot Yesodei HaTorah 5:1–3.
10. *Tshuvot HaRivash* 4.
11. Rambam, *Mishneh Torah*, Hilchot Yesodei HaTorah 5:4.
12. *Tshuvot HaRivash* 4; Tashbetz 3:47.

turbulent times. Rabbi Yitzchak ben Moshe Arama, the Ba'al Ha'Akeida, maintains that the punishment embedded in the phrase "and there you will serve other gods" becomes fully evident only upon reading one of the immediately subsequent verses: "And among the nations you will find no ease and there will be no resting place for the sole of your foot; and there the Lord will give you a trembling heart, longing of eyes and suffering of soul."[13]

The Ba'al Ha'Akeida suggests:

> We may possibly find an allusion in this verse to our exile within which thousands of Jews can be found who have renounced their religion as a result of the suffering and persecution placed upon them. And behold, regarding these apostates the Torah states, "And among the nations you will find no ease…"
>
> Although they would assimilate among the nations, they will not find among them "ease or a place for the sole of their foot," for the nations will still revile them, renounce them and suspect them of being "Judaizers."
>
> …As we have indeed seen in our day, when the smoke [of their torment] ascends heavenward…some have perished in the flames of the Inquisition, some have fled, and yet others continue to live in great fear and awesome trepidation, rising out of the dread of their hearts and the horrors before their eyes.[14]

Whereas the Abravanel emphasizes the psychic suffering experienced by the Crypto-Jews, rising out of the double life into which they are forced, the Ba'al Ha'Akeida stresses the lack of resolution to their physical and social torment, in spite of their apostasy.

———— **D** ————

And yet, as Nehama Leibowitz notes in her analysis of this section of the *tochacha*, the rabbis find a ray of hope, a blessing in the very curse quoted by the Ba'al Ha'Akeida.[15]

Commenting on the symbolism of an event that occurs centuries be-

---

13. Devarim 28:65.
14. Akeidat Yitzchak, Devarim, sha'ar 98.
15. Leibowitz, *Studies in Devarim*, p. 297.

fore the *tochacha* is communicated to the nation, the Midrashic authorities state:

"And the dove [released by Noach from the Ark] found no rest for the sole of its foot, and she returned unto him into the ark."[16]
Rabbi Judah ben Rabbi Nachman stated in the name of Rabbi Shimon: Had the dove found a resting place she would not have returned.
Similarly we find: "And among the nations you will find no ease and there will be no resting place for the sole of your foot..." Had they [the Jewish people] found rest, they would not have returned to their land. Had they been accepted by those around them, they would have assimilated into the surrounding society.[17]

With frightening honesty, the rabbis recognize the blessing in the curse of a torturous exile. Had it not been for the persecution the Jewish people have experienced, we might have disappeared long ago.

Points to Ponder

Changing times, changing questions... The closing comments of our study underscore the unique challenges that face the Jewish community today in countries where we live in freedom. To state the obvious, absent the persecution that has forced us to remain separate from those around us, the Jewish community continues to assimilate into the outside culture at an ever increasing and alarming rate.

While the solutions to this overwhelming problem are complex and elusive, one fundamental point was driven home to me during my recent participation in a multidenominational panel discussing just these issues. As each of the speakers, including myself, discussed practical answers to the question of *how to remain Jewish* in a secular society, I suddenly realized that we were avoiding a much more basic and important question. We were totally ignoring the question of *why be Jewish in a secular society*.

For many centuries of Jewish history we did not have the luxury to ask, let alone answer, this question. Jewishness was not a choice. As we have seen from our study, even when we tragically chose otherwise, our

---

16. Bereishit 8:9.
17. Midrash Rabba Bereishit 33:8.

Jewish identity was often thrust back upon us. Now, however, whether we recognize it or not, the question "why" is being asked, particularly by our children.

I sincerely believe that the answers to the question "why" are there for the taking, in a rich, meaningful, eternal Jewish heritage that today, more than ever, has much to offer to the increasingly secular world around us. I also believe that, with effort and creativity, curricula can be fashioned for our schools, homes and synagogues that can present these answers in ways that will resonate deeply with our youth.

Before we can begin, however, to fashion and offer answers, we must first hear the questions that are being asked. We must first recognize that *in our schools, in our synagogues, in our youth groups, in our Jewish community centers – in our day – the questions have changed.*

Nitzavim-Vayeilech

נצבים־וילך

CHAPTER 29:9–31:30

פרק כט:ט-לא:ל

Parsha Summary

A covenant, assurances and warnings, personal farewells, written records, final laws...

As the curtain rises on Parshat Nitzavim, the last day of Moshe's life dawns. It is destined to be a busy day.

Moshe first gathers the entire nation together for a public ratification of an eternal covenant with God. "And not with you alone do I contract this covenant and oath," he declares, "but with whoever is here, standing with us today before the Lord our God, and with whoever is not here with us today."

Reminding the people of the abominations that they personally witnessed in Egypt, Moshe warns against those who might surreptitiously turn away from God and His law. God's anger will be kindled against such disloyalty, he cautions, resulting in great punishment descending upon the nation.

Turning his attention towards the distant future, Moshe speaks of the nation's eventual repentance after experiencing periods of "blessing" and "curse." The time will come, he predicts, when "you will return unto the Lord your God and listen to His voice...with all your heart and all your soul." As a result, he promises, God will ultimately gather the people from the lands of their dispersion and return them to the land of their forefathers.

With increasing passion, Moshe encourages the people towards observance of the law, emphasizing that the mitzvot are not "distant" but accessible to all. He adjures them to "choose life" by obeying God's will.

The scene changes with the opening of Parshat Vayeilech, as Moshe walks from tribe to tribe in order to inform the people that he has reached the end of his life and to bid them farewell. He encourages the nation with the assurance that God will successfully bring them into the land under Yehoshua's leadership and publicly encourages Yehoshua to be strong and courageous in his new role.

After transmitting a written record of the Torah to the Kohanim, Moshe commands the nation concerning the mitzva of Hakhel, the public reading from the Torah once every seven years on the festival of Succot.

God appears to Moshe and Yehoshua in a pillar of cloud at the entrance of the Mishkan and informs them that the nation is destined to grievously sin and to be severely punished. He commands Moshe to write Shirat Ha'azinu, the song recorded in the next parsha (Ha'azinu) as timeless testimony to the nation that their fate will be determined by their loyalty to God's law. After fulfilling this directive, Moshe commands the Levi'im to place the Torah scroll at the side of the Holy Ark. He then commands the gathering of all the tribal elders and officers for a public recitation of Shirat Ha'azinu.

1 I Want My Lawyer!

Context

On the last day of his life, Moshe assembles the entire nation together in the plains of Moav to publicly ratify a covenant with God. In powerful terms, this great leader emphasizes the ongoing, eternal nature of this contract:

> You are standing today, all of you before the Lord your God: your leaders, your tribes, your elders, your officers, every man of Israel; your children, your wives, and your stranger who is in the midst of your camp, from the hewer of your wood to the drawer of your water.
>
> So that you pass into the covenant of the Lord your God and into His oath which the Lord your God contracts with you today, in order to establish you today as a people to Him and that He be to you a God, as He spoke to you and as He swore to your fathers, to Avraham, to Yitzchak and to Yaakov.
>
> And not with you alone do I contract this covenant and oath, but with whoever is here, standing with us today before the Lord our God and with whoever is not here with us today.[1]

Questions

Jewish law remains the primary vantage point from which the rabbis will view any contract or agreement. Pushing past the passionate poetry of Moshe's words and striking to the core of their content, therefore, the sages raise fascinating challenges to the Nitzavim covenant.

By what legal right does the generation of the wilderness obligate all Jews of all time to a contract that only they are present to hear and accept? Under God's direction, Moshe shapes the relationship between God and

---

1. Devarim 29:9–13.

the Israelites as a relationship based upon mutual agreement and acceptance. No parent, however, has the right to obligate non-present progeny
to specific personal behaviors. Halachically, an agreement such as the one
contracted in the beginning of Parshat Nitzavim would never pass muster.[2]

Even if the Nitzavim covenant can be legally validated, why is this
agreement necessary? An eternal covenant had already been contracted
between God and the nation during the Revelation at Sinai.[3] Why must this
agreement now be renewed? Any eternal covenant that requires renewal
in the next generation can hardly be considered eternal.

Approaches

—— A ——

The Abravanel approaches the issue of the covenant's validity by drawing a
clear distinction between a verbal commitment and a debt. While it is true,
this sage explains, that an individual cannot legally bind his descendents to
specific personal behaviors through a promise or an oath, *a debt incurred
by a parent does pass to his progeny*. If an individual, for example, borrows
money from another, the borrower's heirs are obligated to repay the loan,
even if they were not alive at the time the debt was incurred.

The Israelites incur a debt to God, the Abravanel maintains, through
their personal salvation during the Exodus. At that point, God acquires
"title" to their physical service, as indicated by the biblical statement "for the
Children of Israel are slaves unto Me; they are My slaves whom I brought
out of the land of Egypt."[4] An additional debt is then added to the nation's
ledger during the Sinaitic Revelation when, by conferring spiritual perfection upon the Israelites through the giving of the law, God acquires "title"
to their souls. The people's acceptance of this dual obligation is reflected
in their famous response at Sinai: *Na'aseh v'nishma*, "We will do and we
will hearken."[5] *With our physical beings we will do and serve, as servants*

---

2. Talmud Bavli Eruvin 46b and elsewhere.
3. Shmot 24:6–9. Note: The Midrash maintains, in fact, that two covenants were contracted at Sinai, one before and one after the sin of the golden calf (Midrash Tanchuma
   Nitzavim 3).
4. Vayikra 25:55.
5. Shmot 24:7.

to their master. With our souls we will hearken and believe, as students to their teacher.

Now, as the nation stands in the plains of Moav poised to enter their land, yet another debt is incurred. God is about to grant them the Land of Israel, not as a gift, but as a loan, on trust that they will continue to obey God's will and pay homage to no other gods.

The Jewish people are eternally bound, the Abravanel insists, not by the verbal commitments expressed by their ancestors, but by the successive debts incurred to God through the Exodus, the Revelation at Sinai, and the entry into the land.

—— **B** ——

In a lengthy exposition, the Malbim offers three defenses for the eternal validity of the Nitzavim covenant.

In his first approach, this sage turns to the mystical realm. Jewish tradition expresses, the Malbim explains, a firm belief in the eternal nature of the soul. All souls exist in God's realm both before they enter physical bodies and after they depart. This belief enables the Talmud to famously claim that the souls of all Jews of all generations were present at Sinai.[6] Similarly, says the Malbim, mirroring a tradition in the Midrash,[7] all souls of all Jews of all generations were also present during the ratification of the covenant in the plains of Moav.

Nonetheless, one could argue that a soul absent physicality cannot accept a physical commitment. This difficulty can be addressed, the Malbim maintains, by recognizing that just as a parent tree contains within itself the potential of all future seedlings, each individual human being contains the potential of all future progeny. Once, therefore, the souls of all future Jews were present to accept the Nitzavim covenant directly, the physical obligations included in that covenant could be accepted for them by those physically present.

In his second approach, the Malbim returns to the realm of halacha. While the law prohibits the *obligating* of someone who is not present to a specific responsibility or task, an individual can be legally *benefited* in his

---

6. Talmud Bavli Shevuot 39a.
7. Midrash Tanchuma Nitzavim 3.

absence.[8] Since those faithful to God's law are rewarded for their loyalty in many ways, the Malbim contends, the individuals present in the plains of Moav were fully allowed to accept that law for future generations as well as for themselves.

Finally, in his third approach, the Malbim totally redefines the nature of the covenant between God and the Israelites. An all-powerful God, the Creator and Sustainer of all, the Malbim argues, does not need "agreement" or "acceptance" from His subjects when He obligates them to a particular task. The Israelites would have been required to observe God's law whether they "accepted" the covenant or not. The purpose of the covenant was instead to involve them, to enable them to view their newfound responsibilities as a product of their voluntary choice. Such a perception would serve to root these obligations more firmly in their hearts and in the hearts of their children across the generations. Those present in the plains of Moav do not accept the obligations of the Nitzavim covenant for their children in their children's absence. The obligations exist with or without their agreement. The Israelites of Moses' generation are instead teaching themselves and their children to view God's law as a gift they would have chosen to accept, even had they not been obligated to do so.[9]

— C ———————————————————————————————————

An imaginative interpretation of the Nitzavim covenant is suggested by Rabbi Yitzchak Arama, the Ba'al Ha'Akeida.

This sage maintains that the eternal character of this covenant reflects the natural instinct for survival implanted by God within the nation's heart. Just as every species in creation possesses a natural instinct to survive and would not knowingly self-destruct, the Israelites are bound by the protective power of God's covenant.

By way of explanation, the Ba'al Ha'Akeida offers the following parable: A talented, capable royal officer earns the envy of his colleagues to the point where his safety is threatened. Seeking the assistance of the king, this officer agrees to obligate himself and his heirs to the king's service in return for continued protection. The agreement is ratified and lasts for a few generations. Ultimately, however, the descendents of the officer ques-

---

8. Talmud Bavli Eruvin 46b and elsewhere.
9. Malbim, Devarim 29:14.

tion their ancestor's decision and rebel against continued service to the king. The king agrees to release these descendents from their obligations but, in consequence, lifts his continued protection from them, leaving them vulnerable to attack.

Similarly, argues the Ba'al Ha'Akeida, the Nitzavim covenant obligates the nation to God's service in return for His continued protection across the generations. The abrogation of this covenant by the Israelites would therefore be an act of national suicide. Given the natural instinct for self-preservation embedded in the psyche of all living creatures, this is a step that the nation will never take.[10]

——— **D** ———

Turning to the question of the need for the Nitzavim covenant, in light of the already existing Sinaitic Covenant, Rabbi Joseph Soloveitchik draws a powerful distinction between the two agreements.

The covenant at Sinai is a collective agreement representing the "sanctity of the patriarchs." Through this covenant each member of the Jewish people, whether a member by birth or by choice, becomes included in an *inherited shared sanctity* passed down from generation to generation. The unbreakable character of this sanctity is mirrored in the Talmudic contention that "a member of Israel, even after sin, remains a member of Israel."[11]

The Nitzavim covenant, the Rav maintains, is vastly different. This covenant represents a *direct agreement between God and each Jew*, individually, across the face of time. The terms of the agreement are personal and reciprocal, as each Jew is divinely invested with individual sanctity in return for his commitment to observe the mitzvot. Moshe thus states to the nation, concerning the Nitzavim covenant alone, that the agreement is contracted directly, not only with those present, but also "with whoever is not here with us today." When a Jew sins, in any generation, the Rav continues, this personal covenant is damaged and must be repaired.

The Sinaitic covenant and the covenant enacted in the plains of Moav, the Rav argues, are both essential components in the ongoing relationship between God and His people.

Each Jew enjoys the automatic benefits that come from "belonging,"

---

10. Akeidat Yitzchak, Devarim, sha'ar 99.
11. Talmud Bavli Sanhedrin 44a, based on a passage in Yehoshua 7:11.

from sharing a part in the inherited, unbreakable "sanctity of the patriarchs" passed down from generation to generation. Each Jew, however, is also a "signatory" to a personal agreement with God, dramatically contracted in the plains of Moav on the last day of Moshe's life. This personal agreement with the Divine carries clear responsibilities and must be perpetually maintained.[12]

—— E ——

These and other rabbinic observations concerning the historic covenants enacted between God and Israel reflect the seriousness with which these agreements must be considered.

Moshe is not simply waxing poetic as he stands before his people in the plains of Moav on the last day of his life. He is contracting an eternal contract between God and His people – a contract that, to the rabbinic mind, must withstand legal scrutiny, as well as the test of time.

---

12. Peli, *On Repentance*, 214–20.

2 Beyond Forgiveness

Content

After ratifying the covenant between God and the nation, Moshe offers a sober warning, "lest there be among you a man or woman, or a family or tribe whose heart turns away today from the Lord our God to go serve the gods of those nations, lest there be among you *shoresh poreh rosh v'la'ana* (a root bearing gall and wormwood)."[13]

Outlining the logic that such an individual might use to rationalize his evil actions, Moshe continues: "And it will come to pass that when he hears the words of this oath, he will bless himself in his heart, saying: 'Peace will be with me, even if I walk according to the dictates of my heart, *l'ma'an sefot harava et hatzmeia* (so that the watered will be added with the dry).'"[14]

God's reaction to such an individual, Moshe concludes, will be swift and severe.

> The Lord will not be willing to forgive him, for the anger of the Lord and His jealousy will smoke against that man, and the entire curse that is written in this book will descend upon him, and the Lord will erase his name from under the heavens. And the Lord will separate him for evil from among all the tribes of Israel, according to all the curses of the covenant that is written in this book of the Torah.[15]

Questions

In the most dramatic terms possible, Moshe describes a sin, its supposed rationale, and the consequent divine punishment. So severe is this sin, so warped its rationale, that the fullest extent of God's wrath will be released upon the perpetrator.

---

13. Devarim 29:17.
14. Ibid., 29:18.
15. Ibid., 29:19–20.

Obviously, it is critical that we understand the nature of this sin that "God will not forgive," if only to avoid our own possible transgression. And yet, given the language used by Moshe in his presentation, the full specifics of this case are difficult to comprehend…

In particular, what does Moshe mean when he warns, "lest there be among you a root bearing gall and wormwood"?

And what element of the perpetrator's rationale is described in the phrase "so that the watered will be added with the dry"?

Approaches

Recognizing the need to move beyond the picturesque character of Moshe's terminology and strike to the practical core of his powerful words, the rabbis offer various interpretations for the two phrases in question.

1. "Lest there be among you a root bearing gall and wormwood"

—A—

Numerous commentaries maintain that by referencing "a root bearing gall and wormwood," Moshe warns against *a sinner whose very presence among the people directly jeopardizes all those around him.*

Rashi, for example, interprets the phrase "a root bearing gall and wormwood" to mean "a sinner who fruitfully produces and spreads wickedness in your midst,"[16] while the Ibn Ezra simply states that the effects of "gall" are contagious, "infecting the healthy, as well."[17] In even stronger terms, the Sforno explains that, with this phrase, Moshe figuratively describes an offender "who deliberately plans to sway many others towards his destructive ideas."[18]

Moving in a slightly different direction, the Chizkuni suggests that the societal threat posed by the sinner emerges from his cunning, secretive ways. Just as "a root" is at first hidden in the ground and only later bears its produce, this offender "hides his sin in his heart," doing his damage surreptitiously and with impunity, beyond the reach of the law.[19]

---

16. Rashi, Devarim 29:17.
17. Ibn Ezra, Devarim 29:17.
18. Sforno, Devarim 29:17.
19. Chizkuni, Devarim 29:17.

———— **B** ————————————————————————

Other authorities offer a totally different take on the phrase "a root bearing gall and wormwood." From the perspective of these sages, this phrase describes *an individual whose capacity for sin is not yet fully realized.*

The Malbim, for example, interprets Moshe's words as follows.

"Lest there be among you a man or woman, or a family or tribe whose heart turns away today from the Lord our God to go serve the gods of those nations." *Perhaps there is among you, even now as we contract this eternal covenant with God, an individual or individuals who have already turned towards idolatry...*

"Lest there be among you a root bearing gall and wormwood." *And even if not...perhaps there is among you an individual within whom the roots of such actions exist – roots that will bring forth actual sin in the fullness of time.*[20]

Writing centuries earlier, the Ramban takes this idea one step further. With the phrase "a root bearing gall and wormwood," this scholar maintains, Moshe adds a new, concrete dimension to his earlier claim of the covenant's eternality, that the agreement with God is being contracted with "whoever is here, standing with us today before the Lord our God, and with whoever is not here with us today"[21] (see previous study).

After alerting the people to the covenant's lasting nature, the Ramban explains, Moshe proceeds to inform them of the tangible effect that their own thoughts and actions will have upon future generations. He warns them of "a root bearing gall and wormwood" not only to caution them concerning the negative effects that they can have on their progeny, but also to emphasize the converse: *from a sweet root no bitter plant will issue.*[22]

Your own attitude today, at this pivotal moment, will affect not only your lives but the lives of generations to follow. If your hearts are whole with God as we contract this covenant, your descendents will continue in your ways. If you personally commit to this covenant without hesitation and without reservation, you will guarantee the future of our people.

I challenge you today: Will each of you be the sweet root from which sweet plants will emerge, or will you, God forbid, be the "root bearing gall and wormwood"?

---

20. Malbim, Devarim 29:17.
21. Devarim 29:14.
22. Ramban, Devarim 29: 14–17.

II. ...l'ma'an sefot harava et hatzmeia, "so that the watered will be added with the dry"

—A—

The rabbis intensify their struggle to interpret Moshe's words as they turn to the even more puzzling phrase "so that the watered will be added with the dry." This phrase is presented in the text, it would initially seem, as part of the sinner's rationale for his actions.

Onkelos, in his classic Aramaic translation of the text, deepens the mystery by interpreting the phrase in a way that seems both arbitrary and mysterious. Instead of literally translating the phrase *l'ma'an sefot harava et hatzmeia* to mean "so that the watered will be added with the dry," Onkelos renders this phrase as "*so that the unintentional sins will be added upon the intentional sins.*" This great sage, however, offers no clue as to the impetus for – or the significance of – this translation.

Rising to the challenge, Rashi defends and accepts Onkelos's interpretive translation. According to Onkelos, Rashi explains, *this phrase is not part of the rationale* offered by the sinner for his actions at all. Instead, these words comprise *an introduction to God's severe response.*

So serious is the current transgression of this sinner, Rashi explains, that his culpability for past inadvertent sins will no longer be mitigated due to their unintentional nature. Instead, in response to the offender's rebellious intent, God will reclassify all such sins as fully intentional, and will punish the offender accordingly.

On a technical level, Rashi explains that Onkelos defines unintentional sins as "watered" because they are committed unwillingly, as if in a drunken stupor. Intentional sins, on the other hand, can be characterized as "thirsty," because they are performed willingly, out of desire.

—B—

In a striking move, the Rashbam openly contradicts his grandfather Rashi's interpretation of this text.

While Rashi accepts and explains Onkelos's translation of the term *rava* (watered) as referring to unintentional sins that carry lesser culpability, and the term *tzmeia* (thirsty) as referring to sins that are more severe, the Rashbam completely reverses the terminology. The text's term *rava*, this sage maintains, refers to sins committed with full intent and premeditation.

This analogy is appropriate, the Rashbam explains, because such transgressions are committed at a point when the sinner is "watered," satiated and comfortable. Sins referred to in the text as "thirsty," in contrast, are committed out of compulsion, rather than out of a sense of rebelliousness. While such lust-driven transgressions are not unintentional, they are, nonetheless, less severe than fully intentional crimes.

Far from arbitrary, the switching of terms on the part of the Rashbam has a major effect on the thrust of the passage before us. While Onkelos and Rashi translate the phrase to mean "*so that the unintentional sins will be added upon the intentional sins,*" the Rashbam apparently renders the phrase in the reverse, "*so that fully intentional sins will be added upon those which are less severe.*" While the Rashbam does not elaborate, this variation allows this phrase to be viewed as part of the sinner's rationale, rather than as an introduction to God's response, as had been suggested by Rashi. According to the Rashbam, the sinner apparently reasons: *I will sin intentionally, yet somehow successfully pass off my transgressions as less severe acts, performed out of compulsion, rather than with full intent.*

This approach maintains the cohesiveness of the verse describing the sinner's rationale and is, therefore, in greater consonance with the flow of the text. One can thus understand why the Rashbam chooses this interpretation, even if it means disagreeing with his illustrious grandfather. As we have often noted in the past, the Rashbam is the *pashtan* par excellence, the classical commentary most consistently loyal to the *pshat*, the straightforward meaning of the text.

— **C** —

Numerous other commentaries depart entirely from Onkelos's translation of the text and offer a variety of interpretations for the phrase *l'maan sefot harava et hatzmeia*, "so that the watered will be added with the dry."

Rabbi Ovadia Sforno, the fifteenth–sixteenth-century Italian commentator, agreeing that the phrase is to be viewed as part of the sinner's rationale, maintains that the sinner hopes to escape punishment through an insincere acceptance of the covenant with God. *By openly pledging fealty to God and His law,* the individual reasons, *I will attach my "watered" soul, sated and satisfied from all my transgressions, to a "thirsty" people, who separate themselves from physical excess. This public pledge will enable me to share in the blessings that God will bestow upon His people, without truly committing myself to join them in following God's law.*

Following a similar line of reasoning, the Ibn Ezra, after considering a few alternative approaches to the text, explains that the sinner simply reasons that his transgressions will be overshadowed by the general righteousness of the nation. "I will walk according to the dictates of my heart," the sinner reasons. *And even though I will surrender to the destructive desires of my heart,* "the watered will be added to the thirsty," *the overwhelming virtue of the righteous (those who are "watered") will protect and enable me (the "thirsty") to survive. They, after all, are many, and I am a solitary sinner.*

————— **D** —————

In a striking departure from the approach of his colleagues, the Ramban views the phrase "so that the watered will be added with the dry" neither as part of the sinner's rationale nor as part of God's response to the transgression. Instead, the Ramban argues, God uses this phrase to *warn the nation of the ease with which any individual can descend into devastating sin.*

The term *rava* (watered), the Ramban explains, refers to a "satisfied soul," an individual who experiences no desire for that which is spiritually harmful. The term *tzmeia* (thirsty), in contrast, refers to a "desiring soul," an individual who seeks to satisfy his destructive cravings.

The Torah warns that if a slight "thirst" for the forbidden enters the heart of a satisfied, "watered," individual and causes an individual to transgress, the destructive desire will only grow. The taste for the forbidden will become increasingly intoxicating and minor transgressions will lead to greater ones. This reality is reflected in the Talmudic contention regarding sexual craving: "The more one satisfies it, the more it hungers…"[23]

The Ramban thus interprets the passage as follows: "…he will bless himself in his heart, saying: 'Peace will be with me, even if I walk according to the dictates of my heart.'" *If an individual allows himself to follow the dictates of his heart, surrendering to even the minor cravings that afflict his soul, then…* "The watered will be added with the dry…" *Those forbidden things for which he had no previous desire – concerning which, until now, his soul had been "watered," satiated and satisfied – will inexorably be added to the "thirsty." He will now desire more and more, spiraling down a path leading to ever greater sin.*

---

23. Talmud Bavli Sukka 52b.

——— E ———

Finally, we close our study of the verse *l'ma'an sefot harava et hatzmeia*, "so that the watered will be added with the dry," with a lovely interpretation suggested by Rabbi Dr. Barry Freundel, a distinguished rabbinic colleague and my *chavruta* (study partner) for much of my high school and college career. Rabbi Freundel's approach speaks to a common human failing, familiar to us all, and again demonstrates how new, practical insight into the eternal words of the Torah can be uncovered in each generation.

Most of us can clearly identify those mitzvot that we perform reasonably well and those areas of halachic observance concerning which we "could use some improvement." Instead of exerting the effort to focus on our weaker areas, however, we tend to rationalize: *Nobody's perfect. God will forgive me my trespasses. He knows, after all, how dedicated I am in other realms of observance… L'ma'an sefot harava et hatzmeia, "so that the watered will be added with the dry…" That which I do well, that which is "watered" in my life, will more than compensate for that which is "thirsty and dry," for any failings I may have.*

Such thinking undermines any possibility of improvement on the part of the sinner, dooming him to spiritual stagnation, with the resultant unfortunate consequences.

Points to Ponder

Confronted, once again, with enigmatic language in the text, we find ourselves wondering: *Which interpretation of the phrases spoken so long ago by Moshe is accurate? What did this great leader really mean with his words?*

As we near the end of the book of Devarim and the Torah text as a whole, it is important to underscore that while, on one level, such questioning is understandable, on quite another level, the answer is immaterial.

We have learned that in the halachic realm, the operant principle is *Eilu va'eilu divrei Elokim chaim*, "These and these are the words of the living God." All positions arrived at through the loyal application of the legal process, at the hands of scholars, are "true" (see *Shmot*: Yitro 5, *Approaches* B; Mishpatim 5, *Points to Ponder*). Similarly, in the realm of textual interpretation, all legitimate attempts to arrive at the true meaning of the text have something to teach us.

Shrouded in the mists of history, the one single true intent of Moshe's words will become accessible to us only when God sees fit to reveal it. *Perhaps, however, at that time we will actually discover that all the lessons derived by the scholars across the ages were really components of the text's original intent.*

3 Going Somewhere?

Context

As the Torah continues to chronicle Moshe's activities on the last day of his life, Parshat Vayeilech opens with the statement *Va'yeilech Moshe…*, "And Moshe went and he spoke these words to all of Israel."[1]

Questions

In a clear departure from form, the Torah amends its customary introductory statement *va'yedaber Moshe*, "and Moshe spoke," with the addition of the phrase *va'yeilech Moshe*, "and Moshe went."

Strikingly, however, the text then fails to tell us where this great leader "went." Where did Moshe "go"?

Approaches

—— A ——

Almost all the classical commentaries perceive the same poignant picture emerging from the two simple words *va'yeilech Moshe*. On the last day of his life, Moshe deliberately and painstakingly walks from tribe to tribe within the Israelite camp in order to inform the people of his impending death and to bid them all a personal farewell.

Each of these commentaries, however, building on the surrounding context, adds a slightly different nuance to this heartrending scene. Some of their comments are complementary, others contradictory. Taken together, however, the poignant observations of these scholars provide a sense of the multiple agendas to be fulfilled and the manifold emotions that must have been felt by Moshe and the Israelites as the moment of their parting neared.

---

1. Devarim 31:1.

1. Ramban: Once Moshe concludes the public ratification of the covenant with God in the plains of Moav, the people disperse and return to their tents. Moshe then walks from the camp of the Levites to the Israelite camp in order to show the people respect as he prepares to depart from their midst, "*as would someone who wishes to take leave of his friend and approaches him to ask his permission to do so.*"[2]

2. Ibn Ezra: Moshe walks from tribe to tribe to inform them of his impending death and to strengthen them with his charge to Yehoshua.

Alternatively (and preferably, in the Ibn Ezra's opinion), Moshe *personally blesses the people at this time*, tribe by tribe, with the blessings later recorded in the final parsha of the Torah, Parshat V'zot Habracha.[3]

3. Sforno: The term *va'yeilech* is often used in the text to signify "strengthening oneself" towards the performance of a specific, challenging task. Having concluded the ratification of the covenant, Moshe now "strengthens himself" towards the task of *personally consoling the nation over his imminent death.* This great leader does not want the nation's sorrow over his impending demise to diminish the joy they should feel over establishing a permanent covenant with God.[4]

4. Chizkuni: Moshe goes from tribe to tribe because *he no longer possesses the authority to convene the nation in assembly.* In fulfillment of the prophetic phrase "and there is no authority on the day of death,"[5] God has commanded Moshe to set aside the *chatzotzrot*, the trumpets used until now to direct the nation's movement in the wilderness.[6]

As a result of divine mandate, Moshe's leadership has already begun to slip away...

(See *Bamidbar*: Beha'alotcha 4, for a discussion of the fact that the *chatzotzrot* fashioned by Moshe could not be used by the next generation. These trumpets, alone among the utensils created in the wilderness, had to be made anew in each generation).

5. Rabbi Naftali Tzvi Yehuda Berlin (the Netziv): Throughout Moshe's years of leadership, God miraculously speaks through him to the people. As part of this incredible phenomenon, Moshe's voice carries to the entire na-

2. Ramban, Devarim 31:1.
3. Ibn Ezra, Devarim 31:1.
4. Sforno, Devarim 31:1.
5. Kohelet 8:8.
6. Chizkuni, Devarim 31:1.

tion. As the end nears, however, Moshe's heaven-sent powers slowly begin to weaken. Although his words are still divinely inspired, he can no longer physically project those words to the entire nation at once. He is therefore forced to walk from tribe to tribe, in order to share his final messages.[7]

As a result of divinely ordained weakening, Moshe's leadership has already begun to slip away…

6. Rabbi Shimshon Raphael Hirsch: Moshe deliberately chooses not to use the *chatzotzrot* to assemble the people. He instead travels to them, "*in the simplest manner, quite in the way which characterizes the most modest of men, to bid farewell to them.*"[8]

7. Kli Yakar: Moshe wants the nation to understand that *his imminent descent from leadership will not be caused by any personal weakening or inability but will, instead, stem from the divine decree prohibiting him from entering the land.* This great leader, therefore, walks from tribe to tribe with his customary energy, in order to demonstrate that his personal powers have not waned in the slightest.[9]

8. Rabbi Zalman Sorotzkin: Moshe travels from tribe to tribe in fulfill-ment of the mandate "One may not appoint a leader over the community, unless one consults the community."[10] As the time comes for Moshe to hand over the reins of leadership to Yehoshua, he feels *compelled to obtain the community's acquiescence.*

Moshe does not want to consult with the nation publicly, however, lest an issue embarrassing to Yehoshua be raised. Ever humble in his personal dealings, Moshe also refrains from conducting a public referendum in Yehoshua's absence. Instead, with great humility, this great leader person-ally walks from tribe to tribe to obtain their agreement concerning the leadership transition.[11]

In the eyes of these and other commentaries, the phrase *va'yeilech Moshe* indicates that whether by choice or by force of circumstance, Moshe's goodbyes to his people become as personal as possible on the last day of his life.

---

7. *Ha'amek Davar*, Devarim 31:1.
8. Rabbi Shimshon Raphael Hirsch, Devarim 31:1.
9. Kli Yakar, Devarim 31:1.
10. Talmud Bavli Brachot 55a.
11. *Oznaim LaTorah*, Devarim 31:1.

—— **B** ——————————————————————————————————

Other scholars, however, offer wide-ranging alternative explanations for the enigmatic phrase *va'yeilech Moshe*. A representative sampling of their thoughts reflects the many lessons, from the practical to the mystical, that can be drawn from this two-word introduction to Moshe's actions on the last day of his life.

1. Targum Yonatan: The phrase *va'yeilech Moshe*, "and Moshe went," must be amended through the addition of the words *l'Mishkan beit ulpana*, "to the Sanctuary, the house of instruction."

On the last day of his life, *Moshe naturally gravitates to the Mishkan*, the symbol of God's presence in the Israelite encampment. From there, this great leader speaks his final words to the people.[12]

2. Ohr Hachaim: The Torah's statement *va'yeilech Moshe*, "and Moshe went," *does not refer to Moshe in a physical sense but, instead, references his spiritual essence*.

The Zohar maintains that forty days before a person's death, his soul temporarily travels from his body in order to discern its eventual place of rest in the heavenly spheres. Due to their heightened spiritual sensitivity, the righteous can detect this phenomenon and they can, therefore, sense when the end of life is drawing near. Moshe, who achieved spiritual heights beyond those of any other mortal, was even able to discern the exact date of his death.

The text therefore states, *va'yeilech Moshe*, "and Moshe went." The life spirit that defined Moshe "went" to discern the place of its eventual rest, as is the way of all souls close to death. Sensing this phenomenon, Moshe understood that this was the last day of his life and he began to share his final words with his people.[13]

3. Anonymous sources (quoted in *Iturei Torah*): Talmudic scholars maintain that *an individual should engage in a halachic discussion with his friend as he prepares to take leave of him*. By doing so, the rabbis explain, he will ensure that his friend remembers him.[14]

Moshe, the greatest of our scholars, certainly follows this mandate. The Torah, therefore, states, *va'yeilech Moshe*, "and Moshe departed, through

———————————————

12. Targum Yonatan ben Uziel, Devarim 31:1.
13. Ohr Hachaim, Devarim 31:1.
14. Talmud Bavli Brachot 31a.

the sharing of halacha." The term *va'yeilech* is to be viewed in this context as the root of the word *halacha*.[15]

4. Early Chassidic sources (quoted in *Ma'ayana shel Torah*): The closing words of this biblical passage explain its opening. The text thus reads *va'yeilech Moshe...el kol Yisrael*, "and Moshe went...to all of Israel."

Moshe entered the heart and spirit of each Israelite. "In the deepest recesses of each Jew, in his blood and in his soul, in all generations and in all times, a spark of Moshe, our teacher, can be found."[16]

—— C ————————————————————————————————

Finally, we close with an idea that we have suggested previously in greater depth (see *Shmot*: Shmot 2, *Approaches* D, E, *Points to Ponder*).

A striking textual pattern encapsulates Moshe's life. The story of this great leader begins and ends with the enigmatic application of the term *va'yeilech*.

Moshe's birth is heralded by the statement *Va'yeilech ish mi'Beit Levi va'yikach et bat Levi*, "And a man went from the House of Levi and he took a daughter of Levi,"[17] anonymously referring to Moshe's parents, Amram and Yocheved.

And now, Moshe's impending death is heralded by the statement *va'yeilech Moshe*, "and Moshe went."

Together, these statements marking the endpoints of Moshe's life enable the Torah to subtly convey the remarkable sense of *halicha* (movement) that characterizes the career of this great leader. Moshe's continuous spiritual growth and development is captured in the verb *lalechet* (to go), which encloses his story in the text. At every critical moment of Moshe's life – when he leaves Pharaoh's palace to view the suffering of his brethren, when he turns aside to view the burning bush, when he ascends Mount Sinai before God summons him, when he breaks the tablets at the foot of Mount Sinai in response to the sin of the golden calf, when he repeatedly prays to God on behalf of the wayward nation – this great leader seizes the initiative and acts.

---

15. Greenberg, *Iturei Torah*, p. 192.
16. Alexander Zusia Friedman, *Ma'ayana shel Torah* (Tel Aviv: Pe'er Publishing House), p. 134.
17. Shmot 2:1.

Moshe's final day therefore, is once again marked by the term *va'yeilech*, connoting the sense of movement that has marked his entire life.

Could it possibly be otherwise?

Points to Ponder

What would you do on the last day of your life?

The very question is, of course, rhetorical. None of us are granted the prescience to discern the exact day of our death.

Nonetheless, the activities of Moshe on the day of his passing provide us with a window into the priorities of this great leader – priorities that might well inform, for each of us, not the day of our death, but the days of our lives.

A powerful yet puzzling passage from Pirkei Avot can perhaps best make our point: "Akavia the son of Mahalalel says, 'Consider three things and you will never fall into the grip of sin. Know from where you came, and to where you are going and before Whom you are going to experience a *judgment and a reckoning*…'"[18]

At face value, Akavia seems to have the order wrong. Why does this sage speak first of a judgment and then a reckoning? Won't the Heavenly Court, in each of our cases, *perform the necessary reckoning concerning our deeds before issuing its judgment upon us*?

A powerfully profound answer to this question was suggested to me a number of years ago. *Two verdicts will be eventually handed down by the Heavenly Court upon each of us at the end of our lives.*

The first of these verdicts will be immediately determined by God, in consideration of our actions and our activities throughout our stay on earth. The second heavenly ruling, however, will wait for an ongoing "reckoning," as God determines what happens on earth *after we die, as a result of our having lived*. Whose hearts did we touch? How many lives did we shape and enrich? What acts of kindness did we perform that made a real difference? What lasting human legacy did we leave behind?

This second "reckoning" continues ad infinitum. Each person that we affect during our lifetime goes on to touch the lives of countless others – individuals whom we never knew and will never know – who then go on

---

18. Pirkei Avot 3:1.

to affect still others. This precious personal heritage marks our passage in the world more powerfully than any other phenomenon.

On the last day of his life, the greatest leader our people has known, a man whose countless contributions will shape the world in monumental ways, takes the time to cement his personal relationships with those whom he has encountered during his worldly passage. By doing so, he reminds us of the personal "reckonings" that will determine the true value of our lives, in the fullness of time.

4 Too Much Information

Context

As the final preparations for Moshe's departure and Yehoshua's ascension to leadership continue to unfold, God summons the two leaders to the Sanctuary. There, from the midst of a cloud, God speaks to Moshe:

> Behold, you will lie with your fathers, and this nation will rise and stray after the foreign gods of the land into whose midst they will come; and they will forsake Me and annul the covenant that I have established with them.
>
> And My anger will be kindled against them in that day and I will forsake them, and I will hide My face from them and they will be as prey, and many evils and troubles will come upon them. And they will say on that day: "Is it not because my God is not in my midst that these evils have come upon me?"
>
> V'anochi haster astir panai ba'yom hahu, and I will certainly hide My face on that day, on account of all the evil that they will have done, in that they turned to other gods.[1]

God continues by instructing Moshe to record and vigorously teach a specific "song" to the nation, "that this song may be a witness for Me against the children of Israel."

"And it will be," God concludes, "when many evils and distresses come upon them, then this song shall testify before them as a witness, for it shall not be forgotten from the mouth of their offspring…"[2]

[Note: As we will see in the next study, questions emerge concerning the nature of the song that Moshe is commanded to record and teach. For the purpose of this study we will accept the most obvious

---

1. Devarim 31:14–18.
2. Ibid., 31:19.

interpretation: that God is referring to Moshe's song, recorded in the next parsha, Ha'azinu.]

Questions

Moshe is about to die; the fulfillment of this great leader's dreams will now rest with the nation. God summons him for one final message...

The message that God delivers is nothing less than devastating. He informs Moshe that the nation is destined to sin grievously and to be terribly punished. He further tells Moshe that He will "certainly hide [His] face" from the people, a divine act that, as we have seen, carries the gravest of consequences (see *Bereishit*: Bereishit 1, *Approaches* A).

Is this information truly necessary? The Torah has spoken before, in great depth, specifically in the *tochachot*, of the potentiality of grave sin on the part of the nation and of the inevitable consequences of that sin. Now, however, on the eve of Moshe's death, God speaks not of potentialities but of certainties. *The nation will sin*, God informs Moshe on the last day of his life, *the nation will grievously suffer*. Is it necessary to inform Moshe of these facts, specifically now? The only consolation available to Moshe at this sad moment might emerge from a belief in the nation's success after he is gone. Now, it would seem, even that comfort is denied him.

We can only imagine the deep pain that the devastating news of the nation's certain failure brings to this great leader, at a time of already heightened emotion and personal grief.

One might argue, as it appears from the text, that God shares this information with Moshe so that this great leader can personally prepare the nation for the predicted challenges and calamities. God thus commands Moshe to record, teach and "place in the people's mouth" Shirat Ha'azinu, the song recorded in the next parsha.

We could counter, however, that these tasks could have been accomplished without the accompanying pain. God could have commanded Moshe to prepare the nation for the possibility of *potential backsliding*. The future could have been shared, as in earlier passages of text, as a possibility, rather than as a certainty.

What, then, is God's purpose in imparting this definitive, devastating vision of the future to Moshe, particularly at this sensitive moment?

Approaches

———**A**———

The classical commentaries are strikingly silent concerning the issues we raise. Nonetheless, I believe that a critical, relevant message lies at the heart of God's communication to Moshe on the eve of this great leader's death.

Our approach begins far afield, with ideas that are related to our text by an apparent coincidence of the calendar. At the beginning of each Jewish year, two powerful streams converge. The parshiot of Nitzavim, Vayeilech and Ha'azinu are read on the Shabbatot surrounding the sanctified days of Rosh Hashana, Yom Kippur and Succot. As a result of this convergence, Moshe's last days serve as a backdrop to the holiest period of the Jewish year. I would argue that, as is often the case in Jewish experience, what seems coincidental is not. A connection can be drawn between the concepts critical to this holiday period and the character of Moshe's final journey.

———**B**———

Consider initially a symbol that appears towards the holiday cycle's end: the *succa*, the booth built on the holiday of Succot, in commemoration of the nation's wilderness journey. Strikingly, the halachic approach to the symbol of the *succa* seems to break the normative mold. Generally, *hiddur* (beautification) is a requisite component in the observance of mitzvot. Each Jew is mandated, within reason, to fulfill each mitzva in as complete and beautiful a manner as possible.

When it comes to the the *succa*, however, the halachists seem to go out of their way to "cut corners" (pun intended). The law mandates that an acceptable *succa* need not possess four walls – that it even need not, in fact, possess three walls. A *succa* is halachically acceptable, the rabbis maintain, as long as it consists of two full walls and a portion of a third.

Ironically, the other mitzvot of the Succot festival, the *arba minim*, the four species that are held during portions of the prayer service, are often cited as the prototypes of halachic *hiddur*, beauty and completeness. The days before the Succot festival are marked by the search for a "perfect" *etrog* (citron); a straight, tight *lulav* (palm branch); and well-leaved *hadassim* and *aravot* (myrtle and willow stems). The *etrog*, in fact, is referred to simply in the Torah as a *pri etz hadar*, the fruit of a beautiful tree. If the pursuit of perfection is so critical in the general performance of mitzvot, why is the halacha so clearly satisfied with an imperfect *succa*?

— **C** ————————————————————————————————————

Various technical answers to our question can be proposed from the texts that shape the construction and significance of the *succa*. I would like, however, to suggest a symbolic answer.

I have long felt that, on one level, the *succa* represents the prism through which we are meant to reenter "the real world," after coursing through the "rarefied atmosphere" of Rosh Hashana and Yom Kippur – the Yamim Noraim, the Days of Awe. Much of the symbolism of the *succa*, in fact, serves to counterbalance the powerful experiences and emotions of these sanctified days. Our annual struggle on the Yamim Noraim to *control the uncertainty of our lives* through prayer and repentance is now replaced by our *embrace of that very uncertainty* on the Succot festival. We not only recognize but actually celebrate the limitations of our power. We enter our frail booths, open to the heavens, and eschew the "artificial permanence" of our year-round existence. We acknowledge that the only truly permanent aspect of our lives is the divinely directed journey of our people across time, a journey largely governed by forces that remain beyond our control.

Central to the process of reentering our worlds and beginning our year is the admission that *we have no right to expect a perfect succa*. No matter how hard we prayed over the sanctified Yamim Noraim, some of our prayers will be answered to our liking and others will not. No matter how hard we worked on ourselves over Rosh Hashana and Yom Kippur, we will succeed in some of our newfound resolutions and we will fail in others. The physical *succot* that we build are "whole" when imperfect, because they represent our own inescapably imperfect worlds.

The lesson strikes deeper still. The imperfection of the *succa* is not simply an unfortunate fact of life. On the contrary, this very imperfection powers our growth. One of the most critical lessons of the entire Yamim Noraim experience is that *failure refines*. Our greatest growth occurs when we "pick ourselves up" after a fall, when, in the face of challenge, we not only persevere but triumph. For this reason, the Talmud informs us that with complete *tshuva*, repentance and return, an individual's past transgressions are transformed into mitzvot. An individual who strives, fails, and then builds from that failure stands on a higher spiritual plane than an individual who never fails at all.

Life in a perfect succa, however tempting, would be stagnant and stifling. The impetus to grow, to reach beyond ourselves, emerges as a result of the uncertainties and imperfections of life.

——— **D** ———————————————————————

We can now begin to understand God's powerful message to Moshe, as this great leader's last hours draw to a close:

Were I to tell you, Moshe, that your nation will never stumble nor fail after your death, I would not only be lying but I would be delivering "bad news." The absence of failure in human experience is possible only in situations of torpor and stagnation.

Your people will fail, Moshe, and they will suffer dearly for that failure.

I promise, however, that in the end they will prevail, better for having stumbled and risen. They will ultimately succeed against all odds because they will prove loyal. The song of testimony that you write "will not be forgotten from the mouths of their offspring" until their journey ends.

God could not have delivered more honest nor more reassuring news to Moshe at this time.

Points to Ponder

A critical observation concerning parenting in our day…

We too often try to *protect our children from failure* when we should, instead, be preparing them to *deal with failure*.

Consider this litmus test: How many of us have ever done our children's projects and homework, filled out their school or work-related forms, written their college admission essays, injected ourselves into their disputes with others, tried to solve their problems for them, tried to shield them from any possible struggle and pain?

And as the years go by, how many of us buy our older children cars, rent or purchase their homes, continue to support them after marriage? After all, we reason, why should our children be forced to struggle as we did?

We often forget, however, to our children's detriment, that we are better people for having struggled. We learned to appreciate what we have by earning it, and any bounty that we may now enjoy is that much more precious because we "started small and worked our way up."

Protecting our children from struggle and failure is not only impossible, but the attempt itself is ultimately damaging, as we deny them the refining experience of meeting their own challenges and create unreasonable expectations that simply cannot be fulfilled.

Twice within three sentences of Parshat Vayeilech – once when speaking to the nation and once when speaking to Yehoshua – Moshe offers the reassuring words *lo yarpicha v'lo ya'azvecha*, "[God] will neither weaken you nor abandon you."[3]

At first glance, one half of this promise seems abundantly strange. Moshe's guarantee that, in spite of their sins, God will not abandon the nation is understandable. Why, however, must Moshe reassure the people that God will not "weaken" them? Why would the people even assume that God would deliberately damage them in such fashion?

In light of our observations, I believe, the text becomes abundantly clear. Two potential dangers exist in any relationship with a powerful authority figure. On the one hand, as we have noted, the threat certainly exists that the authority figure will pull away, abandoning his dependent completely to his own devices. On the other hand, however, equally present is a separate danger that the authority figure will foster *too much reliance*, that he will "weaken" the dependent through the stifling of any independent initiative on the dependent's part, that he will smother the charge with "too much care."

Moshe, therefore, reassures the nation before his death: *God will strike the appropriate balance in His relationship with you. He will never abandon you, but neither will He weaken you. He will give you the space you need to develop on your own, to succeed or fail through your own efforts. He will let you become the people you need to become.*

In our relationships with our children, we must learn to do the same...

---

3. Devarim 31:6, 8.

5 The Last Mitzva?

Context

As Moshe's departure from leadership looms, concern for the perpetuation of his legacy becomes increasingly paramount. On four separate occasions during the last day of this great leader's life, therefore, reference is made in the text to the creation of a written record.

1. "And Moshe wrote this Torah and gave it to the Kohanim, the sons of Levi, the bearers of the Ark of the Covenant of the Lord, and to the elders of Israel."[1]

2. "And now write for yourselves this *shira* and teach it to the children of Israel; place it in their mouths, in order that this song shall be for Me as a witness against the children of Israel."[2]

3. "And Moshe wrote down this *shira* on that day, and he taught it to the children of Israel."[3]

4. "And it was when Moshe finished writing the words of this Torah onto a book, until their completion, and Moshe commanded the Levi'im, the bearers of the Ark of the Covenant of the Lord, saying: 'Take this book of the Torah and place it at the side of the Ark of the Covenant of the Lord your God, and it shall be there for you as a witness.'"[4]

Numerous commentaries accept the most obvious approach to these passages, that *two separate written texts* are completed and transmitted by Moshe on the last day of his life: the Torah and the *shira*.

The term *Torah*, these authorities maintain, refers to the entire Torah "from the beginning of Bereishit until the words 'before the eyes of all Israel' [the concluding verse of our Torah text]." At the end of his life, Moshe completes the recording of the complete text,

---

1. Devarim 31:9.
2. Ibid., 31:19.
3. Ibid., 31:22.
4. Ibid., 31:24–26.

334

including the material that will be contained in the coming, final two parshiot of the Torah.[5]

The term *shira*, on the other hand, refers specifically to *Shirat Ha'azinu*, the Song of Parshat Ha'azinu, the next parsha in the Torah. In addition to its inclusion in the entire Torah text, this song is also commanded by God to be recorded separately, as testimony to the nation in anticipation of their future sins (see previous study).[6]

This seemingly straightforward approach to the text, however, is contradicted by a mandate found in the Talmudic tractate of Sanhedrin: "Even though an individual has received a Torah scroll from his ancestors, *he is obligated to sponsor the writing of a new scroll from his own resources*, as the text states, 'And now write for yourselves this *shira* (song)...'"[7]

Based on this Talmudic passage, the halachic codifiers, with few exceptions, list *ketivat sefer Torah*, the writing of a Torah scroll, as an independent mitzva, incumbent upon all male Jews across time.[8] According to most of these authorities, this is the last of the 613 mitzvot to emerge from the Torah text.[9]

Questions

At face value, God's commandment "and now write down for yourselves this *shira*" seems to deal solely with the recording of Shirat Ha'azinu, a specific section of text. Nonetheless, most halachic authorities reinterpret this passage as a positive mitzva to *write a Torah scroll*.

What motivates this reinterpretation?

Is there such a mitzva in our day? If so, what are its full origins and parameters?

---

5. Ramban, Devarim 31:9.
6. Ibid., 31:19.
7. Talmud Bavli Sanhedrin 21b.
8. Rambam, *Sefer Hamitzvot*, positive commandment 18.
9. *Sefer Hachinuch*, mitzva 613.

Approaches

——**A**————————————————————————————————————

A terse rabbinic interchange in the Talmudic tractate of Nedarim may offer early insight into the derivation of the mitzva to write a *sefer Torah.*

The Talmud suggests that Moshe's general obligation to *teach the entire Torah to the Israelites* can be derived from the divine commandment "And now write for yourselves this *shira* and teach it to the children of Israel…"

An objection, however, is raised: *This commandment seems to focus solely on the recording and teaching of Shirat Ha'azinu and thus cannot be cited as a source for the obligation to teach the entire Torah.*

The Talmud responds by quoting God's stated purpose for the recording of the song, "in order that this song shall be for Me as a witness against the children of Israel." *Standing alone,* the Talmud argues, *Shirat Ha'azinu cannot serve as effective testimony.* While this song clearly establishes the relationship between the nation's ultimate fate and their adherence to God's law, the substance of that law is absent from the *shira.* Knowledge of God's law requires familiarity with the remainder of the Torah text. *The commandment to record and teach the* shira *thus proves Moshe's obligation to teach the entire Torah to the nation.*[10]

Some later authorities interpret the Talmud's final argument as proof that the mandate of *ketivat sefer Torah* emerges directly from the commandment to record Shirat Ha'azinu. Full, lasting testimony to the nation, these scholars claim, requires not only the teaching of the entire Torah but the *creation of a written record of its text.* By stating that Shirat Ha'azinu is designed to serve "as a witness," the text effectively broadens the commandment to include the writing of the entire Torah.[11]

Other authorities, however, find this proof less than compelling. The Talmudic discussion, they argue, centers on the issue of Moshe's obligation to verbally teach the Torah to the nation. The Talmud's conclusion, according to these scholars, can be interpreted as follows: God commands Moshe to write Shirat Ha'azinu down as testimony to the nation of their obligation to observe the mitzvot. Such testimony is meaningless, however,

---

10. Talmud Bavli Nedarim 38a.
11. Ran, Nedarim 38a, as interpreted by Rabbi Shimshon Raphael Hirsch, Devarim 31:19 and others.

without transmission of the mitzvot. The commandment to record Shirat Ha'azinu thus serves as proof of Moshe's obligation to *teach the entire Torah*. This Talmudic discussion, however, does not weigh in at all concerning the mitzva to *write an entire Torah*.[12]

B

The Rambam, both in his *Sefer Hamitzvot* and in his *Mishneh Torah*, derives the mitzva of *ketivat sefer Torah* in a very different way. Halacha, the Rambam explains, prohibits the writing of partial Torah scrolls containing only specific portions of Torah text.[13] God's commandment "and now write down for yourselves this *shira*," therefore, cannot be understood as an imperative to record Shirat Ha'azinu in isolation. Such an act is, by definition, prohibited. Instead, the commandment must be interpreted as a directive to record an *entire Torah scroll, including Shirat Ha'azinu*.[14]

Numerous later authorities, including the Chatam Sofer, Rabbi Baruch Halevi Epstein and the Netziv, question the Rambam's contention. God clearly has the right to define His own law. Perhaps, these scholars argue, the divinely ordained law concerning Shirat Ha'azinu parallels the laws regarding the portions of text that are placed in tefillin and mezuzot. Just as those passages may be recorded in isolation on separate scrolls, so too, the Torah mandates that Shirat Ha'azinu should be recorded separately as well.[15]

The severity of these questions leads some authorities to maintain that the Rambam is not positing his rationale in isolation, but only to further buttress other, more foundational explanations for the origin of the mitzva of *ketivat sefer Torah*.[16]

C

Numerous later commentaries struggle to define the mysterious origin of the commandment to write a *sefer Torah*. The comments of a series of late eighteenth- to early nineteenth-century European scholars illustrate these efforts.

---

12. *She'eilot U'tshuvot Sha'agat Aryeh*, Yoreh Deah 34.
13. Talmud Bavli Gittin 60a.
14. Rambam, *Sefer Hamitzvot*, positive commandment 18; *Mishneh Torah*, Hilchot Tefillin, Mezuza, V'sefer Torah 7:1.
15. *She'eilot U'tshuvot Hachatam Sofer*, Yoreh Deah 254; *Ha'amek Davar*, Devarim 31:19.
16. Nachshoni, *Hagot B'parshiot HaTorah*, vol. 2, p. 830.

Rabbi Yaakov Tzvi Mecklenberg, for example, dismisses all questions concerning the derivation of this mitzva. Immediately after the close of Shirat Ha'azinu, Mecklenberg notes, Moshe commands the nation: "Direct your hearts towards all the words that I testify to you today, that you should command them to your children, to observe and to perform this entire Torah."[17] Moshe thus defines the *shira* as a *warning to observe the Torah as a whole*. Once this warning is issued, Mecklenberg maintains, the obligation to record the Torah in writing is self-understood. What, after all, is the value of a written warning, this sage asks, without an accompanying document detailing the obligations to which the warning applies?[18]

Rabbi Meir Dan Plotski cites a series of scholars who claim that the obligation to write a Torah scroll is simply derived through the classical Talmudic tool known as a *kal va'chomer*, an *a fortiori* argument. The logic of a *kal va'chomer* maintains that, barring any external factors, a law that applies in a "weak" situation must also apply in a "strong" situation. If the Torah commands the written recordation of Shirat Ha'azinu, the testimony concerning observance of the Torah, these authorities maintain, *kal va'chomer,* by definition, the Torah must obligate the written recordation of the Torah itself as well.[19]

In his major work, the *Torah Temima*, Rabbi Baruch Halevi Epstein connects the origin of *mitzvat ketivat sefer Torah* to the Talmudic observation that the Torah was transmitted to Moshe over time and was recorded by this great leader section by section, on separate scrolls. Now that Moshe has reached the end of his life, Epstein maintains, God commands him to record the penultimate Torah section of Ha'azinu, to add this section to all that has already been written, and to teach the Torah in its entirety to the nation. The commandment to record Shirat Ha'azinu is thus fundamentally *a commandment to complete the Torah*. From this commandment of completion, the rabbis derive an ongoing obligation to record the entire Torah, across the ages.[20]

For his part, the Netziv, Rabbi Naftali Tzvi Yehuda Berlin, maintains that numerous commandments in the book of Devarim reflect dual levels of obligation simultaneously. The commandment to "write this *shira*," the

17. Devarim 32:46.
18. *Haktav V'hakabala*, Devarim 31:19.
19. *Kli Chemda*, Devarim 31:19.
20. *Torah Temima*, Devarim 31:19.

Netziv maintains, exemplifies this phenomenon. The first requirement emerges from the straightforward reading of the text, as God issues a one-time imperative to Moshe to record Shirat Ha'azinu before his death. A second obligation, however, surfaces when God defines the *shira* as testimony to the people concerning general Torah observance. This definition broadens the commandment's scope, the Netziv explains, and conveys the ongoing mitzva of *ketivat sefer Torah*.[21]

Finally, numerous commentaries note the Torah's framing of this commandment in the plural, rather than the singular, as further impetus for the Talmud's expansion of the law from a temporal mitzva directed to Moshe alone to an ongoing mitzva incumbent upon the Jewish people in perpetuity.[22]

—— **D** ————————————————————————————

Moving from origin to application, fascinating discussions develop over the years concerning the purpose, scope and practical parameters of the mitzva of *ketivat sefer Torah*.

A short passage in the Talmudic tractate of Menachot, for example, becomes critical to our understanding of this mitzva:

> Rav Yehoshua stated in the name of Rav Gidel who stated in the name of Rav: "An individual who purchases a *sefer Torah* from the marketplace is considered to have grabbed a mitzva from the marketplace. An individual who writes a *sefer Torah* is considered to have received it from Mount Sinai."
>
> Rav Sheishet stated: "An individual who corrects one letter is considered to have written the entire Torah."[23]

Rav clearly shows a marked preference for writing, as opposed to simply purchasing, a *sefer Torah*. A critical debate, however, develops among the classical commentaries over his contention that an individual who purchases a Torah scroll "is considered to have grabbed a mitzva from the marketplace."

---

21. *Ha'amek Davar*, Devarim 31:19.
22. Nachshoni, *Hagot B'parshiot HaTorah*,vol. 2, p. 831.
23. Talmud Bavli Menachot 30a.

Rashi interprets this phrase to mean that while the purchaser of a completed Torah scroll does not follow the optimal path, he nonetheless *fulfills the mitzva* of *ketivat sefer Torah*.[24] The essential mandate of this commandment, according to Rashi, is *not to write a Torah scroll*, but to *own a Torah scroll*. Centuries later, the Gaon of Vilna will count himself among those who codify the halacha according to Rashi and maintain that the mitzva of *ketivat sefer Torah* can be fulfilled by purchasing an already completed Torah scroll.[25]

Numerous other scholars, however, adamantly disagree with Rashi's interpretation of Rav's words. By stating that an individual who purchases a Torah scroll "is considered to have grabbed a mitzva from the marketplace," these authorities maintain, Rav indicates that in his opinion, the mitzva of *ketivat sefer Torah* cannot be fulfilled through such a purchase. Given that the biblical commandment emerges from the statement "write for yourselves this song," an individual can only fulfill the mitzva by writing or retaining someone to write a new Torah scroll. *Critical to the fulfillment of this mitzva, according to these scholars, is the creation of a new Torah scroll through one's own efforts.*

Centuries later, in his gloss to the *Shulchan Aruch*, Rabbi Moshe Isserles, the Rema, codifies the halacha according to this latter position. *An individual who purchases an already completed sefer Torah, this sage mandates, does not fulfill his obligation.* The Rema does, however, factor in Rav Sheishet's Talmudic position that an individual who corrects one letter of a *sefer Torah* is considered to have written the entire scroll. *If an individual purchases a flawed Torah scroll and facilitates its repair, the Rema maintains, he has fulfilled his obligation.* Having made an unusable *sefer Torah* functional, he has effectively created a new Torah scroll.[26]

—— E ——————————————————————————

In the fourteenth century, the anonymous author of the *Sefer Hachinuch* offers a position that seems to combine elements of Rashi's view with those of his adversaries. The Ba'al Hachinuch opens his discussion of the mitzva

---

24. Rashi, Menachot 30a.
25. Biur HaGra, Yoreh Deah 270:3.
26. Rema, *Shulchan Aruch*, Yoreh Deah 270:3.

of *ketivat sefer Torah* by maintaining, like Rashi, that the Torah obligates each individual to *possess* a *sefer Torah*.

The Ba'al Hachinuch, however, then goes on to maintain that an individual should preferably *write this sefer* by his own hand and, if he cannot, should hire someone to write it for him. Mirroring the Talmudic mandate (see above), this scholar emphasizes that an individual is obligated to write a *sefer Torah* even if he has inherited such a scroll from his ancestors. This obligation exists, explains this sage, so that more scrolls will be written and available for those unable to write or buy. The existence of new scrolls, he adds, will increase excitement and interest in Torah study.

Apparently, according to the Ba'al Hachinuch, the mitzva of *ketivat sefer Torah* consists of *two critical components: creation of the scroll and possession of the scroll*. To fulfill the mitzva, an individual must write a *sefer* Torah, or cause a *sefer Torah* to be written. His obligation, however, does not stop there. To fulfill the mitzva, he must also retain possession of the scroll that he has written, so that he will be able to learn from it on a regular basis.

"The foundations of this mitzva," the Ba'al Hachinuch explains, "emerge from the realization that people will generally do what is convenient for them. Therefore the Holy One, Blessed be He, commanded that each individual should have a Torah scroll ready at hand, so that he will be able to read from it at all times and he will not be forced to go to his neighbor's home..."[27]

After establishing these points, the Ba'al Hachinuch uses this mitzva as a platform from which to encourage the creation and purchase of other volumes related to Torah study. Although *the fundamental biblical requirement of ketivat sefer Torah is limited to the creation and possession of an actual Torah scroll,* this sage maintains, *an individual should purchase and catalyze the creation of as many books of Jewish scholarship as he can.*[28]

——— **F** ———————————————————————————————

It remains, however, for Rabbi Yaakov ben Asher, the Ba'al Haturim, also writing in the fourteenth century, to go a dramatic step further than the Ba'al Hachinuch with a startling claim in his codification of the law, the *Arba Turim*:

———————————

27. *Sefer Hachinuch*, mitzva 613.
28. Ibid.

And my revered father, the Rosh (Rabbi Yaakov ben Asher), of blessed memory, wrote [that the obligation to write an actual Torah scroll] applied in earlier generations, when it was common practice for individuals to write a Torah scroll from which they would learn directly.

In our day, however, when the Torah scrolls that we write are placed in the synagogue for public reading, it is a positive mitzva, incumbent upon each individual within Israel capable of doing so, to write the five Chumashim (the five books of the Torah in book form), the Mishna, the Gemara, and the commentaries thereon, so that he and his children may study from them.[29]

His father's position, the Ba'al Haturim explains, emerges from the understanding that *the ultimate purpose* of the mitzva of *ketivat sefer Torah* is *to enable and inspire the personal study of Torah.* This intent is clearly reflected in the Torah's formulation of the commandment: "And now write for yourselves this *shira*, and teach it to the children of Israel, place it in their mouths..."[30]

In biblical times and during the years that followed, the Ba'al Haturim continues, when individuals studied directly from a Torah scroll, the mitzva consisted of writing such a scroll. By the thirteenth century, however, Torah scrolls are no longer used for personal study. The mitzva, therefore, morphs into *an obligation to record those texts that will be used for such study.*[31]

The Ba'al Haturim's citation of his father's position on the mitzva of *ketivat sefer Torah* sets off a firestorm of debate among the halachists. *How can the Rosh*, later authorities ask, *suggest a rewriting of a Torah law based on his understanding of the reasons for that law? If the Torah commands the writing of an actual Torah scroll, that obligation exists in perpetuity, no matter the changes in circumstance.*

So serious are these objections that many later scholars adopt an interpretation of the Rosh's view suggested by Rabbi Yosef Caro in his commentary on the *Arba Turim*, the *Beit Yosef.* Caro completely rejects the notion that the Rosh and the Ba'al Haturim would exempt individuals from the biblical mitzva of writing a Torah scroll due to changing circumstances.

---

29. Arba Turim, Yoreh Deah 270.
30. Ibid.
31. Ibid.

Instead, he explains, these sages retain the original obligation to write a Torah scroll *but understand that obligation as expanding, appropriately to the times, to include the writing of additional works essential to Torah study.*[32]

Other authorities, however, accept the statement of the Ba'al Haturim at face value. The mitzva to write an actual *sefer Torah*, these authorities maintain, *remained in force only as long as actual Torah scrolls were used for personal study.* Once texts became available in book form for such study, however, the personal use of a Torah scroll was considered beneath that scroll's dignity. From that point on, these scholars insist, the mitzva of *ketivat sefer Torah* must be fulfilled *through the creation and acquisition not of a Torah scroll, but of those texts appropriate for personal study.*[33]

──G──

Debate continues to our day concerning numerous practical issues surrounding the fulfillment of the mitzva of *ketivat sefer Torah*. As a case in point, consider the halachic questions surrounding the prevalent custom of honoring individuals with the writing of letters towards the completion of a Torah scroll at the time of its dedication. Do the participants in this ceremony, the rabbis wonder, fulfill any mitzva at all?

As noted above, the Talmud records the opinion of Rav Sheishet that an individual who corrects one letter of a Torah scroll is considered to have written the entire Torah. This position, however, would seem to be true only when the correction of that letter makes the scroll functional. If an individual corrects only one of numerous invalidating imperfections in a Torah scroll, the scroll remains unusable and the individual has halachically accomplished nothing at all. One might argue, therefore, that of all the participants at a *sefer Torah* dedication, *only the individual who fills in the last letter of the text actually fulfills a mitzva.*

Conversely, however, the argument can be made that each individual participant who writes a letter during a Torah dedication ceremony fulfills a mitzva. Ultimately, all the letters of the text are completed and the scroll is rendered functional. *As each letter plays a vital role in that process, perhaps the mitzva is shared by all.*

---

32. Beit Yosef, Yoreh Deah 270.
33. See Siftei Kohen and Turei Zahav, Yoreh Deah 270 for a review of the various points of view.

Another issue, however, must be considered in the case before us. As noted above, some authorities consider ownership of the Torah scroll to be a critical component in the performance of the mitzva of *ketivat sefer Torah*. According to these scholars, the honorees in the dedication ceremony can only be counted as participants in the mitzva *if they are granted partial possession* of the *sefer Torah*. Failing such an arrangement, each individual would be judged as a scribe, engaged in the holy work of facilitating a mitzva, but not personally fulfilling that mitzva with his act. Furthermore, even if each participant is granted partial ownership in the Torah scroll, the question then arises as to whether an individual can fulfill the mitzva of *ketivat sefer Torah* in partnership with others. This latter question is also debated by the scholars.

— **H** —————————————————————————————

As can be seen from the above example, the issues surrounding the mitzva of *ketivat sefer Torah* remain intricate and complex. Questions of origin, purpose, and application will continue to be debated, as this last mitzva of the Torah is translated from theory into practice during the years to come.

Points to Ponder

Why must it be so difficult?

I am certain that, after coursing through our study, you would agree that the Torah could have made its last mitzva much easier to "pin down."

In spite of the many explanations reviewed for this commandment's origin, for example (and those reviewed are only a small sample of the many actually authored by the scholars), the derivation of this mitzva from the phrase "and now write for yourselves this *shira*" remains vague. If God's intent is that each individual Jew should write a *sefer Torah* during his lifetime, why doesn't the text simply say so?

Concerning the parameters of the mitzva, surely the Torah could have been clearer, as well. Does the commandment obligate an individual to create a Torah scroll, possess a Torah scroll, or both? Can the mitzva be fulfilled in partnership with others? Can it be fulfilled through the writing or acquiring of other scholarly texts? In our day, is this mitzva only satisfied through the writing or acquiring of such texts?

And, finally, what is/are the purpose(s) of this mitzva? Is this commandment designed to encourage the creation and proliferation of Torah scrolls in the world? Are we enjoined to own a Torah scroll for personal use and study? Have we fulfilled our obligation if we donate the scroll to the synagogue for communal use?

Perhaps, on some level, we have already answered our questions…

While we cannot presume to know God's mind, and we will therefore never know with certainty why He frames this last mitzva as He does, we can, nonetheless, note the results of its framing. *By leaving the last commandment of the Torah open to analysis, God encourages discussions like the one in which we have been engaged.* Consider some of the critical issues that have surfaced in our study: the role of each individual in the concrete perpetuation of communal legacy, the overwhelming importance of personal Torah study, potential shifts in communal need over time, the responsibility of each individual to increase the opportunity for others to engage in Torah study, personal responsibility versus shared participation in the performance of mitzvot, and so much more…

As the Torah text reaches its conclusion, God grants one final commandment that seems designed to keep the conversation going, a mitzva that keeps the Torah "open" even as it draws to a close.

We have no way of knowing whether that was truly God's intent, but we can attest to the fact that if it was, it worked!

6 Striking a Balance 1: The Last Two Mitzvot

Context

In the previous study, we reviewed the mysterious origin and complex application of the last mitzva in the Torah, the writing of a *sefer Torah*.

The immediately preceding, penultimate mitzva of the Torah emerges more clearly, through Moshe's instructions to the nation:

> At the end of seven years, on the occasion of the Sabbatical year, during the festival of Succot – when all Israel comes to appear before the presence of the Lord your God, in the place that He will choose – you shall read this Torah in the presence of all Israel, in their ears.
>
> *Hakhel et ha'am*, gather together the people, the men, the women, the small children and the stranger who is within your gates, so that they will hear and so that they will learn, and they shall fear the Lord your God and conscientiously perform all the words of this Torah.
>
> And the children who do not know shall hear and shall learn to fear the Lord your God, all the days that you live on the land to which you are crossing the Jordan, to possess it.[1]

Further details concerning this mitzva, known as Hakhel (gather together), are outlined in the Mishna. The Hakhel ceremony took place at the close of the first day of the festival of Succot, on the year immediately following Shmita. During the ceremony, the king, while seated on a wooden platform erected in the Temple courtyard, publicly read specific selections from the book of Devarim, including the first two paragraphs of the Shma.[2]

---

1. Devarim 31:10–13.
2. Mishna Sota 7:8.

Questions

Why does God choose the mitzvot of Hakhel and *ketivat sefer Torah* as the last two commandments to be delivered by Moshe to the Israelites?

Is there any relationship between these two extraordinary final mitzvot?

Approaches

— **A** —————————————————————————

One could argue that the answer to our first question is obvious.

With the text nearing completion, the stage must be set for the future. As suggested in the previous study, every effort must be made to ensure that the Torah will remain an "open book," a text that will be reproduced, studied, analyzed and applied. God therefore chooses not one, but two commandments specifically designed to root the Torah text in the hearts and minds of the nation.

Every seven years, the people will assemble in force, young and old alike, to participate in the mitzva of Hakhel, to witness its most powerful political figure pledging allegiance to God and His law through the public teaching of Torah text. And throughout the years, the mitzva of *ketivat sefer Torah* will apply, involving each household in the production, study and analysis of sacred texts, weaving God's word into the daily life of each Jew.

— **B** —————————————————————————

I believe, however, that an even deeper message is struck by the balance created between the last two mitzvot of the Torah.

With these commandments, God brings the Torah text full circle.

Towards the beginning of the Torah's narrative in the book of Bereishit, Parshat Noach chronicled the tragic stories of two doomed civilizations: the generation of the flood and the generation of dispersion (the Tower of Bavel). Based on the text and rabbinic sources, we suggested that these stories reference the pivotal tension between two potentially opposing forces that course across the face of human history: *the needs of the individual and the needs of the community* (see *Bereishit*: Noach 1, *Approaches* D–F).

In order to create and maintain rules necessary for communal governance, society must, of necessity, place limits on personal freedoms. At the same time, however, society must limit the restrictions it places upon its citizens in order to allow for individual freedom of expression and action.

The two civilizations described in Parshat Noach reflect polar extremes. The society of Noach's time was characterized by individual greed at the expense of communal structure. The generation of dispersion, on the other hand, was willing to sacrifice individual life to the creation of society. Each of these societies was, therefore, punished accordingly. The generation of Noach, marked by individual greed and corruption, could only be addressed through total destruction. The problem with the generation of dispersion, however, lay in the society, not the individuals. In this case, therefore, only the society was destroyed.

The Torah's message is clear. The balance a particular society strikes between individual and community will, in large measure, determine the character of the society itself. Only those societies that succeed in striking a healthy balance will eventually endure.

The cautionary tales in Parshat Noach are immediately followed by the introduction of the first patriarch, Avraham, and the launching of Jewish history. In the aftermath of the failures of both the generations of the flood and dispersion, a new society emerges. This society, guided by Torah law, will recognize and cherish the invaluable contributions of both individual and community and will strike a healthy balance between them.

—— C ——

Centuries later, as the Torah draws to a close, the stage must be set to ensure the continuing primacy of the text in the lives of the Jewish people. God therefore issues two final commandments designed to *involve both the individual and the community in the task of perpetuating the law*. He commands the mitzva of Hakhel, the public reading of the Torah in the presence of the entire nation, thereby injecting the community into the realm of textual study, often seen only in personal terms. And He commands the mitzva of *ketivat sefer Torah*, obligating each individual Jewish male to "write" a Torah scroll, thereby directing the individual towards the task of textual preservation, often seen only as a communal obligation.

God's message to the nation through these mitzvot could not be clearer: *Community and individuals must work together, hand in hand.*

I command you, therefore, to periodically gather in full force as a community – young and old, men and women. Inject the mitzva of Torah study,

most often seen in personal terms, into the public sphere. Let the most power-
ful among you read the text, an act that will underscore your responsibility
to build a society based upon the dictates of Torah law. Cherish and sustain
that communal structure. Recognize its essential role in the analysis, practice
and transmission of the law.

I then command you to return home and fulfill your individual obligation
to write a sefer *Torah. Through this mitzva, individualize the responsibility*
for the text's perpetuation – a responsibility that you might otherwise see
only as communal. Recognize the personal obligation that each of us bears
for the continuity of Jewish thought and idea. Touch again the lesson that I
have taught you on so many occasions and in so many ways: unity does not
connote uniformity. Your handwriting is your own. The scrolls you "write"
will be identical in content, but will vary in style. The flavor of your personal
observance, the contributions that you make to Jewish thought, the teach-
ings that you share with your children will all enter the flow of your nation's
journey and will help shape your people's character. Each of you is cherished
and each of you can make a unique contribution to the whole.

—— **D** ————————————————————————————

God closes His list of 613 mitzvot with two carefully chosen commandments. Each of these mitzvot is certainly important in its own right. Taken
together, however, their significance multiplies immeasurably.

These commandments strike the balance between individual and
community – a balance that will prove to be crucial throughout the rich,
enduring journey of an eternal people.

Ha'azinu-V'zot האזינו־ Habracha וזאת הברכה

CHAPTER 32:1–34:12

פרק לב:א-לד:יב

Parsha Summary

Song, blessing, a leader's final journey...

Beckoning the heavens and the earth to hear his words, Moshe raises his voice in song as he shares Shirat Ha'azinu, the song recorded in Parshat Ha'azinu, with the Israelites on the last day of his life. Over the course of this song, designed to serve as eternal testimony to the nation, this great leader recalls God's kindnesses to the people and predicts their future sins, punishment and eventual redemption. In spite of national failure, suffering and exile, Moshe proclaims, the bond between the Jewish nation and its God will never be severed.

Upon concluding Shirat Ha'azinu, Moshe encourages the people to preserve its message across the ages.

God commands Moshe to ascend to the summit of Mount Nevo, in order to view the land of Canaan from afar immediately prior to his death.

The last parsha of the Torah, V'zot Habracha, opens as Moshe turns to the nation for a final farewell. After bestowing a short collective blessing on the people as a whole, he proceeds to bless the tribes individually. He then closes with another short collective blessing.

As per God's instructions, Moshe ascends Mount Nevo. From the mountain's summit, God shows him the entirety of the land of Canaan, identifying it as the land promised to the patriarchs.

At the age of 120, Moshe dies on the summit of Mount Nevo. The Torah testifies that "no man knows his burial place to this day." For thirty days, the nation mourns the passing of the only leader that they have known.

Yehoshua Bin Nun rises to leadership and is accepted by the nation.

The Torah closes with a clear declaration of Moshe's unique place in history, testifying that "never again has there arisen in Israel a prophet like Moshe, whom the Lord had known face-to-face."

1 Striking a Balance 2: Song and Blessing

Context

Moshe's final communications to the nation are delivered through two specific mediums: *shira* and *bracha* (song and blessing).

In Shirat Ha'azinu, the song recorded in Parshat Ha'azinu, Moshe reviews God's past kindnesses towards the nation and applies the theme of divine reward and punishment to the people's future.[1]

In Parshat V'zot Habracha, Moshe bestows prophetic, individualized blessings upon each of the tribes.[2]

Questions

In addition to the messages that can be gleaned from the content of Moshe's final communications to the nation, can lessons be learned from the modalities through which those messages are conveyed? Why, once all his eloquent farewell addresses have been completed and delivered, does Moshe ultimately bid a final farewell to his people *specifically through song and blessing*?

Approaches

—A—

I would suggest that the manner in which Moshe delivers his final words to the nation is far from accidental. Even now, in his last public appearances, this great leader finds a way to educate through example. By saying goodbye to the nation through *shira* and *bracha*, Moshe models *two very different yet equally essential ways of relating to the world around us.*

---

1. Devarim 32:1–47.
2. Ibid., 33:1–29.

—— **B** ——

The realm of *shira* focuses on the heart…

Many of the earliest songs of our people are born spontaneously, with no reasoned forethought or considered calculation. The participants in these *shirot* are immersed in the unfolding story. Moved beyond measure by specific experiences, events or feelings, an individual or a group "erupts" in song, expressing through word the unprompted emotions of the heart.

These early *shirot* – such as the Az Yashir, the song of the Israelites on the banks of the Reed Sea, and Shirat Devora, the victorious song of the prophetess Devora – are fundamentally subjective and reflective, mirroring unfolding events from the perspective of the *meshorer* (songwriter). No attempt is made through the *shira* to objectify, control or determine the course of these events. In this early realm of song, existing reality is accepted, recorded and spontaneously celebrated or mourned.

Going a step further, other songs are consciously evocative in character. Here, the *meshorer* deliberately sets out not only to mirror unfolding events and ideas, but to draw the listener into the *meshorer's* subjective reality. Through the use of poetry, symbolism and music, these songs, such as King Shlomo's Shir Hashirim, are carefully designed to touch the hearts of each listener, inducing emotions that could not be effectively conveyed through any other medium.

—— **C** ——

The realm of *bracha* is vastly different. Here the *mevarech*, the individual reciting the blessing, *takes a step back* to objectively study, analyze, quantify and at times even try to control the reality around him.

While many different types of blessings are found within Jewish tradition, they all share one specific feature. In each case, the *mevarech* utters the blessing *from a distance*, gaining perspective as he determines the proper response to an experience, event or challenge.

—— **D** ——

The earliest *brachot* found in the Torah text are interpersonal in nature. From the blessings recited in the patriarchal era, parent to child, to the obligatory Birkat Kohanim recited by the priests over the nation, each of these blessings marks an attempt by the *mevarech* to affect the course of the unfolding reality, to sway God's will in favor of those being blessed.

As noted previously, the origin of such blessings traces to the divine promise bestowed upon the patriarch Avraham at the dawn of Jewish history: "And you will be a blessing."[3] The rabbis, in the Midrash, interpret this pledge to mean, "Blessings are given to your hand. Until now they were in My [God's] hand. I blessed Adam and Noach. From this time on, you will bless whom you wish."[4]

By granting man the power to bless, God grants effectiveness to our prayers, both on behalf of ourselves and for the welfare of others (see *Bereishit*: Toldot 3, *Approaches* A; Ekev 1, *Points to Ponder*).

— E —

A major shift in the course of *brachot*, however, emerges in Parshat Ekev, with the advent of the mitzva of Birkat Hamazon, Grace after Meals (see Ekev 1).

For the first time, an ongoing obligation devolves upon man to "bless God," in response to the bounty that he receives. As we have noted, various different interpretations are offered to explain this new obligation. At its most basic, however, Birkat Hamazon forces man to pause and gain a clearer awareness of and perspective on the natural gifts bestowed upon him by God.

Using Birkat Hamazon as a template, the rabbis enact a myriad of obligatory blessings designed to punctuate the daily life of the Jew.

Birchot hanehenin, blessings of benefit, for example, are recited before an individual benefits from a specific aspect of his environment. Even the most natural of actions, such as eating and drinking, are preceded by these *brachot*, as the observant Jew pauses to understand the experience involved, to realize that the bounty that he receives is a gift from God, and to show *hakarat hatov* (appreciation of the good) to his Creator for this gift.

Birchot hamitzva, blessings concerning commandments, are recited in connection with the performance of specific mitzvot. Through these blessings the *mevarech* expresses gratitude to the Creator for sanctifying the Jewish nation through the bestowal of the divine commandments. The rabbis specifically decree that each of these *brachot* should be recited

---

3. Bereishit 12:2.
4. Midrash Rabba Bereishit 39:11.

over l'asiatan, before the performance of the specific mitzva.[5] Once again, therefore, the recitation of these blessings provides each individual with the mandated opportunity to consider the true significance of the act that he is about to perform.

Birchot hoda'a, blessings of thanks, for their part, are recited to express gratitude to God for specific life experiences, from the mundane to the extraordinary. One of the most powerful of these blessings, for example, is the *bracha* of *asher yatzar* (He Who fashioned). This blessing, regularly recited by observant Jews after attending to bodily functions, thanks the Creator for the miracles embedded in the intricate ongoing physiological processes of a human being. While the very existence of such a blessing seems strange to the uninitiated, its rabbinic authors clearly felt that nothing could be more natural than a *bracha* that fosters man's recognition of his dependence upon God for the everyday miracles of life.[6]

While the blessings cited above are designed to grant the *mevarech* a clearer objective perspective on the experiences and events that touch his life, many *brachot*, including the formal Birkat Hamazon recited today, go a major step further. The texts of these blessings include elements of *bakasha*, request, as the *mevarech* strives to *control, and even change, the reality that confronts him.*

Following the model of the earliest interpersonal blessings of the Torah text, these *brachot* represent an attempt by man to sway God's will, whether towards the benefit of the *mevarech* himself, his people as a whole, or other individuals. The formalization of these blessings into the daily liturgy, most notably in the wide-ranging requests found in the Amida prayer, also trains the *mevarech* to recognize his dependence upon God for the many phenomena that he would otherwise take for granted and teaches him to "ask" for what is truly important.

---

5. Talmud Bavli Pesachim 7b; Sota 39a; Megilla 21b; Menachot 35b.
6. See Kenneth Prager, MD, "For Everything a Blessing." This beautiful article, written by a renowned physician and esteemed member of my own Englewood congregation, shares a powerful personal perspective on the *bracha* of *asher yatzar*. Originally printed on the op-ed page of the *New York Times*, this article can be accessed on many websites including www.Torah.org/features/firstperson/everythingablessing.html.

—— F ——

We can now begin to understand why Moshe bids farewell to his people with song and blessing. By doing so, he implicitly directs the people towards two critical abilities that they will be required to perfect as they face the years ahead – two essential ways of relating to the world.

My children, you will be challenged across time to respond on multiple levels to an ever-changing world. To succeed you will have to strike the balance between bracha *and* shira.

Always remember to bless, to take a step back for careful objective consideration of the world around you. Pause, gain perspective and recognize the true import of each facet of your reality. Cultivate an awareness of your dependence on God and express gratitude for those gifts that you might otherwise take for granted. And don't be afraid to push the envelope. Plan and dream for yourselves, your loved ones, your entire people, and request from God that He grant you the continuing ability to fulfill those plans and dreams.

At the same time, don't lose heart; don't forget to sing. Periodically, suspend calculation and intellectual attempts to objectify and redirect reality. Even with all your striving, much will remain beyond your control. Immerse yourselves in the moment. Feel with your heart and touch the hearts of others. Never lose your sense of wonder in the beauty that surrounds you each day. And just as I sing to you now of the challenging road that lies ahead, celebrate it all: the gifts from God, the challenges, the struggle, the joys, the pain, the faith in your ultimate redemption…

As I sing and bless you today, always find a way to bless and to sing.

2 A Glaring Omission

Context

The first section of Shirat Ha'azinu, Moshe's dramatic song recorded in Parshat Ha'azinu, summarizes the past kindnesses bestowed by God upon the nation. After a short passage extolling God, chastising the nation for their failures, and inviting them to consider the lessons of the past, Moshe begins to recount the nation's shared history from the moment of their being "chosen" by God.

> He [God] found him in a desert land, and in the desolation, a howling wilderness, He encompassed him, He instructed him, He guarded him as the apple of His eye.
>
> As an eagle arousing its nest, hovering over its young, spreading its wings and taking them, bearing them aloft on its pinions, God alone did lead him.[1]

Questions

An obvious, glaring omission emerges when we consider Moshe's words. As this great leader begins his brief historical overview, he makes no mention of either the Exodus from Egypt or of the Revelation at Sinai, the two towering events that he has personally shared with his people and that have shaped their birth as a nation. Instead, this great leader apparently chooses to begin his historical narrative with the Israelites' wilderness wanderings.

Moshe's stated purpose at this point in Shirat Ha'azinu is to recall the divine kindnesses bestowed upon the nation.[2] Why then does he omit the Exodus, the Revelation at Sinai and all the monumental miracles that accompanied those events?

---

1. Devarim 32:10–12.
2. Ibid., 32:7–9.

Approaches

—A—

The Midrash avoids this problem entirely by completely reinterpreting the opening of Moshe's historical overview. Moshe, the Midrash explains, truly begins at "the beginning," by referencing the much earlier patriarchal era of Jewish history. *God's choosing of the Israelites,* Moshe emphasizes, *actually originates in this pre-national period with His selection of their progenitor, Avraham*:

> "And He found him in a desert land…" This refers to Avraham. The matter can be compared to a king who, together with his cohort, goes off into the wilderness. Ultimately, the king's legions abandon their monarch, leaving him isolated in a place of grave danger, enemy armies and thieves. One loyal hero, however, remains with the king, reassuring him, "Do not despair and have no fear. By your life, I will not leave you until you return to your palaces and sleep upon your bed." Thus did God say to Avraham, "I am the Lord your God, Who took you out from Ur Kasdim…"[3]

God's choice of Avraham, the Midrash explains, effectively saves the Patriarch from the evil forces of his day, ensuring that he will not fade into obscurity beneath the mists of history. With this divine kindness bestowed upon their ancestor, Moshe declares, God's benevolence towards the Israelites begins.[4]

—B—

While some later commentaries accept the Midrashic explanation that Moshe opens his historical review with the patriarchal era,[5] most authorities gravitate towards the more obvious interpretation of the text. The phrase "and He found him in a desert land," they maintain, references God's care for the nation during their wilderness travels. Moshe's apparent omission

---

3. Bereishit 15:7.
4. Sifrei, Devarim 313.
5. Meshech Chochma, Devarim 32:10.

of the Exodus and Revelation thus remains, for these scholars, an issue to be addressed.

Nehama Leibowitz briefly entertains the possibility that Moshe omits the Exodus from his presentation because of the nature of his audience. This great leader addresses the second generation of Israelites, who did not experience the Exodus personally and for whom the wilderness wandering, replete with all of its miracles, has been formative.

Leibowitz herself, however, quickly dismisses this approach, noting that throughout the book of Devarim, Moshe speaks to this second generation and yet "there are many places in the Book of Devarim where the Exodus heads the list of miracles and kindnesses performed by God."[6]

——— C ———

Some authorities maintain that, contrary to appearances, *Moshe does, in fact, allude to at least some of the formative events of Jewish nationhood.* Rashi, for example, contends that the phrase "He found him in a desert land" is to be understood as implicit praise for the Israelites' ready acceptance of the Torah at Sinai: "He found *them faithful* in a desert land, as they accepted upon themselves His Torah, His sovereignty, and His dominion, something that Yishmael and Esav had refused to do."[7]

Rashi's interpretation is based on a well-known Midrashic observation rooted in Moshe's subsequent blessing to the nation: "Hashem came from Sinai, having shone forth to them from Seir, having appeared from Mount Paran."[8]

According to the Midrash, this sentence references God's initial approaches to the nations of Edom in Seir and Ishmael in Paran, requesting that they accept the Torah. When these nations and all other nations of the world reject God's offer, refusing to obligate themselves to the personal restrictions that such acceptance would entail, God turns to the Israelites, who readily bind themselves to God's law.[9] It is this laudatory act on the part of the Israelites, Rashi maintains, that is referred to by Moshe as he begins his historical overview in Shirat Ha'azinu.[10]

---

6. Leibowitz, *Studies in Devarim*, p. 343.
7. Rashi, Devarim 32:10.
8. Devarim 33:2.
9. Sifrei, Devarim 343.
10. Rashi, Devarim 32:10.

The Ramban strongly objects. Rashi's suggestion that Moshe praises the Israelites in the opening of Shirat Ha'azinu, this scholar argues, fails to pass muster contextually. The entire tone of the *shira* is one of reproof, as Moshe admonishes the nation for their ingratitude and for their failure to appreciate the kindnesses bestowed upon them by God. A commendation for the Israelites' actions at Sinai, the Ramban insists, would therefore be totally out of place at the beginning of this song.[11]

— D —

Other commentaries follow Rashi's lead, if not his conclusions, as they attempt to discern allusions to the Exodus or Revelation in Moshe's words at the beginning of Shirat Ha'azinu.

The Abravanel maintains, for example, that Moshe views Revelation as a key component in the fabric of God's protection during the Israelites' wilderness wanderings. As the people travel through a physical and spiritual wasteland, a wilderness where man's connection to God would normally be severely strained, God responds on all levels to their spiritual and physical needs.

"He encompassed him." *God encompassed the people with His divine Providence.*

"He instructed him." *God bestowed upon them His Torah and commandments.*

"He guarded him as the apple of his eye." *God protected them from the physical dangers common to the wilderness: serpent, scorpion and devastating thirst.*[12]

The Ralbag takes a different tack, detecting within Moshe's poetry references both to the Israelites' positive response at Sinai and to their subsequent failure.

"He found him in a desert land." *The Israelites found their God in the wilderness, where they experienced His wondrous acts.*

"And in the desolation, a howling wilderness." *The nation then, however, turned against God through the unjust complaints and baseless protests that characterized the sin of the spies.*

"He encompassed them." *God's plan to bring the nation directly into the*

---

11. Ramban, Devarim 32:7.
12. Abravanel, Devarim 32.

land of Canaan after Revelation could, therefore, not be brought to fruition. Instead, God had to "encompass them," to lead the nation in circuitous fashion, during forty years of wilderness wandering.

"And instructed them." Throughout this punishment period, however, the seeds of hope were sown. God instructed the next generation in critical areas of wisdom, preparing them for nationhood.[13]

—— **E** ——

Yet other commentaries approach Moshe's words in the beginning of Shirat Ha'azinu in a totally different way, thereby explaining Moshe's concentration on the wilderness period. In the eyes of these scholars, Moshe is not simply offering a historical review. This great leader, instead, couches wide-ranging philosophical and ethical teachings within this portion of his song. A beautiful interpretation in this vein is offered, for example, by the towering nineteenth-century German scholar and rabbinic leader Rabbi Shimshon Raphael Hirsch.

Hirsch maintains that as Shirat Ha'azinu opens, Moshe specifically focuses on the singular development path of Jewish national identity. Other peoples' nationhood, Moshe declares, develops with their acquisition of a geographical homeland, as God "directs the nations to their inheritance"[14] and "sets up the boundaries of the nations."[15] The moral, spiritual and social culture of these nations is, therefore, rooted in and shaped by their relationship to their land.

Not so, the Jewish people…

God forges the national identity of the Jewish people through the giving of His law, *prior to their entry into the Land of Canaan.* As a result, "God's portion is His people, Yaakov is the measure of His inheritance."[16] God becomes for the Jewish people, Hirsch explains, what "the soil of their land is for other nations."[17] In contrast to the geographical forces that govern and shape the identity of other peoples, the central force uniting the Jewish nation, on or off its land, will always be the relationship of the Jews to their Creator and their adherence to His law.

---

13. Ralbag, Devarim 32:10.
14. Devarim 32:8.
15. Ibid.
16. Devarim 32:9.
17. Rabbi Shimshon Raphael Hirsch, Devarim 32:9.

Within this context, Hirsch continues, Moshe's statement "He found him in a desert land, and in the desolation, a howling wilderness"[18] speaks to the unique role that the wilderness plays in developing the national character of the Jewish people. Unlike other nations who acquire their identity "with firm land under their feet," the Jewish people are forged "where no verdant meadows and no town stand out, where man is forsaken by all help from nature and fellow man." They become a nation in "the desolation… where man is thrown back to his inner self, is alone with his own inner self and God."[19]

Hirsch explains that the powerful imagery of Moshe's further depiction, "As an eagle arousing its nest, hovering over its young, spreading its wings and taking them, bearing them aloft on its pinions…,"[20] describes the Jewish nation's singular spiritual strength due to its "wilderness training":

Just as the eagle does not bear its young aloft sleeping or in a passive condition but rather first stirs the nest up and then spreads its wings *not under but above* its nestlings, so that…they fly up to rest on the mother's outspread wings awaiting them from above….

So did God first awaken His people and get them used to [having] the courage to trust themselves with free-willed decision and full consciousness to His guidance.

Only a young eagle has the courage to leave the firm, warm, secure nest and trust himself to the upward flight into the isolating heights where his parent hovers.

And it does require courage…to sacrifice all the life of purely material human greatness and imagined security, and bring into it all that is spiritual and moral of the life men are meant to live…and it does require courage to deny this worshiping of nature and men and to reach the lofty heights of mind and morals which Man can and should soar up to…to turn from the geniuses of the world, and alone with one's God give oneself over to the Almighty wings of the One unique God.[21]

In Hirsch's eyes, the early portions of Shirat Ha'azinu are not simply meant

---

18. Devarim 32:10.
19. Rabbi Shimshon Raphael Hirsch, Devarim 32:10.
20. Devarim 32:11.
21. Rabbi Shimshon Raphael Hirsch, Devarim 32:11.

to chronicle the known events of Jewish history, but instead to underscore the lasting effects of the nation's unique origins. *By shaping you as people through your wilderness travels*, Moshe declares to the Israelites, *God has fashioned you into a nation that can free itself from the worship of the material world and soar to great spiritual heights.*

──── **F** ────────────────────────────────

Finally, we might add to all the above approaches by suggesting that Moshe omits any mention of the Exodus and Revelation from his narrative simply in order to *stay on message*.

Standing before the Israelites during the final hours of his life, this great leader has a single agenda. He desperately wants to convince his people to keep faith with their God, to remain loyal to their Creator and to His law over the long term.

As he fashions his song to the nation, therefore, he deliberately emphasizes those past events that will best convey this message: *As I have told you before* (see *Vayikra*: Behar-Bechukotai 4, *Approaches* B, *Points to Ponder*), *trust is the most critical element in any relationship. The quality and strength of your relationship with another is determined by whether or not your partner can trust you to "be there."*

During the years that have brought you to this point, the most important lesson you have learned is that you can trust in God's constant presence and personal care. True, He performed momentous miracles for you during the Exodus and Revelation. Those events, however, as important as they were, were singular and fleeting. The true measure of God's love for you has been shown through His constancy, through His personal care for you over the course of your wilderness wanderings, day after day.

And now, the same will be asked of you. You cannot fulfill the obligations of your relationship with God simply by "being there" during the dramatic moments when you need Him most. God has shown you constancy; now you must show Him the same.

Day after day, year after year, century after century, you must prove to God that He can trust you.

3 Final Blessings

Context

The time has arrived for the final parting. Moshe faces his people one last time and, after issuing a collective blessing, proceeds to bless the nation, tribe by tribe. He then concludes with a short, final collective blessing.[1]

A striking symmetry thus marks the close of two critical periods in the Torah. The patriarchal era ends as Yaakov blesses each of his children from his deathbed.[2] The period of Moshe's leadership closes as he blesses the people he has led from slavery into nationhood.

The Midrash discerns a textual nuance connecting these two scenes, centuries apart. Yaakov's blessings close with the statement *"V'zot (And this is) what their father spoke to them."*[3] Moshe's blessings are introduced with the statement *"V'zot (And this is) the blessing that Moshe spoke."*[4]

At the close of the patriarchal era, the Midrash explains, Yaakov turns to his sons and declares: *In the future, a man like me is destined to bless you; and from the place I end, he will begin…*[5]

Questions

Centuries apart, the *brachot* of Yaakov to his sons and the *brachot* of Moshe to the nation provide snapshots of two critical moments of Jewish history, two separate occasions when a leader bids farewell and an era draws to a close.

What correlations and/or contrasts can be drawn between these two sets of blessings? How do Yaakov's prophecies, dreams and hopes for his

---

1. Devarim 33.
2. Bereishit 49:1–26.
3. Ibid., 49:28.
4. Devarim 33:1.
5. Sifrei, Devarim 33:1.

children connect and compare with those of Moshe for his people, centuries later? What has remained constant over the years? What has changed?

While a full comparison of these sets of blessings remains beyond the scope of our study, we will consider some of the significant connections and contrasts that emerge when four *brachot* bestowed by each of these leaders are reviewed side by side.

Approaches

——**A**————————————————————————————

Yaakov: "Reuven, you are my firstborn, my might and the first fruits of my strength. Unstable as water, you shall not lead, for you mounted your father's bed, then you desecrated him who ascended my bed."[6]

Moshe: "May Reuven live and not die, and may his population be considered in this count."[7]

The first words of Moshe's cryptic blessing to the tribe of Reuven, "May Reuven live and not die," are puzzling. Does this great leader harbor a specific concern for this tribe's safety? If so, what are the sources of this concern?

A number of commentaries, including Rashi, adopt a Midrashic approach that connects Moshe's concern for the tribe of Reuven's survivability to a sin mentioned in Yaakov's blessing to his firstborn son, the original Reuven, centuries earlier. The book of Bereishit records that after the death of his mother, Rachel, Reuven has relations with his father's concubine, Bilha.[8] While the specifics of this sin are vigorously debated by the authorities, all agree that Reuven's reactions were impulsive and precipitous, earning him his father's reprimand, "you shall not lead, for you mounted your father's bed"[9] (see *Bereishit*: Vayechi 3, *Approaches* A).

Centuries later, Rashi maintains, Moshe prays that the tribe of Reuven be spared the continuing ramifications of the grievous sin committed by its ancestor.[10]

A fascinating twist on this approach is offered by the Malbim, who

---

6. Bereishit 49:3–4.
7. Devarim 33:6.
8. Bereishit 35:22.
9. Ibid., 49:4.
10. Sifrei, Devarim 33:6.

connects the tribe of Reuven's vulnerability not to a *specific sin* committed by their progenitor but to a potentially *inheritable trait* attributed to
him, also mentioned by Yaakov. In his blessing to Reuven, the patriarch
describes his oldest son as "unstable as water."[11] As we have noted before,
this description apparently refers to Reuven's impetuous nature. Over and
over again, the Torah chronicles that the firstborn son of Yaakov "rushes
like water," acting with good intentions but failing to carefully consider the
consequences of his words and actions.[12] Because of his reckless, impetuous nature, Reuven loses the leadership role that, as firstborn, should have
rightfully been his (see *Bereishit*: Bereishit 3, Approaches c).

As Moshe stands before Reuven's descendents, generations later, the
Malbim maintains, this great leader is concerned. He knows that individuals who possess Reuven's trait of impulsivity will often "lead difficult lives
and are wont to place themselves in danger."[13] Moshe, therefore, prays that
the descendents of the original Reuven be spared the consequences of this
trait of impulsivity. He bestows upon the tribe of Reuven the blessings of
peaceful, fulfilling lives, protected from danger.

Numerous other authorities, however, reject any direct connection
between Moshe's blessing to the tribe of Reuven and the actions or traits
of that tribe's ancestor who lived 250 years earlier. Moshe's concerns for the
tribe of Reuven's safety, these scholars contend, are current, concrete, and
rise out of the tribe's own decisions and actions. The members of Reuven
have exposed themselves to danger as a result of their previously contracted
controversial agreement concerning the conquest of Canaan. In return for
permission to settle on the East Bank of the Jordan (outside the original
borders of Canaan), this tribe has contracted, together with the tribe of
Gad and one half of the tribe of Menashe, to fight in the vanguard of the
Israelite army during the conquest of Canaan. Leaving their families and
possessions behind in the Transjordan, the soldiers of these tribes will
return only after the subjugation of the land is complete (see *Bamidbar*:
Matot-Masei 3).

Moshe, therefore, now prays that the tribe of Reuven be protected from
the dangers inherent in this agreement, that the warriors of Reuven be

---

11. Bereishit 49:4.
12. Bereishit 35:22; 37:22–29; 42:37.
13. Malbim, Devarim 33:6.

spared the casualties expected by front-line soldiers in battle and that the families of these warriors remain safe from attack during their absence.[14]

Perhaps we can argue that even this controversial decision on the part of the tribe of Reuven to remain in the Transjordan can be traced to the impulsivity inherited from their ancestor, and that this generations-old trait now causes the tribe to choose the fertile land before them in the face of the divine mandate to settle in Canaan. The commentaries are silent on the matter, leaving such possibilities to our own consideration...

—— **B** ——————————————————————————————————

Yaakov: "Yehuda, you, your brothers will acknowledge; your hand will be on the neck of your enemies; your father's sons will bow down to you. Yehuda is a lion's cub; from the prey, my son, you have gone up. He stooped down, he crouched as a lion, and like a mighty lion, who dares arouse him? The scepter shall not depart from Yehuda, nor the ruler's staff from between his feet, until Shiloh will arrive and to him the nations will turn. He will bind his foal to the vine, and his donkey's colt to the vine branch. He will wash his garment in wine, and his mantle in the blood of grapes. His eyes shall be more sparkling than wine, and his teeth whiter than milk."[15]

Moshe: "And this to Yehuda, and he said: 'Hear, oh Lord, the voice of Yehuda and bring him to his people; may his hands fight on his behalf and may You be a helper against his enemies.'"[16]

Moshe's one-line blessing to the tribe of Yehuda stands in stark contrast to the more intricate *bracha* bestowed by Yaakov upon his son, the original Yehuda, centuries earlier.[17] In recognition of Yehuda's powerful journey of personal growth, Yaakov's blessing granted his fourth son the leadership role lost by his older brother, Reuven. The patriarchal *bracha* thus foreshadowed the enduring royal rule destined to descend from Yehuda through his progeny, the members of the Davidic dynasty (see *Bereishit: Vayechi 3, Approaches* c, *Points to Ponder*).

Centuries later, however, in his short blessing to the tribe of Yehuda, Moshe makes no clear reference to Yehuda's all-important leadership role.

---

14. Da'at Zekeinim Miba'alei Hatosafot, Devarim 33:6; Abravanel, Devarim 33:6.
15. Bereishit 49:8–12.
16. Devarim 33:7.
17. Bereishit 49:8–12.

Have the descendents of Yaakov's heroic son lost their leadership privileges?

Most commentaries maintain that, far from contradicting Yaakov's blessing to Yehuda, Moshe simply picks up where the patriarch left off. Implicitly acknowledging the tribe of Yehuda's leadership position, Moshe beseeches God to grant them success in fulfilling this inherited role. While Yaakov bestowed the *privileges of leadership* upon his son, Moshe focuses on the *challenges of leadership* that will now confront that son's descendents.

Moshe's specific concern rises out of a fundamental aspect of Israelite leadership that he himself earlier emphasized in his request from God for an appropriate successor: "May the Lord…appoint a man over the assembly who will go out before them and come in before them, who will take them out and bring them in…"[18] Rashi, quoting the Midrash, explains that Moshe prays for a leader who, unlike the leaders of other nations, *will personally lead his people in battle.*[19] To be a true leader of the nation, one must be the first to take risks.

Standing before his people on the eve of their entry into the land, Moshe thus recognizes the grave military dangers that will, by necessity, accompany Yehuda's leadership role. He therefore prays, "and bring him to his people": *allow the members of this tribe to return safely from the forefront of the battlefield.*[20]

The Ibn Ezra and the Tosafists interpret the blessing's strange opening, "and this to Yehuda," in this vein as well. This phrase, these scholars maintain, connects Yehuda's blessing to the previous *bracha* bestowed upon Reuven: "May Reuven live and not die." Moshe now extends this plea for divine protection on the battlefield to Yehuda as well.[21]

———— C ————

Yaakov: "Shimon and Levi are brothers; weapons of violence are their means of acquisition. Let my soul not come into their council and my honor not be identified with their assembly, for in their anger they slew men and at their whim they hamstrung an ox. Accursed be their anger, for it is fierce,

18. Bamidbar 27:16–17.
19. Rashi, Bamidbar 27:17.
20. Rashi, Rav Saadia Gaon, Ramban and others, Devarim 33:7.
21. Ibn Ezra, Devarim 33:7; Da'at Zekeinim Miba'alei Hatosafot, Devarim 33:7.

and their wrath for it is harsh. I will separate them within Yaakov, and I will disperse them in Israel."²²

Moshe: "And of Levi he said: 'Your Tumim and Urim befit your devout one, whom you tested at Masa, and with whom you contested at Mei Meriva. Who says of his father and mother, "I did not see him," and his brothers he did not recognize and his children he did not know; for they have guarded your promise and now watch over your covenant. They shall teach your laws to Yaakov and your Torah to Israel; they shall bring incense for your perception and burnt offerings on your altar.'"²³

The contrast between the *brachot* of Yaakov and those of Moshe is nowhere more apparent than with their respective blessings of Levi.

Yaakov chastises both Levi and Shimon for their rage and violence, and prophesies that they will be divided and scattered within the nation. Moshe, in contrast, is profuse in his praise of the tribe of Levi and speaks glowingly of its place at the helm of the nation's ritual worship. Bewilderingly, the tribe of Shimon *is completely omitted from Moshe's blessings.*

— **D** ————————————————————

Many commentaries believe that the source(s) of Levi's transformation is/are referenced in Moshe's blessing itself. Over the generations following Yaakov's *brachot*, these scholars maintain, the members of the tribe of Levi prove themselves worthy of positive blessing through the quality of their actions.

The Ibn Ezra, for example, interprets the phrase "whom you tested at Masa" as referencing the many trials successfully met by the Levites during the nation's wilderness wanderings. The subsequent phrase "and with whom you contested at Mei Meriva" indicates that the one "failed test" associated with this tribe has already been "paid for." God has decreed that Moshe and Aharon, members of the tribe of Levi, will not enter the land due to their culpability in the sin at Mei Meriva (see Bamidbar 3).

The Ramban, in contrast, maintains that the statement "whom you tested at Masa and with whom you contested at Mei Meriva" presents a partial defense of Moshe and Aharon's actions at Mei Meriva. The term *Masa*, the Ramban explains, specifically refers to the events shortly after

—————————

22. Bereishit 49:5–7.
23. Devarim 33:8–11.

the Exodus at Refidim, a location that becomes known as Masa U'meriva. On that occasion, God commands Moshe to strike a rock and miraculously bring forth water.[24] Moshe and Aharon's unquestioning loyalty in that instance proves their faith in God's ability to produce water in this fashion. The subsequent "failure" of these leaders under similar circumstances at Mei Meriva, therefore, is clearly not a product of their own lack of belief, but is caused by the pressure placed upon them by the nation's rebellious murmurings.[25]

Finally, Rashi quotes a Midrashic tradition that perceives Moshe raising the issue of seemingly inequitable punishment meted out against Aharon at Mei Meriva: "You [God] seized the opportunity to act against him [Aharon]. For while Moshe was guilty of chastising the people [and deviating from God's commandment to "speak" to the rock], what sin did Aharon and Miriam commit?"[26]

———— **E** ————

The immediately subsequent puzzling passage in Moshe's blessing to Levi, "who says of his father and mother, 'I did not see him,' and his brothers he did not recognize and his children he did not know," is likewise interpreted by many commentaries as a positive statement concerning the tribe's past behavior.

The Midrash maintains that this statement references the loyalty of the Levi'im during the sin of the golden calf. Not only do the members of this tribe refrain from active participation in this tragic sin, but they also unhesitatingly respond to Moshe's call to punish the perpetrators, even those who are related to them by blood.[27] The Ibn Ezra, for his part, interprets the same phrase in a totally different direction as referring to the dedication of those Levites – such as the prophet Shmuel – who entered into the Temple service at a very early age and consequently never really knew their families.[28]

---

24. Shmot 17:1–7.
25. Ramban, Devarim 33:8.
26. Sifrei, Devarim 33:8; Rashi, Devarim 33:8.
27. To make this interpretation work, the Midrash explains the terms "father," "mother" and "children" as referring to relatives who are themselves not Levi'im, such as a half-brother from the mother and a grandson from a daughter.
28. Ibn Ezra, Devarim 33:9.

—— F ——————————————————————————————

Different schools emerge among the commentaries concerning the glaring omission of the tribe of Shimon from any of Moshe's blessings.

Some authorities explain this phenomenon in technical terms. The tribe of Shimon, these scholars note, does not receive a land inheritance of its own in Canaan. Instead, as the text of the books of Yehoshua and Shoftim relate, this tribe's portion is voluntarily subsumed within the boundaries of the tribe of Yehuda.[29] Moshe's blessings, therefore, dealing in part with the division of the land, do not mention Shimon separately. In this vein, a Midrashic tradition quoted by Rashi and others suggests that a veiled reference to the tribe of Shimon does appear in Moshe's blessing to Yehuda, embedded in the phrase "Hear, oh Lord, the voice of Yehuda and bring him to his people."[30]

Other authorities, including the Ibn Ezra and Rashi, attribute the omission of the tribe of Shimon from Moshe's blessings to this tribe's earlier, active involvement in the sin of Ba'al Pe'or, the devastating climactic episode in the nation's spiritual struggle against the Midianite sorcerer, Bilam, and the Moabite king, Balak (see *Bamidbar*: Balak 5). The primary role played by the tribe of Shimon in this tragic crime, the Ibn Ezra argues, is evidenced in the striking discrepancy in Shimon's numbers over the course of two separate censuses. When counted at the beginning of the book of Bamidbar, before the event of Ba'al Pe'or, the tribe of Shimon numbers 59,300.[31] Immediately after the tragedy, however, a second census numbers the tribe at 22,200, showing a startling loss of 37,100 souls.[32] This overwhelming deficit seems to reflect the horrific price paid by the tribe of Shimon for involvement in the sin. In addition, the Ibn Ezra points out that the most public perpetrator at Ba'al Pe'or, the Israelite killed by Pinchas in a zealous act, was a leading figure from the tribe of Shimon.[33]

So grievous is the sin of Ba'al Pe'or and so great the culpability of the tribe of Shimon, the Ibn Ezra, Rashi, and others maintain, that this tribe is completely omitted from Moshe's final blessings.[34] The silence created by

29. Yehoshua 19:9; Shoftim 1:3.
30. Sifrei, Devarim 33:7; Rashi, Devarim 33:7.
31. Bamidbar 1:23.
32. Ibid., 26:14.
33. Ibn Ezra, Devarim 33:6.
34. Rashi, Devarim 33:7; Ibn Ezra, Devarim 33:6.

such an omission is an even more devastating statement than any negative comment might have been.

————— **G** —————————————————————————

Finally, a beautiful Midrash connects and contrasts the fates of the tribes of Levi and Shimon, based upon their actions during the generations between the blessings of Yaakov and those of Moshe. In a brilliantly creative stroke, the Midrash builds its point on the striking similarity between the name Levi and the Hebrew term *lilvot* (to borrow).

The Midrash declares that both Shimon and Levi "drank of the same cup," when, with violence and deceit, they wrought vengeance upon the city of Shechem in response to the rape of their sister, Dina. For this reason, both are chastised in the same breath by their father, Yaakov, when he opens his blessing to them with the declaration, "Shimon and Levi are brothers; weapons of violence are their mode of acquisition."[35]

The Midrash continues by comparing the unfolding story of these two brothers to the parable of two men who both borrow money from their king. Eventually, one individual not only pays his obligation, but then proceeds to actually lend of his own funds to the monarch. The second individual, however, fails to pay back his loan, and then borrows again from the king.

Shimon and Levi, the Midrash explains, both incur a moral debt when, through deceit and violence, they wreak vengeance on the inhabitants of the city of Shechem in response to the rape of their sister, Dina (see *Bereishit*: Vayishlach 4).

Ultimately, however, the tribe of Levi redeems its debt at the foot of Mount Sinai, not only by refraining from participation in the sin of the golden calf, but also by responding to Moshe's call to action in the sin's aftermath. Arming themselves at Moshe's instruction, the Levites proceed to defend God's honor by summarily executing the active perpetrators in the sin. Furthermore, through the daring actions of one of its own, the tribe of Levi subsequently goes a step further and, in the terminology of the Midrash, "advances a loan" to God.[36] As the nation's leadership stands paralyzed in the face of the devastating effects of the sin of Ba'al Pe'or,

———————————
35. Bereishit 49:5.
36. Sifrei, Devarim 33:8.

Aharon's grandson, Pinchas, zealously takes the law into his own hands and strikes down the two most public perpetrators. His courageous actions save the nation from further destruction and earn him significant divine reward (see *Bamidbar*: Pinchas 1, 2).

The tribe of Shimon, in contrast, not only fails to redeem the moral debt incurred at Shechem, but adds to that debt through the active involvement of its members in the sin of Ba'al Pe'or (see above).[37]

From the Midrashic perspective, based upon the clear evidence of the text, "Shimon and Levi are brothers,"[38] with a shared striking tendency towards zealousness. The tribes' respective fates are ultimately determined by *how their members apply this inherent trait in their dealings with the world around them.*

The descendents of Shimon, whose violent tendencies lead them again and again towards sin, are omitted entirely from Moshe's blessings and fail to receive a discrete geographic inheritance in the land of Canaan. The descendents of Levi, who apply the same tendency for zealousness towards good in their pursuit of God's honor, earn one of the most beautiful of Moshe's blessings and attain the coveted leadership role at the nation's spiritual helm. *In contrast to his brother, Levi has more than "redeemed his debt" to the Almighty.*

Upon consideration, the destiny of these two tribes might seem to have been determined by the end of the patriarchal era. As a result of their violent actions at Shechem, both Shimon and Levi will be "scattered" across the nation, Yaakov predicts in his blessing.[39] The patriarch's prophetic prediction is, in fact, realized. The actual character of that realization, however, is determined by the continuing actions of the tribes themselves, as they apply their singular traits towards entirely different ends. Shimon disappears as an independent entity, swallowed within the geographical boundaries of Yehuda. Levi rises to prominence, its members spread throughout the nation with highest honor as spiritual leaders.

The contrasting fates of the tribes of Shimon and Levi thus reflect a fundamental truth that we have previously found woven into the very fabric of the world's creation. No aspect of man is inherently evil. The same trait

---

37. Ibid.
38. Bereishit 49:5.
39. Ibid., 49:8.

that can lead to grievous sin, when properly channeled, can lead to the greatest good (see *Bereishit*: Bereishit 1, *Approaches* F).

—— **H** ——

Yaakov: "Zevulun shall dwell by the seashores, and he shall be a shore for ships, and his border shall stretch to Zidon. Yissaschar is a strong-boned donkey, crouching between the sheepfolds. He saw a resting place that it was good and the land that it was pleasant, and he bowed his shoulder to bear and became an indentured servant."[40]

Moshe: "And to Zevulun he said: 'Rejoice, Zevulun, in your going out, and Yissaschar, in your tents. The tribes will assemble at the mountain; there they will offer righteous offerings, for by the riches of the sea they will be nourished, and the hidden treasures of the sand.'"[41]

If dissimilarity marks the blessings of Yaakov and Moshe to Levi, their blessings to Zevulun and Yissaschar seem markedly alike. As the Rashbam and other adherents to the *pshat* of the text note, both leaders clearly contrast the tribe of Zevulun's role as seafaring merchants with Yissaschar's character as workers of the land. Additionally, both of these leaders textually juxtapose their blessings to these tribes in order to highlight this disparity.[42]

In spite of these clear parallels, however, one major difference between the words of Yaakov and Moshe does emerge with the passage of the centuries. *Yaakov bestows individual blessings on each of these tribes. Moshe includes both in one blessing.*

This contrast suggests that Moshe takes a major step forward in his blessings to Zevulun and Yissaschar. While Yaakov stops at recognizing the disparate character of these tribes, *Moshe moves to forge an essential partnership between them.* This great leader deliberately includes both tribes in one *bracha* in order to underscore the interdependent nature of their blessings.[43] The seafaring merchants of Zevulun, Moshe prophesizes,

---

40. Ibid., 49:13–15.
41. Devarim 49:18–19.
42. Rashbam, Bereishit 49:13, 14.
43. Although the concept of a partnership between Zevulun and Yissaschar is mentioned in the Midrashic comments on Yaakov's blessings to his sons (see Midrash Rabba Bereishit 99:9), Targum Onkelos and other biblical commentaries find this partnership rooted in Moshe's blessings to these tribes. Our interpretation follows their approach.

will provide locally unavailable goods to the tribe of Yissaschar. In return, the farmers of Yissaschar will supply their brothers in Zevulun with the provisions needed for their ongoing journeys.

Many commentaries, however, take a significant further step by following a Midrashic tradition that thrusts the proposed partnership between Yissaschar and Zevulun into an entirely different realm. Central to this approach is the interpretation of Moshe's statement "and Yissaschar in your tents" as specifically referring to this tribe's constant presence in *batei midrash* (houses of study). This explanation is consistent with the Midrashic understanding of the term *ohel* (tent), in a number of other settings, as referring to a house of Torah study.[44]

In his blessing, these scholars maintain, Moshe predicts that the tribe of Yissaschar will be characterized by the extraordinary Torah scholarship of its members. Yissaschar's commitment to constant study, however, will only be made possible by the tribe of Zevulun's equal commitment to provide for the protection and sustenance of their scholarly brothers. In the course of this joint venture, both those "learning" and those "providing" will gain an equal share in the unfolding Torah study. This suggested fraternal partnership finds textual support in two verses recorded in Chronicles that describe the members of the tribe of Yissaschar as "men who had understanding of the times, to know what Israel ought to do," and the members of Zevulun as "[individuals who] went forth to battle, experts in war, with all instruments of war."[45]

Once established at the dawn of Jewish history, the symbiotic model of Yissaschar-Zevulun cooperation continues to be cited across the ages as a paradigm for Jewish communal collaboration. In countless communities throughout the Jewish world, the establishment and maintenance of *batei midrash*, yeshivot and *kollelim* (institutions of continuing Torah study for older students) has historically been enabled by the generosity of benefactors, large and small. These patrons have been encouraged in their largesse by the fundamental assurance that their financial contributions to the furtherance of Torah study grant them a real stake in the study itself.

Even the best of partnerships, however, must be carefully calibrated. While the Yissaschar-Zevulun model has certainly been critical to the

---

44. Rashi and others, Bereishit 25:27, based on Midrash Rabba Bereishit.
45. Divrei Hayamim I 12:33–34.

perpetuation of Jewish scholarship across the ages, issues surrounding communal support for full-time Torah scholarship have also been the subject of vociferous debate. As we have previously noted, various opinions are offered in halachic literature both concerning the suitability of a scholar's acceptance of communal funds to enable his full-time study and the appropriate extent to which a community should allocate such funds (see *Bereishit*: Toldot 3, *Points to Ponder*; *Shmot*: Beshalach 4, *Approaches* D, *Points to Ponder*). In our time, these issues continue to be a source of contention in Israeli society, further stressing the natural fault line between the religious and secular components of the population.

By blessing the tribes of Zevulun and Yissaschar with the wisdom to partner, Moshe emphasizes the critical role that internal partnerships can play in strengthening the nation as a whole. The careful forging of such partnerships continues to be a challenge that the Jewish community faces to this day.

— I —

As our study has shown, Moshe's blessings on the day of his death relate in different ways to Yaakov's final *brachot*, centuries earlier. In some cases, Moshe builds upon the earlier blessings; in other cases, he adjusts them to changing circumstances.

Two sets of temporally distant blessings, one from a father to his sons and the other from a leader to his nation, remain connected at their core. Currents from the past meld with realities of the present, as Moshe shapes the thoughts that will serve as his final farewell to the people. Beyond the specifics of his *brachot*, Moshe thus conveys an overarching, enduring lesson.

Our relationship with the past is complicated. Some elements of the past must be built upon, others must be overcome. The past, however, can never be ignored.

Recognize and build upon your inherited strengths; face the responsibilities that legacy brings; overcome failures of the past and you will succeed in meeting the challenges ahead.

Moshe's message remains as current for us today as it was for a fledgling nation on the eve of their entry into their land.

4 Beginning with God, Ending with Man

Final Points to Ponder

At first blush, one cannot help but feel a bit "let down" by the closing verses of the Torah text: "And never again has there arisen in Israel a prophet like Moshe whom the Lord had known face-to-face, in all the signs and wonders that the Lord sent him to perform in the land of Egypt, to Pharaoh, to all his servants, and to all his land, and in all the mighty hand and awesome power that Moshe performed before the eyes of all Israel."[1]

Is this a fitting close to God's book, the text that majestically began with the words *b'reishit bara Elokim*, "In the beginning God created..."?

Certainly, an understanding of Moshe's exclusive place in history is critical and must be elucidated in the text. Clearly, the Torah must also establish this great leader's uniqueness in order to cement the eternal nature of its own text, as a tome that cannot be contradicted by later, lesser prophets. But why here, at the Torah's close, where God's last words to man would seem to carry such weight?

One might have expected more: a final divine communication to send us on our way, a last splendid lesson to ring in our ears... *Shouldn't God's book end with a parting message from God*?

As if these problems are not enough, Rashi's closing comments on the text compound our questions.

Rashi is among a series of scholars who parse each phrase of the Torah's last sentence in an attempt to pinpoint the exact meaning of the words. Through the application of textual sources and their own logical reasoning, these commentaries offer opinions as to which of *Moshe's miraculous deeds* are specifically emphasized by the Torah as the text draws to a close. Reviewing their efforts, we can almost hear the insistent voices of these scholars declaring: *These are the final words of the Torah. We must*

---

1. Devarim 34:10–12.

understand them clearly and precisely: "...and in all the mighty hand and awesome power that Moshe performed before the eyes of all Israel."[2]

The phrase "and in all the mighty hand" alludes, according to Rashi, to the receiving of the Torah by Moshe's "hand"; according to the Ramban and the Ibn Ezra, to the wonders performed at the Reed Sea; and according to the Sforno, to a series of miracles including the parting of the sea, the opening of the earth to swallow Korach and his followers, and the miracle of the heavenly food, the manna.[3]

The phrase "and awesome power" refers, according to Rashi, to the miracles performed during the nation's wilderness wanderings; according to the Ibn Ezra, to the parting of the sea; according to the Ramban, either to the parting of the sea or to Revelation; and according to Sforno, to Revelation.[4]

When we reach the Torah's last phrase, "before the eyes of all Israel," however, something extraordinary happens. Rashi separates himself from the pack.

Other commentaries continue on the path that they have already mapped out, discerning textual references to miraculous acts or events associated with Moshe's leadership. The Sforno, for example, interprets the words "before the eyes of all Israel" as referring to the rays of light that emanated from Moshe's visage following Revelation, while the Ramban sees this phrase as reflecting back upon all the previously mentioned divine miracles in which Moshe played a role.[5]

Rashi, however, in his very last comments on the Torah text, chooses a different path: "'Before the eyes of all Israel': [This phrase alludes to the fact that Moshe's] heart moved him to *shatter the Tablets of Testimony before their eyes*, as the text states, 'and I shattered them before your eyes.'"[6]

According to Rashi, the last phrase of the Torah references Moshe's controversial shattering of the Tablets of Testimony at the foot of Mount Sinai, upon witnessing the Israelites' involvement in the sin of the golden calf (see *Shmot*: Ki Tissa 4). Rashi concludes his remarks by quoting the Talmudic contention that God retroactively agrees with Moshe's dramatic

---

2. Ibid., 34:12.
3. Rashi, Ramban, Ibn Ezra, and Sforno, Devarim 34:12.
4. Ibid.
5. Ramban, Devarim 34:12; Sforno, Devarim 34:12.
6. Rashi, Devarim 34:12.

act. When God informs Moshe that He will inscribe the second tablets with the words that were on *luchot harishonim asher shibarta*, "the first tablets that you shattered,"[7] the rabbis explain the divine intimation to be, *Yiyasher kochacha she'shibarta*, "You are to be congratulated for having shattered them."[8]

Rashi's comments are startling. Is this, in Rashi's opinion, the way that the Torah wants us to ultimately remember Moshe: as the destroyer of the Tablets? Given all of Moshe's momentous accomplishments, is this act meant to be his final legacy?

Ironically, Rashi's puzzling approach to the last words of the Torah text may help us understand not only how the Torah wants us to remember Moshe, but why God chooses to close His Book with specific references to this great leader.

According to Rashi, the Torah wants us to remember Moshe as great, *but not as greater than life.* The Torah wants its last snapshot to picture Moshe not in his role as a prophet, not in his role as a miracle worker, *but in his role as a man, making real-life decisions in real-life situations.* By emphasizing Moshe's mortality and the aspect of commonality that he shares with us all, the Torah allows us to learn critical personal lessons from this great leader as he exits the historical stage.

In all probability, none of us will be faced within our lifetimes with the challenges of parting a sea, bringing forth water from a rock or summoning food from heaven. *God will expect us, however, to consistently act in consonance with Torah values and traditions, even when the path before us is not clear and the decisions to be made are difficult and complex.* The Torah therefore focuses in the end on the single most important independent act performed by Moshe during his leadership career: a non-miraculous act – a voluntary step taken when he stands alone, without guidance from God, with *everything hanging in the balance.*

Descending from Mount Sinai to the stark scene of debauchery that surrounds the golden calf, Moshe reacts. Instinctively he realizes that the people cannot now receive the Torah, and that were he to transmit the law to them under the present circumstances, the law itself would become an

---

7. Shmot 34:1; Devarim 10:2.
8. Rashi, Devarim 34:10, quoting Talmud Bavli Yevamot 62a, Bava Batra 14b, Menachot 99b.

aberration, misunderstood and misused. Without a second thought, Moshe shatters the tablets "before the eyes of all Israel" and then proceeds to begin the process of spiritual repair (see *Shmot*: Ki Tissa 4).

There could be then no more appropriate close for the Torah, Rashi believes, than a reference to the shattering of the tablets. The lessons that emerge during this episode, both from Moshe's personal example and from the message that his actions convey, strike to the very core and purpose of God's Book. *Ultimately, the Torah's goal is the refinement of man: the shaping of individuals and communities who will naturally "do the right thing" and thereby sanctify God's name.* The text, therefore, closes its narrative by referring to the episode that best exemplifies this goal "before the eyes of all Israel."

At the foot of Mount Sinai, Moshe imperils everything he has worked for, in one single autonomous act. There have been other times when Moshe has acted of his own accord – when he left Pharaoh's palace to witness the pain of his brothers, when he turned aside to view the burning bush, when he ascended Mount Sinai without invitation – and each of these decisive acts and others like them marked critical, life-changing junctures in Moshe's journey (see *Shmot*: Shmot 2, *Approaches* D–F, *Points to Ponder*). Never before, however, has Moshe risked what he risks now, as without divine instruction, he smashes the God-given tablets to the ground. In that wrenching moment, he reaches heights beyond those he attains in all the miraculous moments of his career. For he shows his willingness and ability, *as a mortal man*, to discern and do what is right, no matter the cost. And, in doing so, he sets a personal example for all of us across time to follow.

The significance of this event, however, strikes much deeper. Lessons are also to be learned not only from Moshe's courageous example but also from the message embedded in his actions. Moshe understood that had he not shattered the tablets, had he handed over the law to a nation dancing around a golden calf, the Torah would not have been the Torah; God's hopes for us and our world would have been thwarted.

The message that Moshe conveys to the nation when he denies them God's tablets is so lasting and important that God would have us contemplate it as the text reaches its conclusion. It is the lesson that we have previously referred to as the lesson of context (see *Shmot*: Ki Tissa 4, *Approaches* E; Eikev 2, *Approaches* D).

The Torah cannot do its job in a vacuum. If the Torah does not find a ready home in our hearts – if we are unwilling to accept the possibility that God's text can shape our character, thoughts and actions, if we insist on keeping God's laws separate from our lives, denying their potential to transform us into individuals who strive to do what is right, no matter what the sacrifice or what the cost – then, as Moshe realizes during that fateful moment at the foot of Sinai, it is better that the Torah not be given.

The Torah starts with God and ends with man, challenging us to recognize that when all is said and done, the value of God's Book depends upon us. The Torah acquires its significance in this world when its lessons and laws shape our lives.

The Torah starts with God and ends with man to teach us that God's Book is just the starting line from which man's real journey begins…

Sources

Abravanel – Rabbi Don Yitzchak Abravanel; biblical commentator, philosopher, statesman, diplomat (Portugal, Spain, Italy, 1437–1508).

The last great figure of Spanish Jewry, the Abravanel served during his lifetime as finance minister to the kings of Portugal, Spain and Italy. The Abravanel used his high position and great wealth to benefit his brethren and spared no effort in petitioning the Spanish king and queen, at the time of the Spanish Inquisition, to reverse the edict banishing the Jews from Spain. Failing in that effort, the Abravanel himself suffered expulsion in 1492 with the rest of the exiles.

The Abravanel authored many works including major commentaries on the Torah, other books of Tanach, *Pirkei Avot*, the Haggada and the Rambam's *Guide to the Perplexed*. His commentaries are divided into chapters, each of which is introduced by the list of questions and problems which he intends to address in the chapter. The Abravanel often applied the lessons learned from Scripture to issues confronting the Jewish society of his day.

Abudarham, David ben Yosef – Liturgical commentator (Spain, fourteenth century).

A member of a distinguished family, the Abudarham authored *Sefer Abudarham*, an important guide to the laws, customs and texts of the Jewish prayer service. His work was designed to address a declining understanding of the meaning of the prayers and of the rituals associated with them.

The Abudarham drew upon sources in the Talmud Bavli, the Talmud Yerushalmi, Geonic literature and earlier and later commentaries. He makes extensive use of the Siddur of Rav Saadia Gaon and may well have been the last to see an original of this book.

The *Sefer Abudarham* remains a critical source for Spanish, Provencal, French and Ashkenazi practices and customs surrounding the prayer service.

Albo, Yosef – Rabbi, philosopher, preacher (Spain, circa 1380–1444).

A student of Rabbi Chasdai Crescas, one of the leaders of the Jewish community in Christian Spain, Albo is best known for his major work, *Sefer Ha'ikkarim*, the Book of Principles. In this treatise, Albo critiques earlier attempts, such as that of the Rambam, to identify the fundamental principles of Jewish faith. Albo suggests his own formulation, reducing Jewish dogma to three basic principles from which, he claims, all else flows: the existence of God, divine revelation at Sinai, and reward and punishment.

While many details of Albo's personal life remain unclear, his participation in specific events is recorded. He played a prominent role in the Disputation of Tortosa (1413–1414) and was still active in 1433, when he delivered a sermon at a circumcision.

Alshich, Moshe – Rabbi, scholar, halachist, commentator (Turkey, Israel, Syria, 1508–1593).

Born in Adrianople, Turkey, the Alshich emigrated at a young age to Tzfat, Israel, where he studied under and was ordained by Rabbi Yosef Caro. The Alshich gained such prominence as a teacher, orator, halachic authority and communal leader that he was granted the title *Hakadosh* (the holy one), a title reserved for a few select rabbinic figures across Jewish history. The Alshich's last years were spent in Damascus, Syria.

Among other works, the Alshich published volumes of his popular lectures and sermons relating to various sections of Tanach (Torah, Prophets and Writings). Particularly noteworthy is his commentary on the Torah, *Torat Moshe*, which follows a homiletic approach and is filled with practical lessons on ethics and morals.

Altschuler, David and Hillel – Biblical commentators (Galicia, seventeenth–eighteenth centuries).

Hillel Altschuler finished the commentary begun by his father David Altschuler on Nevi'im (Prophets) and Ketuvim (Writings), designed to promote increased study of the text. The work, which relies heavily on the observations of earlier commentators, consists of two parts: *Metzudat David* (Fortress of David), an elucidation of the *pshat* of the text, and *Metzudat Tzion* (Fortress of Zion), an explanation of difficult individual words.

The Altschulers' commentary attained great popularity and continues to appear in many printed editions of the Tanach.

Avot D'Rabi Natan – An interpretive expansion on the Mishnaic tractate of *Pirkei Avot* (see below).

Apparently dating from the Mishnaic period, *Avot D'Rabi Natan* is essentially a companion piece to *Pirkei Avot*.

In many cases, *Avot D'Rabi Natan* acts as a commentary to the existing text of *Pirkei Avot*, elaborating on and enriching the Mishna through anecdotes and exegetical interpretation. On other occasions, each of these texts presents material not found in the other.

Ba'al Ha'Akeida – Rabbi Yitzchak ben Moshe Arama; biblical commentator, Talmudic scholar, rabbi (Spain, 1420–1494).

Yitzchak ben Shlomo Arama served as the principal of a rabbinical academy at Zamosa and as rabbi of the communities of Tarragon, Fraya and Calatayud. He is most well known for his lengthy philosophical commentary on the Torah, *Akeidat Yitzchak*, which earned him the title Ba'al Ha'Akeida (author of the Akeida). This work consists of 105 "portals," each of which contains two sections: *derisha* (investigation) and *perisha* (exposition). In the first of these two sections, Arama examines a philosophical idea reflected in his chosen text. He then, in the second section, uses this philosophical idea to address and solve problems in the text itself.

The skillful manner in which Arama joins these two sections creates the template for Jewish preaching across the ages.

Ba'al Hatanya – Rabbi Shneur Zalman of Liadi, Talmudic scholar, philosopher, founder of the Chabad-Lubavitch branch of Chassidic Judaism (Belorussia, Ukraine, Russia, 1745–1813).

Born in the small town of Liozna, Belorussia, Shneur Zalman displayed extraordinary aptitude at a very early age. After his marriage, he devoted himself totally to Torah study. Drawn to Chassidic philosophy, he became one of the youngest members of the circle of Rabbi Dov Ber, the Maggid of Mezritch, then the leader of the Chassidic movement. So impressed was the Maggid by his young student that he charged him with the composing of a new, up-to-date *Shulchan Aruch* (Code of Jewish law). Published portions of this work became known as the *Shulchan Aruch Harav* and reflected the young *rav*'s superb scholarship and teaching ability.

In 1788, the Ba'al Hatanya was appointed head of the Chassidic community in Reisin, where he composed the *Tanya*, a major work comprised of his collected teachings. Through this work and other sources, it became clear that he had developed a new type of Chassidism, to become known as Chabad.

After bitter accusations against him from Jews opposed to the Chassidic movement, the Ba'al Hatanya was twice imprisoned by the non-Jewish authorities and released. He settled in the town of Liadi, Russia, and became known as the rabbi of Liadi. A supporter of Russia during the Franco-

Russian war, the Ba'al Hatanya fled with the defeated Russian armies and died on the journey.

One of the most influential Jewish scholars of his day, the Ba'al Hatanya evidenced a unique combination of deep Judaic scholarship; wide knowledge of the sciences and mathematics; clear, incisive teaching ability; great personal charisma; common sense and mystical understanding.

Ba'al Haturim – Rabbi Yaakov ben Asher; halachist, Talmudic scholar, biblical commentator (Spain, 1270–1340).

Third son of the major Talmudic commentator Rabbi Asher ben Yechiel (the Rosh), the Ba'al Haturim emerged to make towering contributions of his own to Jewish scholarship. His greatest work was the *Arba Turim* (Four Rows), a pivotal codification of practical Jewish law that continues to serve as a basic text for the study of halacha to this day. This code was divided into four basic sections and was the precursor of Rabbi Yosef Caro's *Shulchan Aruch*.

The Ba'al Haturim wrote a comprehensive commentary to the Torah in which he included explanations from the works of previous scholars such as Rashi, Ramban, Radak, Ibn Ezra and others. To whet the reader's interest, he prefaced each section of this commentary with an "appetizer" – a segment featuring *gematria* (observations based on the assignment of numerical value to the letters of the text), acronyms and other symbolic references. In an ironic twist of fate, these "appetizers" captured popular attention and have been preserved and published to this day as a separate commentary in the Ba'al Haturim's name.

Babad, Yosef – Rabbi, Talmudic scholar, halachic authority (Poland, 1800–1874).

Few life details are known concerning Babad, who served as a rabbi in several cities in Galicia before being appointed chief of the rabbinic court in Tarnopol in 1857.

His primary work was the renowned *Minchat Chinuch*, a major commentary and expansion on the *Sefer Hachinuch*.

Beruchin, Yaakov ben Aharon – Rabbi, Talmudic scholar, halachic authority (Belorussia, Lithuania, 1787–1844).

The scion of a long line of sages, Beruchin studied at the Yeshiva of Volozhin, where he became a close student of the yeshiva's illustrious founder, Rabbi Chaim Volozhiner.

Originally intent on remaining financially independent of communal funds, Beruchin established a successful business, only to suffer a severe setback due to a catastrophic fire. Reluctantly, he entered the professional rabbinate, becoming the rabbi of the city of Karlin and one of the leading scholars of his time. Beruchin was known for his vast knowledge, deep piety and personal kindness.

Beruchin's most important work was the *Mishkenot Yaakov*, a compilation of responsa and halachic commentary, organized according to the sections of the *Shulchan Aruch*.

Carmy, Shalom – Contemporary Jewish scholar and philosopher (America, 1949–).

Carmy serves as chair of Bible and philosophy at Yeshiva College of Yeshiva University, is an affiliated scholar at Cardozo School of Law and current editor of *Tradition*, a scholarly journal published under the aegis of the Rabbinical Council of America.

Carmy received his rabbinical ordination from the Rabbi Isaac Elchanan Theological Seminary of Yeshiva University, where he studied under Rabbi Joseph Soloveitchik and Rabbi Aharon Lichtenstein. He has written extensively on Jewish thought and philosophy and has edited portions of Rabbi Joseph Soloveitchik's work for publication.

Caro, Yosef – Hamechaber (the author); scholar, halachist, author of the *Shulchan Aruch* (Set table), the universally accepted, authoritative code of Jewish law (Spain and/or Portugal, Turkey, Israel, 1488–1575).

Born either in Spain or Portugal, Caro fled to Turkey with his family upon the expulsion of Jews from Portugal, in 1497. Living successively in the cities of Istanbul, Adrianople, Nikopol and Salonika, Caro studied with numerous scholars, many of whom shaped his mystical life perspective.

In 1522, at the age of thirty-four, Caro began to write his monumental *Beit Yosef*, a project which would occupy him for twenty years and which he concluded only after moving to Tzfat, Israel. With this work, Caro strove to create order out of the multiplicity of codes and halachic rulings that had developed in Jewish law over the centuries. Caro traced each law to its origins, discussed the law's development through an analysis of divergent opinions and rendered authoritative practical rulings. In order to avoid unnecessary duplication, Caro fashioned the *Beit Yosef* as a commentary to the *Arba Turim* of Rabbi Yaakov ben Asher.

While the *Beit Yosef* was considered by Caro to be his most important scholarly writing, it is the more succinct digest of that work, the *Shulchan*

Aruch, for which this scholar is eventually immortalized. The *Shulchan Aruch*, with its ordered, succinct presentation of practical Jewish law, quickly became the authoritative legal code for world Jewry and the point of departure for halachic works that followed.

Among Caro's other contributions was the *Kesef Mishneh*, an extensive commentary on the Rambam's *Mishneh Torah*.

Chafetz Chaim – Rabbi Israel Meir HaCohen Kagan, Talmudic scholar, halachist, ethicist (Lithuania, Belarus, 1838–1933).

A towering figure in the development of Orthodox Judaism during the nineteenth and twentieth centuries, the Chafetz Chaim's continued influence is felt in many spheres of Jewish life to this day.

Of humble origin, the Chafetz Chaim was taught by his parents until the age of ten, when his father's death prompted the family to move to Vilna to allow for Israel Meir's continued studies. After his marriage at the age of seventeen, the Chafetz Chaim settled in the town of Radun where he and his wife subsisted on the proceeds of a small grocery store. The Chafetz Chaim's Torah teaching became so popular that students flocked to his side, leading to the eventual establishment of a yeshiva carrying his name.

At the age of thirty-five, he anonymously published his first volume, *Chafetz Chaim* (He who desires life), devoted entirely to the laws surrounding the prohibitions of slander, talebearing and gossip. Eventually his authorship of this work became known and earned him the personal title the Chafetz Chaim. Among many other works, his greatest halachic contribution was the *Mishna Berura*, an extensive commentary and elaboration on one section of Rabbi Yosef Caro's *Shulchan Aruch*. The *Mishna Berura* is widely used as an authoritative halachic guide to this day.

The Chafetz Chaim played a major role in communal and religious affairs of his day and was universally known for his kindness, piety, humility and integrity.

Chatam Sofer – Rabbi Moshe ben Shmuel Sofer; rabbinic leader, Talmudic scholar, halachist, biblical commentator (Germany, Hungary, 1762–1839).

A child prodigy, the Chatam Sofer entered yeshiva at the age of nine and was delivering public lectures by the age of thirteen. After years of intensive study, he assumed rabbinic and teaching positions in several communities before accepting, in 1807, his primary position in Pressburg, Hungary. There he established a major yeshiva which housed, at its height, five hundred students, many of whom went on to become influential leaders in their own right.

Reacting to the newly developing Reform movement, the Chatam Sofer vehemently opposed any changes or innovations in Jewish practice. He is considered by many to be one of the most influential figures in the development of Chareidi Judaism (the most theologically conservative form of Orthodox Judaism today). The Chatam Sofer authored numerous important responsa (answers to halachic questions) as well as oft-studied commentaries on the Torah and Talmud, including *Chatam Sofer al HaTorah* and *Torat Moshe*.

Chazon Ish – Rabbi Avraham Yeshayahu Karelitz, Talmudic scholar, halachic authority (Poland, Israel, 1878–1953).

Born in Kossow, at that time in Austria (later in Poland), Karelitz received his early education from his father, the head of the local *beit din*. A brilliant scholar, Karelitz lived a modest life, devoting himself entirely to Torah study (although he did master such sciences as astronomy, mathematics and botany, believing knowledge of these areas to be critical to a full understanding of Jewish law).

In 1911, Karelitz published his first work anonymously under the title *Chazon Ish*, the name by which he became almost exclusively known. This work, a commentary on portions of the *Shulchan Aruch*, earned great approbation from the rabbinic community of the time.

In 1920, the Chazon Ish moved with his family to Vilna, where he quickly earned a widespread reputation for scholarship and piety. In 1933, he settled in Bnei Brak, Israel, where literally thousands came to seek his advice and guidance.

Although the Chazon Ish held no official post during his lifetime, he earned recognition as a prominent authority in all areas of Jewish law and life. His halachic positions on practical matters held great sway, particularly within the Charedi (fervently Orthodox) community. He wrote over forty volumes in Hebrew, each of which is characterized by its clarity and lucidity.

Chizkuni – Rabbi Chizkiya ben Manoach Chizkuni; biblical commentator (France, thirteenth century).

Almost nothing is known about the personal life of the Chizkuni, a classical biblical commentator who lived in Provence around the year 1250. The Chizkuni's commentary, which focuses on the *pshat* (simple meaning) of the text, is based, according to the author, upon a number of earlier sources. In particular, the Chizkuni often elaborates upon the observations of Rashi.

The commentary of the Chizkuni first appeared in print in Venice in 1524.

Da'at Zekeinim Miba'alei Hatosafot – A compilation of Torah commentary authored by the Tosafists (a large group of twelfth- to thirteenth-century medieval rabbis whose critical and explanatory glosses are basic to the study of Talmud).

The period of the Tosafists began after the completion of Rashi's commentaries; the first Tosafists were actually Rashi's sons-in-law and grandsons. The Talmudic commentaries of the Tosafists are characterized by lengthy analyses of difficult passages and by a willingness to critically review the positions of their predecessors, particularly Rashi.

Preserved in manuscript for centuries, the *Da'at Zekeinim Miba'alei Hatosafot* was first formally published in 1783.

Epstein, Baruch Halevi – Commentator, scholar, author (Russia, 1860–1942).

The son of Yechiel Michel Epstein, Baruch Halevi studied under the tutelage of both his father and his uncle, the Netziv.

Although he was offered numerous rabbinic positions in such major centers as Pinsk, Moscow and Petrograd, Epstein opted to earn his livelihood as a bookkeeper and to devote his free time to Torah study. The author of numerous volumes, he is best known for his monumental *Torah Temima*. In this work, he connects passages of the Talmud and Midrash to their sources in the written text and comments extensively on the topics they raise.

Falk, Yehoshua ben Alexander Hacohen – Rosh Yeshiva, Talmudic scholar, halachic authority (Poland, 1555–1614).

A student of the great luminaries Rabbi Shlomo Luria (the Maharshal) and Rabbi Moshe Isserles (the Rema), Falk served as the rosh yeshiva in the Yeshiva of Lemberg, teaching many students who were destined to become leading scholars of the next generation. The esteem in which Falk was held by his rabbinic colleagues can be seen from his active participation in the Council of the Four Lands (the central body of Jewish authority from 1580 to 1764), where many of his proposals were adopted.

Falk firmly opposed those halachic authorities who, in his estimation, were "content to base their halachic decisions on the *Shulchan Aruch* alone without investigating the sources." He therefore authored two compilations on the *Arba Turim* – the *Perisha* and the *Derisha* – and an even more important commentary on the Choshen Mishpat section of the *Shulchan*

Aruch, the *Me'irat Einayim*. Falk penned numerous other works, many of which were tragically destroyed by fire.

Hacohen, Meir Simcha of Dvinsk – Rabbi, talmudic scholar, biblical commentator (Latvia, Lithuania, 1843–1926).

Renowned as a brilliant Talmudic scholar and beloved as a compassionate leader, Rabbi Meir Simcha served as rabbi of the city of Dvinsk for forty years. In 1906 he turned down a rabbinic position in Jerusalem as a result of the entreaties of the Dvinsk community who argued that his departure would "destroy" not only their community but the entire diaspora. During World War I when most of the Jewish community fled Dvinsk, leaving behind only the poorest inhabitants, Rabbi Meir Simcha remained, declaring that as long as there were nine Jews in the city he would be the tenth.

Among his most important works were the *Meshech Chochma* and *Ohr Sameach*, commentaries on the Torah and on the Rambam's *Mishneh Torah*, respectively.

Hirsch, Shimshon Raphael – Rabbi, biblical commentator, rabbinic leader, philosopher (Germany, 1808–1888).

In the wake of the emancipation, traditional Judaism was desperately in need of a powerful leader to guide the transition of Orthodoxy into a new world marked by greater freedom. Rabbi Shimshon Raphael Hirsch successfully filled that role.

In 1851, Hirsch relinquished a prominent rabbinic post to become the rabbi of eleven individuals who had separated from the general community of Frankfurt am Main in response to that community's shift towards Reform Judaism. From those humble beginnings, Hirsch built a model Orthodox community of five hundred members.

Hirsch developed a philosophy of *Torah im Derech Eretz* (lit.: Torah and the way of the land) which envisioned a relationship between traditional observant Judaism and the modern world. Much controversy exists today as to the exact dimensions of the relationship envisioned by Hirsch. There is no question, however, that Hirsch's contributions were instrumental in the development of German Orthodox Jewry and paved the way for the development of today's Modern Orthodox community throughout the Jewish world. Hirsch published many works including *Nineteen Letters*, in which he brilliantly responds to the major philosophical questions of his day; *Horeb*, a text outlining his approach to Jewish belief and practice; and an extensive, thought-provoking commentary on the Torah.

Hoffman, David Tzvi – Biblical and Talmudic scholar and commentator, halachic authority (Germany, Hungary, Austria, 1843–1921).

Educated in Hungarian yeshivot, as well as the Hildesheimer Seminary in Eisenstadt, Hoffman later studied in the universities of Vienna, Berlin and Tübingen.

Hoffman lectured at the Hildesheimer Rabbinical Seminary in Berlin and assumed the position of the seminary's rector upon Hildesheimer's death in 1899. By the end of his life, Hoffman was recognized as the preeminent halachic scholar of the German Orthodox Jewish community and regularly fielded questions on a wide array of subjects from rabbis throughout Germany.

While Hoffman was a violent opponent of the Reform Jewish movement, his responsa show great awareness of contemporary concerns and evidence a willingness to show leniency, where possible, in areas of halacha. His commentaries on the books of Vayikra and Devarim demonstrate deep knowledge of rabbinic sources as well as a facility with the archaeological data of his time.

Ibn Ezra – Rabbi Avraham ben Meir Ibn Ezra; biblical commentator, philosopher, poet, grammarian, physician, astronomer/astrologer (Spain, Egypt, North Africa, Italy, France, England, Israel, 1092–1167).

Over the course of an impoverished and itinerant life, the Ibn Ezra made a profound contribution to Jewish scholarship. A prolific poet, the Ibn Ezra produced treatises on Hebrew grammar, mathematics, astronomy/astrology and philosophy.

The Ibn Ezra's greatest contribution, however, was made through his renowned commentary on the Torah and other books of Tanach (an acronym for the biblical canon – Torah, Nevi'im, Ketuvim: the five books of Moses, the Prophets and the Writings). This work, which inspired numerous supercommentaries, is singular for its strong use of grammatical principles to uncover the *pshat* of the text. While the Ibn Ezra's commentary included a great deal of exegetical material authored by his predecessors, he did not shy away from offering his own original observations.

Kli Yakar – Rabbi Ephraim Shlomo ben Chaim of Luntshitz; *dayan*, biblical commentator, orator (Poland, Bohemia, 1550–1619).

At an early age, the Kli Yakar earned a reputation as a spellbinding speaker and traveled in that capacity through numerous cities and towns. Subsequently, he served as rosh yeshiva and *av beit din* (head of the Jewish court) in Prague.

His renowned commentary on the Torah, the *Kli Yakar*, is largely homiletic in style.

Kook, Avraham Yitzchak Hacohen – Leading rabbinic authority, scholar and halachist; first chief rabbi of the newly established Jewish presence in the land of Palestine (Lithuania, Palestine, 1865–1935).

Born in Griva, Latvia, Kook quickly earned a reputation as a child prodigy and, early on, showed great independence of mind and thought. He studied briefly at the famed Yeshiva of Volozhin under the tutelage of the Netziv and in 1887, at the age of twenty-three, assumed his first rabbinic position in Zaumel. This was followed by a rabbinic position in Baumel in 1895.

In 1904, Kook moved to Palestine (then under Ottoman rule), where he assumed the rabbinic position in Jaffa. There he became heavily involved in outreach to Jews of all walks of life and religious backgrounds. He identified with the Zionist movement, seeking a greater role for Torah and halacha in the Jewish settlement in Palestine.

World War I found Kook in Europe (having traveled there to foster Zionist ideology within the religious community), unable to return to Palestine. He accepted a temporary position in London during the war years and returned to Palestine after the conclusion of hostilities. Upon his return, Kook was appointed to the chief rabbinate in Jerusalem and, with the formation of the position in 1921, was elected first Ashkenazic chief rabbi of Palestine.

Kook's influence upon twentieth-century Jewish thought was profound, as he mapped out a unique path in support of religious Zionism. He was able to blend mystical speculation with practical activity and managed to see good in all participants in the Zionist enterprise, across the religious spectrum. At the same time, he did not shy away from encouraging secular Jews towards greater piety and the Orthodox community towards greater involvement in national and world affairs.

Kook's deep love for the whole of the Jewish people and his vision of the newly established Jewish presence in Palestine as the beginning of divine redemption laid the groundwork for the developing character of the Religious Zionist movement in the decades that followed.

Lamm, Norman – Rabbi, scholar, educator, author, communal leader (America, 1927–).

One of the major figures of the Modern Orthodox movement, Lamm received his *smicha* in 1951 from the Rabbi Isaac Elchanan Theological

Seminary of Yeshiva University, where he studied under the renowned sage Rabbi Joseph Soloveitchik. He also holds a PhD in Jewish philosophy from the Bernard Revel Graduate School of Jewish Studies, Yeshiva University.

A pulpit rabbi for twenty-five years, Lamm served as rabbi at Congregation Kodimoh in Springfield, Massachusetts, and at the Jewish Center in New York. In 1976, he was elected the third president of Yeshiva University, the first to be born in the United States. He also served as chancellor of the University and as rosh yeshiva of its Rabbi Isaac Elchanan Theological Seminary from 2003 until his retirement in 2013.

Renowned as an eloquent spokesman for the Modern Orthodox approach to Jewish thought, Lamm consistently preaches Yeshiva University's mantra of *Torah u'madda* (Torah and modern culture), acknowledging the legitimacy of both Torah learning and secular knowledge and the capacity of each sphere to inform the other. Lamm maintains that the methodology of *Torah u'madda* can be traced to the Talmud and the Rambam, and that it is more recently reflected in the teachings of Rabbi Shimshon Raphael Hirsch and Rabbi Joseph Soloveitchik.

Lamm has authored over ten books, penned countless articles, and edited or coedited more than twenty volumes.

Leibowitz, Dr. Nehama – Biblical scholar and commentator, teacher (Israel, 1905–1997).

Born in Riga, Latvia, Nehama Leibowitz was awarded a doctorate from the University of Berlin in 1930 and emigrated that same year to the British Mandate of Palestine. Over the course of her career, Leibowitz taught for decades at a Religious Zionist teachers' seminary, lectured at Tel Aviv University, where she was appointed full professor, delivered regular radio addresses on Voice of Israel radio and lectured in a multitude of settings throughout the country.

Leibowitz is best known for her *gilyonot* (lit.: pages), stencils on the weekly Torah reading which she distributed to all interested. Her incisive analytical approach to text made these *gilyonot* immensely popular and through their distribution she rekindled intense interest in the study of biblical text and commentary throughout the Jewish world. Later Leibowitz produced formal studies, which were eventually collected into books on the Torah. Leibowitz was awarded the Israel Prize for education in 1957.

Levi Yitzchak of Berdichev – The Kedushat Levi; rabbi, Chassidic master (Poland, Ukraine, circa 1740–1810).

One of the most famous personalities in the third generation of the Chassidic movement, Rabbi Levi Yitzchak was born into a distinguished rabbinic family in Galicia. After his marriage, he moved to his father-in-law's home in Lubartow, Poland, where he was introduced to Chassidism by Rabbi Shmuel Shmelke Horowitz of Nikolsburg. In 1766, Rabbi Levi Yitzchak went to study under Rabbi Dov Ber, the Maggid of Mezritch, becoming one of his closest disciples.

After serving in a number of prior rabbinic posts, Rabbi Levi Yitzchak became rabbi in Berdichev in the Ukraine in 1785, where he remained until his death. There he earned great renown as a rabbi, Chassidic master and scholar.

Rabbi Levi Yitzchak was known for his singular love of the Jewish people and for his stress upon ecstasy and joy in prayer and in the performance of mitzvot. His work *Kedushat Levi* – on the Torah, festivals, *Pirkei Avot* and other topics – is considered one of the essential works of Chassidic literature.

Lichtenstein, Aharon – Talmudic scholar, philosopher, rosh yeshiva (America, Israel, 1933–).

After studying under the renowned scholar Rabbi Yitzchak Hutner, Lichtenstein received his *smicha* at Rabbi Isaac Elchanan Theological Seminary of Yeshiva University, where he became a devoted student of a great luminary, Rabbi Joseph Soloveitchik. Lichtenstein subsequently received a PhD at Harvard University in English literature. In 1960, he married Dr. Tovah Soloveitchik, the daughter of his mentor, Rabbi Joseph Soloveitchik.

Lichtenstein served for a number of years as a rosh yeshiva of Yeshiva University, where he quickly earned wide respect for the breadth of his scholarship and the incisive quality of his thinking.

In 1977, Lichtenstein accepted the invitation of Rabbi Yehuda Amital to join him as co-rosh yeshiva of Yeshivat Har Etzion in the Gush Etzion region of Israel, a position that Lichtenstein holds to this day. In this capacity, Lichtenstein has instructed thousands of students from across the globe and has garnered a worldwide reputation for his great scholarship, towering intellect and deep grasp of complex issues. His opinion is widely sought by many in all areas of Jewish law and thought. Lichtenstein has also served as rosh kollel of the Caroline and Joseph S. Gruss Institute in Jerusalem, an affiliate of Yeshiva University.

Lichtenstein has published extensively in many settings and is widely considered one of the preeminent scholars of the Modern Orthodox/ Religious Zionist community today.

Lubavitcher Rebbe – Rabbi Menachem Mendel Schneersohn, prominent Torah sage and Jewish leader of the twentieth century (Russia, America, 1902–1994).

Born in the town of Nikolaev, Ukraine, Schneersohn was the son of Rabbi Levi Yitzchak Schneersohn, a renowned Talmudic scholar and authority on Kabbala and Jewish law. Menachem Mendel showed prodigious talent at an early age, and by the arrival of his seventeenth birthday had mastered the entire Talmud. In 1923, Menachem Mendel visited the sixth Lubavitcher Rebbe, Yosef Yitzchak Schneersohn, and met the Rebbe's daughter, his own future wife, Chaya Mushka.

After their marriage in 1928, the couple moved to Berlin, where Schneersohn studied mathematics, physics and philosophy at the University of Berlin. During the same period, he authored hundreds of pages of original Torah studies, corresponded with many leading European rabbinical figures, and completed numerous scholarly and communal tasks requested of him by his father-in-law. In 1933, after the rise of the Nazi Party in Germany, the Schneersohns moved to Paris, where Schneersohn continued all his activities and studies. In 1940, days before the city's fall to the Nazis, the couple fled Paris and ultimately left Europe for America, in 1941.

Shortly after his arrival in America, Schneersohn was appointed by his father-in-law to a number of tasks and increasingly became seen as his father-in-law's spokesman. Upon his father-in-law's death in 1950, Schneersohn initially resisted the great pressure placed upon him to become the next leader of the Lubavitcher movement, finally agreeing to become the Rebbe only a full year later.

Under the new Rebbe's leadership, the Lubavitcher movement gained tremendous influence and power, touching the lives of Jews throughout the world and influencing the ethical and moral development of the world community at large. Driven by his deep love for every Jew, observant and nonobservant alike, the Rebbe placed tremendous emphasis on outreach, training thousands of young Chabad rabbis and their wives to serve as shluchim (emissaries) to promote Jewish observance and education across the globe. Under his aegis, the Lubavitcher movement connected with Jews under Communist rule in the Soviet Union and other endangered com-

munities, playing a major role in perpetuating their Judaism. He oversaw
the establishment of schools, community centers, youth camps, campus
programs, Chabad houses and more. The Rebbe took a great interest in
the affairs of the State of Israel and reached out to the non-Jewish community, as well, preaching ethical and moral behavior on the part of all.

Passing away in 1944, the Rebbe was buried next to his teacher and
father-in-law, the previous Lubavitcher Rebbe, at Montefiore Cemetery
in Queens, New York. So great was the Rebbe's personal charisma and
influence that, to date, no successor has been named to his position. Some
members of the Lubavitcher movement continue to maintain a controversial belief in his identity as the messiah, in the face of great opposition
from within the Jewish community at large.

Luzzatto, Shmuel David – Shadal; philosopher, scholar, biblical commentator,
poet (Italy, 1800–1865).

Over the course of a prolific literary career, Luzzatto produced a great
number of works in both Hebrew and Italian including a commentary on
the Torah, commentaries on numerous books of the Prophets, a treatise
on Hebrew grammar, a guide to the understanding of Targum Onkelos,
essays and poems.

While deeply traditional, Luzzatto was unafraid to challenge established
ideas. He subjected the commentary of the Ibn Ezra to scathing attack
and, while he greatly admired the Rambam for the latter's halachic contributions, he did not hesitate to criticize that great scholar for adopting
elements of Aristotelian philosophy.

In 1829, Luzzatto was appointed professor at the rabbinical college of
Padua. He contributed to most of the Jewish periodicals of his time, corresponded voluminously with contemporaries and wrote on an extremely
wide range of Jewish topics.

Maharal – Rabbi Yehuda Loew; rabbi, Talmudic scholar, philosopher, commentator (Poland, Bohemia, 1525–1609).

Born to a noble family that traces its lineage to King David, the Maharal
was one of the most influential Jewish thinkers of the postmedieval period.
So expansive was his influence that Rav Avraham Yitzchak Hacohen Kook
(the first chief rabbi of Israel) once proclaimed that the Maharal was "the
father of the approach of the Vilna Gaon on the one hand and the father
of the Chassidic movement on the other."

After serving as rabbi of Nikolsburg in the province of Moravia for twenty years, the Maharal moved to Prague in 1573, there opening a ye-shiva and mentoring numerous outstanding disciples. After leaving for a brief period to serve as rabbi in the city of Posen, the Maharal returned to Prague in 1598 to assume the position of chief rabbi.

A renowned educator, the Maharal criticized his contemporaries for not heeding the advice of the Mishna which counsels that children should be taught subjects that are age appropriate. "The fools nowadays," he pro-claimed, "teach boys Torah with the commentary of Rashi, which they do not understand and also Talmud which they cannot yet grasp." (The Maharal's supercommentary on Rashi is entitled *Gur Aryeh*.) While clearly rooted in the world of Torah, the Maharal embraced the study of secular subjects, particularly mathematics.

A prolific writer, the Maharal was held in high esteem by Jews and non-Jews alike. His statue was erected in 1917 at the entrance to the province town hall by the municipal authority, and his synagogue, the Altneu Shul, stands to this day.

Mecklenberg, Rabbi Yaakov Tzvi – Rabbi, biblical commentator (East Prussia, 1785–1865).

Mecklenberg began his rabbinic career in 1829 when he became the assistant to the rabbi of Koenigsberg, the capital of the German province of East Prussia. In 1831, he graduated to the role of rabbi and remained in that position until the day he died.

Mecklenberg's major work was *Haktav V'hakabala*, a commentary on the Torah which stressed the indivisibility of the Written and Oral Law. Responding to the emerging claims of the Haskala (Enlightenment) move-ment that the traditional explanations of the Torah were outdated and far-fetched, Mecklenberg demonstrated the authentic textual and linguistic basis for traditional interpretation.

Midrash Hagadol – Collection of Midrashim compiled in the late thirteenth century by the Yemenite scholar Rabbi David ben Avraham Adani.

This work, culled from ancient Tannaitic (Mishnaic) sources, was preserved in manuscript for centuries and studied primarily within the Yemenite community. European scholars, within the last 150 years, have printed carefully edited versions of the text. The Midrash Hagadol serves as a significant record of many teachings from the Mishnaic and Talmudic period which are found in no other source.

Midrash Lekach Tov – A Midrashic commentary on the Torah and the five-Megilla scrolls.

Also known by the title *Pesikta Zutarta*, this work was compiled by the Bulgarian rabbinic scholar Tuvia Ben Eliezer in the late eleventh century.

Midrash Rabba – A collection of Midrashic anthologies on various books of Tanach.

Although the title "Rabba" is shared by all of these anthologies, they are not a cohesive work but a series of Midrashic texts edited in different centuries and in various locales. Bereishit Rabba (Midrash Rabba Bereishit) was compiled in the sixth century and consists of wide-ranging ethical teachings, homilies, maxims, parables and metaphors all connected (albeit sometimes loosely) to the text of Bereishit.

Midrash Tanchuma – A compilation of Midrashim, many of which are ascribed to the Talmudic sage Tanchuma bar Abba.

Rav Tanchuma bar Abba, who lived in Israel during the second half of the fourth century CE, was a student of the renowned sage Rav Huna and a major author of *aggadot* (Midrashic tales). The text ascribed to his name has appeared over the centuries in various versions.

Midreshei Halacha – A group of Tannaitic expositions on the Torah designed to identify the sources of the 613 mitzvot within the Torah text.

In contrast to *Midreshei Aggada* (homiletical Midrashim such as the Midrash Rabba, Midrash Tanchuma, etc.), *Midreshei Halacha* are primarily halachic in purpose. Nonetheless, they contain much aggadic material, as well. While the contents of the *Midreshei Halacha* date to the Mishnaic period, the redaction of the extant texts apparently occurred much later. Numerous theories, in fact, concerning the categorization and dating of these Midrashim have been offered by scholars and historians.

Because practically no halachic legislation derives from the book of Bereishit, *Midreshei Halacha* are only found in connection with the books of Shmot, Vayikra, Bamidbar and Devarim. These Midrashim are referred to by various titles such as *Mechilta*, *Sifra*, *Sifrei* and *Torat Kohanim*.

Mishna – First official written summary of the Oral Law.

The editing of the Mishna by Rabbi Yehuda Hanasi at the end of the second century CE marked a major transformation in the mode of transmission of Jewish tradition. Until this time, the distinction between Written Law (*Torah She'bi'chtav*) and Oral Law (*Torah She'b'al Peh*) had been studiously maintained, the latter memorized and transmitted verbally across the centuries. Driven by the fear, however, that the Oral Law would be lost if not recorded in writing, Rabbi Yehuda developed the six "orders" of the Mishna. This pioneering sage, however, preserved the character of the Oral Law by recording the Mishnaic edicts in short, cryptic style which requires immediate further oral explication.

The sages of the Mishna are known as the Tannaim.

Mizrachi, Eliyahu – Talmudic scholar, biblical commentator, rabbi, rosh yeshiva, halachic authority (Turkey, 1450–1526).

Born and educated in Constantinople, Mizrachi rose to become the foremost rabbinic authority in the Ottoman Empire of his day. Mizrachi was firm and unbending in his legal positions and responded to halachic queries addressed to him from far and wide. His grueling daily schedule encompassed communal leadership, the stewardship of a yeshiva, extensive teaching, the rendering of legal decisions and scholarly writing.

In addition to his major achievements in the area of Jewish scholarship and communal leadership, Mizrachi also studied and wrote on secular subjects, particularly mathematics and astronomy.

Mizrachi's crowning achievement – and the project which he personally considered his most important – was his monumental supercommentary on Rashi. This extensive work became the basis for continued study and analysis by later commentaries.

Munkatcher Rebbe – Rabbi Chaim Elazar Shapira, Talmudic scholar, halachic authority, communal leader (Hungary, 1868–1937).

A Rebbe in the Munkatcher dynasty, in 1931 Shapira assumed the position previously held by his father and grandfather in 1913. Combining vast knowledge in Talmud, halacha and Kabbala, Shapira exerted great influence over the entire Hungarian Jewish community. A strong opponent of innovation in Jewish practice and a fierce foe of the Zionist movement, Shapira believed that redemption was to be a miraculous and not a man-initiated phenomenon.

Under Shapira's leadership, the Jewish community of Munkatch thrived and, by the time of his death, fully one half of the city was Jewish. Hundreds of students from throughout eastern Europe flocked to study in his yeshiva, Darkei Tshuva, many of them becoming the rabbis, teachers and community leaders of the next generation.

Nachshoni, Yehuda – Contemporary biblical scholar and commentator (Israel).

Nachshoni is the author of one of the most comprehensive works on the weekly parsha, *Hagot B'parshiot HaTorah* (available in an English translation by Shmuel Himelstein: *Studies in the Weekly Parashah: The Classical Interpretations of Major Topics and Themes in the Torah*, ArtScroll Judaica Classics [New York: Mesorah, 1989]). In this work he presents a series of essays on each parsha, raising critical questions and offering a wide array of approaches from the classical to the contemporary.

Netziv – Rabbi Naftali Tzvi Yehuda Berlin; Talmudic scholar, rosh yeshiva, biblical commentator (Poland, Russia, 1817–1893).

For forty years beginning in 1854, the Netziv served as the rosh yeshiva of the Yeshiva of Volozhin. The Netziv's scholarship, coupled with a deep personal love for all of his students, transformed the yeshiva into the largest such institution of its time and a major spiritual center for the Russian Jewish community. His opposition to the secularization of the yeshiva eventually brought him into conflict with government authorities and, according to some versions, led to the yeshiva's closing in 1892 (others suggest that the closure was due to internal upheaval). The Netziv was one of the early supporters of Jewish settlement in the Land of Israel.

Among the Netziv's publications was his popular biblical commentary, the *Ha'amek Davar*, in which he emphasized the consonance between Talmudic interpretation and the *pshat* of the Torah text.

A son of the Netziv's first marriage was Rabbi Chaim Berlin, who became chief rabbi of Moscow and subsequently chief rabbi of the Ashkenazic community in Yerushalayim; a son of his second marriage was Rabbi Meir Berlin (later Bar-Ilan), a leader of the religious Zionist Mizrachi movement who inspired the creation of Bar-Ilan University (named in his memory).

Ohr Hachaim – Rabbi Chaim Ibn Attar; rabbi, biblical commentator, Talmudic scholar, kabbalist (Morocco, Israel, 1696–1743).

One of the most prominent rabbis in his native land of Morocco, the Ohr Hachaim decided in 1733 to resettle in the Land of Israel. He was, however, detained along the way in Livorno, Italy, by leading members of the Jewish community who established a Talmudic academy for him. Finally arriving in Jerusalem in 1742, the Ohr Hachaim served as the head of the Beit Midrash Knesset Yisrael until his death.

The Ohr Hachaim's commentary on the Torah combines textual analysis with Talmudic and kabbalistic insights. Over the years, this commentary has become particularly popular within the Sephardic and Chassidic communities.

Onkelos – Convert to Judaism, scholar and author of the seminal Aramaic translation of the Torah, Targum Onkelos (Rome, Israel, 35–120 CE).

According to tradition, Onkelos was the nephew of the Roman emperor Titus (who, as a general, was responsible for the destruction of the Second Temple).

After his conversion, Onkelos authored Targum Onkelos, a monumental interpretive translation of the Torah into Aramaic. This translation, which received the approbation of Onkelos's teachers, the Mishnaic scholars Rabbi Eliezer and Rabbi Yehoshua, offers striking insights into the text. So authoritative did this work become that the rabbis of the Talmud decreed that the weekly reading of the Torah portion should include the reading of the Targum, as well. Targum Onkelos is included in almost all published editions of the Torah today.

Palagi, Chaim – Rabbi, scholar, halachic authority (Turkey, 1788–1869).

Born in Izmir, Turkey, Palagi rose to successive positions of increasing rabbinic authority in his native town and its environs, culminating with his ascension to the rank of *chacham bashi* (chief rabbi) of Izmir at the age of seventy-seven. Temporarily removed from this position due to controversy instigated by communal leaders against whom he had ruled, Palagi was ultimately reinstated due to overwhelming popular support.

A prolific writer, Palagi published twenty-six works. Many of his other manuscripts were lost to fire or remained unpublished.

After a brief additional controversy following Palagi's death, his son, Abraham, was appointed to the position of *chacham bashi* of Izmir, a position that he held for close to thirty years.

Peli, Pinchas – Scholar, author, poet (Palestine/Israel, 1930–1989).

Born in Jerusalem to a Chassidic family by the name of Hacohen, Peli adopted his pen name, which means "wonder." Peli combined a traditional yeshiva education with advanced academic degrees from Hebrew University in Jerusalem and a doctorate received under the tutelage of Rabbi Abraham Joshua Heschel in America.

Peli served as professor of Jewish thought and literature at the Ben-Gurion University in the Negev and as visiting professor in numerous universities in the United States, Argentina and Japan. During his tenure as visiting professor at Yeshiva University from 1968 to 1970, Peli developed a close relationship with Rabbi Joseph Dov Soloveitchik and eventually published a volume based on the Rav's oral discourses entitled *Al Hatshuva,* (*On Repentance*).

Peli authored numerous other volumes, poems and short stories.

Pirkei Avot – Mishnaic tractate containing the ethical pronouncements of the Tannaitic sages.

Pirkei Avot is singular within the Talmud in its focus upon ethical maxims as opposed to legal stricture. Many of Judaism's best-known proverbs and moral observations are contained within this tractate.

Elsewhere, the Talmud proclaims, "He who desires to be pious, let him practice the teachings of *[Pirkei] Avot.*"

Plotski, Meir Dan – Rabbi, Talmudic scholar, rosh yeshiva, communal leader (Poland, 1866–1928).

Author of the *Kli Chemda*, a commentary on the Torah, Plotski occupied rabbinical positions in Warta and subsequently in Ostrow. In 1926, at the age of sixty, he resigned from the rabbinate and was appointed to head a large yeshiva in Warsaw, known only as "the Mesivta."

Plotski served as chairman of the executive committee of the Rabbinical Council in Poland and as the emissary of Agudat Israel in Belgium, England and the United States.

Rabbeinu Bachya – Rabbi Bachya ben Asher; biblical commentator, *dayan*, preacher (Spain, 1263–1340).

A disciple of the renowned Talmudist Rabbi Shlomo ben Aderet (the Rashba), Rabbeinu Bachya served as a preacher and a *dayan* (rabbinical judge) in Saragossa, Spain. Rabbeinu Bachya is best known for his commentary on the Torah, which combines *pshat*, Midrash, philosophy and Kabbala. Each weekly parsha is introduced by an ethical discussion citing a verse from Proverbs.

Rabbeinu Bachya Ibn Pakuda – Philosopher, poet (Spain, second half of the eleventh century).

Little is known about the life of this Spanish scholar whose major work on ethics was originally published in Arabic in 1040. Subsequently translated into Hebrew by Judah Ibn Tibbon in 1161 under the title *Chovot Halevavot* (Duties of the Heart), this work achieved great popularity and had a powerful influence upon later Jewish ethical literature.

Ibn Pakuda felt that the inner, spiritual responsibilities of Judaism had been sorely neglected by his predecessors and contemporaries, who, in his estimation, focused solely on the outer trappings of religious observance. *Chovot Halevavot* is thus divided into ten "gates" or chapters, each of which focuses on a specific inner milestone to be attained in a Jew's quest for spiritual perfection.

Rabbeinu Chananel – Rabbi Chananel ben Chushiel; Talmudic scholar, halachic authority, commentator (Tunisia, 990–1055).

Rabbeinu Chananel lived in the city of Kairouan, Tunisia, where he studied under the tutelage of his father, Chushiel ben Elchanan, head of the Kairouan yeshiva. Following in his father's footsteps, Rabbeinu Chananel eventually earned the title *Reish Bei Rabbanan* (chief among the rabbis), accorded by the Babylonian academies of his day.

Rabbeinu Chananel wrote the first authoritative commentary on the Talmud, great sections of which are preserved and recorded on the actual pages of specific Talmudic tractates. In contrast to the later commentary of Rashi, Rabbeinu Chananel's work is not a running interpretation of the entire text. Instead, he summarizes and explains the main arguments of the Gemara and issues halachic decisions on the matters in question. He relies greatly on the positions of the Babylonian Geonim, and thus serves as an important bridge between the teachings of the Geonim and the scholars of North Africa and those of the scholars of Europe and Israel. Many later commentaries rely heavily on his work.

Rabbeinu Chananel also wrote a commentary on the Torah, only portions of which have been preserved.

Rabbeinu Yonah – Rabbi Yonah ben Avraham Gerondi, philosopher, Talmudic scholar, moralist (Catalonia, France, Spain, c. 1200–1263).

Born in Gerona, Catalonia, Rabbeinu Yonah studied in the French yeshivot and was the most prominent pupil of Rabbi Solomon of Montpellier. Deeply influenced by the latter's hostility to the Rambam's philosophical works, Rabbeinu Yonah participated in the campaign against the Rambam's thinking which culminated in the public burning of the latter's works by the Parisian authorities in 1233. When, a few years later, tractates of the Talmud were burned in the same square, Rabbeinu Yonah recognized the danger of involving Christian religious authorities in areas of Jewish doctrine and, according to tradition, publicly repented over his attacks against the Rambam.

Rabbeinu Yonah taught and preached extensively in a number of communities, including his native Gerona, Barcelona, and Toledo, where he remained until his death in 1263. Renowned as one of the greatest Talmudists of his day, Rabbeinu Yonah also acquired enduring fame for his ethical teachings and writings.

Rabinovitch, Nachum – Rosh yeshiva, educator, Talmudic scholar (America, Israel, 1928–).

Rabinovitch is the rosh yeshiva of Yeshivat Birkat Moshe in Ma'aleh Adumim, Israel, and one of the leading figures in the religious Zionist movement today. He is considered an authority on the Rambam's philosophy and has published extensively on topics in that field.

Rabinovitch received his *smicha* from Rabbi Yaakov Yitzchok Ruderman at Yeshivas Ner Israel, in Baltimore, Maryland, and a PhD in statistics and probability from the University of Toronto. Prior to his current position, Rabinovitch served as a pulpit rabbi in Charleston, South Carolina, from 1952 to 1963, and in Toronto, Canada, from 1963 to 1971. He also occupied the prestigious position of dean at Jew's College in London, from 1971 to 1982.

Radak – Rabbi David Kimchi; biblical commentator, philosopher, grammarian (France, 1160–1235).

Best known for his commentary on the books of the Prophets, the Radak also wrote commentaries on Psalms, Proverbs and Chronicles. His commentary on Bereishit stresses the ethical underpinnings of the narrative and includes mystical interpretations of specific biblical stories.

The Radak's works, in general, are noteworthy for their stress on grammar, language and literal meanings of words in the text. He distinguished between interpretations which conformed to the *pshat* and homiletical *drashot* (which he often included for added interest).

Radbaz – Rabbi David ben Shlomo Ibn Abi Zimra; Talmudic scholar, halachic authority, community leader (Spain, Israel, Egypt, 1479–1573).

The Radbaz was born in Spain to wealthy parents, but, at the age of thirteen, was forced into exile as a result of the Alhambra Decree (the expulsion of the Jews from Spain in 1492). Together with his family he emigrated to Tzfat, Israel, where he studied under Joseph Sargossi. Moving for a short time to Jerusalem, the Radbaz ultimately emigrated to Egypt, where he remained for forty years, first in Alexandria and then in Cairo. After the conquest of Egypt by the Turks in 1517, the Radbaz became the head of the Egyptian Jewish community, serving in numerous capacities, including *dayan* (judge), head of a yeshiva and administrator of charitable collections. These offices were honorary in nature, as the Radbaz was independently wealthy. Revered beyond the borders of Egypt for his vast knowledge, personal integrity, rigorous scholarship and deep humanity, the Radbaz regularly responded to legal and religious questions sent to him from other communities. Although a kabbalist, the Radbaz introduced Kabbala into his halachic decisions only when there was no contraindicating Talmudic position.

Shortly before 1553, the Radbaz resigned his position as chief rabbi of the Egyptian Jewish community and traveled back to Israel, settling for a short time in Jerusalem and then returning to Tzfat, where he remained until his death.

Ralbag – Rabbi Levi ben Gershon; Talmudic scholar, commentator, philosopher, mathematician, astronomer/astrologer (France, 1288–1344).

Little is known about the life of this revolutionary Jewish philosopher who authored works ranging from biblical commentary to acclaimed philosophical and mathematical treatises. His major philosophical text, *Sefer Milchamot Hashem* (The wars of the Lord), was composed over a twelve-year period and earned the Ralbag renown well beyond the Jewish community.

In opposition to the generally accepted position of classical Judaism, the Ralbag maintained that God deliberately limits His own omniscience with regard to His foreknowledge of human acts. By stating that God knows the choices available to us but consciously chooses not to know the specific decisions that we will make, the Ralbag addressed the age-old dilemma of how man's free will can exist in the face of God's omniscience.

Rambam – Rabbi Moshe ben Maimon, also known as Maimonides; widely recognized as the greatest post-Talmudic authority on Jewish law and thought (Spain, Morocco, Egypt, 1135–1204).

The Rambam's works include *The Guide to the Perplexed*, a philosophical work on Jewish theology; *Sefer Hamitzvot*, a compendium of the 613 commandments of the Torah; a commentary on the Mishna; and his magnum opus, the *Mishneh Torah*, a masterful, comprehensive code of Jewish law. In his commentary on the Mishna, the Rambam delineated thirteen principles still considered to be the cornerstones of Jewish belief. His *Mishneh Torah* launched the course for halachic codification across the ages and served as the forerunner of other essential texts such as the *Arba Turim* and the *Shulchan Aruch*.

A royal physician and world-class philosopher, the Rambam made a monumental impact upon the development of Jewish tradition and law, reflected in the well-known dictum inscribed on his tomb: "From Moshe (Moses) to Moshe (Rambam) no one arose like Moshe."

Ramban – Rabbi Moshe ben Nachman, also known as Nachmanides; biblical and Talmudic commentator, scholar, physician (Spain, Israel, 1194–1270).

The Ramban's commentary on the Torah combines *pshat*, Midrash and kabbalistic insights. A towering figure in the history of Jewish scholarship, the Ramban authored numerous works on the Talmud as well as Jewish law and thought. His vigorous defense of Judaism in the face of Christian attack culminated in a public disputation with the Jewish apostate Pablo Christiano, in the presence of King James of Spain in 1263.

The Ramban's deep love for the Land of Israel is manifest in his writings and in his philosophy of Jewish law. In 1267, at the age of seventy-two, the Ramban settled in the Land of Israel and worked vigorously to rebuild Jerusalem's Jewish community.

Ran – Rabbi Nissim ben Reuven; Talmudic scholar, rabbi, halachist, philosopher, physician (Spain, 1290–1380).

Widely recognized as the greatest rabbinic authority of his time, the Ran served as rabbi of Barcelona and responded to thousands of halachic inquiries from across the Jewish diaspora. The Ran is best known for his practical commentary on the halachic work of Rabbi Yitzchak ben Yaakov Alfasi (the Rif). Through this commentary, the Ran achieved a revered position in the world of Talmudic scholarship. The Ran's compendium of sermons, *Drashot HaRan*, provides insight into many of the basic tenets of Jewish faith.

Rashba – Rabbi Shlomo ben Aderet, Talmudic scholar and commentator, halachic authority, rabbi (Spain, 1235–1310).

A student of the illustrious sages Rabbeinu Yonah and the Ramban, the Rashba rose to great prominence as one of the foremost scholars of his day.

In his early years, the Rashba was involved in business, but eventually withdrew in order to pursue a rabbinic career. Appointed to the position of chief rabbi in Barcelona, he established a yeshiva and remained at his post for over forty years. Before he reached the age of forty, the Rashba became the acknowledged leader of the Spanish Jewish community. As his reputation continued to grow, halachic queries were sent to him not only from across Spain, but from all corners of the Jewish world, including Germany, France, Bohemia, Sicily, Crete, Morocco, Algiers, Portugal and Israel. He demonstrated a keen knowledge of economics, Roman law and local Spanish custom, combined with an uncanny grasp of the vast panorama of halachic literature. He was strong and clear in his positions, steadfast in judgment yet warm, humble and caring.

The Rashba's works include thousands of responsa, a critically important commentary on the Talmud, and halachic works on the laws of kashrut, marital relations, the Shabbat and festivals, mikveh, *eruvin* and more. His halachic positions exerted great influence upon later legal decisions and many of his rulings were included in Rabbi Yosef Caro's *Shulchan Aruch*.

Rashbam – Rabbi Shmuel ben Meir; biblical commentator, Talmudic scholar (France, 1080–1158).

The Rashbam, Rashi's grandson, was a leading member of the Tosafists (a large group of medieval rabbis whose critical and explanatory glosses are basic to the study of the Talmud). The Rashbam's commentary on the Torah is remarkable for its bold adherence to *pashut pshat* even when the *pshat* leads to controversial conclusions. The Rashbam took issue with his renowned grandfather's periodic Midrashic interpretation of the text and, in fact, claimed, "I debated with him [Rashi] and he admitted to me that, if he had the time, he would be obligated to author other commentaries based upon the straightforward explanations of the text...."

So great was the storm concerning some of the Rashbam's views that his commentary on the first chapters of Bereishit was omitted in many earlier editions of the Bible.

Rashi – Rabbi Shlomo Yitzchaki; arguably the greatest of all biblical and Talmudic commentators (France, 1040–1105).

Rashi's commentary on the Torah, considered an essential companion to the study of the text, combines *pshat* with the periodic referencing of Midrash (when he feels such referencing is necessary for textual comprehension).

In addition to commentaries on the Prophets and Writings, Rashi also authored an indispensable running commentary on the Talmud, known for its brevity and clarity.

No course of study in the Torah or Talmud is considered complete without the accompanying study of Rashi's commentary.

Rema – Rabbi Moshe Isserles; Talmudic scholar, *dayan*, rosh yeshiva, preeminent halachic authority for Ashkenazic Jewry (Poland, 1520–1572).

Born in Cracow, Poland, the Rema studied in Lublin where he married the daughter of Rabbi Shalom Shachna, the rosh yeshiva. Upon his wife's untimely death at the age of twenty, the Rema honored her memory with the building of a synagogue which stands in Cracow to this day. The Rema's second wife also came from a scholarly family.

The Rema distinguished himself as an outstanding scholar at an early age and by 1550 was a member of the Cracow Beit Din (religious court). He established a yeshiva in Cracow, supported its students through his own resources and earned a worldwide reputation as a brilliant and effective *posek* (halachic arbiter). Humble and self-effacing, the Rema was, nonetheless, so confident and incisive in his halachic positions that he became known to his contemporaries as the "Maimonides of Polish Jewry." Like Maimonides, the Rema also pursued secular knowledge through the study of history, astronomy and philosophy.

While the Rema authored many works, he is best known for his *Mapa* (Tablecloth), a series of annotations inserted into the body of Rabbi Yosef Caro's halachic compendium, the *Shulchan Aruch* (Set table). These glosses append the legal positions and customs of Ashkenazic Jewry to Caro's Sephardic-oriented work, thus transforming the *Shulchan Aruch* into the primary universal code of law for the entire Jewish nation.

Rif – Rabbi Isaac ben Yaakov Alfasi, Talmudic scholar and commentator, halachic authority and codifier (Tunisia, Morocco, Spain, 1013–1103).

A critical transitional figure between the halachic periods of the Geonim and the Rishonim, the Rif wrote the *Sefer Hahalachot*, the most important halachic code prior to the *Mishneh Torah* of the Rambam. In this work, the Rif follows the flow of the Talmud and extracts the accepted halachic decisions from the lengthy discussions of the Talmudic sages. In this way, the Rif produced a digest of Jewish law that then paved the way for the later codes of the Rambam, the Ba'al Haturim and Rabbi Yosef Caro. In addition, the Rif's rulings themselves became critical sources for later halachic decisions. Overall, the Rif's contributions to the development of Jewish law were monumental.

The Rif studied in Kairouan, Tunisia, under the great sages of his day, Rabbi Nissim Gaon and Rabbeinu Chananel. In 1045 he moved with his family to Fez, Morocco, where he remained for over forty years. The Fez community financially supported the Rif's scholarly efforts and founded a yeshiva in his honor. Among his most renowned students were Rabbi Yehuda Halevi, author of the *Kuzari*, and Rabbi Yosef Ibn Migash (the Ri Migash) who himself became the teacher of Rabbi Maimon, the father and teacher of the Rambam.

In 1088, accusations were leveled against the Rif in the royal court and he was forced to flee to Spain, where he became the rosh yeshiva in the town of Lucena.

Rivash – Rabbi Isaac ben Sheshet Perfet; Talmudic scholar, halachist, rabbi (Spain, Algiers, 1326–1408).

A student of renowned scholars, including Rabbi Nissim ben Reuven (the Ran), the Rivash earned his own scholarly reputation at an early age. Nonetheless, he led a private life, assuming his first rabbinic position approximately at the age of fifty. His communal career was marked by controversy and false accusation resulting, in one instance, in imprisonment for several months. The anti-Jewish riots of 1391 forced the Rivash to leave Spain and to finally settle in Algiers where, after some initial difficulty, he eventually enjoyed the deep affection and respect of the Jewish community.

The greatest contribution of the Rivash lay in his responsa, which greatly influenced the subsequent development of halacha.

Rosh – Rabbi Asher ben Yechiel, Talmudic scholar and commentator, halachic authority, rabbi (Germany, France, Spain, 1250 or 1259–1327).

Trained in the Franco-German Tosafist school of rabbinic thought, Rabbi Asher moved to Worms, where he became a prized student of the great sage Rabbi Meir ben Baruch (the Maharam of Rothenberg). Upon Rabbi Meir's imprisonment by the gentile authorities, Rabbi Asher became the acknowledged leader of German Jewry and spearheaded the ultimately unsuccessful attempt to secure his mentor's freedom.

In the face of continuing German persecution of the Jewish community, Rabbi Asher fled to Spain and assumed the rabbinic position in Toledo in 1305. He was welcomed in Spain with great honor by the towering sage Rabbi Shlomo ben Aderet, and, after the latter's death, became widely acknowledged as the foremost halachic authority of his generation.

Rabbi Asher demonstrated a unique blend of personal humility, a willingness to consider the positions of others, and a strong firmness, when necessary, in defense of his halachic positions. Communities across Spain referred their halachic questions to him and students were drawn to his yeshiva from all corners of Europe. He published over one thousand responsa and a critically important commentary on the Talmud that wove together the approaches of the Franco-German and Spanish schools of halachic scholarship. In this Talmudic commentary, Rabbi Asher cites the salient halachic points of each Talmudic discussion and includes the observations of the other scholars. Rabbi Asher's halachic rulings and commentaries had a major influence on the unfolding of Jewish law in subsequent generations.

Saadia Gaon – Talmudic scholar, philosopher, halachist (Egypt, Babylonia, 882–942).

Arguably the greatest scholar of the Geonic period (late sixth–eleventh centuries), Saadia Gaon is also considered by many to be the "father of Jewish philosophy." Sensing the twin dangers posed to rabbinic Judaism by Karaism (a movement that accepted the Written but not the Oral Law) and rationalistic thought, Saadia developed a systematic philosophy of Judaism which examined its truths and teachings in the light of reason.

Saadia played a major role in a calendar controversy between the Jerusalem and the Babylonian scholarly communities which threatened to create a dangerous schism concerning the fixing of festival dates. At the request of the Babylonian scholars, Saadia effectively refuted the position of Aharon ben Meir, the head of the Jerusalem Academy, and solidified the supremacy of the Babylonian scholars. Both as a result of this effort and in the merit of his extraordinary abilities, Saadia was appointed head of the famed Babylonian Academy of Sura in 928, at the age of forty-six.

So important were Saadia's contributions to Jewish thought that, centuries later, the Rambam proclaimed in his *Iggeret Teiman*: "Were it not for Saadia, the Torah would almost have disappeared from among Israel."

Sefer Hachinuch – Systematic analysis of the 613 commandments of the Torah, published anonymously in thirteenth-century Spain.

Following the order of the Torah text, the Ba'al Hachinuch (as the anonymous author of the *Sefer Hachinuch* is called) links each mitzva to the parsha in which it is found and discusses both the philosophical underpinnings and halachic parameters of that mitzva.

Sfat Emet – Rabbi Yehuda Aryeh Leib Alter; Chassidic leader, Talmudic scholar, biblical commentator (Poland, 1847–1905).

One of the greatest Talmudic scholars of his generation, the Sfat Emet assumed the leadership of the Ger Chassidic movement in 1870. His works on the Talmud became renowned well beyond his own Chassidic community and are studied today by serious students throughout the Jewish world. His monumental commentary on the Torah, based on homilies delivered over the course of his life, was published posthumously and is arranged according to the weekly Torah readings and festivals. The Sfat Emet stresses the moral and ethical lessons to be derived from the text.

Sforno – Rabbi Ovadia Sforno; biblical commentator, Talmudic scholar, philosopher, physician (Italy, 1470–1550).

The Sforno's broad-based education earned him recognition in many fields including law, philosophy, mathematics, medicine, Hebrew language and Hebrew literature. When the famous German humanist Johan Reuchlin desired to perfect his knowledge of Hebrew literature, Cardinal Domenico Grimani advised him to approach the Sforno. A prolific writer, the Sforno is best known for his clear commentary on the Torah and many books of Tanach. These works reflect great respect for the *pshat* of the text and are written in a beautiful, almost lyrical style.

Sha'agat Aryeh – Rabbi Aryeh Leib ben Asher Gunzberg, Talmudic scholar, halachist, rabbi, rosh yeshiva (Lithuania, 1695–1785).

Over the course of a tumultuous life, Gunzberg served as rabbi and rosh yeshiva in various Lithuanian communities. Renowned for his incisive intellect and brilliant scholarship, he became known by the title of his major work the *Sha'agat Aryeh* (Roar of the lion). Published while Gunzberg served as rabbi of Volozhin, this work features a number of the author's responsa and complex halachic discussions on the Orach Chaim section of the *Shulchan Aruch*.

In 1776, Gunzberg was appointed rabbi of the community in Metz, France, where he served until his death in 1785. In addition to the *Sha'agat Aryeh*, Gunzberg also produced a number of commentaries on the Talmud and other halachic works. An additional volume of Gunzberg's responsa was published posthumously in Vilna in 1874.

Shach – Rabbi Shabbetai ben Meir Hacohen; Talmudic scholar, *dayan*, halachic authority and commentator (Poland, Lithuania, 1621–1662).

Born in Amstivov, Lithuania, Shabbetai moved to Poland, studying in Tykocin, Krakow and Lublin. While still young, he returned to Vilna, where he married a woman from a wealthy family, descended from the Rema (Rabbi Moshe Isserles). Financially supported by his father-in-law, the Shach was able to devote his time solely to study.

After serving for a period of time in the *beit din* (rabbinical court) in Vilna, Shabbetai returned to Krakow where, in 1646, he published his classic work, the *Siftei Kohen*, a commentary on the Yoreh Deah section of the *Shulchan Aruch* (thus he became known by the title the Shach, comprised of the initials of the title of this work). Towards the end of his life, Shabbetai expanded his commentary to include the Choshen Mishpat section of the *Shulchan Aruch*, as well. The *Siftei Kohen* revealed Shabbetai's towering intellect, incisive mind and mastery of Jewish law and is widely accepted as an authoritative source for halachic decisions.

Shabbetai was forced to flee repeatedly in order to escape the religious persecution and slaughter of Polish Jewry during his lifetime. In 1651, he published *Megilat Eifa*, which portrays the suffering of the Jewish community at the hands of Chmielnicki and his followers.

Shafran, Avi – Rabbi, communal leader, educator (America, twentieth–twenty-first centuries).

Shafran serves as the director of public affairs for Agudath Israel of America, the leadership and policy umbrella organization for Chareidi Jews in the United States. Widely respected for his articulate and incisive observations, Shafran regularly lectures and writes in a variety of settings. His comments are often directed towards those outside the Orthodox community, in an effort to explain traditional Jewish practice and thought to nontraditional Jews.

Prior to his present position, Shafran served as principal of Providence Hebrew Day School in Rhode Island.

Siddur – The Jewish prayer book.

The Siddur mirrors the historical journey of the Jewish people. While the earliest prayers were primarily spontaneous, prayer services became codified over time, stemming from various sources.

Biblically mandated prayers include the Shma Yisrael, the Birkat Kohanim (priestly blessing) and the Birkat Hamazon (grace after meals). The central prayer of the Jewish liturgy, known as the Amida (the standing [prayer]), was edited by Rabbi Gamliel and his colleagues in Yavne, after the destruction of the Second Temple.

The earliest true Siddur was drawn up in the ninth century by Rav Amram Gaon, at the request of the Jewish community of Spain. One hundred years later, Rav Saadia Gaon compiled a Siddur, as well. Critical to the development of the Jewish prayer book was the Machzor Vitri, edited in the eleventh century by Simcha ben Shmuel, a student of Rashi. The Machzor Vitri contained all the regular prayers according to the custom of northern France.

The Siddur continues to evolve to this day, as evidenced by prayers included in many contemporary prayer books relating to the welfare of the State of Israel and its armed forces.

Soloveitchik, Yosef Dov – The Rav; rabbi, pioneering spiritual leader of the Modern Orthodox movement in America and throughout the Jewish world (Lithuania, America, 1903–1993).

Scion of a two-hundred-year-old rabbinic dynasty, the Rav arrived in America in 1932 armed with an education that combined traditional Lithuanian Talmudic studies and a PhD in philosophy from the University of Berlin. He assumed a rabbinic position in Boston where he established the Maimonides School and played a major role in many facets of the community's development. In 1941, he succeeded his father, Rabbi Moshe Soloveitchik, as the head of the Rabbi Isaac Elchanan Theological Seminary rabbinic school of Yeshiva University. For decades thereafter he commuted weekly between Boston and New York.

The Rav combined vast Torah and secular knowledge, a deeply analytical mind, powerful teaching ability and majestic oratorical skill with a magnetic leadership personality. Through his classes, widely attended public lectures, writings and policy decisions, he furthered the philosophy of encounter between the highest form of Torah knowledge and the best secular scholarship of Western civilization. Advisor and teacher to tens of thousands, the Rav shaped the course of Modern Orthodox philosophy through the twentieth century and beyond.

Sorotzkin, Rabbi Zalman – Rabbi, Talmudic scholar, communal leader (Lithuania, Poland, Israel, 1881–1966).

After beginning his studies under the guidance of his father, the rabbi of Zakhrina, Russia, Sorotzkin continued his education in the yeshivot of Slobodka and Volozhin. His renown as a brilliant student earned him the hand of the daughter of Rabbi Eliezer Gordon, the rosh yeshiva of Telz.

Sorotzkin served as the rabbi of the Lithuanian towns of Voronova and Zhetel, where he established educational institutions. The outbreak of World War I forced him to flee to Minsk. During the war years, he devoted himself to communal activities. Shortly after the end of World War I, Sorotzkin was appointed rabbi of Lutsk, Poland. He remained in Lutsk until World War II, when he escaped to Israel.

Sorotzkin helped found numerous communal institutions and served in many leadership capacities. He enjoyed personal relationships with other Torah luminaries of his day including the Chafetz Chaim, the Chazon

Ish and Rabbi Chaim Ozer Grodzinski. He authored the works *Oznaim LaTorah*, a commentary on the Torah, and *Moznaim LaTorah*, concerning the Jewish festivals.

Talmud Bavli – Babylonian Talmud; foundational compilation of the halachic (legal) and aggadic (ethical-homiletical) discussions of the sages of the Babylonian academies from the second through the fifth centuries CE.

The scholars of the Talmud, known as the Amoraim, expound at great length upon the concise teachings of the Mishna, often digressing to discuss loosely related issues and ideas. Structurally, the style of the Talmud Bavli can best be described as "conversation in suspended animation," reflecting the origin of its subject matter, which was memorized and transmitted orally for centuries before its eventual written recordation.

Together with the Mishna, the Talmud Bavli serves as the basic source for the continually developing Oral Law.

Talmud Yerushalmi – Jerusalem Talmud; collection of the teachings of the sages of the Israeli academies from 200 to 350 CE.

Like the Talmud Bavli, the Talmud Yerushalmi centers on the discussions of the Amoraim (Talmudic scholars) concerning the Mishna. The Talmud Yerushalmi, however, is smaller in scope, more fragmented, and more difficult to study than its Babylonian counterpart; consequently, over the centuries, the Yerushalmi has exerted less influence upon the development of Jewish law. The return to the land of Israel in recent years has given birth to a renewed interest in the Talmud Yerushalmi and the laws it contains pertaining to the land.

Targum Yonatan – Interpretive Aramaic translation of the Torah commonly attributed to Yonatan ben Uziel. The correct name of this translation, according to most biblical scholars, is Targum Yerushalmi (Jerusalem Targum [translation]). Probably due to a printer's error (in Hebrew, as in English, the first letters of Targum Yerushalmi and Targum Yonatan are the same), the work was mistakenly labeled Targum Yonatan and attributed erroneously to Yonatan ben Uziel, an outstanding pupil of the renowned Mishnaic sage Hillel. Yonatan ben Uziel did produce a famous translation of the books of the Prophets which, according to the Talmud, reflects the interpretation of the prophets Chagai, Zacharia and Malachi. The Talmud makes no mention, however, of a Targum on the Torah produced by this sage. The erroneous attribution is perpetuated in many current Chumashim. To address the issue, scholars refer to this biblical translation as the Targum Pseudo-Yonatan.

The Targum Pseudo-Yonatan contains much aggadic material from various sources and is both translation and commentary. The actual date of its composition remains a matter of dispute.

Taz – Rabbi David ben Samuel Halevi, rosh yeshiva, Talmudic scholar, halachic authority and commentator (Poland, Galicia, Ukraine, 1586–1667).

The son-in-law of the renowned halachic authority Rabbi Yoel Sirkes (the Bach), Rabbi David held positions as rabbi and rosh yeshiva in numerous locations, including Kraków, Putalicze, Posen and Ostraha. Following a miraculous escape during the Chmielnicki pogroms of 1648–1649, he wandered from place to place, eventually returning to Poland in 1654 to assume the position of rabbi of Lemberg. He participated in the meetings of the Council of the Four Lands (the central body of Jewish authority in Poland from 1580 to 1764) and was a signatory to many rulings issued by that body.

In 1646, Rabbi David published the first installment of his classic commentary on the *Shulchan Aruch*, the *Turei Zahav* (he became known by the title the *Taz*, comprised of the initials of the title of this work). This first installment consisted of studies on the Yoreh Deah section of the *Shulchan Aruch*. His commentary on the other portions of the *Shulchan Aruch* was published, in stages, after his death. Halachic rulings in succeeding generations were greatly influenced by his works.

Vilna Gaon – Rabbi Eliyahu ben Shlomo Zalman (Lithuania, 1720–1797).

Also known by the acronym the *Gra* (Gaon Rabbi Eliyahu), the Vilna Gaon is considered one of the greatest Talmudic scholars of the past two centuries and is recognized as the "founding father" of the Lithuanian (non-Chassidic) yeshiva movement.

The Gaon demonstrated extraordinary ability as a youngster, delivering a learned discourse in the Great Synagogue of Vilna at the age of six and a half.

A man of iron will, the Gaon devoted every waking moment of his life to all facets of Torah study. He reportedly never slept for more than two hours in a twenty-four-hour period and studied in an unheated room in the winter, placing his feet in cold water to prevent himself from falling asleep.

The Gaon's Talmudic methodology was sharp and incisive, standing in stark contrast to the lengthy *pilpul* (discussion) approach of the Polish yeshivot. He was a harsh opponent of the Chassidic movement, believing that the Chassidim replaced serious intellectual search with a superficial emotional approach.

The Gaon's influence upon the trajectory of modern Jewish scholarship cannot be overstated. He reframed the approach to Talmud study, authored over seventy works on wide-ranging aspects of Torah thought and mentored select students who became foremost Torah scholars in their own right.

Wurzburger, Walter – Rabbi, scholar, philosopher (Germany, America, 1920–1998).

Born in Munich, Germany, in 1920, Wurzburger emigrated to America in 1938. He received his rabbinic ordination from the Rabbi Isaac Elchanan Theological Seminary of Yeshiva University and a PhD in philosophy from Harvard. At Yeshiva University, Wurzburger studied under Rabbi Joseph Soloveitchik, and remained one of the Rav's most ardent students throughout his life.

Wurzburger earned a reputation as one of the most important rabbis and intellects of the Modern Orthodox movement in the latter half of the twentieth century. Author of numerous articles and volumes on Jewish philosophy, Wurzburger served as editor of the scholarly Orthodox periodical *Tradition*, published under the aegis of the Rabbinical Council of America.

Wurzburger held rabbinic positions at Shaarei Shomayim Congregation in Toronto from 1953 to 1966 and at Congregation Shaarey Tefila in Lawrence, New York, from 1967 until 1994. He taught philosophy at Yeshiva University for many years and served as president of both the Rabbinical Council of America and the Synagogue Council of America.

Yalkut Shimoni – An important, comprehensive Midrashic anthology compiled in the twelfth or thirteenth century.

The *Yalkut Shimoni* contains over ten thousand aggadic and halachic observations on the entire Torah text. Both the authorship and the exact date of the *Yalkut's* publication are the subject of dispute.

Zohar – Central work in the literature of Kabbala (Jewish mysticism).

The Zohar is essentially a collection of several sections containing Midrashim and discussions on a wide array of topics.

The Zohar's main section is arranged according to the parshiot of the Torah text, although the latter part of the book of Bamidbar and the book of Devarim are not completely covered. Other portions of the work include the teachings and experiences of the second-century Tanna Rabbi Shimon bar Yochai; mystical studies on specific sections of the Torah and other books of Tanach; and discourses on a variety of topics including the nature of God, the origin and structure of the universe, good and evil, man's relationship to God, etc.

While the authorship of the Zohar is subject to dispute, many traditionalists have, for centuries, traced its origins to Rabbi Shimon bar Yochai.

Index

Praise for *Unlocking the Torah Text*

"Rabbi Goldin's superb collection of essays in *Unlocking the Torah Text* illuminates basic themes in Vayikra. Through careful reading of the Torah text, especially through the prism of Chazal, he interprets what to some might seem philosophically remote. His scholarship and pedagogy make the Torah text…easily accessible and alive. It is a wonderful and inspiring read."

– **Rabbi Menachem Genack**
General Editor, OU Press

"I have found in Rabbi Goldin's volumes a fascinating mix: his thoughts are refreshingly original, while being well grounded in the classic commentaries; his conclusions are profoundly relevant to the contemporary scene, while remaining true to our age-old traditions."

– **Rabbi Dovid Miller**
Rosh Yeshiva and Associate Director
Yeshiva University's Joseph S. and Caroline Gruss Institute, Jerusalem

"Rabbi Goldin performs his task with consummate skill and in a style of writing that will appeal both to the scholar and to the ordinary reader interested in gaining an insight into the Torah text. The result is a grand tapestry of *pshat* and *drash*, classic exegesis and original thought, biblical narrative and issues facing our own society today."

– **Moshe Aumann**
Former Israeli Consul General to the United States
Counselor for Relations with the Christian Churches, *Jewish Press*

"[A] challenge to the reader, a challenge well worth taking. Rabbi Goldin is both a skillful teacher and writer…. [T]he book will serve as a valued resource in better understanding all the events of the Exodus, Matan Torah (Giving of the Torah) and the Mishkan's construction, as well as the incident of the Golden Calf."

– **Alan Jay Gerber**
"Kosher Bookworm," *Jewish Star*

"Rabbi Shmuel Goldin demonstrates in his volumes of *Unlocking the Torah Text* a remarkable knack for identifying [compelling] topics. He surveys the classic approaches to the issues addressed and then adds a new and often surprising layer of interpretation that addresses contemporary concerns and sensibilities. Many of Rabbi Goldin's novel insights serve as a springboard to vigorous classroom discussion and debate. The combination of the old and the new provides for an enriching and vigorous learning experience for a wide range of audiences.... [A] major contribution to serious study of Chumash in our day."

– **Rabbi Chaim (Howard) Jachter**
Rebbe, Torah Academy of Bergen County
Co-rabbi, Shaarei Orah, the Sephardic Congregation of Teaneck
Dayan, Beth Din of Elizabeth; author, three volumes of *Gray Matter*

"Rare is a study of the weekly parsha which speaks to all the generations. Rabbi Goldin's *Unlocking the Torah Text* breaks new ground not only in its clear, fascinating insights into the Torah text but in its compelling appeal to young and old alike. Many of our school's parents use Rabbi Goldin's books as the basis of their Shabbat dinner Torah discussions and have shared with me how much their children look forward each week to the challenging and dramatically presented questions which Rabbi Goldin explores. For any parent and Jewish educator seeking to inspire their children with the love of Torah, *Unlocking the Torah Text* is essential."

– **Dr. Elliot Prager**
Principal, The Moriah School, Englewood, NJ

והאמרי והפרזי והחוי והיבוסי אל ארץ זבת
חלב ודבש ושמעו לקלך ובאת אתה וזקני
ישראל אל מלך מצרים ואמרתם אליו יהוה
אלהי העבריים נקרה עלינו ועתה נלכה נא
דרך שלשת ימים במדבר ונזבחה ליהוה
אלהינו